Computers and Information Systems in Business

Second Edition

Computers and Information Systems in Business

George J. Brabb · *Illinois State University*

HOUGHTON MIFFLIN COMPANY · BOSTON

Dallas   Geneva, Illinois   Hopewell, New Jersey   Palo Alto   London

Library of Congress Catalog Card Number: 79-88716
ISBN: 0-395-28671-9

Contents

Preface

In the preface of the first edition of this text we wrote: "The information system function in organizations has increased in importance as the world has become more complex and dynamic. Managers must adjust more quickly than ever before to rapid changes in their environment. The electronic digital computer can be of great assistance in speeding the processing and analysis of data to create information that management can use in reaching its decisions. However, if not properly managed (used and controlled), the electronic digital computer increases the complexity of the manager's environment without providing assistance in dealing with that complexity. Misuse of this marvelous tool occurs most frequently because managers and their information systems and data processing staffs do not understand the real nature and purposes of the data processing and information systems functions. This text introduces the reader to business data processing and management information systems, including their creation and control, and to the electronic digital computer and its use in such systems." This new edition of *Computers and Information Systems in Business* is also based on these beliefs.

Part 1 (Chapters 1–4), which defines data processing and management information systems, has been improved in two major ways. The treatment of data processing concepts in Chapter 2 has been expanded to include modern file design and processing concepts. This expansion includes the modern concepts underlying the use of integrated data bases and the need for data and data base administration. Data dictionaries and data base management languages are also explained. Chapter 4 on functional information systems is new in this edition. It provides a realistic, system-level view of information systems for the functions of finance, marketing, production, materials control, personnel, and planning.

Part 2 (Chapters 5–7) discusses the analysis and design of information and data processing systems. The emphasis is still on overall system design rather than computer program design, which is covered in Part 3. A discussion of system control is included in Chapter 6.

Computer hardware and software (programs) are covered in Part 3 (Chapters 8–14). The discussion has been updated to reflect the current state of technology. Chapter 11, Microprocessors, Minicomputers, Teleprocessing, and Networks, has been added to cover these important topics more thoroughly than in the first edition. The discussion continues to relate changing patterns of computer use to changes in the design of computer hardware and software. Other unique features carried over from the first edition include guidelines for selection of computer systems (Chapter 12) and programming languages (Chapter 14). Chapters 9 and 10 describe input/output devices and electronic storage devices in some detail. Students who have previous knowledge of computer hardware or who do not need such detailed knowledge can safely omit these chapters. Chapter 13 covers the development of computer programs and presents tools and techniques, including structured programming, that are useful in the initial development and in the debugging of computer programs.

The final section, Part 4 (Chapters 15 and 16), deals with the computer in the organization. Chapter 15 concentrates on the effects of the computer on the accounting function, with emphasis on the control and auditing of electronic accounting systems. Problems in accounting for computer costs are also covered. Chapter 16 discusses the effects of the computer on management, including the special problems of managing the information system function. Alternatives to the internal computer department (service bureaus and facilities management services) are included.

Questions at the end of each chapter have been expanded and rewritten to increase their usefulness as a learning tool for students. Several questions are designed to integrate learning across several chapters and some of these can be used as major term projects. The Instructor's Manual specifically identifies the questions that can be used as term projects or as discussion cases.

This text can be used in courses with differing objectives. Although each part of the text has been carefully organized to yield maximum student understanding, each part of the text can stand alone. For example, if a course were to emphasize computers and computer programming, the following design might be used:

Topic	Chapters or Part
I. Introduction	Chapter 1
II. Computer Hardware and Software	Part 3
III. Programming Language	Language Text
IV. Data Processing and MIS	Chapters 2, 3, 4
V. Analysis and Design	Part 2
VI. More Programming Language	Language Text
VII. Computer Impact	Part 4

Other possible course organizations are presented in the instructor's manual.

A bibliography of selected references is given in the appendix. A glossary of technical terms is also included.

Stanley J. Birkin of the University of South Florida, Jack A. Fuller, who is now at the University of Northern Iowa, and John J. Neuhauser of Boston College provided useful reviews of materials for the first edition.

James C. Hershauer of Arizona State University, David M. Dougherty of the University of Maryland, and John J. Neuhauser of Boston College also provided useful reviews of the materials for the second edition. Any errors that remain are solely my own and I accept full responsibility for them. I am especially grateful to my wife Betty for her patient and unflagging assistance in composing, typing, and proofing. Without her assistance and support this book would never have been completed.

G. J. B.

Computers and Information
Systems in Business

Part 1

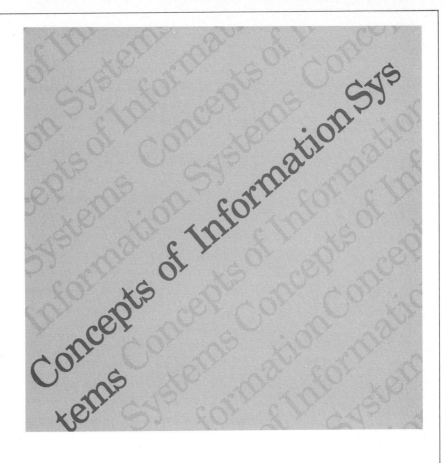

Concepts of Information Systems

Most laypeople would suppose an information system to be some sort of organized process for providing information. They would be right. Few would restrict their definition to systems using a particular means to attain the information sought. Again they would be right. Many information system technicians would think in terms of a computer-based processing system. They would be partly right. Many businesspeople would equate the terms *information system* and *data processing system*. They also would be partly right.

A basic concern in the so-called computer age for managers of business organizations is the impact the computer will have on the business organization. To many, "the boundless age of the computer" is "the blundering age of confusion." Assured that computers are marvelous tools capable of solving almost any problem, managers are plagued with late reports and irate customers suffering late deliveries or incorrect billing, and the excuse is "The computer goofed." It is our contention that there are two reasons for this state of affairs: (1) managers (and computer "experts") do not understand the true nature and purpose of business data processing, and (2) data processing "experts" (and managers) do not understand computers. It is one purpose of this work to remove this confusion.

This section defines some basic concepts and removes some of the confusion that leads otherwise knowledgeable persons to fail to distinguish *data* from *information* and *data processing systems* from *information systems*. The concepts and definitions developed are largely independent of the means used to obtain information by the processing of data. They apply to manual processing systems featuring the traditional figure wearing a green eyeshade and sleeve protectors and hunched over a set of handwritten records. They apply equally to the latest computerized system featuring automated entry and immediate recall of stored information.

The first chapter in this part defines the true nature and purpose of *data processing*. Chapter 2 continues the discussion of data processing by introducing and defining important *data processing concepts*. The vocabulary developed there will be used throughout the remainder of the book. Chapter 3 defines the nature and purpose of a *management information system*. It includes a definition of the management information system as a data processing system, thus serving to place these concepts in clearer perspective. Chapter 4 presents a system-level view of the six major *functional information* subsystems found in most modern manufacturing firms. The six functions are financial, marketing, production, materials control, personnel, and planning. The six system descriptions further illustrate the basic structure of information systems identified in Chapter 3.

One

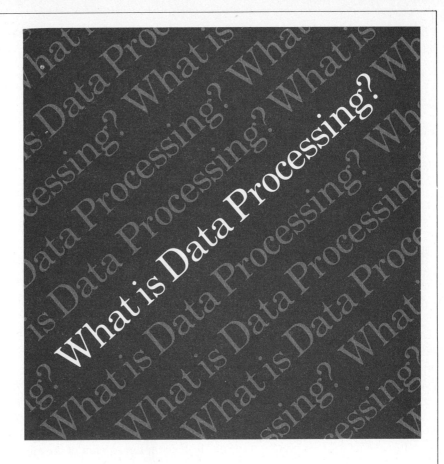

It is the purpose of this chapter to define the nature and purpose of *data processing*. *Note that this discussion will deal with data processing in general*, not just computerized or electronic data processing.

The Purposes of Data Processing

An important question to answer as a basis for putting this discussion in perspective is: Why are business data processed? Every business transaction can be described by a variety of facts. The sale of a dress to a customer in the local department store can serve as an example. *Facts* concerning this transaction *could* include:

1. Name and address of person buying the dress
2. Whether or not this is a credit transaction
3. If this is a credit transaction, who is to pay the bill

4. The identity of the clerk making the sale

5. The department of the store in which the sale is made

6. A description of the dress (color, size, and style)

7. The selling price of the dress

8. The cost to the store of the dress

9. The color of the purchaser's hair

10. The sex of the salesclerk

11. How the dress was packaged for the customer (box, paper bag, etc.)

12. Whether or not the sun was shining

13. The level of bank debits in the community this month

By the application of a little imagination, the reader can extend this list ad nauseam. It is obvious that all of these facts are not of equal value to the management of the store. However, some of these facts are of vital importance. Trends in colors, sizes, and styles of dresses sold are important in planning future purchases. Sales generated by each department and each salesperson in the store are important in planning changes in store layout, changes in personnel assignments, and evaluation of personnel practices. When accumulated for all such sales, the difference between purchase cost and sales price is important in determining margins of profit and in preparing tax reports and statements to stockholders. Over time, these facts accumulate to indicate whether or not the store should be expanded or similar stores should be established elsewhere.

Specific data on the amount of the sale are necessary in order to bill customers for their credit purchases. Information on factors external to the store (such as bank debits) can be important in explaining why total sales reached the level they did. Planning for future sales may be improved by noting general economic conditions in the community.

The reasons for capturing the facts associated with any business transactions and processing them can be grouped in three general categories.

1. Some data must be collected and analyzed to *provide information for management planning and control activities.*

Management must plan for future activity and exercise control over current activity if plans are to be carried out successfully. Such actions determine the profitability (success) of the enterprise.

2. Some data must be collected as a basis for the *custodial processing* activity.

Just as the buildings, furnishings, and heating systems of an organization must be taken care of, *documents* (sales slips, paychecks, purchase orders, receiving slips, tax reports, etc.) must be prepared and their contents recorded, manipulated, and compared in order to carry on the daily business routine. Employees must be paid, and customers must be billed. Purchase orders must be prepared for vendors and vendor invoices recorded as goods are received. Legal reporting requirements must be met if the enterprise is not to be forced to close down. Such activities are necessary to the operation of the enterprise, although they contribute only indirectly to profit (success). Data generated by transactions and contained on such documents *may* serve as the basis for information reports to management, but the processing necessary to their production and use (completing a purchase order, for example), while required to keep the operation going, is not a basic planning or control activity of management.

3. Data must be collected and retained to *provide historical facts* as a basis for the other two types of activity.

Planning cannot be rational without historical data to use in establishing past and current trends and tendencies. Further, adequate management control of any activity requires the recognition of performance standards. Such standards are most often obtained from the analysis of past (historical) behavior. Legal requirements exist for retaining past data as a basis for tax and other reports.

It is not accidental that three reasons for data processing are listed in the order given. This order reflects their relative importance. The most important use of business data is in providing management with the information necessary to recognize trends and patterns in the activities of the enterprise and in the environment within which it operates. Such recognition is necessary if the business is to successfully and continuously adapt to these changing patterns and trends. Without a well-informed management, the enterprise will almost surely fail. Without preplanning of activities and later control over physical operations to see that those plans are being carried out, day-to-day operations very well may cease.

Emphasis on management information does not really come at the expense of the other needs for data processing. A data processing system that collects and preserves the proper facts to provide adequate information for management planning and control will of necessity perform the necessary custodial processing required to keep the enterprise in operation. However, a system designed primarily for efficient custodial processing need not provide good management information. The custodial approach tends to put major emphasis upon reducing the cost of inescapable processing activities. Putting management information needs first emphasizes the importance of considering profit motives in striving for improvement in data processing procedures.

A Systems View of Data Processing

Another way in which to state the argument of the previous section comes from viewing data processing as a three-phase process or system as sketched in Figure 1.1. It should be emphasized that the same basic inputs are required to provide any of the three types of outputs. The processing *activities* in phase 2 also are required (in varying degrees) to obtain each of the outputs.

Another data processing concept is found in the systems view of Figure 1.1, namely, the concept of a difference between *data* and *information*. If there were no difference, all activities in phase 2 other than storage and retrieval and communication would not be required. Classification and sorting, summarization, and analysis would be superfluous. What, then, is this difference?

Data are raw facts. They may or may not be information, since they are the raw material from which information is created.

Information is communicated knowledge expressed in a form that makes it immediately useful for decision making. This definition is not easy to grasp unless we see what each part of it actually means. First, *knowledge* means a novel or new fact for the recipient, something previously unknown to the recipient. Second, *communicated* knowledge is a novel or new fact which has been *sent, received* by the person to whom it is directed, and *recognized and accepted* by that person for what it really is. Third, this knowledge must be so stated that *further processing is not necessary* in order to use the information for decision making.

FIGURE 1.1   *The data processing function as a three-phase system*

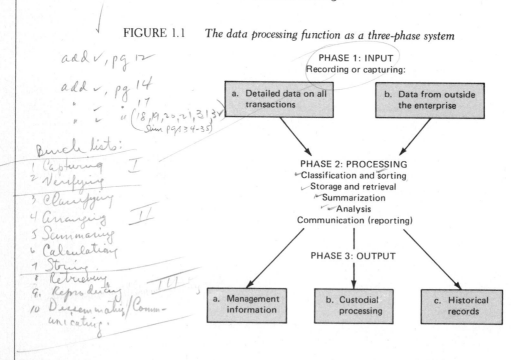

Consider the manager who receives a report but does not read it because it is out of date, referring to what happened two months ago. Information in our sense has not been created. The recipient did not *accept* the knowledge (if any) contained in the report. Or consider the sales manager who receives a quarterly report on sales of each product by each salesperson in his or her sales group, then summarizes the data and plots them on a graph to compare them with performance in the same quarter of the previous year. The data processing system that creates information in this case includes the sales manager, undoubtedly a high-priced data processing clerk. Finally, consider the general manager who receives a report stating that production in the previous month totaled 144 tons, a fact this manager was told by an assistant ten days ago. Again, no information was imparted by this fact, since the manager already knew it.

As another example, consider the case of one manager who regularly received a suggested weekly production schedule based on a mathematical programming model of the operation under her control. Unfortunately, this manager had never been trained to interpret the output of such an analysis and also was not familiar with the basic model used in the analysis. This manager continued to use standard charting and rule-of-thumb techniques to schedule the operation. Or consider the factory manager who each month received a detailed report showing production and cost relationships for every operator and machine combination in the factory. This report was filed away, and all cost control decisions were based on a summary report organized to show cost per unit for producing each of the twelve products manufactured in the plant. In both of the last two examples, information in our sense has not been created, because the report was not accepted for use by the recipient.

The last two examples illustrate an important feature of the stated definition of information. Information cannot be created unless the abilities and desires of the recipient come into play. The mere transmittal of relevant and timely *facts* is not enough. Unless those facts are accepted as a basis for action, they are *not* information.

Data Processing Operations

The specific operations that comprise data processing activities were listed in Figure 1.1. Regardless of how the data processing is accomplished, by humans using pencil and paper or by the most sophisticated electronic equipment, these basic activities are performed. Each of these operations is designed to increase the usefulness of the data by adding time, place, or form utility.

Time utility refers to giving an item value by making it available at a point in time other than the time at which the item originally occurs. Thus storing fruit and vegetables after harvest for use at a period of the year (such as winter) when they would not otherwise be available adds value to the fruits and vegetables.

Place utility refers to making an item available at a place of use different from that at which the item naturally occurs. An example would be the transport of fruits and vegetables from the region(s) where they are grown to cities (or arid regions) for sale to ultimate consumers. The value of the fruits and vegetables is greater at the new locations due to their being brought to where they are needed.

Form utility refers to changes in the physical form of an item in order to make it more useful or desirable. Thus canning or freezing fruits and vegetables so that they may be stored safely until needed gives the fruits and vegetables greater value.

In the discussion below, each data processing operation is labeled as providing one form of the three types of utility, time, place, or form. Only the most important type of utility provided by each operation is indicated.

PHASE 1: INPUT

Originating (Recording)   Data describing a transaction or the conditions of the environment within which the organization operates must be captured (recorded) in some form for processing. (*Time* utility.)

Often transactions data are captured on handwritten or typed forms such as sales tickets, purchase orders, invoices, or checks. In a manual processing system, these documents are passed on to a clerk for sorting and entry into the appropriate accounts. If the data are to be processed by machine, they must be transcribed or converted to some machine-readable form. Increasingly, data are captured by special recording devices and entered directly into some electronic storage medium such as a magnetic disk. When data are not entered directly into some such device, a machine-readable medium such as a punched card, punched paper tape, or magnetic tape is created as a by-product of the operation producing the original transaction document (sales slip, purchase order, etc.). Sometimes the document itself is prepared in a form that can be "read" by a special input device. Examples are checks with the account identification and amount written in magnetic ink and cash register tapes written in a special kind of type so that they may be read by an optical character reader. Whatever the means of processing, the data must first be recorded on some medium that can be entered into the manual or machine processing cycle. This activity preserves the original data and gives it time utility. Changes in form necessary for this preservation are incidental.

PHASE 2: PROCESSING

1. Classification and Sorting Recorded data must be classified by type and then physically arranged (sorted) into particular sequences or groupings if they are to be useful in guiding management decisions. (*Form* utility.)

Classification can take many forms. Data can be classified by source or by immediate importance. Obviously, the most useful classifications are those with some logical relevance to the planning and control functions of management. Thus customer records at the department store can be classified by frequency of purchase, average amount of purchase, and whether or not the customer is paying on time. Sales records can be placed in categories (classified) by department, by salesperson, and, perhaps, by specific item. Classification changes the physical ordering or arrangement of the data and provides form utility.

Data can also be classified by the response they require. *Action data* require a response. Some action data items require an immediate response — for example, a customer request for delivery of a specific item. The occurrence of other facts (the presence of a specific datum) may lead to a delayed action. For example, the fact that a salesclerk reported on time and worked for a full day will mean that he will have to be paid for the day's services, but not until the next payday arrives. *Inaction data* require no action. For example, if an employee cashes her paycheck, no action is required. However, if the employee fails to cash the paycheck, action could be required, since accounting entries would need to be adjusted, and so on.

The actual physical process of placing data in classifications (arranging data) is called *sorting*. Not all sorting is done for the purpose of classification. For example, the day's credit sales at the department store may be arranged in account number sequence before being used to update customer account records. The processing is more efficient when the input file (the accounts to be updated) is arranged in account number sequence. Such ordering has no significance other than the increase in processing efficiency that results. Sorting provides form utility to data to the extent that it increases the value of the data by either revealing its meaning or making it easier (cheaper) to process.

2. Storage and Retrieval Data must be retained in some accessible form after their initial recording until they lose their usefulness. (*Time* utility.)

Returning to the department store example, account records must be maintained to show in detail each customer's transactions with the store. Customers often wish to confirm the details of these transactions. A simple statement of the amount owed is not always sufficient. Management also has need of details concerning when amounts were charged and billed and if and when payment was made. Accounts for those no longer customers of the store need to be deleted (purged) at periodic intervals.

Planning decisions are apt to be based on an analysis of sales trends in total and in detail by department and/or specific items as indicated earlier. This means that these data must be retained (stored) somewhere so that they can be retrieved when needed. The form of the storage medium and the method of retrieval will depend on the frequency with which the data file must be queried and the detail required in each response. Obviously, the value of storage and retrieval is to provide time utility to the data by making them available when needed.

3. Summarization The simplest form of data analysis is accumulating details to obtain totals. This also includes the process of computing an arithmetic average, since such an average is merely a rescaled sum. (*Form* utility.)

The management at the department store needs information on the total amount of income and expense for the whole store, for individual departments, and even for individual employees, in order to do rational planning. Such data, when expressed in the form of rates (averages), can be used to check on progress toward a goal (total) as time passes. Standard accounting reports such as income statements and balance sheets also represent this type of processing activity. Note that these processes are primarily descriptive and do not usually reveal reasons for (cause of) particular results. A sum or an average is a different form of the data than a simple listing, however, and can give added value or information (form utility) to the extent that the new form is more useful.

Totals are also a standard method for checking on the completeness of processing. For example, the total(s) of processed items must be equal to the total(s) of recorded items.

4. Analysis To reveal the full informational content of data, the underlying relationships they contain must be identified. (*Form* utility.)

Mere summations usually reveal little more than the symptoms of success or failure. The underlying causes of such results can be found only by examining underlying relationships. For example, the ratio of liquid assets to liabilities helps to reveal whether or not a firm is able to meet its debts. However, a complete analysis of this issue involves a comparison over time of the flows of money into and out of the firm. More basic relationships such as those between advertising expenditures and amount of sales require more sophisticated analysis. Modern management science involves the use of complicated techniques for modeling and analysis, such as mathematical programming and computer simulation. If the data in the new form created by the analysis have value, form utility has been added.

5. Communication Processing results are worthless if not sent to and accepted by someone who can use them. (*Place* utility.)

As was indicated earlier in defining *information*, facts do not become information until received and accepted by someone with the responsibility, ability, and desire to use them in decision making. By the same token, any report, whether its contents are useful in decision making or not, is not truly an information report until communicated to a responsible recipient. By communicating the facts and relationships to someone who can use them, place utility is created.

File Processing Organization of Data Processing

Data processing systems are *file oriented*. The basic data storage unit is a file made up of individual records. More specifically:

A record is a related collection of data about a single entity or event.

For example, the charge account maintained for Adam Jones at the local department store which records his purchases, returns, and payments is a *record*.

A file is a collection of records relating to similar elements or transactions.

For example, the records for all charge customers at the local department store collectively form the *accounts receivable file*. Thus, Adam Jones's account is an *accounts receivable record*.

A record that describes a single business activity is called a *transaction record*. Thus, when Adam Jones buys a new suit on credit, the salesclerk writes up a credit sales ticket as a *transaction record*. The total set of credit sales tickets for that day would collectively comprise a *daily credit sales transaction file*.

The major jobs of data processing are to capture data from each transaction, use them to update the related permanent (*master*) record and create management reports from the flow of transactions and the changed status of the master records. Thus, Adam Jones's purchase of a suit creates transaction data that are used to update his record in the accounts receivable file. A daily credit sales report summarizing and classifying the credit sales by department, product classification, and salesclerk could be prepared by processing the credit sales transaction *file*. A credit analysis report could be prepared by summarizing and classifying the records in the accounts receivable file according to balance owed for each account and the amount of time since the last payment (the delinquency status of the accounts).

In addition to keeping master records up to date and preparing reports, data processing may also be called upon to respond to inquiries about record or file status. For example, before completing the sale of a suit to Adam Jones on credit, procedures for credit control may have required that the salesclerk check that the charge for the suit would not push Jones's balance above his credit limit with the store. A method for locating the Jones record and ascertaining its current balance and credit limit (*accessing* the file) must be available.

Note that all of the processing activities just described involve the processing, or accessing, of files. File processing is more completely defined in Chapter 2.

Desirable Characteristics of Data Processing Systems

An effective data processing system will possess the characteristics of timeliness, pertinence, precision and accuracy, and economic feasibility and efficiency.

Timeliness refers to the data processing system capturing current data and producing current information. Periodic accounting and management reports highlight historical facts. For example, the department store manager who receives an analysis of departmental sales for the previous quarter one month after its close would be reacting to situations that may very well have changed dramatically during that month. This manager is in the same position as an automobile driver negotiating the freeway at rush hour but able to see only through the car's rear view mirror. Timely processing that reflects current conditions can assist the manager in performing his or her duties just as being able to see out the front and side windows as well as the rear view mirror aids an automobile driver.

Ideally, data should be processed into information fast enough to have some effect on the physical operation that generated the data. In such a case, information would be fed back in time to affect the situation from which the raw data were generated. Such a data processing system would be a *real-time data processing system*. This concept will be discussed more fully in Chapter 3.

Pertinence refers to a data processing system producing the proper information and doing the proper custodial processing. A system for evaluating performance of the shoe department in the department store should not be overly concerned with reporting the color of each pair of shoes sold. The system should, however, attempt to capture data on the extent to which customers found shoes in the colors they wanted — that is, the reasons why potential customers were not served. On the other hand, the manager of the shoe department should not receive personnel performance reports relating to the personnel in the women's ready-to-wear department.

Precision and accuracy refer to two aspects of what the layperson thinks of as accuracy (*correct* values). *Precision* as used here refers to the value being correct within the limits of allowable error. For example, the manager of our mythical department store does not need to know that total sales in the notions department this year were exactly $182,134.69, and would probably remember this figure as either "$182,000" or "about $180,000." For the manager's purposes, the $180,000 figure may be sufficiently *precise*, sufficiently close to the exact value. However, he or she would be disturbed to find that through a consistent clerical error, this figure included sales made in the men's clothing department each month. Such a *lack of accuracy*, that is, the presence of a consistent error (*bias*) in the reported figures, could be very misleading. Other forms of such bias, or lack of accuracy, could arise in the way various indirect costs were charged to the individual operating departments of the store.

The degree of acceptable precision and accuracy in management information depends upon how the information is to be used. For planning purposes, accuracy is definitely important, but great precision is not required. In controlling detailed operations at the department level, however, a high degree of both precision and accuracy is required.

Economic feasibility and efficiency can be summarized in two statements: (1) the cost of the data processing system does not place an excessive burden on the physical operation generating the data to be processed; (2) the data processing system gives the most information for the dollars expended. The second statement says that it would not be possible to change an efficient system to get *more* information without spending more money. The first statement is more complex. If processing costs are too high, the physical operation will eventually have to cease. However, just because the returns from the physical operation are sufficient to cover the associated processing costs does not mean that the level of processing is appropriate. The general relationship between cost and value of processing is shown in Figure 1.2. This is an application of the principle of diminishing returns. As the cost of processing increases, the value of the information received for each dollar of expense tends to increase, but at a rapidly decreasing rate. Eventually, very little additional information is being obtained for each addition to processing costs. Ideally, investment in the process is stopped at the point where the value of the last unit of information generated is just equal to the cost of obtaining it.

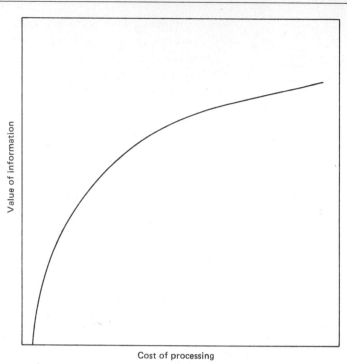

FIGURE 1.2   *Relation of the cost of processing and the value of information*

Summary   *Data processing* consists of a set of procedures (recording, classification and sorting, storage and retrieval, summarization, and analysis) used to process *data* (raw facts) to produce *information* (communicated knowledge expressed in a form that makes it immediately useful for decision making) for management planning and control, to produce custodial documents, and to provide historical records. Data processing systems are *file processing* systems. Data on business transactions are collected and used to update the affected permanent records in the master file. Management reports are then created from the flow of transactions and the changed status of the master records. An effective data processing system will possess characteristics of timeliness, pertinence, precision and accuracy, and economic feasibility and efficiency.

Questions   1. Define the following as briefly as possible and then use a short paragraph to clarify each definition.

a. Data processing
b. Data
c. Information
d. Custodial processing

e. Input
f. Output
g. Real-time data processing system
h. File

i. Transaction   k. Record

j. Master file   l. File processing

2. For each pair of concepts listed below, carefully explain the difference between the two concepts. (Use the definitions developed in question 1 to clearly identify how each concept differs from the other member of the pair.)

    a. Data and information   e. Precision and accuracy

    b. Classifying and sorting   f. Economic feasibility and

    c. Summarization and analysis   economic efficiency

    d. Communicating and reporting

3. List, in order of importance, the three reasons for processing business data and briefly justify your choice of order.

4. Why must the concept of information as used here include each of the following characteristics?

    a. Novelty

    b. Communication

    c. Form of information

    d. Decision making

5. What are the three phases of the data processing system?

6. How do the economic concepts of time, form, and place utility enter into the concept of information?

7. What are the desirable characteristics of a data processing system?

8. Which of the desirable characteristics of a data processing system relates to:

    a. Time utility of information?

    b. Place utility of information?

    c. Form utility of information?

    Carefully justify each of your choices.

9. As assistant to the president of HAFM Corporation (a diversified holding company), you have been directed to collect the information needed to decide whether or not HAFM should acquire the BBFM Company, a building construction firm.

    a. What kinds of data would you collect?

    b. How would you process each type of data before presenting it to the board of directors as a basis for decision making?

    c. How might a computer be used in processing the data? Would it be necessary?

10. The local mayor and city council are faced with a decision about whether the city should provide garbage service or leave the provision of this service to private firms.

    a. What types of data might be obtained in order to develop information on which to base this decision?

b. What processing might be performed on these data before their presentation to the mayor and city council?

11. Adam Jones receives a bill from the local department store, compares its entries to his copies of the sales tickets contained in a file folder labeled "Current Unpaid Bills," finds it is correct, and sends a check for the balance to the store. He notes the check number on the portion of the billing statement he retains, attaches the copies of the sales tickets, and files the packet in a file folder labeled "Bills Paid." Referring to Adam's data processing system:

   a. What master file(s) can you identify?
   b. What transaction file(s) can you identify?
   c. What data processing procedures can you identify?
   d. What improvements can you suggest?

Two

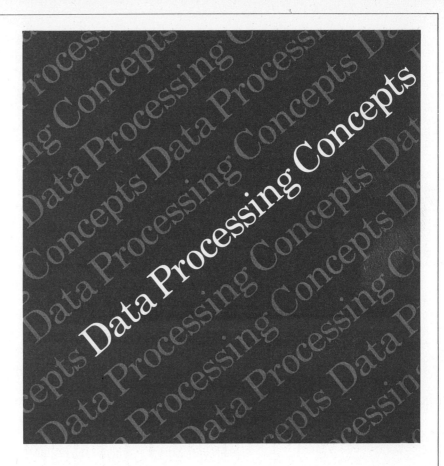

Data Processing Concepts

However, **D**ata processing in operation is a very complex activity. The few data processing concepts introduced in the previous chapter are insufficient as a basis for a full understanding of this activity. In order to be implemented, desirable properties of data processing systems must be identifiable as operable procedures. To fit individual data processing operations into a system that will produce desired results requires a clear understanding of how these operations are carried out. Files must be designed and procedures for updating and accessing them established. This requires an understanding not only of the structure and processing of individual files, but also of the design and use of interrelated sets of files (data bases) as well. It is the purpose of this chapter to provide this understanding.

Data Structure

For example,

In data processing there exists a structure by which data are described and organized. The smallest element in this structure is called a *bit*. This term is a contraction of the phrase *"binary digit."* A bit is the smallest recognizable element into which data can be separated.

Combinations of bits make up *characters*. In electronic data processing, the bit is a binary digit — a 0 (zero) or a 1 (one) — and each character is a combination of 0's and 1's. In general, a character consists of one or more bits. Several codes have been used in combining the binary digits to form characters. Figure 2.1 briefly illustrates some common binary based codes. A more complete example of binary data codes is given in Figure 8.1 in Chapter 8.

The minimal combination of characters with subject matter meaning is called a *word*. A word is made up of one or more characters. A character, in turn, is made up of one or more bits. Therefore, it is possible that a word could be formed by a single bit. Note that a "word" can be numerical as well as verbal.

Data *fields* are formed by groupings of one or more words making up a particular data module. For example, a person's name is usually composed of three words — the first name, the middle name, and the surname. On a data processing form, the name field often specifically provides for those three words.

Fields are aggregated into *records*. A record is a unit (related collection) of data about a thing of interest. For example, a student's transcript is a record of his or her school performance and is identified as a "student record" in a school's "student record file."

A *file* is a collection of records about similar entities or transactions. For example, the student record file referred to above would contain the transcripts for all students.

A file is sometimes subdivided into groups of records called *blocks*. This is usually done to facilitate processing. Thus, in a manual system, a file of departmental accounts in a university could be separated into several groups

FIGURE 2.1   *Examples of bit structure of characters*

Character	Binary code
A	110001
B	110010
C	110011
1	000001
2	000010
3	000011

File element	Example of element
File	The whole set of accounts receivable data. (There is *one* file.)
Block	All accounts for customers whose names begin with the letters A and B. (Each file contains one or more blocks.)
Record	The account for Lois Jane Friedman. (Each block contains one or more records.)
Field	The space for the name in the account record. (Each record contains one or more fields.)
Word	The first name in the name field, Lois. (Each field contains one or more words.)
Character	The first letter in the first name, L. (Each word contains one or more characters.)
Bit	The recognizable "pieces" making up each character. (Each character contains one or more bits.)

FIGURE 2.2   *Elements of an accounts receivable file*

and each group assigned to a particular accounting clerk. Processing would be speeded as each accounting clerk became intimately familiar with the transactions carried out by the few departments whose records he or she was assigned.

The hierarchy of data structure described above is illustrated in Figure 2.2, where the structure is defined by examples from an accounts receivable file. The differences between fields, words, characters, and bits are further illustrated in Figure 2.3, where a possible physical structure of a record is shown.

File Organization

A file of records can be organized in many ways. All ways involve ordering the records into the file through use of the *major record key* for each record. The major record key is a field within the record used as the primary iden-

FIGURE 2.3   *Physical structure of a record*

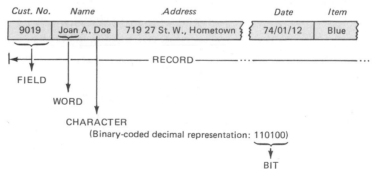

tifier for that record. Thus, in the accounts receivable file referred to in the previous chapter, each record may be principally identified either by the name of the customer to whose account the record corresponds or by the customer number. The major key is also referred to as the *control field* of the record, or simply as the *file key*.

Records within a file are usually accessed by the control field for routine processing activities. However, any field (or word) within the record may serve as a *sorting key*. Thus if the accounts receivable records were being *aged* (classified by the extent to which they were delinquent), the delinquency status field would be used as a key in sorting the records into delinquency classes.

SEQUENTIAL FILE ORDER

may also be sequentially ordered, in which case the

Sequentially ordered files are simply arranged in ascending or descending order of the major record key. Thus, for the accounts receivable file, if the key were the customer name, the records would be arranged in the alphabetic order of customer names. If the key were the account number, the records would be ordered in the numerical sequence of the account numbers. Use of an appropriate alphabetically related coding scheme in assigning the account numbers could result in simultaneously ordering by number and name but will allow sorting on the number alone.

INDEXED-SEQUENTIAL FILE ORDER

Further, a file may be set up in

In a file organized by the indexed-sequential method, the individual records are arranged into sequence by the control field and grouped into *blocks* for storage. An index containing two entries is created. The first entry indicates the starting point of the block. The second contains the control entry (major key) for the last record in the block. Within the block the records are arranged sequentially according to control field content. Access to an individual record is gained by looking up the block location in the block index table and then reading sequentially through the records in the block until the desired record is found. A sequentially ordered file stored in a set of steel file drawers is a common example of an indexed-sequential file. Each drawer is labeled with the major-key identifier of the first and last records the drawer contains. These labels on the outside fronts of the file drawers form the block index table. The labels on the tabs of the folders within the drawers are the sequentially indexed keys within each block.

INDEXED-NONSEQUENTIAL FILE ORDER

A nonsequential file can also be indexed. The index table will contain an entry for each and every item in the file, however. A familiar example of an indexed-nonsequential file is the storage system for books in a library. Consider each book as a record, the card catalog as the index, and all the books on the shelves as the file. Each book is assigned an identifying major key (Dewey Decimal Code or Library of Congress Code) according to its general content. Each book is listed in the catalog both by author and by title in alphabetic order. The books are stored on the shelves (arranged in the file) in order of their master keys (by order of their identifying code). The author and title cards in the index (the catalog) locate each book by its coded major key.

Note that the index in this case does not specify an exact physical location. Rather, the major key identifies only the shelf on which the book can be found. When an individual volume is added or deleted, only one shelf unit needs to be rearranged. If all the books were arranged in the same order as one of the indexes (alphabetically by title, for example), a much larger number of books would have to be moved each time a book was added or deleted.

RANDOM FILE ORDER

Records may be entered into a file without reference to order. To be able to retrieve an individual record, however, we must know where that record is. Therefore, the location of each record in a randomly ordered file is based in some fashion on the record key. Usually a formula is applied to each record key to obtain the location on the storage device in which to store the record. A record is retrieved from the file by recomputing its location. Actually, in most such filing systems the records are not truly ordered randomly into the file. Rather, the formula and the key assigned to the record are carefully chosen so that frequently used records can be found and retrieved in the least amount of time. Most such systems compute *symbolic* locations from which the physical location is then determined. They are really *direct addressing methods*, rather than random addressing methods. They allow each record to be located *directly*, rather than in relation to other records.

Direct Relation Addressing The simplest direct addressing method is *direct relation addressing*, which assigns the record to a location corresponding to the major file key of the record. Whenever a record is added to the file, it is assigned the address of the serially first empty location in the file as its record key. For example, suppose a customer account is being added to the accounts receivable file. The first empty location on the storage device has the address of 2017. The number 2017 would be assigned to the record and the record stored in the location with the address of 2017. The limitations of this method are that the record key is required to be numerical and that storage space can be wasted. Enough space must be allocated initially to hold the total file. Reassignment of keys that become available when a record is deleted can often cause problems of identity at a later date unless they remain empty for a time.

Key Transformation Processes More random methods of providing direct addressing are the *key transformation processes*. Two of these processes are illustrated in Figure 2.4. Both locate *relative addresses*, that is, addresses relative to the first physical location used by the file. Note that in the example of the division method, we have used the number of locations in the file as the divisor. The remainder can then vary from 0 to one less than the divisor. Since we add 1 to the remainder, the relative addresses obtained can vary from 1 to 3000, the number of locations to be used for the file. The divisor does not have to be the number of storage locations. Prime numbers (numbers evenly divisible only by themselves and by 1) are often used as the divisor to guarantee that the minimum identifying number (key) contains a specific number of digits.

The second example extracts digits from the record key to form a location. In some forms of this technique, a two part process is used, where two sets of digits are extracted and added together to find the location.

Logical Calculation Another form of direct addressing locates the record address through *logical calculation* of its relative address. This method is

FIGURE 2.4   *Two examples of record location by key transformation*

---

1. Division: The record key is divided by a number, the quotient is discarded, and the remainder, plus 1, becomes the relative storage location of the record.

    Example: Record Key = 7628
                   Number of locations needed = 3000

$$\frac{2}{3000\overline{)7628}}$$
$$\underline{6000}$$
$$1628 = \text{Remainder}$$

                   Relative address of record = 1628 + 1 = *1629*

2. Extraction: The storage location is developed from a set of digits extracted from the record key.

    Example: Record Key = 518782496
                   Extract second, fourth, sixth, and eighth digits to obtain storage location: *1729* is the record location.

---

particularly useful when the file can be considered to be a matrix (table) of two or more dimensions. The process involves counting rows and columns of the table to find the location of the desired data item or record. For example, suppose we wish to access a daily sales record file with entries for daily sales of 25 products by each of 10 sales representatives. We wish to find the sales amount for the fifth sales representative ($R = 5$) on the tenth working day ($D = 10$) of the second month ($M = 2$) for product 17 ($P = 17$). Each record contains 32 characters ($L = 32$). The relative address, RA, of the record can be obtained from the following calculation:

$$RA = 25(R - 1)(L)(M) + (P - 1)(L)(D) + 1$$
$$= 25(5 - 1)(32)(2) + (17 - 1)(32)(10) + 1$$
$$= 6400 + 5120 + 1$$
$$= 11,521$$

This relative address (11,521) would be added to the address of the first character in the file to find the *physical address* where the record being sought actually begins.

Buckets To overcome the inflexibility of the direct addressing techniques, the physical file is often divided into *buckets*, each of which will store a fixed number of records. A direct addressing technique is used to obtain the address of one of these buckets, and the record is stored in the first empty location found in the bucket. If the bucket is full, the record is placed in either the serially next bucket or an *overflow* bucket whose address is recorded in a *pointer* field at the end of that bucket.

LIST ORGANIZATION FOR FILES

The key idea leading to the development of list organization (and processing) of files was the *pointer* referred to in the discussion of buckets. Records are stored in physical locations on a storage device. Thus they are given a *physical relation* to one another by the physical ordering of the locations in which they are stored. The physical order need not control the order of access, however, particularly if pointers are included with each record to identify other records that have a *logical relation* to the particular record. Thus, the record in the first physical location in a file need not be the *logically first* record in the file nor must it be followed, *logically*, by the second record.

The basic list structure is a *simple list* in which a file is logically ordered by a file key. Suppose, for example, that employees are each given an identification number that indicates the position where they work (division, department, level) and a unique identifier in that department (the seventeenth or twenty-second employee). For ease in file maintenance, however, the record for each new employee is added to the payroll file in the first open position available. If we consider only employee number and name as contents, the file would look something like this:

Name	Identification number	Physical location	Logical order	Pointer
Joan R. Bradley	617584	1	5	*
Penny Schwartz	511303	2	2	4
Juan N. Mendoza	608215	3	4	1
Kevin Kelly	511304	4	3	3
Tom Longo	412413	5	1	2

Logically, these records relate to one another by identification number. Thus Penny Schwartz and Kevin Kelly are in the same division and department, work at the same level, and were hired in sequence. In order to access the records in *logical order*, a pointer is added to each record indicating in which physical location the next logical record will be found. Note that the last record in the file is given a special symbol as its pointer to indicate it is the last record.

Insertion and deletion of records in a simple list is relatively easy. Suppose we add the record for Shirley A. Miller to the above file. Shirley works at level four in department twelve of division five and is the twenty-second employee in that department. Her identification number would be 512422, placing her fourth in logical order. The file would now look as follows:

Name	Identification number	Physical location	Logical order	Pointer
Joan R. Bradley	617584	1	6	*
Penny Schwartz	511303	2	2	4
Juan N. Mendoza	608215	3	5	1
Kevin Kelly	511304	4	3	6
Tom Longo	412413	5	1	2
Shirley A. Miller	512422	6	4	3

Suppose the record for Joan R. Bradley is deleted because she leaves for another job. This time, the logically last record will be the record of Juan N. Mendoza, and the file will appear as follows:

Name	Identification number	Physical location	Logical order	Pointer
Penny Schwartz	511303	2	2	4
Juan N. Mendoza	608215	3	5	*
Kevin Kelly	511304	4	3	6
Tom Longo	412413	5	1	2
Shirley A. Miller	512422	6	4	3

Sometimes there is a need for more than one pointer in each record. For example, a record in the customer order file is logically related to the customer's record in the customer file and to the record for the item ordered in the item (inventory) file. Two pointers would be needed to show those relationships. The creation of such *multilists* can usefully decrease duplication across a set of files, but makes the insertion and deletion of records more difficult. A special type of multilist is the *two-way list,* which contains not only forward pointers but also backward pointers. A two-way list can be entered at any point and scanned logically forward or backward. The listing system used to make it possible to enter a list at any point and process through it is the *ring list.* In the ring list, the last logical record points back to the first logical record.

INVERTED FILES

The file organization and access methods discussed above implicitly assume that the files are standard files in which each record contains the attribute values for a particular file entity and the indexes used showed where to find each record (set of attribute values). In the inverted file, this process is reversed. Indexes are constructed with attribute values in order to identify the entities (records in the file) that possess those attribute values. For example, we might prepare indexes for the payroll file used above using employee level (grade) and division as indexes. The indexes for the next-to-last version above (which contains six entries) would look like this:

Employee grade	Employee number	Division	Employee number
2	608215	4	412413
3	511303	5	511303
	511304		511304
4	412413		512422
	512422	6	608215
5	617584		617584

The standard method of file indexing is good for answering the question: What are the attribute values of a given entity? The inverted file is designed to answer the question: Which entities possess a particular attribute?

A *fully inverted* file would index the entity identifiers for each and every attribute value in the file. A *partially inverted file* is more common and indexes only the entity identifiers for certain major attributes, not for all attributes.

File Processing

A business data processing application requires that one or more master files are established, that data on business transactions and changes in the environment are captured (recorded) and processed against the master files to update those files, and that management and custodial reports are developed from the flow of transaction and change data and the changed status of the master files. As indicated in Chapter 1, these processes are really a series of *file processing operations*:

1. Master files are developed.

2. Processes are developed for capturing transaction data and environmental data and using them to update the master files.

3. Reporting processes are set up to derive needed reports from the flow of transactions and changes and from the changed status of the master files.

PROCESSING MODES

Basically, business or administrative data processing consists of recording pertinent data on each transaction and using the recorded data to update records (files) to reflect the effects of the transaction.

The specific processing methods used to carry out the updating of files vary with the nature of the transaction causing the update. For example, the factory worker on an hourly wage who finishes a shift and punches out on the time clock is completing the recording of data indicating how long he or she has actually worked that day. The period of work started when the worker punched in at the start of the shift. This transaction record may not be processed any further at the time. At the end of the pay period, however, the worker's time card is collected along with the time cards of the other hourly production workers and processed to update the payroll accounts and develop paychecks for the workers. At that time, the data may be processed not only to produce paychecks and related withholding records but also to produce management reports such as a labor cost distribution report. Such a report would charge the wages and benefits of each hourly employee (individual labor costs) to the department(s) and/or product(s) where the effort was expended. Similarly, at the department store the credit sales will be accumulated throughout the day and processed to update the accounts receivable, inventory, and sales records at the end of the day (perhaps on the next business day). Data from transactions are often accumulated over a period of time (*batched*) in this manner and then processed as a group (a *batch*). Such *batch processing* is very common when the effects of the transaction need not be reflected immediately in the affected files. Another example of batch processing is customer billing systems that accumulate charges daily but bill the customer only once a month.

Processing costs are often less when data from transactions can be accumulated over a period of time (batched) and then processed together. Another significant advantage of batch processing is that the data relating to transactions can be sorted into the same sequence as the file before processing takes place. This reduces the complexity of the processing operation. Also, *sequentially ordered* files can usually be stored on a less expensive storage medium — magnetic tape rather than magnetic disk, for example. Finally, not only is there a cost saving in storing the current (active) file, but it is also less costly to save earlier versions of the file and the transactions that have been passed against it. Thus in case of accidental destruction the current file can be recreated more easily.

Not all batch processing operations involve sequential processing. In those cases in which the proportion of records to be changed on a processing run is low, processing time can be saved by storing the file in a *random-access* mode. This mode differs from *sequential access* in that individual items in a sequentially accessed file must be accessed in sequential order. All items preceding the one being accessed must be passed to reach that item. Punched paper tape and magnetic tape are good examples of sequentially accessed media used for sequential storage of files. A *randomly accessed file* is one in which any individual record can be accessed directly and in approximately the same amount of time. Very few pure random-access file devices exist (magnetic-core memory is an example), but several essentially direct-access devices do exist (magnetic disks, magnetic-drum memories, and tub files). These *modified random-access files* feature *direct* access with random access to blocks of records and sequential access within each block. Such direct-access devices also include such data storage devices as tub files, rotary punched-card stores, and microfilm files.

Direct-access files are necessary for efficient *inline processing*, where transactions are processed in the order in which they occur. Inline processing usually does not involve batch processing, although it may. *Quick-response systems* (such as airline seat reservation systems) require inline processing against directly accessed files.

The airline seat reservation systems are also examples of *electronic online* processing systems, when the data are fed directly into a computer that has all the necessary files stored in electronic random-access storage devices physically attached to and under the control of the computer. Such *online* systems are being increasingly used in all phases of business data processing as their cost per transaction and their reliability improve. A major reason is that the immediate availability of updated records leads to more efficient control of the physical operation and to increased profits.

Data Processing Systems Orientation

As indicated earlier, data processing systems may be oriented primarily toward satisfying management information requirements or toward satisfying custodial processing needs. Systems also may be either *integrated* or *applications-oriented*. An *applications-oriented system* emphasizes the efficient handling of each particular subsystem. Thus there could be an accounts receivable subsystem, an inventory subsystem, and a sales analysis subsystem for handling the data generated by a charge sale at the department store. An *integrated system*, on the other hand, tends toward viewing the total processing system as a single system. But there are degrees of integration. *Technically*, an *integrated data processing system* is one in which there is a single recording of the basic data from each transaction in a common classifying code for the purpose of making maximum use of the data with a minimum number of human operations. This can consist simply of multiple copies of a single input document (the sales slip at the department store), which become the basic input for several processing subsystems. In a *fully integrated* data processing system, the data from the sales transaction would be entered once and *all* files (sales, inventory, accounts receivable) affected by the transaction would be updated in one complex operation.

In an *integrated electronic system*, the transaction record for the department store sale would usually be transcribed to an input medium (punched cards, magnetic tape, magnetic disk) that could be used separately with each of the subsystem programs or once with a more complicated program. Currently, more *fully integrated electronic systems* are available that include point-of-sale entry devices that capture all the data in an electronic form at the clerk's station (cash register) on the sales floor. All files affected by the transactions are then updated from that record. Completely integrated systems do not exist today, but highly integrated systems are growing in number and sophistication.

An integrated data processing system does not have to be oriented to providing adequate management information. However, it is necessary to define the relationships between separate files and the impact of data from a particular transaction on *all* files to develop such a system. This definition tends to lead to a fuller recognition of management's information needs, since it encourages the consideration of the total organization as an interrelated whole. Attention naturally swings toward controlling that total system to gain desired objectives. This in turn encourages definition of those objectives.

When the initial development expense can be carried by the operation and when the volume justifies the operating expense, a fully integrated system tends to be more efficient and less costly than an applications-oriented system. This is because the integrated system eliminates duplication in the content of files and reduces the processing time required to update those files.

Integrated Data Base

Historically, a data element (for example, the balance due) belonged to the department or application (accounts receivable) that created it. Labor cost data belonged to payroll; sales data belonged to the marketing group; financial data belonged to the finance department; and so on. As new applications were developed for the computer, analysts came to realize that, even in different departments, the same data elements were useful in several applications. Thus data developed from a credit sale transaction affect accounts receivable, sales analysis, inventory, personnel (who is doing the sales job), and payroll (if sales commissions are paid). The *integrated data base, a set of interrelated files containing at least one element in common,* was born. The philosophy underlying the integrated data base concept recognizes data as a resource and *assigns applications to data elements rather than elements to applications.* However, integrated sets of basic data files in which each data element appears only once, in which related data are cross-referenced, and in which related data elements can be located by starting from any one of the individual elements, don't just happen. They must be planned and created. To create a usable integrated data base, a data inventory must be created, data and information needs must be analyzed, the necessary data base files must be designed, and the procedures to maintain the data base must be established.

DATA INVENTORY

The inventory of data available in a firm is contained in the *data dictionary* for that firm.

The Data Dictionary Basically, the data dictionary is a listing of all the data elements found in the organization and usually shows the following for each data element:

1. name (e.g., credit sale amount)
2. form (e.g., numeric)
3. size (the number of characters, e.g., 7)
4. primary source (e.g., credit sale ticket)
5. location (e.g., accounts receivable file in the finance department; stored on disk number FIN-100-1)
6. uses (e.g., accounts receivable, sales analysis, cost control, payroll)

Analysis of Data Uses Even though the data dictionary has a listing of the uses for each data element, these uses may not be fully developed at the time a new data base is being created. Data and information uses throughout the organization or function being integrated should be carefully analyzed and each use listed and described as follows:

1. The form of each data or information element in each of its uses (graph, table, document, ratio, or listing)
2. The frequency of use for each report (or inquiry) by individual data element as well as by category
3. The speed with which each recall or other response must be possible

DATA BASE DESIGN

We may have implied earlier that a single integrated data base would be created for the total organization. Seldom can this be done. Normally, all that is envisioned is the integration of one or parts of two functional areas based on one or two common sources of data, such as for integrating all the applications using credit sales data as input. The first step is to segregate the data base into individual files. Each file must be carefully designed to provide proper inquiry response and report-generating abilities. Decisions to be made include:

1. The exact content of each file
2. The storage device for each file
3. The file linkages (file organization)

The answers to these questions will depend upon the volume of data in each file, the frequency and form of access needed, the relationships between the different files and how much cross-referencing is required, and the processing modes that will be used.

MAINTAINING THE DATA BASE

Data base maintenance involves more than updating the records contained in each file. New records must be added and old ones deleted. Addresses, names, and other fixed data elements can change as well. More important, new data elements (fields) can be added to each record and old data elements dropped. In addition, provision must be made for retrieval of data in nonroutine ways in response to unique inquiries. Finally, the security of the data files must be assured, with access controlled so that unauthorized users are not allowed to work with the files and authorized users are not allowed to accidentally destroy or rearrange their content.

Today, a large part of the file management activities are controlled by computer programs (software). Data base management software (languages) allows users to access data elements by name without knowing or caring exactly where the element is physically stored. Data elements (fields) can be removed, added, or rearranged for use with relative ease. Unusual and unique inquiries can be responded to in a short time. The detailed processes of finding, retrieving, modifying, and moving data elements into and among the physical locations on the storage device are handled by the data base management language. We will have more to say about this in Chapter 13.

Management Reporting and Decision Making

As indicated in Chapter 1, a data processing system is not complete unless the outputs produced are fully and effectively communicated to management (that is, unless *information* is created). This implies that the data processing system must be designed to develop informational outputs in response to management's needs and not just for data processing convenience. The timing of the processing cycle must therefore relate to the timing of the physical operating cycle of the operation in which the data originate. Adequate managerial control requires that management be given information about the operation frequently enough to prevent the continuation of undesirable activities.

Historically, reporting to management has been *periodic*. Processing has been largely in the batch mode after the close of an operating cycle or an accounting period. At that point, transactions were processed, all files completely updated, and the condition of the organization or operation determined. The time required to determine the condition of the organization or operation usually meant that reports were available some time after the operating or accounting period being reported on had ended and the next period was well started. Actions taken to correct revealed problems were often incorrect. The nature of the problem had changed, the problem was already solved, or it was too late to do anything about it. The delayed reaction often acted to reinforce and overextend natural corrective actions. Thus the delayed reaction tended to create an unnecessary oscillation in the operation. The formal information system provided information from too far in the past. What is desired is a *real-time response*, a response in time to affect (in a desirable way) an ongoing physical operation.

Still another factor to consider is the quality and form of the response. As indicated in our definition of information, the report must be in a useful form. One useful form of response is to report details on *exceptions* only. Exceptions are the unplanned, unexpected, and unusual results. They have high information content and pinpoint problems with fair precision, and their use reduces reporting requirements. Establishing *exception reporting* as the principal form of management reporting leads to both *effective* (useful to management) and *efficient* (less voluminous and therefore less costly) management information systems.

Modern Management Techniques

Another way in which the data processing function is changing is in response to the development of more structured decision-making techniques of management. The advent of the electronic computer has made the routine use of scientific decision techniques a possibility. Answers to such questions as what mix of products should be produced with available materials and productive capacities to attain a maximum net return or to fill available orders at minimum cost can now be available daily, weekly, or monthly. Changes in product prices and costs of materials can be combined with modifications in productive capacities to determine optimum operating mixes. Warehouse locations that minimize storage and transportation costs and also reduce chances of failing to satisfy customer demands in each area can be found. The number of equipment repair centers and their locations can be so determined as to minimize all costs, including the cost of required service and the cost of downtime while equipment is out of service. Complex projects ranging from constructing a large building to preparing a computer-based data processing system can be so scheduled that the project can be expected to be finished on time and within allowable cost limits. A complete view of all the scientific decision-making techniques available to management is beyond the scope of this text. In fact it is beyond the scope of *any* single text.[1]

---

[1] Some useful texts in this area are included in the bibliography in Appendix A among references for further study of the topics of each part of this text.

Modern management science techniques are most easily classified by the characteristics of the decision problem to be attacked. The decision situation is analytically structured (modeled), and then the appropriate technique is applied. There are three basic types of models.

Stochastic models apply to those situations in which the relationships between controllable variables and outcomes cannot be exactly stated but must be defined in terms of probabilities, or when values of important variables are unknown. Statistical decision and statistical estimation procedures are the major tools applied to such problems. These tools are used to estimate future sales levels, to control physical processes, and to study relationships between variables. Variable values and relational coefficients obtained through the application of statistical analysis are often used in other models.

Deterministic models are used in situations in which the relationships among all pertinent problem variables and the values of pertinent variables can safely be assumed to be known. In these situations it is assumed that setting the values of the controllable variables will completely determine the value of the important variable (or variables) that cannot be controlled directly. Mathematical programming (linear and nonlinear programming, both integer and noninteger) and other mathematical modeling techniques are the major techniques used in this area.

Mixed models apply to complex situations in which some aspects of the problem are subject to analytic treatment using certainty models but other aspects of the situation can only be specified using probabilities. One example of such a situation is the linear programming problem in which coefficients in the model are subject to random fluctuations or are available only as statistical estimates subject to errors whose probability distribution can be specified. Certain network planning methods (for example, PERT) in which the time to accomplish a part of the task can only be specified as a range of values also qualify as mixed models. Queuing models used to study the relationships among customer arrivals, number of servers, and service times usually involve aspects requiring the use of probability distributions to describe performance in some parts of the model. For many such models, no way of obtaining a solution by mathematical analysis of the model exists. However, knowledge of the model structure can improve decisions of managers operating in such situations.

Computer simulation has been valuable when none of the available analytic solution models fit the situation. For very complex situations in which many variables are affecting one another, the best technique for gaining insight is computer simulation. For example, it is valuable in studying the realistic but complicated queuing situations for which analytic models do not exist. In computer simulation, how the situation (problem, organization, market) operates is *described* as fully as possible. Important relationships are stated as explicitly as possible and then "programmed" in a computer language. The simulation model is then operated by the computer. Inputting changes in model parameters and observing the results allow the analysis of the effects of different policies on outcomes.

Management science techniques can also be classified by the *purpose* for which they are used. For *planning,* the techniques applied are highly diversified. They include simple trend or other smoothing models describing movements over time; regression models that forecast variables by studying relationships between the forecasted variable and other variables thought to exhibit a causal relationship to that variable; the various network models (CPM, PERT); and the resource allocation algorithms of mathematical programming.

Control models tend primarily to be statistical. They usually entail developing an optimum or satisfactory range within which variables are to remain, based on some desired optimum or standard. This range is usually in the form of a probability distribution of the relevant controlled variable developed from a statistical analysis of past performance or from an analytic study of design characteristics of the process being controlled.

In any case, the growing use of mathematically oriented management science models and methods to aid management decision making is affecting the establishing, maintaining, and operating of management information systems. Progressive managers are interested in incorporating many of these management science tools as standard parts of the management information system. They expect the analytic use of these tools to be a routine part of management planning and control systems.

Summary

Data must be organized if they are to be stored and retrieved for use in valuable ways. The file is the basic organizational structure for data. Individual records, each containing data on attributes of a specific entity, are organized into files. A *master file* contains the permanent, on-going record for a set of related entities. Temporary files containing records of individual transactions and/or changes in the master records are processed against the permanent master files to update them. Management reports, including responses to nonscheduled inquiries, are developed from the flow of transactions and changes and from the changed status of the master file.

Records may be ordered into a file sequentially, randomly, or as lists. Sequentially ordered files can be stored on any medium, but random and list organizations require a storage device that allows direct access to each location for efficient processing of the file. Direct-access files may be ordered through direct relation addressing, distributed addressing, indexed addressing, or lists. List organization includes simple lists, two-way lists, ring lists, and inverted files. In inverted files, the keys identifying each record (entity) in the file are grouped under individual attributes possessed by the entities. That is, attributes are the file index, and identifying record keys are the index content, a reversal of the normal file index.

Individual files can be organized into *integrated data bases*, which are sets of interrelated files containing at least one element in common. The data base approach developed from the recognition that the same data elements are used in several applications. The result is a change in philosophy. In nonintegrated systems, each data element is "owned" by the application that created it. We now recognize data as a resource and assign applications to data elements, rather than the other way about. This modern approach requires that a data inventory and a complete analysis of data and information needs and uses be developed, that data base files be carefully designed, and that processes and procedures for keeping the data base up to date be coordinated.

The chapter concludes with a few remarks on the nature and purpose of management reports and the increasing importance of modern management science techniques for data analysis to guide management decisions.

Questions

1. Define the following as briefly as possible and then use a short paragraph to clarify each definition.
   - a. Online processing
   - b. Inline processing
   - c. Batch processing
   - d. Real-time response
   - e. Integrated data processing system
   - f. Exception
   - g. Sequential access
   - h. Random-access
   - i. Quick-response system
   - j. Operating cycle
   - k. Indexed-sequential file order
   - l. Inverted file
   - m. File bucket
   - n. File key
   - o. File
   - p. Record
   - q. Direct addressing
   - r. Relative address
   - s. Data base
   - t. Physical address
   - u. Data base management language
   - v. Symbolic location
   - w. List processing
   - x. Data inventory

2. Must an integrated data processing system be an inline system? Explain.

3. Could an applications-oriented system be a real-time system? Explain.

4. If this book were considered a file, what would each chapter be? Explain.
5. Why should exceptions have a high information content?
6. Why is it important that we recognize the increasing use of management science tools by modern managers when studying data processing?
7. Can a batch processing system be a real-time system?
8. Must a real-time system be an online system?
9. Differentiate between deterministic and stochastic models.
10. a. Would the model describing a coin toss game be an example of a deterministic or a stochastic model?
    b. Would you change your answer if you were told that the coin is known to be "fair" (heads and tails are equally likely on each uncontrolled toss) and the toss is uncontrolled?
11. Use an automobile parts inventory accounting system as a source for examples of the elements of a file.
12. What are the advantages of batch processing?
13. What are the advantages of inline processing?
14. Can a batch processing system include inline processing? Explain, citing a specific example if possible.
15. What are the advantages of exception-oriented management reporting systems?
16. Would batch or continuous inline processing most likely be used for handling an application with a large volume of transactions occurring primarily at regularly spaced periods of peak activity? Explain.
17. Would your answer to question 16 change if adequate processing of any individual transaction required knowledge of the effects of previous transactions? Explain.
18. Would batch or continuous inline processing most likely be used for handling a low-volume application where transactions occur —
    a. In bunches at irregularly spaced peak periods?
    b. Individually but at irregular intervals?
19. Can a sequentially ordered file be randomly accessed? Explain.
20. Under what conditions would a randomly accessible file be preferable to a sequentially accessible file?
21. What criteria should be used to decide between inline instantaneous updating of a file and batched sequential updating?
22. The protection of files against accidental or intentional (malicious) destruction is a major concern to many organizations. What are some of the protection techniques that might be suggested?
23. How has the data base concept led to a change in the philosophy of data management?

24. Differentiate the following lists:
    a. Simple list
    b. Two-way list
    c. Ring list
25. What is the purpose of the inverted file organization?
26. How does a file bucket differ from a file block?
27. Briefly describe the four phases of developing an integrated data base.

Three

Management Information Systems

It is popular to link the term *management information system* to the electronic digital computer. The implication seems to be that management information systems are impossible to develop without electronic aids. This is an erroneous view. The *management information system* (MIS) of an organization is merely that combination of people, machines, and procedures used to produce information for management use.

In the most general sense in which it is used in this chapter, *system* stands for a combination of elements, their attributes, and their interrelationships, organized in the pursuit of a common objective. Thus a business firm is a combination of people, machines, money, and procedures for engaging in the pursuit of the objectives of that firm. As a system, the management information system is a subsystem of the firm that is engaged in providing *information* to management as a basis for decision making. In order to understand this concept, we must understand the firm itself. We also must keep in mind the definitions laid out in Chapter 1, where information was defined as *communicated knowledge expressed in a form that makes it immediately useful for decision making.*

The Elements of an Organization

Any organization, whether business, government, or educational, is composed of at least three kinds of interrelated factors, or elements. First, there are the resources and productive factors controlled by the organization. In a business organization these are people, materials, and money that the business organization controls. The second classification of factors is the specific activities to be carried on by the institution. In a business organization these might be manufacturing, marketing, personnel management, and financial operations, for example. The third and final set of factors is the activities of management — defining objectives, developing plans, executing plans, and evaluating the results. The activities of an organization are carried out under the direction of managers. These managers establish objectives and translate them into plans. Managers then attempt to execute these plans and evaluate the results as a basis for further planning.

Figure 3.1 represents the interrelationship of the resources and activities of the business firm and illustrates how complex these relationships really are.[1] However, Figure 3.1 is inadequate in this regard. For example, it does indicate that customers may influence and be influenced by the way in which resources are allocated to the various activities of the firm, but it does not clearly indicate that customers interact with employees in determining consumer acceptance of the firm. Also, the financial resources of the firm are reflected in research methods and manufacturing processes, which are in turn markedly influenced by the quality and quantity of employees. A dedicated and imaginative staff of well-trained researchers and engineers backed up by an efficient marketing organization employing well-trained and dedicated marketing specialists can obviously do a great deal to keep a firm progressively in the forefront of its industry.

Figure 3.1 is inadequate in another way. It does not take into account certain outside (environmental) factors that are extremely important to the business firm. A business organization is affected by the general level of economic activity and the actions of competitors. It is also influenced by political and legislative actions at the national, state, and local government levels. The exact nature of these interactions with outside forces is difficult

---

[1] Figure 3.1 is patterned after a figure prepared several years ago by William Robinson, who was then Director of Financial Systems, Management Systems Operation, Weyerhaeuser Company, in describing the activities of his organization.

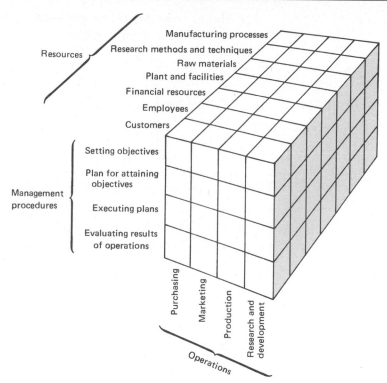

FIGURE 3.1   *Interrelationships of factors and functions of business firms*

to specify. That these outside forces do affect the firm is not a matter of question.

One potential view of the management information system can be drawn from Figure 3.1. This view would see the information system as the creation and/or exchange of information at all the points of interaction among the elements of the organization and between the organization and its environment. Figure 3.1 is particularly inadequate here in that it fails to depict all the points at which the organization interacts with its environment. These latter points are especially important to the information system, for they are points at which the bulk of the business transactions occur that create business data. Figure 3.1 indicates interaction only with customers.

This view of the firm has at least two important implications for the development of management information systems. The first is the complexity of the organization and the many points at which data and information must be available to guide and ease the interaction of the many diverse elements of the firm. The second implication of Figure 3.1 is more subtle but equally important. It requires the recognition that the individual elements of the firm are controlled and operated by *people*. The job of executing

done by management consists largely of hiring, organizing, coordinating, and controlling people. Without sufficient knowledge of what is being done and how it is being accomplished, people do not perform well. Part of the job of the information system must be to get the right data and information to each point at which people interact so that they will be sufficiently informed to perform their individual functions effectively.

The Information System as an Organizational Construct

The information system of an organization obviously reflects the structural organization of the firm. The MIS can thus be viewed as an organizational construct. The organizational structure of information systems can be represented by at least three different organizational patterns.

IDEALISTIC HIERARCHICAL

The first pattern reflects an idealistic organizational pattern for an organization and is represented by the two-dimensional, flat-topped pyramid in Figure 3.2(a). As information about activities moves from the production line or sales room to the position of the chief executive or top executive body of the organization, the information passed upward is continually condensed. Information on individual customers, employees, facilities, and transactions goes to the first-level manager (the foreman or first-line supervisor). Each foreman or supervisor then summarizes this detailed information and passes on that summary to the next management level, his or her departmental or division manager. Administrators at each level summarize and analyze information concerning their individual departments or divisions and pass their summaries on up the chain of command. And so it goes until, finally, the chief executive or chief executive body receives analyzed information for the entire organization or for major activities within the organization. The information supposedly has a form that is useful in assessing overall performance and trends and for setting major goals and policies for the organization. The confusion of detail existing at the first-line level has been sifted and analyzed (refined) to reveal the essence of its overall meaning.

WORST-CASE HIERARCHICAL

Contrasted to the idealistic hierarchical type of information system is that illustrated by the cylinder in Figure 3.2(b). In this information system the detail available at the first-line level is passed upward through the chain of command without analysis and summarization. Such a system is most apt

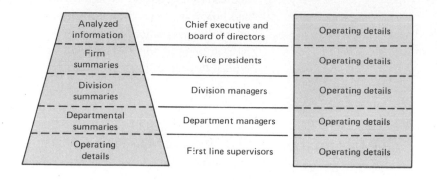

(a) Idealistic hierarchical MIS

(b) Worst-case hierarchical MIS

Analyzed information	Chief executive and board of directors	Operating details
Firm summaries	Vice presidents	Operating details
Division summaries	Division managers	Operating details
Departmental summaries	Department managers	Operating details
Operating details	First line supervisors	Operating details

(c) The true hierarchical MIS

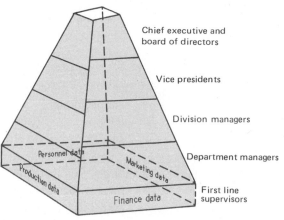

FIGURE 3.2   *The management information system as an organizational construct*

to exist when management positions are filled entirely by promotion from the next lower level. Managers at each level feel that they can adequately assess the performance of the managers reporting to them only if they themselves have all the detail they were used to getting in their old jobs at the level below. This system obviously is ineffective and does not really exist except in small, flat organizations with few levels in the management hierarchy.

THE TRUE HIERARCHICAL MIS

A third organizational pattern for the information system is probably nearer a true picture of existing systems. It is represented by the three-dimensional structure in Figure 3.2(c). The figure indicates that the detailed data generated by the activities carried on by the organization form a base from which the various levels of management extract information for purposes of decision making. The varying widths of the horizontal strata of the pyramid are intended to indicate that the differing levels of management reduce (distill) the information flowing upward to varying degrees. All levels do not contribute equally to the data analysis necessary to getting information in a form suitable for decision making at the higher levels. When the information flow reaches the top level (chief executive and board of directors), much analysis still remains to be done. The lack of a point on the top of the pyramid indicates that not all the information contained in the data base has been distilled out and provided for top-management use. If this had been done, the pyramid would reach a sharp point.

It is also true that each of the functional information subsystems does not do an equally complete job of data reduction and analysis. Different functional subsystems perform at differing levels of efficiency and effectiveness from firm to firm. Some firms have a better marketing information subsystem, others do better with finance, and so on. Most firms do have semi-independent information subsystems for each function or for each division or product, depending on the way they are organized. In any case, these subsystems operate with differing levels of efficiency and none seems to do a complete job.

There are obvious relationships between the hierarchical position of a manager in the organization and the type and form of information that manager should receive. The higher in an organization the recipient, the less detail should be in the reports received. The higher in the organization the manager, the less he or she is involved in execution of plans (supervision) and the more in setting goals and planning to attain them. Top-level managers have primary responsibility for *strategic planning*, deciding what should be done. Middle-level managers have primary responsibility for *tactical planning*, deciding how it should be done. Lower-level managers have primary responsibility for *operational control*, seeing that the plans are carried out. This means that the higher the managers are in the organization, the less their need for detailed data and the greater their need for summarized and analyzed information. This also means that the higher the managers are in the organization, the more they must be involved with how that organization interacts with its environment. They must be aware of how that environment may be changing. Therefore they must be aware of the information drawn from data obtained from sources external to the firm. The informational needs of top management can be fully satisfied only by an information system that captures data about all activities of the organization and about its environment and then combines those data to show not only the outcomes of past actions but also the expected results of future actions.

The decisions in this area tend to be individually unique and the related information requirements more difficult to predict.

Middle-management planning focuses more on individual tasks and elements of the organization. Middle managers attempt to optimize relationships between resource inputs and product or service outputs. They deal with problems such as scheduling of tasks, determining optimal inventory levels, allocation of resources among different tasks, and cost control. The informational needs of these managers require more detail on results of past actions but are more predictable than the informational needs of top management. The decision process can be fully described for many such situations and turned over to a staff clerk or a machine.

Lower-level managers are primarily responsible for supervising employees as they carry out day-to-day tasks. Planning is minimal; the focus is on individual tasks and techniques of performing those tasks. The information needed at this level relates to performance measurement (relation of actual results to previously specified standards for both quantity and quality of output). Figure 3.3 illustrates the relationships among management level, management responsibilities, information detail, and sources of information.

The timing of system response also differs by management level. Planning the distant future does not *require* as current information on past results as does the planning of tomorrow's production schedule. More time can be afforded for analysis of data to be used in long-range (strategic) planning. Tactical planning requires more immediate feedback on operating results. Adequate supervisory control of operations requires immediate feedback on quantity and quality rates.

FIGURE 3.3   *Relationship of detail and source of information to management level and management responsibilities*

Hierarchical management level	Amount of detail	Information sources	Responsibility
Top	Minimum	External environment and internal operations	Strategic planning
Middle	Intermediate	Mostly internal operations	Operational planning and control
Lower	Maximum	Internal operations	Supervision of individual performance

Another important idea involved in the pyramid of Figure 3.2(c) is that the pyramid is not divided (vertically) among the functional areas (or operations). This is because each transaction normally affects more than one function. For example, take a charge sale at a department store. As a result of the sale, inventory is reduced (purchasing); sales are increased in total, for the particular department and for the specific salesperson (sales analysis); and accounts receivable are increased (finance).

The above comments should not be interpreted to mean that the *functional* responsibility of a manager has no influence on that manager's need for information. Marketing managers need information pertinent to the determination of product mix, promotional strategies, and sales quotas. Production managers need information pertinent to setting production goals, inventory limits, and production schedules. The marketing manager is not directly concerned with how many television chassis of acceptable quantity can be produced by the chassis production line in one hour, the production manager is. Conversely, the production manager is not directly concerned with the relative pulling power of a TV advertisement compared to a magazine advertisement, the marketing manager is.

Obviously, then, each manager's need for information is determined by that manager's hierarchical level in the organization and his or her functional responsibilities. Just as obviously, the need for information is influenced by managerial style, by the way the manager manages. Management style, in turn, is determined by the manager's personality, education, and previous experience.

The Information System as a Feedback and Control System

A different but equally instructive view of the information system is provided by cybernetics. In this view, each organization or part of an organization is seen as an operating feedback and control system. As shown in Figure 3.4, each of these systems consists of three elements: the planning and control element, the operating element performing the activity, and an evaluation element monitoring the results of the operation and reporting back to the planning and control element. Planning and control receives inputs from outside the organization (economic conditions, market trends, activities of competitors, and so on) as well as information from within the organization by way of the evaluation element. On the basis of this information, planning and control sets goals, develops policies and operating guides, and issues directives to the operating element. The resulting activity is monitored by the evaluation element and matched against the goals, plans, and directives established by planning and control. Deviations from desired results are reported back to planning and control so that corrective actions can be formulated and undertaken.

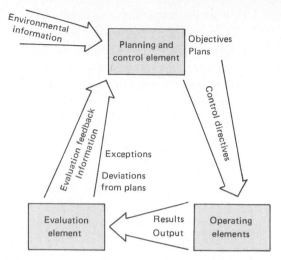

FIGURE 3.4   *The management information system as a feedback and control system*

There are at least two key relationships in the feedback and control loop we have just described. The first of these is *timing*, the second is the nature of the *monitoring* function. It is necessary to know how rapidly feedback must be developed in order to keep the process under control, that is, to keep the system in a stable state. Second, we must know what information must be developed, that is, what elements are critical in providing adequate information for effective planning and control.

The speed with which feedback must be developed depends upon the *cycle time* of the physical operation being controlled, that is, how long it takes the physical operation to run from start to finish. For example, the cycle time on a stock transaction on the New York Stock Exchange is very short. In most instances, when a trader (customer) places an order, it is sent immediately to the trading floor and executed. The cycle time for this physical operation can be less than one minute. On the other hand, a cattle rancher breeding cows to obtain calves which are to be raised and sold as beef cattle has a complete cycle time of three to four years. There are, however, decision points within that overall cycle. The first could be at the time of birth of the calf. The calf is marketable at that point. It might also be marketed at weaning time, as a yearling, or as a mature animal. Even in the last case, the rancher has a choice of marketing the animal as grass-fed only or as fattened (grain-fed) beef. For control of the process, information on ancestors' sizes and health and on the weight gain of each animal at each decision point would need to be considered in developing a feedback and control system for the rancher. However, there would not be any severe time constraint on the system.

Not all data that are recorded about an operation must necessarily be communicated to those responsible for the operation in order for them to adequately plan for and control that operation. Rather, it is apparent that data should be distilled, that their essence should be captured, and that only information that has immediate impact for decision making or planning purposes should be communicated to the people responsible for planning and control functions. Most of our information systems tend to look pretty much like the three-dimensional pyramid of Figure 3.2(c). We have tended to report too many details at all levels. One very important concept has been significantly noteworthy for its absence. This is the concept of *control by exception,* or *management by exception.*

Exceptions are unusual or unexpected things and have very high information content. For example, knowledge that the salespeople who are consistently exceeding their quotas have received a specific type of training, whereas salespeople without that training often fail to achieve their quotas is important information for planning future training programs. As another example, knowledge that certain individuals in management are successful because of specific attitudes, concepts, or skills received from their education is a very important piece of information for selecting management trainees. As a final example, knowing that sales of a particular product are considerably above (or below) expected levels has significance for future production levels and desired inventory levels. Knowing the detailed distribution of these sales by area and salesperson can be important in deciding on the permanence of the high (or low) level of sales. On the other hand, knowing such details about sales that are meeting expectations in total and by area and salesperson would not be as valuable. No corrective action is required, and planning procedures can apparently remain unchanged.

The Information System as a Data Processing System

Still another way to view the MIS is as a data processing system involved with the capture and processing of data to obtain information. Data processing is defined here as the *function of recording, summarizing, analyzing, and reporting data and information concerning activities of an organization* (with *data* and *information* defined as in Chapter 1).

Perhaps the most important concept involved in this area is the principle of *integrated data processing.* Integrated data processing attempts to record each piece of data once, to record it correctly, and then to utilize it in that same form in every way possible to elicit information for the planning and control purposes of the operation. What we are working for is as little duplication as possible. This prevents errors from creeping in. Every time data are converted from one medium to another, every time they are recopied, errors can and will creep in. The more human intervention in the processing of data can be reduced and the more the processing of data can be turned over to machines, the fewer errors there will be in the final results. However, it is also true that the more the ingenuity of humans can be used to plan for full analysis of the information content of any particular set of data, the greater the worth of the final information derived from the system. It therefore seems that we need to proceed on a twofold basis in the design of adequate information systems. On the one side, we need to look at the media requirements for the establishment of an efficient, unified set of basic data files. On the other side, we need to take a look at the informational requirements for efficient administration of current operations and also design routine analytic studies of the proper kinds of correctly captured data to provide the information necessary for future planning.

For an effective information system to be developed, it is required that information be available to all parts of the system. The MIS is a mix of information on employees, products, customers, facilities, and finances. Supporting information must be available on competitors, market conditions, government activities, and general economic conditions.

The needed records can be considered as files for each area. That is, we need files of data about employees, files providing data about facilities, files providing data concerning current products and processes, files presenting data on customers, files presenting budgetary and financial data for the firm, and files presenting data on research and development activities. Stated simply, we need to establish a *data bank* for the organization, a library of files containing all data and information relevant to the organization.

Figure 3.5 gives a diagrammatic view of such a data bank. The total cylinder is the total file system. Each slice of the cylinder represents a different file (or set of files) relating to a different area of the system. Figure 3.5 also indicates the different parts of the decision-making milieu most deeply interested in different aspects of this data bank. We must recognize, however, that each functional activity interacts with other functions; no transaction is solely a "marketing," "production," "finance," or "personnel" activity.

It is obvious that a desirable characteristic from this point of view is that each piece of the original data be captured once, placed in its proper file, and held there until needed or until changed by other transactions. The *information system* would incorporate that piece of data with the other facts in its home file, relate these facts properly to facts in other files, and thus produce *information* for management. It is desirable to recognize that the data associated with each business transaction are a combination of fixed and variable *modules*. Fixed modules (name and address of a credit customer, for example) should not be repeated for every transaction with that customer except insofar as necessary to provide identification. Variable modules (such as units, items, dollar amounts) should be captured for each

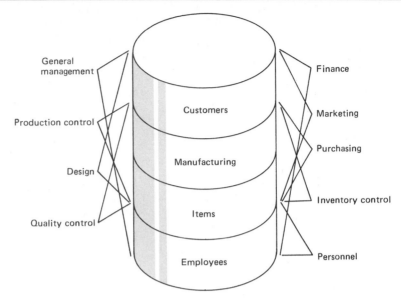

FIGURE 3.5   *Data bank for a management information system*

transaction and used to update the customer account, inventory records, accumulated sales records, and so on.

This data processing view of the MIS of an organization thus recognizes three aspects of the job. First, the data bank, a complete library of relevant files, must be established. Second, procedures must be developed to capture relevant data from transactions and from the environment and use these data to update the data bank. Third, processes must be developed whereby the data bank can be accessed (data contents retrieved) and its contents analyzed and organized and the resulting information reported to management to support its decision-making function.

One area of controversy in the data processing view of the MIS is what should be put into the data bank. Some experts argue that it is appropriate to capture all possible data in the data bank in the expectation that someone in the organization will find a use for each data set included. Others suggest that it is necessary to define what the information outputs will be before the data bank is established; that only those data elements necessary to the provision of the required information be captured and stored in the data bank.

A second area of controversy concerns the accessing of the data bank for development and retrieval of its information content. One group believes that all informational requirements must be fully defined and included in a regularized system of formal reports. A second group believes that managers should define most of their informational requirements as the need arises.

Reports would tend to be unique and be developed "on demand" in the latter system.

It seems rational to adopt an intermediate position on both of the above controversies. All data that can be remotely expected to be useful at some time should be recorded and retained. Data sets not being used immediately might be stored in a less easily accessed form. Access to the data bank should be on a regularized basis for standard reports, but provision should be made for on-demand access for obtaining guidance for unexpected problems or one-of-a-kind decisions.

A third problem to be faced in designing the data bank for an MIS is the level of detail in which the data are to be maintained. For example, should the permanent record for an employee master payroll record for an hourly employee contain only total hours worked, or should it show regular time, overtime, and holiday time? Should the record show where the hours were worked, that is, the department and/or project? Should permanent historical sales records show only total sales by product, area, and salesperson for each time period, or should all the detail of daily activity be retained? It is not always easy to forecast future planning and control needs. Most data bank experts are now encouraging the storage of the detailed data at least on some less expensive medium such as microfilm or magnetic tape.

The basic data processing view of MIS, then, is that of a set of basic files (a data bank) that is modified by current transactions. Actually the data bank is a set of integrated *data bases*. Thus there is a customer data base, a manufacturing (production) data base, a materials control data base, an employee data base, and so on. The structure and interrelations of these functional data bases, which make up the data bank for a business firm, are discussed in greater detail in Chapter 4. The complete differentiation between data banks and data bases is a semantic problem that need not affect our understanding of the philosophy being developed in this chapter. The basic idea is to develop and maintain an integrated set of files. In this process, fixed data modules are captured once and retained, and variable data describing each transaction are captured and used to update all files affected by that transaction. The informational content of the data bank is reported according to management's requirements for that information.

Summary

The major purposes of the management information system are to provide management with information for planning and control, to provide custodial processing required to keep the firm operating, and to provide the historical records necessary as a base for the first two. Thus the MIS must provide avenues of communication between elements of the firm (see Figure 3.1), and the communications must take the form of policies and control directives going down the chain of command and evaluative feedback coming back up (see Figures 3.2 and 3.4). Data processing is concerned with the mechanics by which the capture of data, their evaluation, and the feedback of *information* take place. Thus we see that the MIS is designed to establish a data bank for the organization, capture pertinent data about each transaction and change in the environment (once if possible), use these data to keep the data bank current, evaluate all data to determine their informational content, and communicate each part of that information to the managers having need of that particular information. As good a definition as any for an adequate MIS could be stated as follows:

> *A management information system is the complement of people, machines, and procedures that develops the right information and communicates it to the right managers at the right time.*

Questions

1. Define the following as briefly as possible and then use a short paragraph to clarify each definition.
   a. Management information system
   b. System
   c. Management
   d. Data bank
   e. Feedback
   f. Control
   g. Exception
   h. Integrated data processing
   i. Cycle time
   j. Control cycle
2. Compare the data processing view of a management information system given in this chapter with the systems view of data processing given in Chapter 1.
   a. What are their points of similarity?
   b. In what respects do they differ?
3. Compare the data processing view of a management information system given in this chapter with the *purposes* of data processing identified in Chapter 1.
   a. Are they complementary? If so, how?
   b. Are they in conflict? If so, how?
4. Write a definition of a *fully* integrated (total) management information system.
5. Do you believe that a *fully* integrated (total) MIS can be implemented? Support your answer.
6. Can an MIS be compared to a manufacturing process?

     a. Identify any similarities in general organization and purpose.

     b. Identify any similarities in general procedure.

7. Feedback and control systems are considered to be part of all successful systems. Discuss the application of this idea to an MIS.

8. The following two statements have been made about information and its purpose in organizations:

     a. "Information is the lubrication that keeps organizations functioning smoothly."

     b. "Information is the cement that holds together any organization."

     Can both these statements be true? Explain your answer.

9. Identify four factors that cause the informational needs of managers to differ. Include definitions of these differences in your answer.

10. What is the difference (if any) between a data processing system and an information system? Explain fully.

11. Develop an original example of a specific feedback and control system, defining each part carefully and clearly specifying the cycle time of the operation and the necessary timing of control impulses.

12. It is not unusual for the major assigned "mission" of governmental departments to be significantly modified at least once per year and often more frequently. Would it be possible to develop a working management information system for such an organization? Explain fully.

13. Three different views of a management information system were presented in this chapter. As a manager (actual or potential), do you see any conflicts among these views? Explain fully.

14. What are the advantages and disadvantages of on-demand reporting?

15. Contrast the concepts of a data base and a data bank.

16. Why are exceptions considered to have a high information content?

17. The basic functions of management are popularly designated as planning, organizing, staffing, directing, and controlling. Relate these processes to:

     a. The four steps in the process defined in the discussion of the elements of an organization

     b. The steps in the feedback and control process

18. Refer to questions 9 and 10 at the end of Chapter 1. Is each of the decisions to be made there programmable? Explain.

19. Refer to questions 9 and 10 at the end of Chapter 1. Is each of the decisions to be made there strategic, tactical, or operational? Explain.

20. A local retail hardware chain that operates three stores in the local area is considering expansion to other cities in the region. Provide the president with the following:

     a. A brief description of an information system designed to support strategic decision making for the firm.

b. A brief description of an information system designed to evaluate overall performance of each store and each store manager. Specifically identify any differences in information requirements for these two purposes that might exist. Also indicate who should receive the information developed for each purpose.

c. A brief description of an information system designed to control the level of inventory of items carried in a specific store.

Four

Functional Information Subsystems

It should by now be clear that there is no such thing as *the* management information system for a firm. Rather, there is a collection of subsystems, each integrated in varying degrees into the overall information system of the organization. It is the purpose of this chapter to outline the major subsystems that together provide management with information. These subsystems are most frequently organized around each of the functional subsystems making up the firm. From the descriptions of these functional subsystems and the information subsystems that serve them, a clearer picture of current management information systems should emerge.

Identifying the Subsystems

Our first task is to identify the functional parts (subsystems) of the firm for which information subsystems will be developed. The subsystems can be defined in many ways. We have chosen to recognize six basic functional subsystems:

1. Financial subsystem
2. Marketing subsystem
3. Production subsystem
4. Materials control subsystem
5. Personnel subsystem
6. Planning subsystem

The descriptions of the set of functional subsystems we have chosen are based on the following assumptions:

1. We are dealing with a firm that manufactures and sells a set of related products.

2. The firm is functionally organized (see Figure 4.1).

The major limitation of this approach is that a firm need not be functionally organized. Figure 4.2, on page 57, reflects another common mode of organization, *product* (*project*) organization. A third and more complex organization structure is illustrated in Figure 4.3, on page 58. The structure depicted in Figure 4.3 is a combination of the product and functional structures and is called *matrix* organization. Note that in this latter case, each functional manager for a project has dual allegiance since the manager is simultaneously responsible to the project manager and to the top manager in that functional area. The project manager also is responsible to the president on a line basis. We have chosen to describe a functionally organized firm because in either the project organization or the matrix organization, each project is usually functionally organized. Therefore, the points made in discussing the functional information subsystems are transferable to the other structures.

We have chosen to describe a firm involved in the manufacture and sale of a set of related products because service firms can be viewed as manufacturing and selling services. For example, a financial institution, such as a commercial bank, can be viewed as manufacturing and selling loans to consumers and businesses, demand deposit and time deposit services, and money management (trust) services.

The discussions of each of the individual subsystems will provide the major organizational device for this chapter. Each function is identified in terms of its overall objectives, and its organization into subsystems is outlined. The major information subsystems in the functional area are then similarly defined and outlined.

Special note: Most of the symbols used to describe the functional subsystems and their information subsystems have been taken from a flowcharting template. These special symbols are used partly for clarity and partly for convenience. They should not be interpreted literally. Neither all files nor

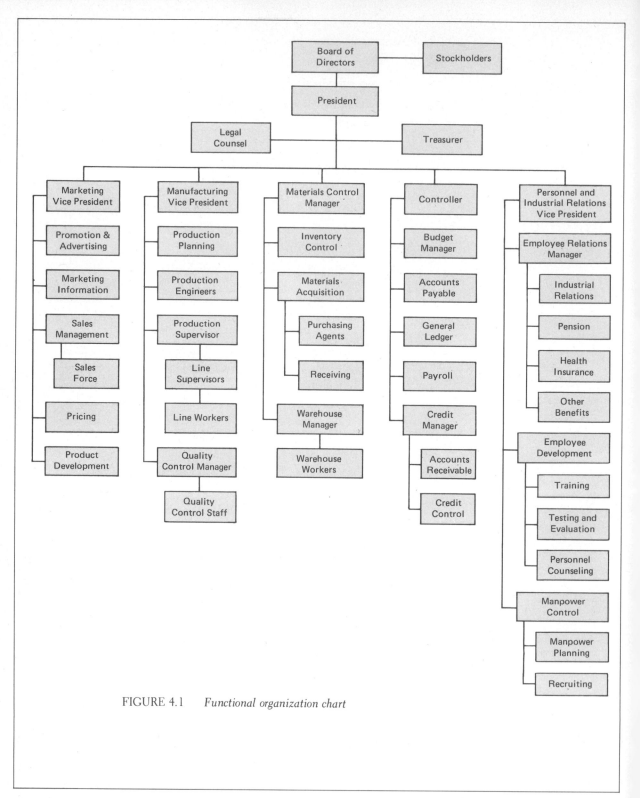

FIGURE 4.1   *Functional organization chart*

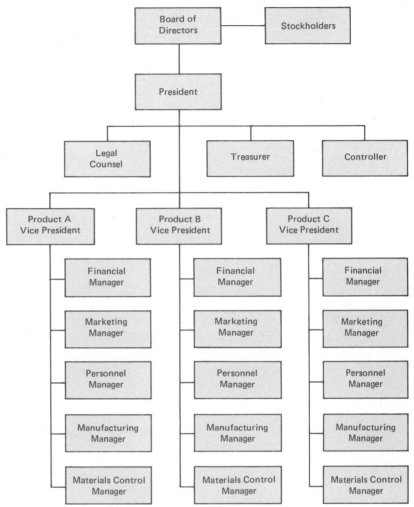

FIGURE 4.2   *Product (project) organization chart*

all processing must be online to a computer, as these charts seem to indicate. Further, all input need not be captured online and all outputs need not be on display terminals. The use of the symbol for an online display terminal is intended to indicate a need for fast response, which could be obtained in other ways.

The Financial Information Subsystem

THE OBJECTIVE OF THE FINANCIAL FUNCTION

The financial function is concerned with the monetary resources of the firm and their acquisition, management, and expenditure in line with the overall objectives of the firm.

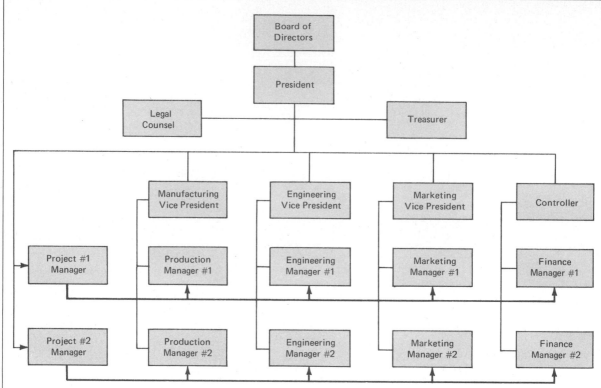

FIGURE 4.3   *Matrix organization chart*

> *The basic objective of the financial subsystem is to meet the firm's financial obligations as they come due, using the minimal amount of financial resources consistent with an established margin of safety.*

The schematic diagram in Figure 4.4 illustrates the activities of the financial subsystem. Money flows into the firm through the sources shown on the left-hand side and out of the firm through the operational activities shown on the right-hand side. The job of the financial manager is to control these flows in line with the goals of the organization.

THE ORGANIZATION OF THE FINANCIAL INFORMATION SUBSYSTEM

The actual data processing and information systems used in controlling the financial activities of the organization are indicated by the functional organization chart shown in Figure 4.5. Each of the subfunctions is designed to handle a particular aspect of the total financial function.

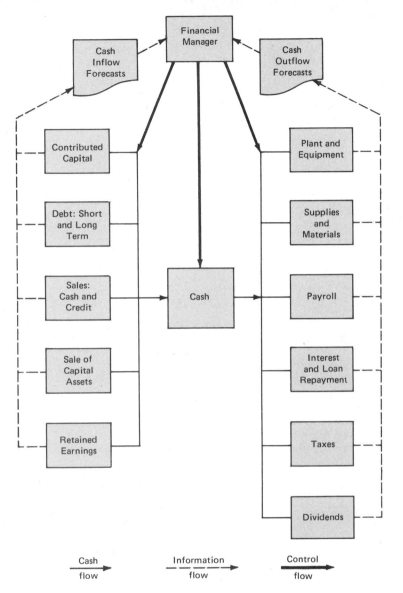

FIGURE 4.4   *The finance function*

Operating and Capital Budgets   A budget is a plan set forth in financial terms. The purpose of a budget is to translate organizational activities and their expected results in a future period into dollar value of expenditures and incomes. The *capital budget* is, rather obviously, the plan for making capital expenditures. *Capital expenditures* refer to purchases of resources (plant,

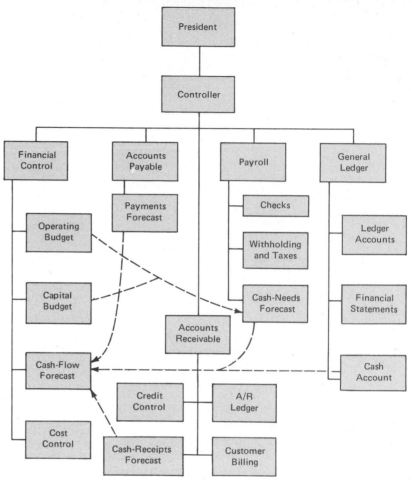

FIGURE 4.5   *The organization of the finance function*

equipment, land) whose benefits are to be realized over a period longer than one year. The *operating budget* is concerned only with *operating* expenditures for resources (labor, materials, supplies) whose benefits are to be realized within a few months.

The preparation of any budget requires that the expected activity level in each area match that in each coordinated area. Thus expected sales levels must be coordinated with production plans, advertising schedules, sales effort, and so on. Production goals must then be coordinated with material and supplies inventories, wage and salary expenditures, and transportation costs. The coordinated planning required in the creation of complete operating and capital budgets forces management to consider future plans carefully and in detail. Obtaining the participation of managers at all levels in the organization gives the managers a sense of involvement and increases their commitment to the plan that is developed. New projects or capital replacements are usually analyzed by comparing their net present value with their cost. If the return on investment is satisfactory, the project will be added to the budget.

Once the budgets have been fully developed, they should become a control standard against which activities and performance levels are measured during the budgetary period. Significant deviations from budget give clear indication that plans either are not being carried through or cannot be carried through because of changed conditions. In either case, adjustments are necessary.

Working Capital Reports   One analysis needed to support budgeting is the working capital report. A firm's balance sheet separates the assets of the firm into current assets and fixed assets. The total of current assets (cash, receivables, inventories, and prepaid expenses) is called the *working capital* of the firm. Changes in the financial health of the firm are indicated by the changes in its working capital. Care must be exercised to determine how these changes are brought about. An increase in liquid assets (working capital) may well be financed by going into debt. Such debts reduce the proportion of the firm's total value that can be considered as belonging to the firm's owners. However, if new working capital is financed by retaining earnings or by increases in capital provided by the owners, the owner's equity is increased. The flow of funds through a firm over a period of time can be determined by comparing its balance sheets at the beginning and end of the period being studied. Such an analysis is illustrated in Figure 4.6. The change in balance sheet items shown in part (a), the flow of funds work sheet, is summarized in the flow of funds statement shown in part (b). This analysis for the MAFM Corporation indicates that working capital has increased by $121,000. Part of this increase has been financed by increases in current liabilities (Accounts Payable and Notes Payable). The *net* increase in working capital, or liquidity, of the firm is only $45,000.

The flow of funds statement indicates the *sources* and *uses* of working capital. Note that changes in part (a) of Figure 4.6 identified as credits are the *sources* of capital. The debits in part (a) show the *uses* of that capital.

Cash Flow Forecast   The cash flow forecast is critical in controlling the financial affairs of an organization. Many basically healthy firms have been forced into bankruptcy or taken over by a more solvent owner because cash outflows temporarily exceeded cash inflows when the physical and financial

MAFM Corporation, Year Ended December 31, 1979

(a) Flow of funds work sheet (all figures in thousands of dollars)

	Dec. 31, 1978	Dec. 31, 1979	Changes Debit	Credit
Assets				
Cash	38	27		11
Accounts receivable	150	215	65	
Inventory	205	264	59	
Building and equipment	89	98	9	
Allowance for depreciation	(16)	(24)		8
Other assets	23	31	8	
Total assets	489	611		
Liabilities and equities				
Notes payable (short term)	9	24		15
Accounts payable	74	126		52
Notes payable (long term)	50	75		25
Other liabilities	19	28		9
Capital stock	125	125		
Retained earnings	212	233		21
Total liabilities and equities	489	611	141	141

	Beginning	Ending	Increase
Total working capital (current assets)	416	537	121
Net working capital (current assets minus current liabilities)	314	359	45

FIGURE 4.6   *Balance sheet changes and flow of funds*

assets of the firm were fully committed and could not be used to acquire added cash. This is particularly prevalent in growing firms. Growth requires increasing investments in receivables, inventories, and fixed assets. In financing these increased needs with short-term debt, a firm can become unable to meet these obligations as they come due. A careful process of estimating receipts and expenditures as they are expected to be distributed through the subsequent planning period can help to prevent such problems. Cash flow can be increased by speeding collections of accounts receivable, reducing cash float with such practices as depositing customer's checks to the firm's account before they are processed, by delaying payments to creditors as long as possible (but without losing any cash discounts), and investing cash in short-term securities. Increased needs for fixed assets should be met

(b) Flow of funds statement (all figures in thousands of dollars)

Sources of funds			
Increases in current liabilities			
Short-term notes payable	15		
Accounts payable	52		
Other liabilities	9	76	
Depreciation (charge to income that did not use cash)		8	
Increase in long-term notes		25	
Increase in net worth		21	
Total sources			130
Uses of funds			
Increase in current assets			
Cash	(11)		
Accounts receivable	65		
Inventory	59		
Other assets	8	121	
Increases in building and equipment		9	
Total uses			130

FIGURE 4.6 (*cont.*)

with long-term financing, through either increases in equity capital (stock sales) or increases in long-term debt.

Cost Control   Costs of performing any activity are subject to control as long as a *standard cost* of performing the activity can be established. Actual costs can then be measured and compared to the standard. Standards are most easily established for repeated activities. However, estimates of costs must be made for every activity as part of the budgeting process. As indicated above, these budgets can then be used as control standards.

In applying cost controls, one must recognize that some variation from the long-term average is natural. Control action should not be instituted unless deviations are large enough to be significant or, although small, have persisted over a significant number of repetitions.

Cost control over larger segments of an organization rather than individual activities is usually a form of budgetary control. Expense data are collected, classified, and summarized for *cost centers*, which may be departments, work stations, or individual activities.

The Accounts Payable Subsystem   An organization must have supplies, materials, parts, and services from other firms. Many of these items are purchased on credit. The accounts payable (A/P) subsystem is responsible for monitoring these delayed expenditures and discharging them by payment at the appropriate time. Its *objective* is to discharge legitimate obligations to the firm's creditors while utilizing a minimum of capital resources. Figure 4.7 presents a system flowchart of such a system.

As shown in Figure 4.7, the transaction inputs to the accounts payable subsystem are requisitions approved for payment, invoices received from vendors, and receiving reports. Using these three inputs, one can determine whether or not an invoice should be paid.

At least three possible outputs are not shown in Figure 4.7. One is the payments forecast for the next planning period. The forecast would be based on expected purchases to support planned production and sales levels beyond currently placed orders. These estimates could then be added to the expected costs of orders already placed. A second missing output is distribution of the costs of invoices paid among the business activities for which the items were purchased (*expense distribution report*). The third missing output is the *vendor profitability report,* an analysis of the differing gains available by taking advantage of payment terms offered by each vendor, adjusted for any cost that might result from receiving low-quality items from each vendor.

The Accounts Receivable Subsystem   The accounts receivable (A/R) subsystem has the basic *objective* of maximizing the transformation of credit sales transactions into cash. The maintenance of a record of the amount owed by each credit customer is a primary function of the subsystem. Accurate accounts promote customer goodwill and provide a source of vital information on this major source of cash inflow to the firm. Regular generation of billing statements to customers obviously assists in the collection of amounts due. Both of these factors are provided for by the system shown in Figure 4.8.

The four basic inputs shown in Figure 4.8 are the credit application, a close or change in an account, a credit sale, and a payment on account. These four inputs make it possible to keep accounts current, bill customers at regular intervals, and control delinquencies. One part of the accounts receivable subsystem is not fully developed in the chart, however. This has to do with customer credit limits. The establishment of such a limit is not indicated at the time an account is opened. Even so, a check for exceeding the credit limit at the time of a sale is indicated. Figure 4.8 does not indicate how this question is answered. Obviously a special inquiry process would have to be used to compare the sum of the previous balance and the current purchase to the credit limit.

The output reports from the A/R systems (credit sales analysis, aging

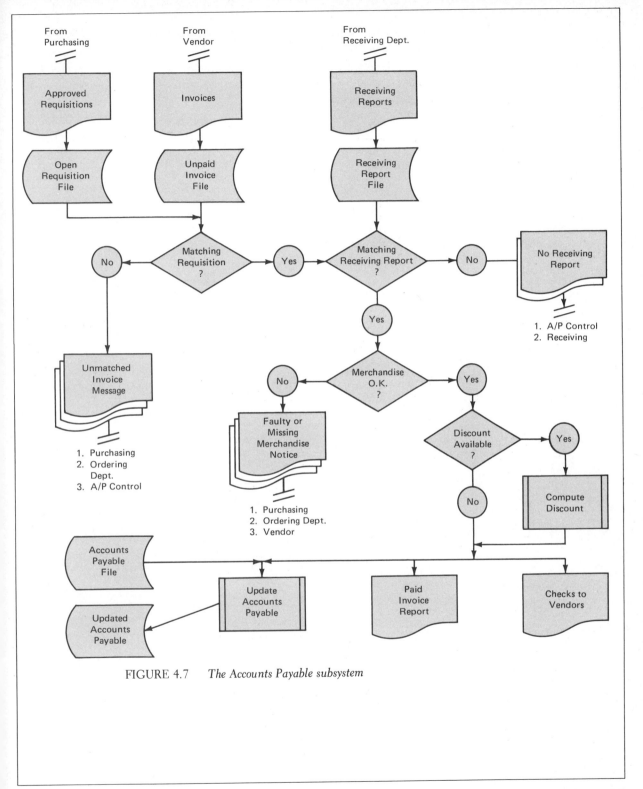

FIGURE 4.7   *The Accounts Payable subsystem*

report, and a credit control report) could be supplemented by a customer activity history report focusing on the activity level of each customer. Good customers who pay promptly could be given advance notice of sales and other special consideration. Inactive accounts could be purged to save processing and mailing costs.

FIGURE 4.8   *The Accounts Receivable subsystem*

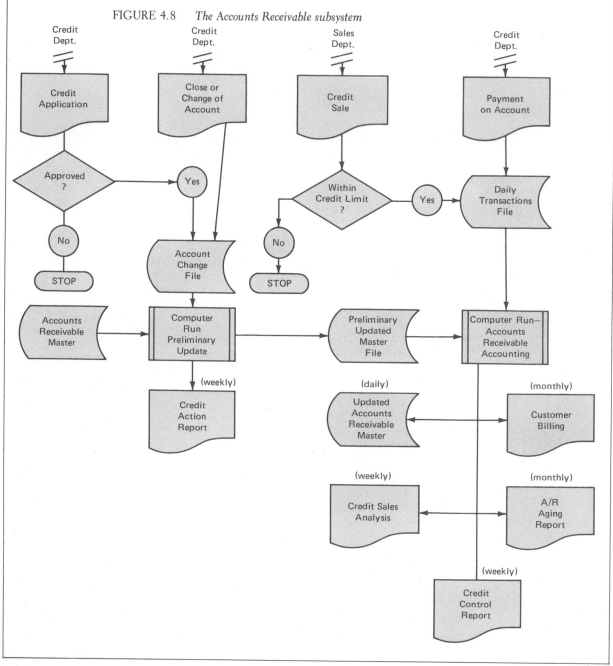

The Payroll Subsystem   The payroll subsystem is an interface between the financial subsystem, the personnel subsystem, and all other subsystems. Its objective is to meet the financial obligations to employees in an orderly and legal fashion consistent with the personnel policies of the firm. Payroll involves the preparation of pay checks for employees and the distribution of labor costs to each of the activities in which the employees work. Payroll is normally a major part of the demand for cash in a firm. Fortunately, it is relatively easy to forecast the cash needs for the subsequent planning period generated by the payroll subsystem. We will look more carefully at an hourly payroll system in Chapters 13 and 14.

The General Ledger Subsystem   A complete set of accounting records is required to prepare a complete set of financial statements. The most common statements are the balance sheet and the income statement. Accounting efforts are devoted primarily to maintaining historical financial records by applying generally accepted accounting practices. Emphasis is on reporting the financial condition of the firm to outsiders. We will have more to say about this part of the accounting function in Chapter 15.

The Marketing Information Subsystem

THE OBJECTIVES OF THE MARKETING FUNCTION

The marketing function must identify the markets or market segments that the firm can serve. It must then manage the firm's resources involved at the interface between the customer and the firm so as to support the attainment of the firm's goals. On the one hand, the marketing function is oriented to identifying and satisfying customer needs. On the other hand, the marketing function is charged with obtaining an amount of sales that maximizes profits for the firm, which is usually indicated to be a *maximum* amount of sales.

> *The objective of the marketing function is to facilitate the flow of goods and services from the firm to satisfy the perceived wants and needs of customers in support of the objectives and goals of the firm.*

The schematic in Figure 4.9 outlines what it is that the marketing function really does. It appears that the marketing function is primarily an information processing operation. Information on the wants and needs of potential and actual customers as developed from population and demographic data, income distributions, broad sales trends (consumer durables and nondurables, and so on), availability of resources and technology, previous sales patterns, and customer reactions and complaints is brought together and sifted, condensed, and evaluated. The intelligence that is developed is used as a basis for choosing, developing, and pricing products; creating promotion and advertising strategies and campaigns; selecting and organizing channels

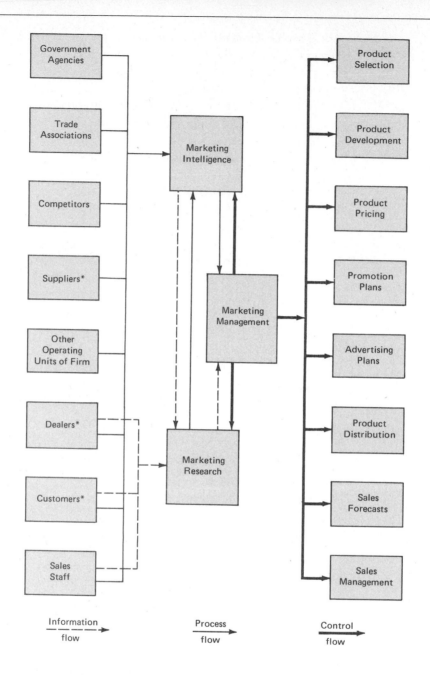

Government Agencies

Trade Associations

Competitors

Suppliers*

Other Operating Units of Firm

Dealers*

Customers*

Sales Staff

Marketing Intelligence

Marketing Management

Marketing Research

Product Selection

Product Development

Product Pricing

Promotion Plans

Advertising Plans

Product Distribution

Sales Forecasts

Sales Management

Information flow

Process flow

Control flow

*Actual and Potential

FIGURE 4.9   *The marketing function*

of distribution; and setting sales goals and supervising the sales efforts designed to reach them.

THE ORGANIZATION OF THE MARKETING FUNCTION

The organization chart in Figure 4.10 presents a possible organization for the marketing function. There are four basic subdivisions, sales management, product management, marketing intelligence, and promotion and advertising. The titles of the subsections may vary, but the subfunctions are similar. For example, the heart of the system, the marketing intelligence subsystem, is often called marketing research.

THE MARKETING INTELLIGENCE SUBSYSTEM

The most obvious major elements in the marketing intelligence subsystem are the intelligence data bank and the marketing research activities. However, there are other custodial and information systems in the marketing area. The major custodial processing and marketing control subsystems are sales planning and sales control.

The Marketing Intelligence Data Bank   The marketing system is a dynamic system serving as the interface between the business firm and its customers. In order to accomplish this task, the wants and needs of customers must be determined for translation into saleable products and/or services. Sources of information here are quite variable. Customer inquiries about actual or potential products or services need to be systematically collected and analyzed. Customer reactions to the goods and services provided for them, both favorable and unfavorable, should be known. Data collected from sales transactions obviously should provide sales amounts by product, territory, and salesperson or other delivery channel. In addition, the firm must know its customers, their ages, sex, income, family status, and personality if promotion and advertising campaigns are to be effective. Whether or not these customers return to the firm is also important; that is, to what extent do sales represent repeat business from the same loyal customers? Information on sales of directly competitive and substitute products and services by other firms is also needed. The size of the total market and the firm's share of that market can reveal the effectiveness of marketing efforts. The profitability of various types of sales — credit versus cash, catalog versus store, and so on — is important. For example, is it more profitable to integrate vertically from manufacturing through retailing or to sell the manufactured goods to wholesalers or jobbers? Finally, what new or improved products or services are possible or are being provided by competitors?

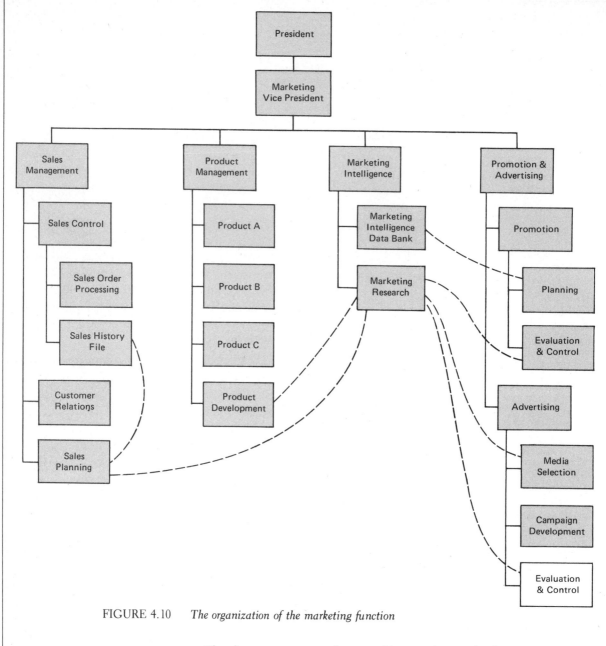

FIGURE 4.10   *The organization of the marketing function*

The data on customer demographics, product technology, market size, and other environmental information is collected from the environment and stored in a *market intelligence data bank*, most likely offline from the computer. After analysis and reduction, these data may enter the formal system for the quantitative marketing models that are used as guides in decision making. In conjunction with data on sales trends and data on customer reactions to advertising and promotion developed from internal sources, these data are used to develop sales forecasts. Sales forecasts can also be derived from estimates made by the sales force. Each individual salesperson or sales office develops an estimate of sales for the particular sales territory, product, or department. These individual estimates are then compared, analyzed, adjusted, and totaled to arrive at an overall sales forecast.

The *sales forecast* is the base from which all sales plans are developed. Promotion and advertising plans (which may modify the initial forecast); sales quotas by territory, product, and salesperson; inventory stock levels; salary and commission budgets; and other sales expense budgets are based on the sales forecast as coordinated with expected production.

The success or failure (effectiveness) of a sales plan is judged by resulting sales. Even if success is gained and all sales quotas are realized, the reasons why should be known. Sales amounts by product and area must be matched with income distributions, prices, actions of competitors, and shifting customer tastes and habits. Only then can the firm be sure that its efforts *caused* success. Promotion and advertising efforts may appear successful when the real cause lies in improving economic conditions, failure of the competition, or a general shift in consumer tastes and habits. For example, the popularity of blue jeans among college and high school students in the 1960s caught many suppliers by surprise. Sales of standard blue jeans skyrocketed while supplies of fashion jeans lay unwanted in the warehouses. Significant changes in production facilities and distribution patterns were required to adjust to this spontaneous shift in customer tastes.

Marketing Research Much of the information on the tastes and habits of potential and actual customers will be collected through *marketing research*. The success of promotion and advertising campaigns, the pulling power of particular media and particular advertisements, and the potential reactions to price changes can best be obtained through well-designed scientific research studies. Market definition, including definition of customers by age, sex, income, location, education, and other factors, can also require specifically designed research efforts. The potential for new or improved products or packaging also needs testing. The marketing research function is a prime source of the data and information in the marketing intelligence data bank. Marketing research is also a prime user of this intelligence. The information that results should be a major guide for marketing decisions.

Marketing research is also responsible for developing tools with which data are analyzed and decision models structured. Market researchers should be well-trained professionals who know how to use statistical tools and mathematic modeling.

THE SALES MANAGEMENT SUBSYSTEM

The internal information system other than marketing research is concerned primarily with actual sales. Many manufacturing firms produce to order rather than to inventory. In those firms, the customer sales orders drive the manufacturing activity directly via the *sales order processing subsystem*. In any manufacturing firm, the amount of production must be related to sales activity. If it is not, inventories will either become depleted and potential sales lost through inability to deliver or increase beyond reasonable levels as sales decline. The simplified customer order processing subsystem shown in Figure 4.11 indicates that the major reports from the system are a goods availability analysis and a sales analysis that reports sales by product, product line, area, and salesperson for cash, credit, and total sales. The sales reports should also compare current sales to sales in the previous period, to sales in the same period one year earlier, and to expected (planned) sales for the period. These latter requirements indicate a need for a complete sales history file to provide the comparable data for past periods. The sales history file is not shown in our simplified system description. The sales history file would also be useful in determining the effectiveness of new methods of promotion, new prices, and other changes in product management. That such requirements are difficult to predict specifically indicates that the sales history file needs to retain a great deal of detailed information. For example, suppose a customer analysis were run to identify major customers. If historical sales data were not available in sufficient detail to classify sales by individual customer, comparative analysis would not be possible.

The Production Information Subsystem

THE OBJECTIVE OF THE PRODUCTION FUNCTION

The production function in a manufacturing firm is the process by which raw materials and purchased parts are operated on by labor and machines (capital) and converted into finished goods. A form of this function is easily recognized in service firms such as insurance companies, governmental organizations, and financial institutions. For example, the insurance company produces a product (the insurance policy) that trades a small certain loss (the premium) for a large uncertain loss (death, fire, accident, and so on). The production function for a retail or wholesale firm is not so easily recognized because it is organized as a sales activity, but it is there. Regardless of the type of firm, however,

> *the objective of the production function is to produce the goods and/or services provided by the firm at the least cost consistent with the firm's goals of quality and quantity.*

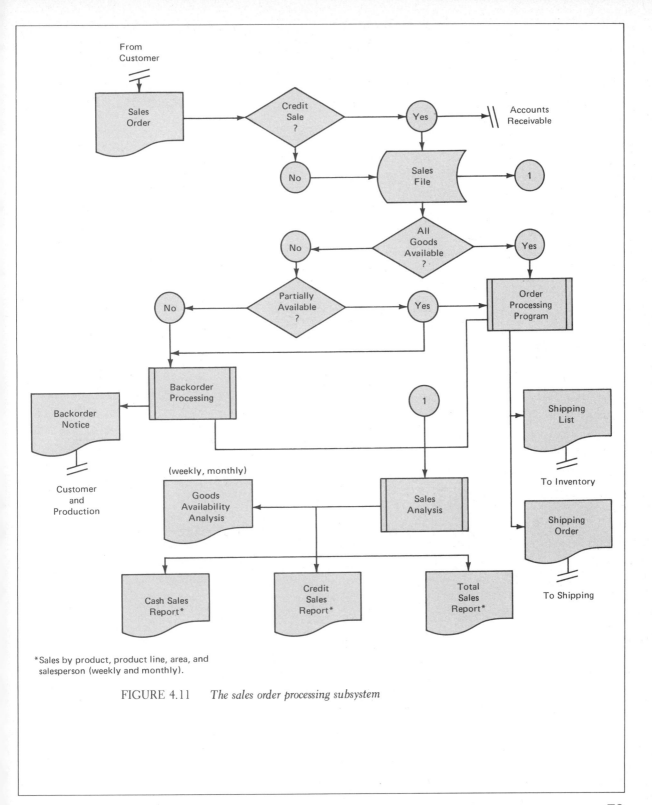

FIGURE 4.11 *The sales order processing subsystem*

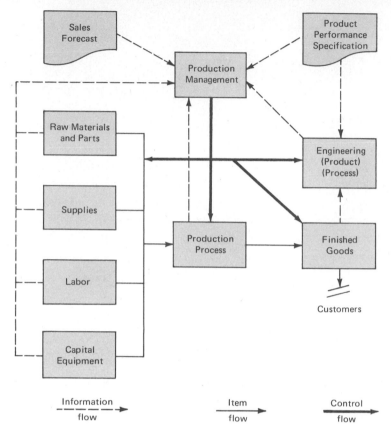

FIGURE 4.12   *The production function*

Figure 4.12 illustrates the nature of the production function. The inputs on the left are converted by the production process into finished goods (or services) for the customer. The entire process is planned and controlled by the production management assisted by engineering. Production planning is also dependent on the input of sales forecasts and product performance specifications from marketing.

THE ORGANIZATION OF THE PRODUCTION FUNCTION

Figure 4.13 presents a typical organization for the production function in a manufacturing organization. It indicates four major subfunctions: engineering, production supervision, production planning and control, and quality control. Many firms also include materials control functions (inventory control and purchasing) under production. We feel that the materials con-

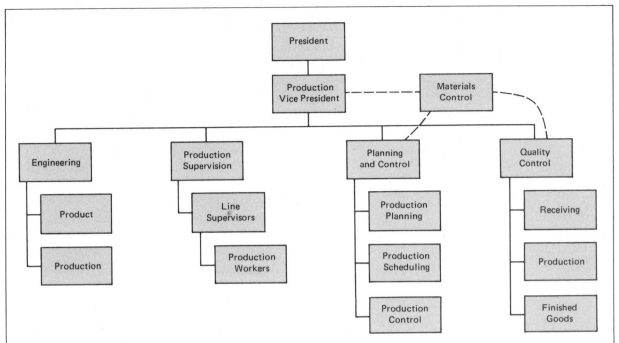

FIGURE 4.13   *The organization of the production function*

trol function is important enough to justify a place as a major functional activity of the organization.

The production information subsystems relate directly to the organizational subdivisions specified above.

Product Engineering   The product engineer is responsible for designing the product. The design of a product is based on product performance specifications (what the product will do and at what cost) and current technology. The performance specifications are usually developed in the marketing function. After a design has been tested and is accepted, the design engineer produces a *bill of materials*, which lists all the raw materials and parts that are needed to produce the product. The bill of materials is an essential input into the production planning process.

Production Engineering   The production process is also designed. If the production process is not efficient, production costs will be too high and profits may disappear as sales are lost to competitors producing more efficiently at a lower cost. Production systems can be classified into two basic types, continuous and batch.

Continuous production processes use raw material and/or parts and modify or assemble them into the final product in a continuous uninterrupted flow. Examples are automobile assembly plants, steel rolling mills, and oil refineries. Such systems use machine processes that require large capital investments and provide high productivity for the labor used, and the production flow follows a fixed path.

The *batch* production systems, as the name implies, involves the filling of individual production orders. Examples are machine shops, the airframe industry, the manufacture of goods affected by style such as clothing and furniture, and building construction. Batch systems use general-purpose machines combined with skilled labor to provide flexibility in production. Capital costs are lower, but unit costs are higher than with a continuous process.

The efficiency of production systems is measured primarily by cost of production. Other measures may be used, however. In situations when some inputs are in short supply, economy in use of the scarce resources may be important. In times of emergency need, cost efficiency may be sacrificed for faster production. Firms facing highly variable product demand may value flexibility in shifting among products or the ability to adjust the production rate over a wide range above minimization of production costs.

One dimension of effectiveness which must be considered for all production systems is quality. Unless the system produces a product (or products) of adequate quality, it cannot be considered. In general an effective production system is able to meet standards of cost and quality over an adequate capacity range.

The results of production engineering are *production routings*, which specify the exact steps to be followed in producing the product. Standards in terms of cost, time, quality, and labor used must be included. Obviously the equipment and tools required are also specified.

The Production Planning Subsystem Figure 4.14 presents a traditional production planning system. Existing sales orders and expected future sales (for the planning period) are translated into actual production requirements. Each request for a unit of finished product is "exploded" into a set of parts to be purchased or manufactured using the bill of materials for that product. Adjustment for existing inventories of finished goods and goods in process gives actual items to be manufactured and assembled. Reference to the manufacturing specifications and standards for each part and product allows creation of the three major production planning outputs — materials requirements, production requisitions or production routing slips, and the planned production schedule.

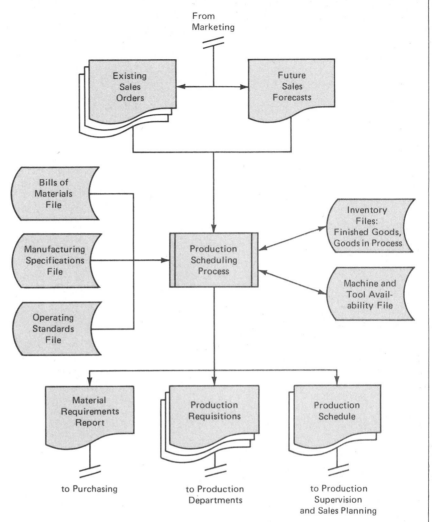

From
Marketing

Existing
Sales
Orders

Future
Sales
Forecasts

Bills of
Materials
File

Manufacturing
Specifications
File

Operating
Standards
File

Production
Scheduling
Process

Inventory
Files:
Finished Goods,
Goods in Process

Machine and
Tool Avail-
ability File

Material
Requirements
Report

Production
Requisitions

Production
Schedule

to Purchasing

to Production
Departments

to Production
Supervision
and Sales Planning

FIGURE 4.14   *The production planning system*

The Production Control Subsystem   Production control is a coordinated activity among the production control, manufacturing supervision, and cost control groups. All of these groups combine to compare actual production volumes, item quality, and item costs to preset time, cost, and quality standards. Deviations from standards are reported to production supervisors for corrective action. The heart of the production control subsystems is the production data base illustrated in Figure 4.15. Note that deviations from the basic plan would require interrogation of current status to determine

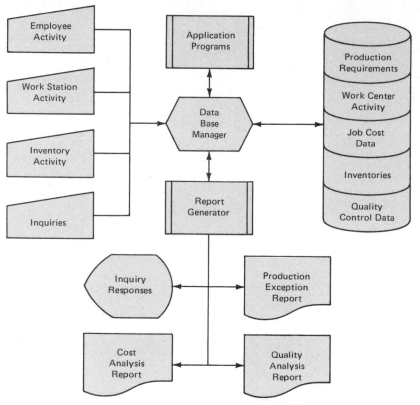

FIGURE 4.15   *The production control data base system*

what changes to make. New inputs might then be made to the production planning system (Figure 4.14) to obtain a revised schedule.

Interruptions to production, such as machine breakdowns, employee absences, and excessive defective items, cannot be specifically planned for. Preventative maintenance and planned excess capacity can be used to reduce these problems but may add more to cost than they are worth. Seldom, however, can a production facility be expected to work at its full rated capacity at expected quality levels over a planning period such as a day or a week. Production plans should reflect the actual production rate that has been attained in the past.

Introducing priority ordering makes scheduling more difficult. Important customers may deserve special consideration and preferential scheduling. Modern management science techniques allow the use of order priorities in scheduling to deal with such situations. Algorithms are available which adjust for such variables as promised delivery dates, order size, and customer rating to determine order precedence relationships.

The Materials Control Information Subsystem

THE OBJECTIVE OF THE MATERIALS CONTROL FUNCTION

The materials control function has responsibility for the selection, acquisition, and storage of materials (raw materials, parts, and supplies) used by the firm. These materials are either being held for sale, being produced for sale, or to be used up in the near future in producing goods or services for sale.

> *The objective of the materials control function is to provide and maintain stocks of raw materials, parts, and supplies of adequate quality in quantities sufficient to accomplish the objectives and goals of the firm at a minimum cost.*

The general processes involved in this function are shown in Figure 4.16. The primary activities are procurement and inventory management.

THE ORGANIZATION OF THE MATERIALS CONTROL FUNCTION

The selection and management of the materials, parts, and supplies flowing through a firm can be subdivided into four parts:

1. Materials requirements planning
2. Procurement (purchasing)
3. Inventory control
4. Receiving and warehousing

FIGURE 4.16   *The materials control function*

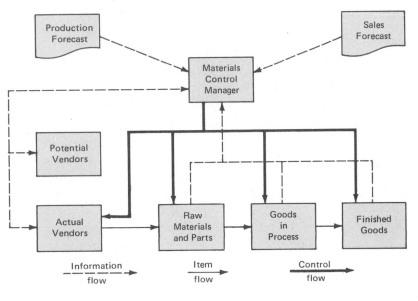

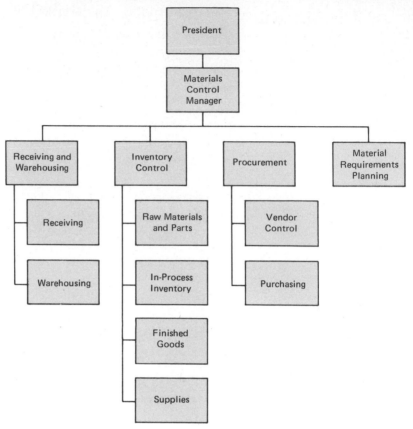

FIGURE 4.17   *The organization of the materials control function*

These subsystems are clearly indicated in Figure 4.17. They are the basis of the information subsystems for the function.

Material Requirements Planning   This process overlaps with and really is a part of production planning and was discussed under a production information subsystem, the production planning subsystem.

The Procurement (Purchasing) Subsystem   Purchasing involves more than just placing orders. A vendor must be carefully selected to obtain the needed item at the lowest possible overall cost. Factors that affect procurement cost include the price of the item, the terms of payment, the quality of the goods supplied, and the time required for delivery. The lowest priced goods are not always the most economical. That is why it is so important to carefully spell out specifications of performance, quality, style, material content, and so on, when requesting bids from potential vendors.

A *vendor history file* should be maintained to continuously define the vendors in terms of their reliability in delivery, the quality of their product, the credit terms they offer, and the care they exercise in meeting all product specifications. Note that the vendor activity file and the vendor evaluation report used in Figure 4.18, on page 65, are points of interface with the financial subsystem for accounts payable (see Figure 4.7).

Carefully designed policies should be developed for approval of all purchase requisitions *before* purchase orders are written. Large or unusual orders should be approved by the chief executive officer of the firm. Intermediate-sized orders might require approval from the head of the department or function that will use the items. Standard items might be ordered in small lots on the authority of the chief purchasing agent after the purchase order has been prepared by the computer.

The Inventory Control Subsystem The term *inventory* includes a variety of subdivisions. In trading firms involved in wholesale or retail trade, the *merchandise held for sale* is the inventory. In a manufacturing firm finished goods are held for sale, goods in the process of being produced form the *goods-in-process inventory*, the raw materials and parts held for future use in production are the *raw materials inventory*, and the consumables to be used to support future production and office activity are the *supplies inventory*. These inventories provide buffers between activities that vary because of transit and production time and seasonal irregularities in demand and supply.

Regardless of the type of inventory, inventory accounting and control will be carried out in much the same way. The accounting portion of the inventory control subsystem measures the effects of inventory activity on the financial condition of the firm and assists in managing the firm's financial assets efficiently and effectively. There are several problems of importance in this area. One is setting a value on the inventory. Tax liability and profit determination are important determinants of the type of valuation scheme used [average pricing; last-in, first-out (LIFO); or first-in, first-out (FIFO)]. It is beyond the scope of this text to fully discuss these considerations. Their existence does indicate a need to know the actual price paid for each item in inventory. This cost history should report not only the price of an item, but also its *net cost* after allowance for quantity and early payment discounts. Note the overlap with the vendor history information referred to earlier.

A simplified inventory control subsystem is shown in Figure 4.18. The

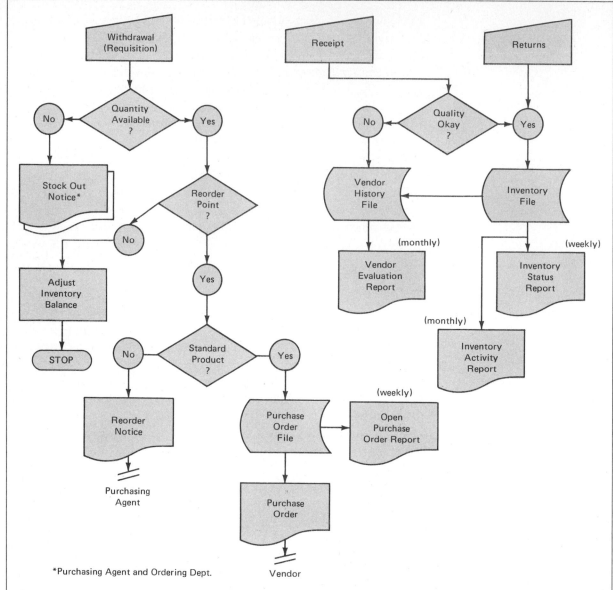

FIGURE 4.18   *The inventory control information subsystem*

major inputs are withdrawals, receipts, and returns. The major outputs are notices of inadequate supplies (stock out reports and reorder notices), purchase orders for standard items, vendor performance evaluation report, inventory status report, and inventory activity report.

To operate such a system efficiently, one would have to make a prior determination of reorder points and reorder amounts. Algorithms exist for determining these amounts, which take into account order cost, delivery time, item cost, quantity discounts, the cost of being out of the item, inventory carrying costs, and the need for a safety stock because of variability in such things as delivery times, quality, and use rates. For parts produced internally, a similar calculation of economic lot size is based on set-up (fixed) and run (variable) costs of production and storage costs.

Most of the reports indicated as output for the system should be self-explanatory, but we will review each briefly.

The *vendor evaluation report* is a performance report that summarizes vendor effectiveness as a supplier of raw materials, parts, or supplies. The report summarizes the response time of the vendor (delivery times) in terms of the average delivery time and its variability. Another important statistic is any lack of performance by the vendor, such as failing to fill an order in full or in part. Also important is the proportion of the items received that were defective in any way. This kind of information, when combined with information on payment terms from the accounts payable subsystem (see pages 63–65) make it possible to determine the time cost of doing business with a particular vendor.

The *inventory status report* reports inventory levels and amounts on order for all items in the inventory. This report can be useful in determining the amount of capital tied up in inventory.

The *inventory activity report* is very useful in controlling inventories. It reports activity by item and should identify clearly those items that are not being used and those items for which activity is increasing.

In combination, the reports on inventory status and activity can be used to perform an ABC *analysis* so that inventory control efforts can be directed at those points at which they will have the most effective impact. In ABC analysis, the items in inventory are separated into three categories:

A items: most active and most costly items.

B items: items of intermediate activity and cost.

C items: least active and least costly items.

It has been repeatedly demonstrated that 20 percent of the items in inventory will account for 80 to 90 percent of the dollar usage per year. Inventory control practices designed to reduce costs should be concentrated on this group of A items. Conversely, items that are not being used can be eliminated from inventory. These items will be found in the C group. Items in the B group are prime candidates for application of programmed processes, such as economic order quantity and economic lot size formulas and exception reporting to management. Items in category A should be continuously monitored. Planning for their control could profitably involve more costly techniques, such as computer simulation and daily control reporting.

The Receiving and Warehousing Subsystem The receiving and warehousing activities serve primarily as a source of inputs to the materials control information subsystem. *Receiving reports* indicate the quality and completeness of shipments received from vendors. *Physical inventory reports* periodically confirm or correct the inventory item balances. Excessive differences between physical and book inventory amounts should be investigated to control inventory *shrinkage* (the loss of items from inventory). Shrinkage occurs because of breakage, spoilage, theft, and misplacement. All of these shrinkage categories must be kept to a minimum if adverse effects on profits are to be kept reasonable.

The Personnel Information Subsystem

THE OBJECTIVE OF THE PERSONNEL FUNCTION

To perform a useful economic function, a firm needs people. As indicated in Chapter 3, managers get things done by, with, and through other people. The personnel function assists management in the acquisition, organization, compensation, training, development, evaluation, and disciplining of employees. As shown in Figure 4.19, the ultimate purpose of all this activity is to obtain an effective organization that performs its economic function. The nature and productivity of its employees, in the final analysis, determines the effectiveness with which the firm attains its objectives. The personnel function is a staff function, however. It does not provide the supervisory leadership; it only facilitates its effectiveness. The firm does not own the human resources it commands. Each employee expects the firm to provide for his or her personal satisfaction and self-realization.

> *The objective of the personnel function is to provide and maintain at a minimum cost the human resources for accomplishing the firm's objectives, while insuring satisfaction and personal development for the individual employee.*

As indicated in Figure 4.19, the personnel function is the interface between the firm and its employees. As such it has dual responsibilities. First, it must provide adequate numbers of productive employees to the firm. Second, it is responsible for seeing that the firm goes as far as possible in establishing a work environment that provides satisfaction and personal development for each employee. These dual objectives need not be in conflict. Well-trained employees acquiring and using expanding skills and increasing responsibilities at a reasonable level of compensation are satisfied and productive employees.

The efficiency and effectiveness of the personnel function can be measured in a variety of ways. These would include:

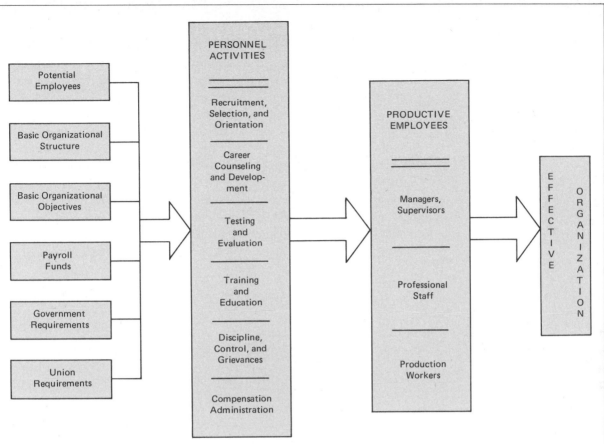

FIGURE 4.19   *The personnel function*

1. Employee turnover rates
2. Average longevity of employment for all employees
3. Longevity by job, department, project, and so on
4. Accidental injury rates
5. The attainment of affirmative action goals

THE ORGANIZATION OF THE PERSONNEL FUNCTION

Historically the personnel function has often been fragmented. Each operating department would hire its own employees, determine their compensation, train them, promote them, and discharge them. The personnel (or industrial relations) department would maintain a few files, negotiate union contracts, and handle employee grievances. This has been changing, and currently personnel functions are being centralized and expanded. Figure 4.20 presents a possible organization of subfunctions for such a centralized personnel department. The major subfunctions are grouped under personnel development, recruitment and staffing, personnel planning, and employee relations. The major files in the system are the employee inventory and the skills inventory. These two files fully identify the employees of the firm, indicating not only who they are and where they live and work, but also what they can do both on and off the job. A well-designed personnel subsystem will keep track of the development of each employee, particularly with regard to newly acquired skills (educational, recreational, cultural, physical, leadership, and so on). It may be, for example, that the firm will need a German-speaking engineer who plays bridge and skis to help it close a deal with an important client. More likely, it will need an engineer with management training and experience to direct the development of a new

FIGURE 4.20   *The organization of the personnel function*

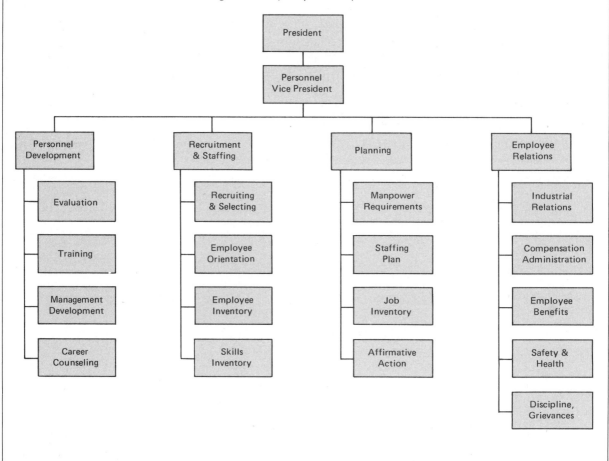

plant or production process. The productive characteristics of individual employees change constantly, and up-to-date knowledge about them is vital to the effective performance of the personnel function.

The personnel function is also responsible for identifying the personnel needs (staff requirements) of the firm and for developing a plan (the staffing plan) for meeting those requirements. Part of that plan should indicate those current employees who will be moved into positions of greater responsibility (promoted). An employee's promotability is a function of the employee's development. The personnel function is responsible for seeing that employees are given the counseling and training that assist them in realizing their individual potential within the firm. Failure to provide such opportunity will mean that ambitious employees will seek promotion elsewhere, and some of the most effective employees will be lost to competing firms.

THE PERSONNEL INFORMATION SUBSYSTEM

As indicated above, the personnel function requires the collection, storage, retrieval, and use of data concerning the performance, skills, education, promotions, and so on, of employees. The information activity in this area is involved primarily with establishing and maintaining a personnel information data base. A computerized personnel data base can provide an easy-to-use and accurate inventory of personnel, skills, and jobs to assist in carrying out the personnel function. Inputs are the changes in personal status, promotion or transfer to different jobs, new hires, resignations, dismissals, retirements, completion of education or training programs or courses, creation of new jobs within the firm, and work activity. The outputs are responses to inquiries by management, analysis of hiring and turnover, affirmative action reports, staffing requirements, staffing plans, wage and salary administration reports, and annual evaluations of each employee's productivity and promotability.

There are at least four files contained in the personnel data base as shown in Figure 4.21. These are the personnel inventory, skills inventory, job inventory, and payroll master.

The Personnel Inventory This file contains each employee's master employee record. Data items found in each employee record include:

Employee identification: name, employee number, social security number, address, telephone, and so on

Personal data: sex, age, family status, number of dependents, and so on

Work history: experience before joining the firm, date of original hire, positions held within the firm (with dates), performance evaluations

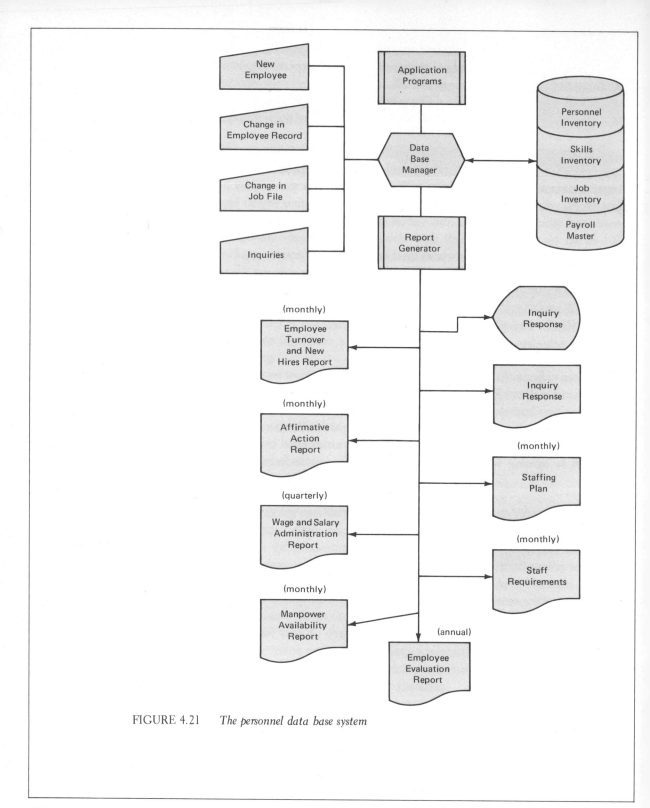

FIGURE 4.21   *The personnel data base system*

Education: degrees (with dates), special training

Special skills: work skills, language skills, recreational skills

Benefits: insurance, retirement, savings plan, and so on

The Skills Inventory   Information taken from the employee inventory file provides efficiency in locating employees with special abilities, talents, or interests.   The skills information from the employee master file is rearranged to list employee identification arranged by skill, interest, or talent category. The skill code is the record key and the employee identification, the data elements of each record.   The rearrangement by skill makes interrogation easier and faster.   Actually, experience has shown that this file need not contain information on every employee but only those at the supervisory level or above.   This reduction in numbers means significant savings in online storage costs without significant loss in needed information.

The Job Inventory   This file contains such descriptive data as location(s), pay scales, numbers of positions, and so on, for each job in the firm.   Each separate job has three subrecords.   One is the *job description*, which tells what activities comprise the job, that is, what the job *is*.   The second subrecord is the *job specification*, which identifies the characteristics persons holding the job must have — education and/or training, physical capabilities, skill levels, and so on.   The third subrecord is the *statistical data*, the location(s) and numbers of positions for each job.

The Payroll Master File   The data this payroll file contains are obvious. This file is the major interface between the finance and personnel functions.

Other Personnel Files   Additional files can, of course, be added.   Data on insurance, retirement programs, and other employee benefits, including accumulated sick leave and vacation time, could be stored in a *benefits file*. Union membership data, identification of union officers, grievance cases, and so on, could be stored in an *industrial relations and grievance file*.

The Planning Information Subsystem

THE OBJECTIVE OF THE PLANNING FUNCTION

Planning is one of the major functions of management.   It is necessary because of the uncertainty about the environment within which the firm operates.   The general social, political, and ethical philosophies of society promote an atmosphere of progress through change.   Rapidly advancing technology is a significant contributor to the instability of the business environment.

The result of planning is, as one might expect, one or more plans. A *plan is a predetermined course of action and the expected outcomes from following that course of action.* Plans provide the coordination among the various parts of the firm.

The objective of the planning function is to set the objectives and goals of the firm and the paths of action that will be followed in seeking to attain those objectives and goals.

As seen in Figure 4.22, inputs to the planning system include the basic objectives of the firm, data from the environment, and internal data. Markets can be identified and market trends established by analyzing environmental data on population (age, sex, geographic distribution); income (total, distribution over the population, variability over time, and so on); technological developments; price relationships; and consumer tastes and habits. In addition, data and coefficients can be developed for formal or informal simulation models that answer questions such as "What is the effect on sales of automobiles of a 1-percent increase in disposable personal income?" "If average mileage per gallon of gas were to increase by five miles per gallon, what would be the effect on demand for gasoline?" "As cars are made smaller and lighter, how does the demand for service, repair, and tire replacement change?" Answers to such questions allow the firm to refine its objectives and to select among its strategic alternatives.

A *strategic alternative* is a general direction of future activity for the firm. It should reflect a realistic joining of an opportunity present in the business environment and the capabilities present in the firm. Thus a firm with no technical knowledge in the field of electronics would be ill-advised to try to get into the manufacture of computer components by designing products, building a plant, and starting to produce. It might be reasonable, however, for that same firm to use its available capital resources to buy control of a firm that is already producing computer components. By acquisition of a viable competitor in that field, the expanding firm could obtain the necessary technical knowledge and skill and a foothold in the market for computer components.

Selecting the strategic alternative or alternative set allows objectives to be further refined and stated as quantitative goals. The strategic plans and the goals then provide the basis for developing operational plans that specify exactly how the goals are to be obtained. Planning has a hierarchical nature that is reflected in the level at which planning occurs, the scope of the plan, the degree of aggregation of the variables used in the planning, and the time sequence in which the planning occurs.

Strategic planning occurs at the top levels of the firm and is concerned only with the overall (global) objectives of the organization. Planning at this level uses aggregate data, much of which is drawn from sources external

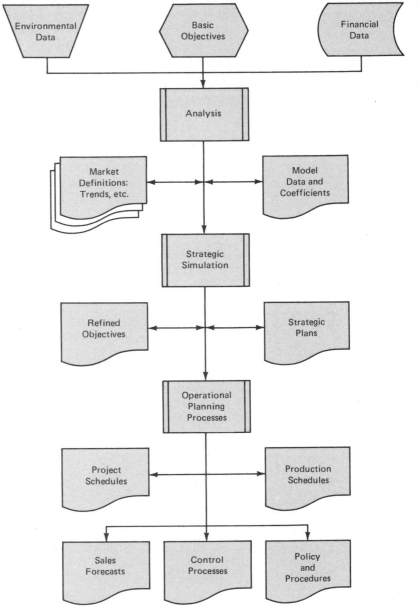

FIGURE 4.22   *The planning function*

to the firm (see Figure 4.22). Strategic planning also takes the long view, several years into the future. The shift of capital resources between two competing uses usually requires efforts spread over several years. Moves to take advantage of newly developing opportunities can take more than a decade, particularly if the tastes and habits of the population must be changed to provide a market for a new product based on new technology. For example, the so-called radar (microwave) oven has been produced for over twenty-five years but has been widely accepted by consumers for less than half that time. Although television was commercially available many years before World War II, it did not become available to the average citizen until after that war. Production processes developed as part of the war effort improved the entire television process, and increases in consumer incomes made the television industry an economic as well as a technological possibility.

Operational plans are made at a lower level. The design and construction of a new plant to increase productive capacity or the development of a marketing organization for a new territory cannot be carried out overnight. The assignment of available workers to machines and the concurrent planning of the flow of available jobs through those machines can be carried out rather quickly, however. Operational plans often are concerned with a single function. At the highest level of operational planning, functions must be coordinated. At the lowest level, each functional activity is independently planned. Thus as planning activity is traced from the top of the organization through middle management to the supervisory level, its time frame shortens, the level of detail in the data used increases, and the span, or scope, of the planning narrows. In addition, if plans are to coordinate activities to attain overall objectives as well as to realize today's production or sales quota, the lower level (operational) plans must be based upon and therefore follow after the highest level (strategic) plans.

THE ORGANIZATION OF THE PLANNING FUNCTION

There is no typical organization of the planning function. Strategic planning is often carried out by the top executive of the firm or by a top-level executive committee. Operational planning is carried out by middle managers at the higher levels and by supervisory personnel at the lowest levels. In well-managed firms, planning is formally organized and its hierarchical nature clearly evident. In smaller firms, planning is often informal and intermittent. Regardless of the size of the firm or the formal or informal nature of the effort, planning must be done. In the process, certain subfunctions must be provided for. The organizational structure shown in Figure 4.23 identifies the necessary subfunctions. Note that the functional subsystems of the firm have primary responsibility for the operating plans. The planning department is responsible for strategic plans on which the operational plans are based, for providing information and analysis needed by the functional units in developing their plans, and for coordinating the total planning effort. The planning function must involve those line officers of the firm who have direct operational responsibilities. The planning depart-

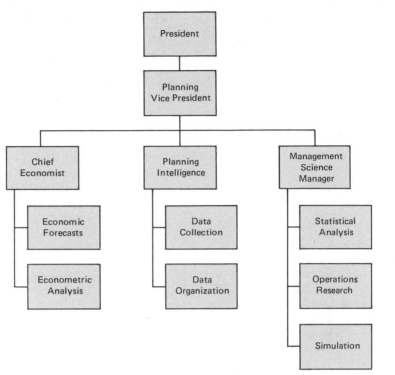

FIGURE 4.23   *The organization of the planning function*

ment is a staff department that assists the line officers in planning. The department provides the organization, analysis, and interpretation of environmental and operational data that provide information on which planning decisions can be based. Line officers with operating responsibilities must be involved in the setting of goals and in planning how they are to be attained if those officers are to be held accountable for reaching the goals established.

THE PLANNING INFORMATION SUBSYSTEM

Plans are, in reality, coordinating communications directed to the various subsystems within the firm. The heart of the planning information subsystem, as shown in Figure 4.24, is composed of three information resource banks:

1. The environmental data bank

   This collection of data on market populations, income distributions, economic activity measures for the economy, competitors, technological developments, and other environmental developments is the primary source of environmental data.

2. The internal data bank

This is really the master files of the firm as defined earlier. It includes data on financial flows, human resources, plant and equipment, products or services produced for sale, research and development activities, and any

FIGURE 4.24   *The planning information subsystem*

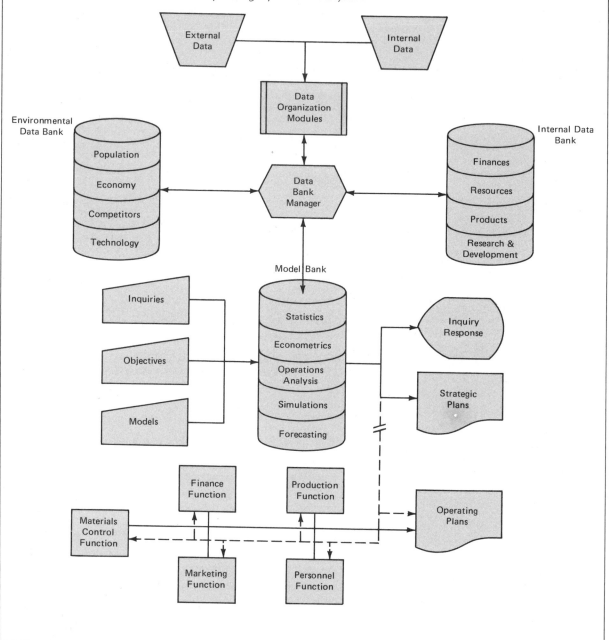

other facts about the firm and its components which can be useful in developing strategic and operational plans.

3. The model bank

This collection provides the tools and techniques for data analysis, forecasting, scheduling, and simulation needed for developing forecasts and for testing strategies and plans. The major tools from each major area are listed below:

I. Statistics
    A. Data Description
        1. Univariate (central tendency and dispersion, frequency distributions)
        2. Multivariate (joint probability distributions, including correlation)
    B. Statistical Inference
        1. Estimation
        2. Hypothesis testing (single and multiple sample)
        3. Decision analysis under uncertainty
        4. Multivariate analysis (analysis of variance, factor analysis, discriminant analysis, and so on)
        5. Regression (simple, multiple, step-wise, robust, ridge, and so on)
        6. Nonparametric statistics (chi-square, runs, and so on)
II. Econometrics
    A. Time Series Decomposition (trend, cycle, seasonal)
    B. Multiple-Equation Models
    C. Input-Output Analysis
III. Operations Analysis
    A. Scheduling [critical path methods (CPM), program evaluation and review techniques (PERT), networks, and so on]
    B. Resource Utilization (mathematical programming: linear, nonlinear, dynamic, goal, and so on)
    C. Queuing
IV. Simulation
    A. Markov Chains
    B. Computer Simulation Modeling using discrete and continuous simulation languages
V. Forecasting
    A. Regression
    B. Time-Series Analysis, Box-Jenkins
    C. Multiple-Equation Models
    D. Exponential Smoothing, Moving Averages

Through the imaginative use of the above tools, a multitude of "what if" questions can be answered. Some repeated planning tasks, such as plant scheduling and inventory control, can be completely routinized and even handled by the computer if demand, prices, and production processes and costs remain unchanged.

Integration of the Functional Information Subsystems

It is obvious that several of the functional information subsystems overlap. Some of the most obvious overlaps are indicated in Figure 4.25. Although these overlaps can be categorized in a variety of ways, a useful one in the analysis and design of information systems recognizes three major categories of overlap:

1. Systems with common data sources.

2. Systems with common master files; that is, systems that share a common data base.

3. Systems that jointly contribute to one or more reports to management.

FIGURE 4.25   *Overlap among functional information subsystems*

	How used in function					
Element	*Finance*	*Marketing*	*Production*	*Mat. cont.*	*Personnel*	*Planning*
Credit sale	A/R	Sales analysis	Product demand	Inventory withdrawal	Sales- person performance	Sales history
Cash sale	Cash	Sales analysis	Product demand	Inventory withdrawal	Sales- person performance	Sales history
Payroll check	Cash	—	Labor cost	—	Pay rate Performance	Cash use
Vendor invoice	A/P Cash	—	Materials parts supplies	Receipts (cost/ value)	—	—
Customer payment	A/R Cash	—	—	—	Salesperson performance	Customer history
Environmental data	Capital budgeting	Marketing intelligence	Process planning	Potential vendors	Wage rates Availability	Environmental intelligence

Summary   The functional information subsystems for finance, marketing, manufacturing, materials control, personnel, and planning have been described and discussed. These descriptions should lead the reader to recognize that these systems have more in common than might be supposed. As was indicated in Chapter 1, each of these subsystems tends to consist of a set of basic records (a data base or data bank) and a method of extracting from business transactions and activity in the environment data that is used to update those data banks. The flow of data and the master files are accessed to develop information for management to use in decision making. Several of the functional subsystems share sources of data or master files and/or make joint contributions to managerial reports.

Questions

1. Define each of the following as briefly as possible and then use a short paragraph to clarify each definition.
   a. Functional subsystem
   b. Functional organization
   c. Matrix organization
   d. Working capital
   e. Standard cost
   f. Bill of materials
   g. Vendor history file
   h. Job specification
   i. Strategic planning
   j. Information Subsystem
   k. Project organization
   l. Budget
   m. Cash flow forecast
   n. Cost center
   o. Production routing
   p. Staffing plan
   q. Job description
   r. Operational planning

2. State as briefly as possible the objective of each of the functional subsystems listed below:
   a. Financial
   b. Marketing
   c. Production
   d. Material control
   e. Personnel
   f. Planning

3. What is (are) the difference(s) between a flow-of-funds statement and a cash flow forecast? Include the purpose of each of these reports as *part* of your answer.

4. Compare the marketing intelligence subfunction and the marketing research subfunction. Do they overlap? Why differentiate between them?

5. Contrast the objectives of the personnel and the materials control subsystems. In what respects are they the same and in what respects do they differ?

6. Identify the four inventories controlled by the inventory control subsystem.

7. How can the efficiency of production systems be measured?

8. How can the efficiency with which the personnel function is carried out be determined?

9. What is (are) the difference(s) between a staff requirements forecast and a staffing plan?

10. What is (are) the difference(s) between each pair of items below? (*Note:* Start by referring to the definition of each item and then look for differences.)

    a. Capital budget and strategic plan
    b. Operating budget and operating plan
    c. Strategic plan and operating plan

11. Discuss in detail the overlap between the planning function, and the

    a. Marketing intelligence subsystem
    b. Budgeting subsystem
    c. Production planning subsystem
    d. Staffing subsystem.

    What general conclusions do you draw from this analysis?

12. List the major data bases (or data banks) identified in this chapter. Clearly identify any overlaps among them. Can any of them be combined?

13. Compare the objectives of the marketing function with the objectives of the personnel function. In what general ways are they the same? In what specific ways are they different? Can you draw any general conclusions from this comparison? Explain.

14. Some firms do not establish an identified planning unit. Why might this be an acceptable organizational structure?

15. How might the effectiveness with which the planning function is performed be determined?

16. After reading this chapter and answering the previous questions, do you think it will ever be possible to have a single, totally integrated MIS for a firm? Support your conclusion as fully as possible.

Part 2

Analysis and Design of Information Systems

Part 1 of this text examines the nature of data processing and information systems. It shows that information systems are merely special forms of data processing systems. Part 2 examines the general processes used in analyzing and designing such systems. Chapter 5 lays out the general process for analysis of existing systems and shows how it is applied to data processing and information systems. In Chapter 6, the process is extended to design of new or different systems. Chapter 7 presents a collection of tools commonly used in these activities. The reader should note that the material in this section is applicable to systems featuring either manual or automated processing of data. In fact, Chapter 6 specifically discusses manual and machine-aided manual data processing devices as well as automated devices.

Five

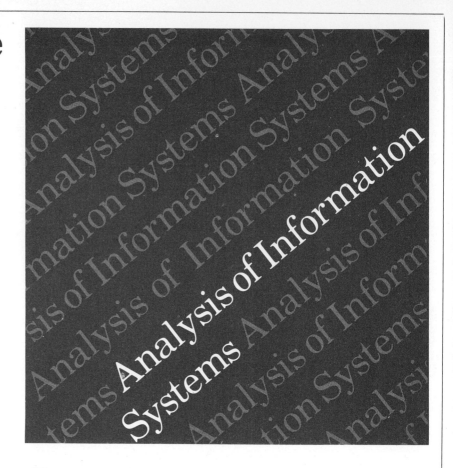

Analysis of Information Systems

$\mathbf{C}$hapters 1–4 examine the nature of data processing and management information systems. This chapter introduces the basic concepts of the analysis of such systems. *Systems analysis* as used here implies an existing system and consists of defining and analyzing the system and making suggestions for its improvement. Systems analysis is applied to the systems that control, service, and coordinate the operations of an organization. Systems analysis is concerned with identifying and analyzing an existing management information system or one of its subsystems. It is not to be confused with *systems design*, the process of creating a new system or deliberately redesigning an existing system.

The Steps in Systems Analysis

The objectives of systems analysis are the identification and evaluation of a system and the formulation of suggestions for its continued effective operation. We define a *system* as a combination of elements, their attributes, and their interrelationships organized in the pursuit of a common objective. A system is defined by its elements, their attributes, interrelationships, and organization, and the objectives of the system. The components of the system, and their characteristics and interrelationships must be identified. The effectiveness of the system in attaining its objectives must be evaluated. Such analysis of a system is best accomplished by adhering to a logical process.

A generalized statement of the format for *any* systems study is presented in Figure 5.1. This figure serves to relate our discussion to the common vocabulary of systems theory for the reader who has had a previous introduction to such theory. Figure 5.1 indicates that systems are made up of *components* found within the *boundaries* of that system. A system also has a set of one or more *objectives* that are related to what is expected of the system in the way of outputs (the *requirements* of the system). It also has a *structure*, a

FIGURE 5.1   *Format of a systems study*

  I. The *system* (a description of what and where the system is, relative to the rest of the environment)
     A. *Boundaries* (what is in the system; what is outside the system)
     B. *Components* (those distinguishable entities that affect the accomplishment of the systems objectives to a specified degree)
 II. System's present *objectives* (a statement of what the system is presently attempting to accomplish)
III. System *requirements* (what it must provide or do)
     A. For the environment
        1. Within the organization
        2. Outside the organization
     B. For itself (self-imposed requirements)
 IV. System *structure* (a description of the organization and interaction within the system)
     A. Hierarchical relationships among components
     B. Interactions of components
  V. System *state* (a description of the system's contents and the characteristics of those contents at this moment in time)
 VI. *Analysis* of system
     A. Its objectives relative to the requirements
     B. Its state relative to its objectives
     C. Its structure relative to its objectives
VII. Suggested modifications
     A. In objectives
     B. In structure
     C. In state (amount of components such as inventory, cash balance, etc.)

SOURCE: Adapted from Table 2.1 in Gene P. Neely, "Relating Systems Theory to Management Concepts," an unpublished professional paper submitted in partial fulfillment of the requirements for the degree of Master of Business Administration at the University of Montana, summer 1972.

set of hierarchical and interaction (effectual) relationships between components. Finally, at any instant of time the system has a *state*, which is the current amounts and/or capacities of each of its components and the specific status of the components relative to one another and to the environment that surrounds the system.

It is important to recognize the importance of time in differentiating between state variables and structural variables in a system. State variables will include certain coefficients or ratios in structural relationships, if those coefficients or ratios are subject to change over time. The capacity or conversion rate of a machine or process may be either a state variable or a structural variable. The specific classification will often be determined by the time frame within which the analysis occurs. This blurring of the difference between system structure and system state is also reflected in their identification. In order to define structure, one must define state, and vice versa. They must be determined together because they are mutually interdependent.

Figure 5.1 indicates that systems analysis consists of a series of activities. These activities overlap, and several steps in the analysis may be carried out simultaneously. Close study of the outline and some hard thinking will reveal that its order could be altered without reducing the value of the analysis. In general, however, we must define the system (define system objectives, system components, system structure, and system state), then analyze the system operation relative to the objectives of the system and the requirements placed upon it by its environment, then suggest improvements. This three-phase process of system definition, analysis of system operation, and suggestions for improvement is the *general* process.

Business systems enable management to fulfill the purposes of the organization; that is, they are the mechanics by and through which any function of the organization is performed. They represent methods of translating management policy into action. Those business subsystems that directly effect changes in the form of the product or produce a service are the sources of information system inputs and/or the destination for information system outputs. Information systems handle only data and information, not physical things.

In the analysis of information and data processing systems, we follow the same three-phase process used in analyzing *any* system: definition, analysis of operation, suggestions for improvement. However, the specific steps (actions) to be taken will *sound* different from those given in Figure 5.1. They represent the specific activities necessary to the accomplishment of the generalized process of systems analysis. Specific steps to be taken in the analysis of information systems are as follows:

1. Define system objectives.

2. Define system components.

3. Define system boundaries and interfaces with other systems.

4. Define system procedures.

5. Define system volumes.

6. Define system timing requirements.

7. Document the system.

8. Analyze system effectiveness and efficiency.

9. Suggest system improvements.

The addition of several steps peculiar to information system analysis that were not specifically suggested in Figure 5.1 should be noted. It should also be recognized that the process being described could be organized in a different sequence of steps. The set given provides the basis of organization for the remainder of this chapter. The information system to be analyzed is not the total information system found in a firm but, at most, an overall subsystem (production or marketing, and so on) of the total system. (Functional information subsystems are covered in Chapter 4.) In the discussion that follows, the term *system* will usually refer to such a subsystem or one of its components (payroll, sales analysis, inventory control, and so forth). If the total information system is being referred to, it will be identified as the total information system.

Defining System Objectives

The first step in the analysis of an information system is to determine the objectives of that system. An adequate determination requires that the purpose of the total system, that is, the purpose of the organization in which the information system is located, be fully understood. The primary purposes of any information system are to provide information as a basis for management planning and control and to carry out custodial processing necessary to the accomplishment of the activities of the organization. If these purposes are to be realized, the information system must provide that information and those processing services that support the real objectives and goals of the overall organization. For example, a business might ostensibly be established to produce and sell television sets. However, its true purpose is to produce and sell its product with a cost–price relationship that provides an adequate return on the required investment of capital and entrepreneurial skills. The information system must provide the kinds and types of information needed by management in attaining the real objective. Thus the total information system must report not only the total cost of resources devoted to production and marketing, but also trends in television technology and patterns of use if the company is to recognize the full potential of the market available and know how to realize that potential. The information system must relate attempts at technological efficiency and leadership to patterns of sales and net returns over time.

The objectives of the organization can be adequately defined only by top management. In a well-managed corporation, this definition will have been formalized in statements of objectives and goals in proceedings of the board of directors. In many organizations, however, such formal statements do not exist, are no longer appropriate, or are incomplete. Top management must then be asked to fill the gap.

The importance of an information system as seen by management is indicated partly by the placement of the system components within the organization. The higher the level at which the system is placed, the greater the emphasis on management information. Similarly, the greater the decision-making power of information systems personnel in defining data processing procedures, the greater the emphasis on processing efficiency. Such conflicts must be balanced if the system is to achieve optimal productivity.

The objectives of the system being studied can also be determined partly by looking at the system itself. The manager of an information or processing system should know what information the system is intended to provide for management and what custodial processing it is to carry out. The outputs of a system (the journals, ledgers, and reports developed by the system) are a clear indication of the objectives as understood by those responsible for operating the system.

Defining System Components

This process and the one that follows are the processes that define what it is that the system does and how the job is accomplished. These two processes are necessary counterparts and should go forward together. The process of identifying system components generally requires the definition of system boundaries, and vice versa. The boundary is defined to include all components that have a significant effect on the system. The components must be known in order to identify the system boundary.

A component should be defined as part of a system only if it contributes to a sufficient degree (determined by the objectives) to system purpose. The methods used to define components are numerous. Spending time with the system supervisor can assist in obtaining an overall picture of the system. It is usually impossible to get a complete picture without spending time at the lowest functional level, however. The supervisor is often too far removed from the daily operations to know the detail of those operations.

An efficient means for gaining an understanding of a system is to "walk" through the basic system flow by following each basic input through the system. For example, in an accounts receivable system, the analyst would follow through all the procedures used to process a credit sale; then follow through a customer payment; and, finally, follow through each type of correction or change data entering the system. Deviations from the main line of flow for each input should be carefully noted as each main track is being identified. Once the main line system has been identified, each of the different *special-action paths* can be examined in detail. Failure to adequately define the special-action deviations from the main system will mean continual system failures and a need for constant revision of any new system that may be developed. At this stage, however, we are trying only to define what is contained within the system and are interested in the detailed activities carried on by components only to the extent that they help us to decide whether each component encountered is or is not in the system.

Components to be identified within the system are the people, machines, and procedures that accomplish the data processing activities within the system. How are data introduced into the system? What media are used for storage and transmission of the data within the system? What devices or machines are used in capturing, storing, transporting, and modifying data within the system? Are these devices special-purpose devices useful for accomplishing only a single activity or are they more general-purpose, capable of a wide range of activities without significant change? Who operates each of these devices and accomplishes the data transfers between devices? A useful way to begin is to think in terms of the three basic components of any processing system, *input*, *processing*, and *output*. This approach is a form of the *black box method*, which is explained more fully later.

If the system being analyzed is only a part of the total information system, its purpose in the overall information system must be recognized if its outputs are to be compatible with total system objectives. Thus it must be recognized that the payroll processing subsystem requires many of the same data inputs as the labor cost control subsystem. These two jobs may be accomplished partly as an *integrated* processing activity. Data on labor time can be collected just once and used for both purposes. If the basic purpose of the total information system is kept in mind, the integrated nature of subsystems and the need for fully processing each data input are obvious.

In defining components, the total system is usually divided into subcomponents, or *work stations*, each responsible for only a single activity or group of interrelated activities. In systems utilizing electronic digital computers, these may not be physical work stations, but computer programs and related offline (noncomputer) activities. In such cases the computer system is a major component and the individual programs are subcomponents of the total system being studied. In systems that are largely manual, a work station may be only a single desk or machine and the person assigned to that desk or machine. Alternatively, a work station may consist of a group of desks (machines) and the individuals performing a single detail operation or a set of related detail operations at those desks (machines).

In summary, the analyst attempts to segregate major and minor groupings of productive factors (people and machines), each of which contributes in a meaningful way to the overall processing accomplished by the total system. Initially, the exact, detailed procedures followed by each group (at each work station) need not be specified, only the general task noted. In this way the major flow can be easily identified and components recognized without getting lost in the details handled at each station.

Defining System Boundaries and Interfaces with Other Systems

Because of the interrelated nature of business transactions (discussed in detail in Chapters 2, 3, and 4 in discussing MIS and data processing concepts) the definition of the boundaries of an information system for analysis is usually arbitrary. It is clear, however, that attempting to analyze the total information system in a single analysis is essentially impossible. The total system can be looked at as a *black box* with grossly specified inputs and outputs. Within that total black box are smaller black boxes with some common boundaries. Efficient analysis requires more detailed analysis of specified subsystems as individual systems. At the same time, it has been clearly demonstrated that the whole is greater than the sum of its parts and that optimizing each minor-detail subsystem may lead to an extremely inefficient total system. The analyst must strive to include in the analysis of a subsystem all the components and procedures that have a *significant* impact on that subsystem. Components and procedures with only minor peripheral impact can be ignored in the early stages of the analysis.

The complications ensuing from the interaction between subsystems can only be handled if the points of interaction are clearly identified. Information and processing subsystems may interface in four basic ways. First, they may share a common master file or set of master files (a data base). Second, two or more subsystems may share the same sources of transaction data. Third, two or more systems may contribute jointly to one managerial report. Fourth, one or more of the outputs of one system may be inputs to another system. These interrelationships must be considered in all aspects of the analysis, but they particularly affect decisions concerning system volume and timing, as will be indicated in subsequent sections.

Defining System Procedures

Once an initial grouping of the people and machines in a system into components has been accomplished and the interfaces of this system with other systems identified, the analyst can start defining the actual processing procedures used in the system. At this stage, it can be useful to follow the input data (usually representing a single transaction and contained on a single input document) through the system in detail, spending enough time at each work station to determine exactly what happens there and why it is done.

Particular attention should be given to control procedures. What keeps the system operating in the way it is supposed to? How is the quality of input data assured? How are errors in processing or analysis prevented? What procedures insure that input data are not lost from the system and never included in output? How is the introduction of fictitious records or data elements prevented?

The analyst must watch for key individuals who handle the major exceptions in the system. There is normally an individual, usually someone who has been around for some time, to whom unusual or incorrect items are referred at any work station. The first such person encountered by the author was a woman in charge of a desk in the corner of the room housing a processing department. This "woman in the corner" was not identified as holding any particular processing responsibility, but she was consulted constantly by other workers in the department about unusual items and served as a significant *special-action path* in the processing. Such a person can be the key to a successful system operation — and its analysis. As an example of this, a company assigned a new analyst to put its sales order processing on the computer. The analyst examined the sales orders as they arrived at the central plant; found them to be generally neat, orderly, and accurate; and proceeded to design a processing system (computer program and related peripheral input-output activities) to handle the sales orders written by the salespeople. To save time, orders were rerouted to go from salespeople directly into the order processing department rather than through the regional sales offices as in the past. The system immediately broke down when it turned out that in each regional office a key employee, usually a former salesperson with a good knowledge of customers and products, rewrote a large portion of the orders sent in by the salespeople. The system was rescued by a costly and time-consuming retraining of salespeople in sales order preparation and the transfer of two of the sales "expediters" from regional offices to central sales order processing to rewrite poorly prepared or obviously erroneous orders.

Defining System Volumes

One key element in determining the most efficient and economical processing procedures and devices to use in an information system is the volume of processing handled by the system. The analyst normally starts with the volume of transactions data inputs. These must be determined for each transaction type. A simple count for some period is not sufficient. The analyst must know not only how many transactions are handled each time period (day, week, month, year) but also how the transactions are distributed within each of those periods. These frequencies must be related to the cycle time of the physical operation. This is discussed in greater length in the next section on determining timing requirements. The problem, basically, is to be able to handle the maximum possible volume in any processing cycle.

Another dimension of the volume determination is the complexity of the processing required. This is also related to the control needs of the physical process that the data reflect. More expensive and sophisticated devices can be economically justified to handle complex analyses at much lower volumes than when the processing is relatively simple. It must be true, of course, that the more complex analysis results in additional information of enough value to offset the cost of obtaining it.

A third dimension of volume is the size of storage files required within the system. This, of course, is determined by not only the number of master records and the size of each such record but also the processing method employed. If data for each transaction must be retained for a time rather than merely used for an immediate update of the related master record, storage requirements increase.

Organizations often pay excessive but unrecognized storage costs because of the failure to recognize that detailed data on each transaction have a limited useful life. Again, this is related to the control requirements of the physical process to which the data apply. *Purging* of detail transaction files as frequently as the situation will allow can often result in significant data processing savings. This usually requires some change in data processing procedures (not necessarily equipment) to be fully effective. Care must, however, be exercised to retain enough detail so that there is little chance of a future need for detail that is no longer available. It should be recognized, however, that it may be possible to clear some details from the *active* master file and retain them only on some inexpensive medium such as microfilm.

Another very important volume consideration related to retention of detail data has to do with the volume of output. Long, detailed reports have a low informational value. Much information can be gleaned from them but only by extensive additional processing. Reports should be kept as brief and simple as possible. This is best done by designing them to highlight the important information contained in the data being analyzed. Averages, time trends, relationships, and unplanned or unexpected occurrences (exceptions) should be clearly identified and reported. Details should be included only when necessary to provide a sufficient level of understanding so that effective decisions can be made. Again, one must understand the underlying physical operation and the requirements for its effective control. In any case, an obvious trade-off occurs between the volume of detail in the report and the size of the storage file and the period of retention of detail data. The greater the detail in the report, the less the need for storage of the same detail elsewhere, and vice versa. However, as noted above, there is a cost to putting detail into a report. The greater the detail, the harder it is to grasp the *information* content. Ease of access to filed data must also be considered in relation to the need for such access in the design of reports and in the design of the data files from which they are developed.

Defining System Timing Requirements

As indicated earlier, system volumes are meaningless unless related to timing. Then, however, we were speaking primarily of inputs; now we are thinking primarily of outputs. The question to be answered is: How soon must the data be processed or analyzed? That is: How soon must follow-on custodial documents or analytic results of the processing be available for use within the operation or for control of the operation? Related questions are: Who is to receive the report, and how does that person use the results? Normally, the closer the recipient of a report is to the actual physical operation, the more quickly that person must be made aware of deviations from plan. Those responsible for controlling the day-to-day physical operation must receive frequent, detailed reports. Those responsible for planning and policy need more fully analyzed (summarized and organized) data and analytic results which show the relationship of the particular activity to other activities of the organization and to long-run plans and overall objectives and goals. For example, in a manufacturing business, those managing the production operation need to know the range of production rates, the product mix being run, the length of the run, and how efficiently each production unit is performing. Policy and planning management in the same firm needs only average costs and production totals, for they reflect directly the objectives and goals set by management. Operating management must know detailed marginal costs and individual unit production to control the operation to reach those goals. Planning and policy management is primarily concerned only with whether or not the goals are being met. Not only must operating managers know the details of the operation, but they must also be aware of them on a current basis. Planning can operate effectively only if the day-to-day fluctuations in the data are not allowed to obscure trends and long-run averages. Only when pursuing an explanation of unexpected or undesired results will planning and policy management be concerned with the day-to-day details of the operation. Routine reports for operating management normally will come with greater frequency than reports for planning and policy management. Both types of reports should include an analysis of expected future developments and the extent of present and foreseen goal attainment.

Documenting the System

The previous steps would provide a general picture of the system being analyzed. This step is involved with the detailed description of the system and the activities carried on within the system. Part of this description would be available from the previous steps, but it must be organized into a consistent, detailed picture. Everything must be recorded in an easily understood form that can still show every component, every procedure, every operation of the entire system. Specific devices to use include organization charts, flowcharts, decision tables, and input-output matrices. The preparation and use of each of these devices is described in detail in Chapter 7. At this time, we merely assert their usefulness in creating a detailed system description.

System documentation should include samples of all input, processing and report forms, copies of procedural manuals and/or computer runbooks and computer programs, and a complete description of flow through the system. It should also include a clear indication of exactly where output documents go and what other systems the system under study either receives data from or sends data to. The worst error that can be made in system analysis is to try to short-cut system documentation. Obtaining complete documentation assures a complete, usable description of the system, which makes analysis of its effectiveness and efficiency possible. The cycle time of a processing operation should be included in its documentation. The frequency with which data are processed and reports disseminated should also be included. Only with complete documentation is effective evaluation of system performance possible.

Analyzing System Effectiveness and Efficiency

Judging a system encompasses two areas, *efficiency* and *effectiveness*. System *efficiency* refers to the technical capability and the cost of doing the processing accomplished by the system. *Effectiveness* refers to the capability of the system in meeting managerial requirements.

SYSTEM EFFECTIVENESS

System *effectiveness* is measured by asking if the system is meeting management's goals. Returning to the reasons for processing business data, we can see a need to answer three major questions: Does the system perform necessary custodial processing? Does the system preserve the necessary historical data? Does the system provide adequate information for management planning and control? Another way to approach this issue is to ask: (1) Does the system provide an adequate data bank (inventory of files) for the organization? Are the data and information that are present in those files relevant and useful? Are all relevant data included? If not, why not? (2) Does the system provide for the continuous capture of data from transactions and the environment to keep the files current (updated)? Are the capture and processing of transactions and environmental data up to date? (3) Does the system provide for the summarization and analysis of the captured data and the reporting of the current status of the operation so as to make timely and relevant *information* available to both operating management and policy and planning management? Are the historical files so arranged and stored that they are accessible to management for obtaining details when routine reports indicate the operation is not going as planned?

Practical Methods A practical method for assessing the effectiveness of a data processing system in providing managerial information involves two tests of its informational output. One test involves obtaining access to the personal copies of all reports already received and used by managers. These reports and related papers, if they can be obtained, quickly reveal the degree to which the processing system has done a complete job. Managers and their secretaries and assistants will routinely perform further processing of these reports in many instances. Ratios and percentages scribbled in the margins or squeezed between the lines, figures for a related past period added as an additional column or line; the plotting of key series or ratios on a graph — all these reveal that the information requirements of a manager result in further data processing, which the manager often supplies personally. This can be very high-cost data processing.

The second test of system effectiveness can be used to determine both its information output and its custodial processing abilities. Basically, the analyst tries to determine how frequently the recipients of the outputs of the system find it necessary to use "informal" methods to obtain needed information or data in order to carry out their responsibilities. Do managers find a need to know certain facts before the system routinely supplies them? Do workers in other systems find it repeatedly necessary to go outside the system to obtain data that routinely come from this system? For example, do clerks dealing with the public repeatedly find it necessary to contact the accounting department to obtain data on a customer because the system does not provide the data quickly enough? Does the marketing manager repeatedly have to "call Harry down in production" to get needed facts about production schedules in time to develop marketing schedules? A change in the length of the reporting cycle might easily obviate this type of difficulty. Sometimes the provision of multiple copies of documents or mutual access to a common data file can significantly improve performance in related systems.

A word of warning: Analysts cannot expect to make the above two practical tests merely by asking for the information. Close observation and detailed analysis, coupled with the development of an attitude of mutual respect and trust between the analyst and the operating personnel, are usually required. Managers will provide the analyst with duplicated copies of the reports they receive when what is needed is a look at the working copies of those reports. Production workers will tend to dismiss as "no problem" the repeated need to visit another department because they enjoy the contact with friends and fellow workers there. These are honest misunderstandings and normal human behavior, not attempts to deceive the analyst.

Reports to Management   One difficult area of analysis is the evaluation of output (management) reports. Is each report necessary? Are reports duplicative and thus redundant? Are they used? Experts have variously estimated that 30 to 60 percent of the reports prepared by data processing departments in business firms and governmental agencies are wasted. Either they are ignored or they do not report needed information. It gets back to the concept of information: Do the reports result in the communication of knowledge that is in a form that makes it immediately useful for decision making? Often reports can be improved by paring out extraneous materials so that the useful information is highlighted. Presenting the information in a graphic form can also be helpful. In any case, the analyst (with the aid of the managers concerned) should concentrate on the feedback of relevant evaluative information that clearly indicates system performance in relation to system objectives.

In summary, then, we ask if the data from all transactions are being handled on a timely basis (are the timing and volume requirements of the system being met?) and if information is being made available so that management can adequately control the physical system from which the data arise. This determination is not as easy to accomplish as it is to specify. Particularly in those situations (which are many) when management has failed to define measurable goals for the system and information needs are largely undefined, the task can be difficult. Evaluation can also be very difficult for sophisticated electronic-based systems, especially online, quick-response systems involving automatic decision making and document preparation by the computer.

SYSTEM EFFICIENCY

System efficiency involves two interacting dimensions, the *technical* and the *economic*.

Technical Efficiency   An evaluation of the technical efficiency of a system can require very detailed analysis involving a high level of technical knowledge. The questions to be answered are: Are system tasks being performed in the *best* way as far as techniques and equipment employed are concerned? Is equipment being correctly used? If a computer is involved, this evaluation can involve very subtle questions. For example, sorting on the computer can be accomplished by a variety of techniques with widely varying time and resource requirements. The appropriate technique for a particular case involves a balance between physical system components, file structure, programming language, computer speed, and frequency of use of the sort. Further, there is still the question of whether the sorting is really necessary or desirable in accomplishing the purpose of the processing.

Evaluating the efficiency of computer processing is a complicated process best carried out by a computer scientist. However, the analyst should at least be satisfied that certain questions have been considered: Is the programming language used in this application suited to the problem? Is the central processor well utilized? Are the peripheral devices suitable to the processing requirements? Is the computer actually up and working a satisfactory portion of the time? Is the hardware–software system designed to require a minimum amount of human effort, or at least so that costs are minimal? Specific tools that can be useful in this analysis are described in Chapters 12 and 14.

Economic Efficiency   Economic efficiency is obviously concerned with getting the required processing done at the lowest possible cost. However, one must consider long-run and short-run costs. The configuration of people and machines providing necessary processing at the lowest cost at a given moment in time may prove to be a false economy if it must be totally replaced at great expense by a different (larger) system when the volume of processing increases at a later date. If continuous growth in processing volumes is to be expected, excess capacity may not be undesirable. Alternatively, the modular nature of computer systems may make desirable a flexible system with increased capacity available through adding units or replacing slower units by faster units. Intimate knowledge of the types of available processing equipment (capacities, capabilities, and costs) and how these are changing is needed. Normally it will be necessary to consult a computer hardware specialist for this information.

A word of warning: Equipment vendor personnel are not always reliable as sources of information about what is available or technically feasible. Their primary job responsibility is, after all, to sell their employers' products; and their training is designed to fit them to that purpose. Their knowledge of alternative methods or new developments can be very limited, and their view of a competitor's products and services is most likely to be biased. Sometimes they do not even know their own employer's total product line. They can be used as sources of information, but the information should be crosschecked and independently verified. They never should be relied upon as the sole source of technical or economic information for this aspect of a system analysis.

Suggesting System Improvements

It is impossible to specify the exact nature of the improvements that might be suggested for a data processing or information system. A few examples must suffice as illustrations of the kinds of improvements that will occur to the analyst who has completed the steps described in previous sections of this chapter.

Are there obvious duplications in the procedures carried out within the system? Can these duplications be eliminated?

What procedural changes might be made to make the system totally effective? Which of these seem to be worthy of consideration?

Are there underutilized components in the system? Are there ways to improve their utilization without increasing costs unduly? Are there any volume or timing bottlenecks in the system? Can inadequate components be replaced by units of greater capacity? Can underutilized resources be used to relieve any of these bottlenecks?

In summary, then, at this stage the analyst sits down and pulls together all the facts learned and sees if they indicate any obvious ways to improve the system. Apparently minor changes often have a significant impact. For example, through-put in one electronic data processing installation was significantly improved by having the receiving clerk take accumulated jobs from the receiving desk to the computer at more frequent intervals. Under the old system, as much as three or four hours of computer work would accumulate at the receiving desk during the first hour of operation. In the meantime, the computer had been idle because no jobs had been delivered to the computer room. Similar rush hours just before and after coffee breaks and the lunch hour and just before closing also contributed to the development of long waiting lines in the computer room at certain periods during the day. Shortening of these lines led to faster service and discouraged users from bunching their deliveries at these times. The net result was a decline in average job turnaround time from about eight hours to a little less than two hours.

Common sense is the analyst's greatest ally here. In many cases application of the analyst's reason, supported by suggestions from people operating the system or from users of the system outputs, will make significant improvements possible.

Summary

The analysis of data processing and/or information systems involves the identification of what is contained in the system (its *boundaries* and its *components*). The *objectives* sought by the system and the organization of the components in pursuit of those system objectives also must be identified. *Procedures* used in processing data within the system must be discovered. *Volumes* of transactions handled by the system and the *time* within which they must be processed and results (control reports and custodial documents) produced are to be established. After all these things are found out and written down (*documented*) in appropriate ways, the system must be evaluated in terms of its ability to meet management needs (*effectiveness*) with low enough costs in the utilization of appropriate processing methods and machines (*efficiency*). Improvements in system organization, system procedures, or system components can then be suggested.

Questions

1. Define the following as briefly as possible and then use a short paragraph to clarify each definition.

   a. Systems analysis
   b. Special-action path
   c. System boundaries
   d. Work station
   e. System components
   f. Cycle time
   g. System structure
   h. System efficiency
   i. System state
   j. System effectiveness

        k. System volumes   n. Technical efficiency
        l. Economic efficiency   o. Documentation
        m. System timing

2. In what sense(s) are timing and volume related in the analysis of system capacity?

3. a. What is the concept of "special-action deviations from the main-line flow"?
   b. Why is this concept important to systems analysis?
   c. What relation does this concept have to system controls?

4. Why is identification of work stations important in the analysis of information and data processing systems?

5. Why is a simple count of transaction volume over a processing cycle inadequate in analyzing a processing system?

6. Discuss the potential trade-offs between detailed reports and detailed data files.

7. How does an analyst get involved with "real-time" concepts in the analysis of an information system?

8. a. Differentiate between system effectiveness and system efficiency.
   b. Why is it useful to make such a distinction?

9. Why should an analyst care that on receiving a report, a manager regularly computes ratios of figures given in it?

10. Why should equipment vendor representatives not be relied upon for system analyses?

11. What is the difference between system analysis and system design?

12. List the steps in systems analysis and write a brief paragraph describing each step.

13. Should the cost of a systems analysis be charged to the analyzed operating department or to company overhead? Explain. Include the following in developing your answer:
    a. What incentives are created under each method (and for whom)?
    b. What effects does the charging system have on relationships between the operating department and the analysis team?

14. One charge leveled against analysts by managers is that analysts seldom solve the "real problems" of the operating unit. Analysts allege that this occurs because "the operating managers do not know what they want from an information or data processing system."
    a. From the analyst's viewpoint, what might be done to resolve this stalemate, if it does exist? Be specific.
    b. From the operating manager's viewpoint, what might be done to resolve this stalemate, if it does exist? Be specific.

15. How can the effectiveness of an information system be measured?

16. What two questions can be used to determine if a system is efficient?

17. What is the difference, if any, between technical and economic efficiency?
18. How does the concept of a work station enter into the definition of system components and system boundaries?
19. Identify and briefly describe three methods of determining the objectives of an information subsystem.
20. Suppose you are assigned the job of project leader in designing and implementing the information systems for the hardware store chain described in question 15 at the end of Chapter 3.
    a. What knowledge and skills would you like included on your project team?
    b. What specific questions would you direct to the top-management team of the chain?
    c. What specific questions would you ask of the managers of the local stores?
    d. What specific questions would you ask of the manager of the housewares department in each store?

Six

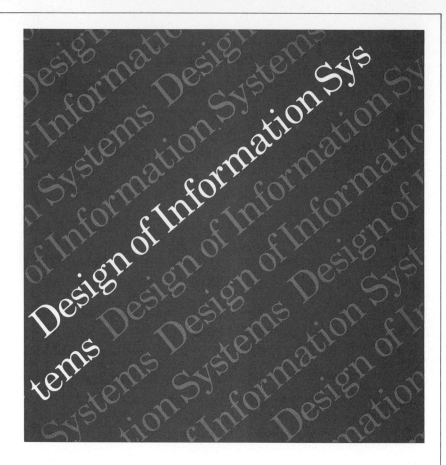

Design of Information Systems

In the previous chapter, dealing with the analysis of information systems, we defined *systems design* as the process of creating a new system or deliberately redesigning an existing system. Design, then, goes beyond mere analysis of an existing system, and starts with the supposition of change. Either an information system is to be created where none existed before, or an existing system is to be rebuilt in whole or in part.

The Steps in Design

The design of a new or different system starts in much the same fashion as a system analysis. Before a rational design can be developed, the objectives of the system must be defined. Limitations imposed on the design by organizational policy, resources available, and technology must also be taken into account. Viable alternatives must be carefully evaluated for each part of the system. It is best to have a definite set of steps or outline to follow. We suggest the following:

1. Analyze the system.
2. Specify system outputs.
3. Define feasible media and devices.
4. Select media and devices.
5. Establish appropriate controls.
6. Recognize human limitations.
7. Establish accountability for system results.
8. Implement the new or revised system.
9. Monitor the results.

This listing provides the organization for the remainder of this chapter.

Analyzing the System

The analysis of an existing system was covered in Chapter 5. We are often faced, however, with the analysis of a *new* system. New systems are needed for new organizations and for major reorganizations of old organizations. One cause of a major reorganization can be the shift from manual or machine-assisted manual processing systems to online integrated processing and information systems. Any major change in technology, whether in information and data processing or in production or delivery systems, will often cause structural changes in the organization.

The analysis for a new information or processing system proceeds in roughly the same steps as for an existing system up to the point at which system improvements are suggested. The order differs, however. The steps in analysis for an existing system are contrasted to the steps in analysis for a new system in Figure 6.1.

Systems design has as its end goal the implementation of a new or changed system. The efficiency and effectiveness of the new or revised system will have to be considered without having actual system outputs to study. The analysis of system effectiveness and efficiency must attempt to relate expected timing of outputs and expected capacities to the requirements established during the analysis phase. Actually, for revised systems, the analysis usually centers on comparing the new system with the old system on the dimensions of volume, timing, quality of output, and cost. If the design is successful, the new system will be superior in all respects except possibly total cost. Seldom can greater effectiveness be obtained for a lower total outlay. However, newer, more effective systems should remove volume, timing, or control limitations and can be less costly per dollar of income or per item processed.

FIGURE 6.1   *Steps in the analysis of an information system*

Existing system (from Chapter 5)	New system
1. Define system objectives.	1. Define system objectives.
2. Define system components.	2. Define general system procedures.
3. Define system boundaries and interfaces with other systems.	3. Define system volumes.
4. Define system procedures.	4. Define system timing requirements.
5. Define system volumes.	5. Define system boundaries and interfaces with other systems.
6. Define system timing requirements.	6. Specify system outputs.
7. Document the system.	7. Choose system components.
8. Analyze system effectiveness and efficiency.	8. Develop system controls.
9. Suggest system improvements.	9. Develop the system.
	10. Analyze system effectiveness and efficiency.

Specify System Outputs

After the objectives of the system and its volume and timing requirements are known, attention should be given to specification of its outputs. It is especially important to involve system users in this activity. Remember, if the reports created by the system are not accepted and used as a basis for decisions, information will not have been created. Attention at this point should be focused on the following questions:

1. Who will use the outputs and for what purpose?

Users may be external to the organization as well as internal. The information needs of these groups may differ a great deal. Most internal users will be involved in planning or controlling operations. External users will be concerned with evaluation of total performance, with primary emphasis on future performance.

2. Is the content of each output directed to the user's need?

Exactly what information or custodial document does each user need? How much detail? If this is an informational output, does it present novel, nonredundant information or only unrefined data?

3. What form should the outputs take?

Here, the questions have to do with presenting outputs that are in a form that makes them available for immediate use. In addition, the output should not be developed in an overly complex analysis. Simple analyses often reveal *most* of the information content contained in a set of data. Complex and difficult analysis often only results in minor refinements of this basic informational content.

4. How frequently must each output be available?

This, obviously, is a reformulation of the timing requirements imposed on the system that identifies, for each specific output, exactly when that output is required.

The form and timing of outputs has primary influence on the selection of system media and devices as will be seen below. Obviously, the requirement of immediate response means online systems and may also dictate a particular delivery vehicle such as a tube display. With longer response times, more traditional reporting media such as printed reports may be considered.

Clearly, the specification of system outputs is important in determining the total design of the system. The form, frequency, volume, and timing of system outputs will be important not only in determining the media and devices used in the system but also in determining the procedures to be used in obtaining outputs that meet the required specifications.

Defining Feasible Media and Devices

A variety of means are available for the capture (recording), processing, storing, and reporting of business data and information. In most cases we have to recognize two general elements, a *medium* and a *device*. The device *reads*, *stores*, or otherwise manipulates the medium and the data or the information it contains. The difference between media and the devices by which they are maintained should become clearer as we proceed.

DATA CAPTURE

Facts from business transactions can be *captured*, or recorded, on many media. Probably the most prevalent medium is the *manually prepared form* such as the sales slip in the department store. At the next level is a *machine-assisted manually prepared document* such as the cash register tape. Finally, there is increasing use of *point-of-action recording* either directly into a computer or onto some machine-processable medium such as punched paper tape or magnetic tape. When to use each of these media and related devices depends upon many factors. Before discussing these factors, we should identify the characteristics of each input medium more fully.

Manually Prepared Forms   The design of printed forms for manual recording of data is a complicated task. Good forms for manual data collection have the following characteristics:

1. Data elements are in a logical order and sequenced left to right and top to bottom.

2. Related data elements are grouped together.

3. Abbreviations and codes used to conserve space while identifying content are logical and nonoverlapping.

4. Adequate space is provided for the insertion of each data element.

5. Major data elements are highlighted and easy to find at the edges of the document, particularly on the right and at the bottom.

6. Forms are easy to correct.

7. Sufficient copies are prepared or duplication is easily effected to provide input data for all processing systems relying on this activity for input.

8. The forms are easy to handle, store, and process.

9. Whenever possible, fixed (nonvariable) data elements are preprinted on the form.

Manually prepared preprinted forms for data collection have the advantages of being easy to set up and easy to use in most business situations. The tools required are simple (pencils or pens and preprinted forms), mistakes are easily corrected, and a permanent record of the transaction is created. These media have the disadvantages of being slow, being subject to error by the human agent involved, and requiring conversion to another medium (for example, to punched cards or magnetic tape) for entry into machine systems.

Machine-assisted Manually Prepared Documents   The data elements that describe a transaction are of two general types, *fixed* data and *variable* data. Fixed data are those elements that do not change from transaction to transaction of the same type. As an example, let us look at the data elements associated with a credit sale at a department store:

Fixed data elements	*Variable data elements*
Customer name and address	Items purchased
Department identification	Units of each item
Salesperson identification	Unit price for each item
	Total sale price
	Date of sale

Through the use of plastic credit cards for customers and an identification card or entry button for each salesclerk, a machine can be used to enter the fixed data elements in one machine cycle. The variable data elements are recorded by the salesclerk. The chance of charging the wrong customer or misspelling the customer name is reduced.

Cash sales in a supermarket are more fully recorded with a machine, the cash register. Buttons on the cash register are used to identify the department and the price of each item and the amount of money received from the customer. In some retail stores, the cash register tapes are recorded in a special-character *font* (typeface) that can be read by an optical reader for entry into a computerized information system.

For inventory control some retail stores affix to each piece of merchandise an identifying tag that is in reality a punched card. These punched cards are accumulated during the day and processed by machine each night to update inventory records and prepare inventory and sales reports for buyers and department managers. When combined with cash register tapes and credit sales slips, they also provide control over cash receipts and credit sales transactions.

Cash registers and other point-of-action devices used to record transaction data have been joined to card and paper tape punches to simultaneously prepare machine-readable input. For example, such an entry device at the teller's window of a savings and loan association creates a punched paper tape record of all transactions. These tapes are transported to a central, computerized data processing facility at the end of each day and processed during the night to update customer records and prepare management reports.

In addition to being equipped to prepare a machine-readable record, some transaction recording devices are programmed to guide the operator in entering the data elements. Lighted messages adjacent to the appropriate keys flash on in the proper sequence as data elements are entered. Attempting to enter data elements out of sequence causes some devices to "lock up" until the proper sequence is restored.

The keying of certain inputs is checked by some input units through the use of a *check digit*. The check digit is obtained as the final digit of a number calculated from the individual digits of the number being keyed in and appended to that number (see Figure 6.2). The calculation process is designed to prevent a significant amount (as many as 98 percent) of the common keying errors (transposition of adjacent digits and keying the wrong digit). The input device contains a special-purpose calculating unit programmed to perform the required calculations to verify the check digit. If a mistake is detected in the keying of the number, the operator is signaled to rekey the data element.

The advantages of using machine assistance in entering data manually is that human activities are reduced or controlled by a machine. Since

FIGURE 6.2   *A common method for computing a check digit*

Initial number: 97822
1. Beginning with first digit, multiply every second digit by 2:
   $$9 \times 2 = 18$$
   $$8 \times 2 = 16$$
   $$2 \times 2 = 4$$
2. Add these products together with the digits not multiplied by 2:
   $$(18 + 16 + 4) + (7 + 2) = 47$$
3. Subtract the units digit of this sum from 10 to obtain the check digit:
   $$10 - 7 = 3$$

---

machines are less error-prone than humans, errors in initial recording of data elements are reduced. An additional advantage is that the recording operation is accomplished in less time. The extra cost associated with the use of more sophisticated devices must be compared to the worth of the improvements that result from their use.

Point-of-Action Recording for Machine Processing   It is becoming increasingly common to record transactions data in a form that allows machine pro-

FIGURE 6.3   *Point-of-sale data entry.* The penlike wand of the NCR 280 Retail System optically reads the bars of coded data for direct entry to the computer from the retail floor. (PHOTO COURTESY OF NCR CORPORATION)

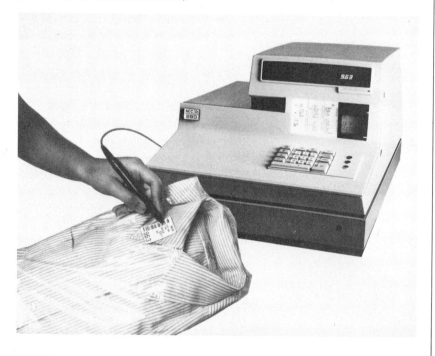

cessing without the necessity of intermediate translation to a machine-oriented medium. The devices used are advanced forms of the machines used to assist manual recording. The data are either recorded directly onto a machine-readable medium (punched card or paper tape, optically or magnetically readable document, and so on); entered directly onto a magnetic storage device (magnetic tape or disk); or immediately processed and all files affected by the transaction updated (online input). Actual devices vary from key-driven devices to special electronic sensors (see Figures 6.3, 6.4, and 6.5).

FIGURE 6.4   *Key-to-disk incremental recorder.* Mohawk data recorder enters data on computer-compatible magnetic disk. (PHOTO COURTESY OF MOHAWK DATA SYSTEMS)

FIGURE 6.5   *Intelligent terminal.* The Burroughs entry-level B 80-20 small computer system, while occupying 50 percent less floor space than earlier models, brings a new level of power and performance to small systems. The system can accommodate up to eight input/output channels and offers a choice of fixed disk, removeable disk-cartridge or mini-disk subsystems. (PHOTO COURTESY OF BURROUGHS CORPORATION)

Key-driven online input devices vary from cash registers and adding machines to special-purpose devices involving associated output display or *hard-copy* (printed output) preparation. The cathode ray terminal (TV screen display and keyboard for input) used by airline clerks at airline ticket counters is one example. Other applications are warehouse receiving systems, order entry systems, and many more.

Special-purpose terminals and point-of-action recorders come in many forms. One example is specialized terminals used in teller cages at banks and savings and loan associations to simultaneously update the internally stored customer record and the customer pass book. Another is the point-of-sale (POS) recorders designed to read magnetic or printed coding on merchandise in retail stores to process the sale transaction and update customer and store records (see Figure 6.3). Limited use is being made of voice input in quality control and point-of-sale applications.

Other means of keyboard entry include the push-button telephone, the portable data terminal, and industrial data collection devices. All are easy to operate and, because they are combined with the computer, can provide automatic editing, validating, and machine recording of transactions data at the point of origin.

Point-of-action recording has the advantage of reducing human intervention in the flow of data processing. This tends to reduce error. However, it also reduces hard-copy records of the entry transaction and makes the errors in entry that do occur more difficult to identify and correct. Expensive computerized error detection processes and "intelligent" entry terminals capable of being programmed to recognize erroneous entries become desirable. So-called intelligent terminals (a minicomputer is involved) can result in savings in total data preparation and communication costs (see Figure 6.5). They provide access to a pertinent data base and to the processing power of a computer that can significantly increase the efficiency of a point-of-action operation.

FILE STORAGE

Data storage devices vary from *manually operated devices* to *machine-assisted manually operated* devices to *automated storage and retrieval* devices.

Manually Operated Devices   The devices used to store data carrying media are even more varied than the media themselves. Most manually operated devices store some type of paper medium, however. An example of this type of device is the standard file cabinet or file drawer. Side-opening versions and rotating versions (tub files) are also available. Rotating multilevel file systems like that pictured in Figure 6.6 are large enough to store thousands of records and provide a number of work stations with easy access to the files. Specialized file cabinets are available for storing punched cards, paper and magnetic tape, magnetic disks, and microfilm.

Primarily because they usually involve paper media, manually operated systems tend to require large amounts of room in relation to the amounts of data they contain. All manually operated systems tend to be unreliable. Records are easily misfiled, lost, or destroyed. They are, however, easy to operate and relatively inexpensive for small systems.

Machine-assisted Manual Devices   These devices substitute electric motors and electronic selection for human effort. Systems can be obtained that store file folders, punch cards, microfilm rolls or cartridges, and so on, so that recall of a particular record requires only the keying of its identifying code (see Figures 6.7 and 6.8). These systems also tend to be bulky and

FIGURE 6.6   *Multiple-station, multiple-tier rotating file.* Centrac Rotary Systems store file folders, manuals, and reference works, as well as the microfilm cartridges shown here, for ready access from as many as ten desks. (PHOTO COURTESY OF ACME VISIBLE RECORDS, INC.)

FIGURE 6.7   *Mechanized filing system.* Conserv-a-Trieve Systems allow storage, retrieval, and replacement of hundreds of storage elements (file drawers, tape or film trays, and so on) from a single location. (PHOTOS COURTESY OF SUPREME EQUIPMENT AND SYSTEMS CORPORATION, BROOKLYN, N.Y.)

FIGURE 6.8   *Microfilm retrieval system*. With the Kodak IMT-150 microimage terminal, individual frames from a microfilm cartridge are key-selected for display on the video screen. (PHOTO COURTESY OF EASTMAN KODAK COMPANY)

somewhat unreliable, since most require that initial entry and later replacement of the records be done by hand.

Automated Storage and Retrieval Devices   Most fully automated systems are electronic and involve computers. However, systems involving microfilm as the storage medium under computer control are becoming increasingly common.

In general, automated devices provide speed of recording and easy retrieval of stored data. Recording is most often through an electronic computer. Storage is often in a direct-access mode where each data element is essentially equally available at any time. The major disadvantages of the electronic systems are cost and the need for highly trained technicians to devise and maintain the systems. All automated systems tend to be uneconomic for low-volume systems. Advances in electronic technology are continuously reducing these costs, at least per transaction; and increasing numbers of trained technicians are available to plan and operate systems. The microfilm systems are less expensive but slower (data access time can be as high as two to three minutes compared with a fraction of a second for electronic random-access devices).

Easily installed and easily operated systems, each specifically designed to provide data storage and retrieval for a particular business or functional subsystem, are being developed. The entire system (hardware and software) can be purchased as a package and is operational as soon as it is installed. We will have more to say about such systems in Chapter 12.

PROCESSING

Actual manipulation of data (and media) can be carried on *manually, manually with machine assistance,* by *electro-mechanical machine,* and by *electronic computers.*

Manual Processing The manual manipulation of data usually occurs when data have been captured initially on manually completed paper forms. Although simple to understand and easy to install, manual processing systems have major deficiencies. Processing tends to be slow and subject to a high error rate. Complex analysis of the captured data is difficult, if not impossible, within a reasonable time frame. The human propensity to make errors is partially offset by the human ability to recognize errors, particularly when individual data elements do not exhibit the proper relationships to each other. Such systems are easy to change, but this is a disadvantage as well as an advantage. The systems tend to change continuously, evolving into less tightly structured and more loosely controlled systems as workers within the system strive for greater speed or more individual autonomy.

Machine-assisted Manual Processing It is not uncommon for human workers to rely on machines such as desk calculators, adding machines, and cash registers to assist in manual processing (see Figure 6.9). The machines speed the work and tend to reduce error. They often produce hard-copy records of arithmetic processes that are useful in controlling the processing. When combined with prenumbered forms, such hard-copy records can be used to guard against losing data on an individual transaction. They can also assist in proving the accuracy and completeness of subsequent processing by providing control totals and record counts. Such devices speed up manual processes by replacing the arithmetic processes of the human processor. They are still relatively slow and expensive per transaction and do not lend themselves well to the application of complex analyses.

Current technology is replacing the old mechanical aids with newer devices. The motor-driven rotary calculator has been replaced by the electronic calculator. Many of the new calculators can be programmed (instructed) to

FIGURE 6.9   *Monroe 2830 desk-top electronic printing calculator.*   (PHOTO COURTESY OF MONROE, THE CALCULATOR COMPANY)

repeat a given set of operations automatically (see Figure 6.10). The more advanced of these systems are in reality small computers. These microcomputers are fully described in Chapter 11.

Electro-Mechanical Machine Processing   Slightly more complex machines (accounting machines) speed routine processing still more. These machines perform standard accounting functions such as posting to individual accounts, computing discounts on payables and receivables, calculating simple payroll deductions, and accumulating totals by categories (see Figures 6.11 and 6.12).

   The most numerous of the electro-mechanical machines are the so-called unit record punched-card systems. The label "unit record" comes from the use of the punched card as a record of each transaction or account (each *unit* of data). Several standard machines are used in such systems.

Key-operated card punches The operator enters data elements onto punched cards from a keyboard. The machine can be programmed to enter constant

FIGURE 6.10   *Hand-held electronic calculator.* The battery-powered Model H-P 38E provides fast, silent operation and instant programming of useful business and financial calculations. (PHOTO COURTESY OF HEWLETT-PACKARD COMPANY)

(unchanging) data elements or to skip certain fields automatically in order to speed up the card preparation process.

The punched card becomes the data carrying medium for further processing. For large-volume installations, card punches are being replaced by key-to-tape and key-to-disk devices that enter the data directly onto magnetic recording data storage devices (see Figure 6.4). These latter devices are faster in preparing media, and data can then be transferred to a computer at much higher speeds (see Chapter 9).

Card sorters The electro-mechanical sorter is used to sort the data entered on punched cards. Cards are separated into "pockets" on the machine according to the data value in a single card column. Repeatedly passing the cards through the machine allows sorting of the contents of an entire field.

Card collators Two or more decks of cards can be automatically merged on such a machine. Thus a *master* deck and a *transactions* deck can be interleaved for a processing run intended to update the master deck. The machine can also be used to separate the two decks.

Reproducing punch This machine can be used to reproduce a card deck exactly or with rearrangement of its contents. It can also be programmed to

FIGURE 6.11   *Small electronic accounting machine.* The Burroughs B 800 Series of small scale computer systems offers wide choice of electronic data entry, inquiry, and file update capabilities. An operator, (left foreground) using a Burroughs TD 830 display terminal, is inquiring into the data base and entering transactions in an interactive processing environment. An operator, (right foreground) using a Burroughs Audit Entry Data Preparation system is entering transactions for subsequent file updating. (PHOTO COURTESY OF BURROUGHS CORPORATION)

punch constant data into each card. When attached to processing equipment capable of addition, it can be used to produce an updated master file deck of cards.

Accounting machine This machine is essentially a card lister that prints out the card contents onto a paper form. It also has the ability to create subtotals and totals and can be used (with the reproducing punch) to create updated master file decks of cards and useful totals by categories for printing activity reports.

Unit record equipment has declined in popularity as a class of data processing devices but is still widely used. Many small computer systems are oriented to the punched card as an input medium. In general, card input is slow compared to input from magnetic data media. Processing by the full line of card equipment is slower and much more limited in complexity of analysis than computer processing. No internal or external storage on a magnetic device is possible. Variable control over machine activity is limited. Programming consists of modifying electrical control circuits by

FIGURE 6.12   *Larger electronic accounting machine.* The Litton ABS/1241 is a minicomputer with 4,096 words of programmable storage and punched paper tape and edge-punched–card input and output, in addition to keyboard entry and a 35-character-per-second printer. (PHOTO COURTESY OF LITTON AUTOMATED BUSINESS SYSTEMS)

changing plug-in wires on a board to cause different sequences of simple machine activities.

Punched cards are bulky to store and require careful handling. Individually, the cards cannot be reused (repunched) or corrected and wear out quickly with repeated handling. However, card systems encourage some degree of integration of processing steps, with the same card serving as initial input of transactions data for several functional subsystems. For example, a single-card record of a sales transaction in the department store might serve as input for inventory update, sales analysis, and accounts receivable processing. The card also provides an efficient *turnaround* document (a bill to be returned with the payment, for example) in many operations.

In general, electro-mechanical equipment has limited speed because most of its processing operations are performed mechanically, and it is limited also in its ability to perform complex analyses. When used properly, it performs routine accounting functions well for small businesses. Even in this use, however, it is being replaced by minicomputers and microcomputers (see Chapter 11).

Computer Processing   The automatic electronic digital computer is a fast, accurate, and flexible machine. As such, it is capable of doing nothing it has not been programmed to do. Even so, the computer serves to extend human calculating and decision-making powers. As a data processing device, it tirelessly performs highly complex analyses or simple, repetitious calculations with both speed and accuracy. Once an appropriate set of instructions (a *program*) has been prepared and stored in the machine's memory, the computer will follow those instructions automatically and correctly with speed and accuracy. The set of instructions in the machine's electronic memory (the program) can be changed and the machine shifted to another job. Modern computers can even switch back and forth among several stored programs (jobs) at a speed that makes it appear all are being performed simultaneously.

A major disadvantage of computers is that they utilize such basic logical processes that few people can perform the programming necessary to harness effectively their great capacity. In business data processing many are used at a level well below their full capability. Coupled with their high cost, such misuse can easily make the computer appear to be an expensive device only capable of speeding up clerical processes. Faulty attempts at sophisticated use lead to missed schedules, erroneous billings, and processing bottlenecks. Such mistakes in design of systems lead to errors in the output of computer systems for which the machine is blamed. When used effectively and efficiently in situations in which volumes are large, timing requirements severe, or needed analysis complex, computers have proved themselves to be effective processing devices in information and data processing systems.

Minicomputers and microcomputers are spreading computer use throughout the business world. Almost any business can now justify the acquisition and use of these small systems. Small firms or organizations and divisions or departments of larger firms or organizations are using computer technology. Many smaller firms are sharing computer processing services. They either send their data to independent service bureaus or *access* (gain access to) remotely located computers through terminals at their own business sites.

RETRIEVAL AND REPORTING

Capturing data, storing them, and processing them are not enough. The results of processing activities must be delivered to final users in a form and in time to make those results useful. A wide variety of media and devices are available. Data and information can be presented on paper, on film, or as pictures on a cathode ray tube (think of the television screen). The time required to respond to a request for data can vary from a fraction of a second to many hours.

In addition to standard management reports, data processing systems must prepare a variety of custodial documents such as checks to reimburse employees and suppliers, invoices to order items from suppliers, and receipts to acknowledge payments made by others or shipments received from vendors. The need for custodial documents may require a paper handling capability whose cost dictates that paper will provide the medium for all information and data presentations from the system. Even so, many different devices are available for preparing paper documents.

Paper Documents   Paper is the medium most widely used for presenting data and information outputs from data processing and information systems. Devices for preparing paper documents vary from pen and pencil to sophisticated chemical and photographic printing processes capable of preparing multiple copies of a document at a speed of thousands of lines per minute. Only those devices considered important because of wide use and/or promise of wide use as they become more familiar will be discussed here.

Typewriter   Probably the most familiar "hard copy" report preparation device is the typewriter, a key-driven printing device.

The manually operated typewriter is slow, error-prone, and relatively expensive on a per copy basis. Its advantages are flexibility and ease of use. Modern versions coupled with electronic control devices featuring magnetic or disk storage decrease per copy costs of documents (such as letters) for which several original copies are required. The use of tape storage and electronic control decreases initial preparation time. The maximum printing speed of such a device is more than double that of the manually controlled electric typewriter (see Figure 6.13). Typewriters coupled with punched paper tape can be used to prepare documents offline from a computer system. They operate at 15 to 30 characters per second.

Word processing systems   The automatic typewriter is being linked with microcomputers and minicomputers to provide systems to relieve stenographic bottlenecks.

Rough drafts are entered into electronic storage from typewriter-like keyboards, then corrected, modified, combined, and otherwise put into final form with the aid of the data-manipulating power of the computer. Error-free copies can then be produced by the computer using typewriter-like devices or special printers. Multiple copies of form letters, individualized to the recipient, can be created rapidly. Document content can be stored indefinitely on electronic storage devices and recalled for use at any time. Manuscripts for complete reports, or even books such as this one, can be electronically stored and edited, then sent directly to an electronically controlled printer with line length, color, and pagination controlled by the

FIGURE 6.13   *Automatic word processor.* The IBM mag card reader and automatic typewriter. (PHOTO COURTESY IBM)

computer. The capacity of some of these "word processing" systems allows several stenographers to work on different projects at one time.

Printers Printers are output devices that present data and information outputs on paper. There are many types.

Typewriter and typewriterlike terminals (including the so-called character printer) prepare paper documents at speeds measured in characters per second. They are commonly used as output devices for minicomputers and remote-terminal setups. When operated manually they are error-prone, slow, and relatively expensive per copy produced. They are capable of speeds of 10 to 300 characters per second. The fastest devices of this type are electronically controlled.

Punched card and other electro-mechanical accounting machines (discussed above as processing devices) are the simplest character or line

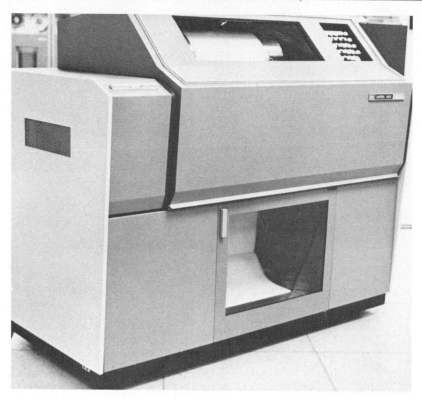

FIGURE 6.14   *The CDC Model 9370 line printer.* (PHOTO COURTESY OF CONTROL DATA CORPORATION)

printers. They print at 100 to 300 lines per minute. The noncard machines are quite limited and are usually used only in the preparation of custodial documents.

Line printers print a whole line on each machine cycle. Speeds vary from 300 up to 3,000 lines per minute, with the most common speeds being 1,000 and 1,200 lines per minute. They are usually part of a computer system, although offline versions that print from magnetic tape are common (see Figure 6.14). More recently electrostatic line printers capable of much higher speeds have become more dependable and are becoming increasingly popular.

Page printers, which also are becoming increasingly popular, use some form of an electrostatic or photographic process to print an entire page during each print cycle. They usually print single copies only. They are extremely fast, reliable enough, produce good quality printing, and have come into limited general use. Expense is the major deterrent to their wider use. They are more expensive than line printers and require highly skilled operators and specially prepared paper.

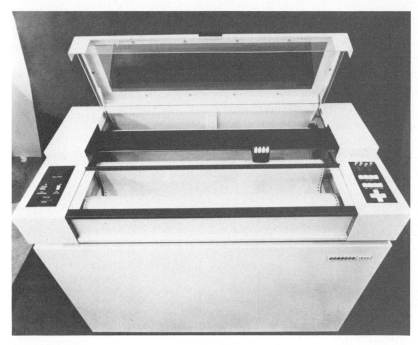

FIGURE 6.15   *Drum plotter.* The CalComp Model 1055 plots at a drawing speed of 76.2 centimeters (30 inches) per second with four pens that allow multiple line weights and colors. (PHOTO COURTESY OF CALIFORNIA COMPUTER PRODUCTS, INC. [CALCOMP])

Plotters are, in effect, special-purpose printers that output line drawings. There are two general types, the table (flat-bed) plotter and the roll plotter (see Figure 6.15). Roll plotters tend to be smaller and cheaper. In general, roll plotters move the paper past a stylus (pen) that can move back and forth across the paper in a single dimension. The combined movement of the paper and the stylus is controlled by the computer output directly or by instructions from the computer that have been written onto a magnetic tape. The controller for the plotter reads the tape and follows the instructions given there. A table plotter, on the other hand, moves a stylus in two dimensions as instructed by the computer, but the paper remains fixed on the flat bed (table) of the plotter. Both types vary widely in size and speed, and some models allow multiple styluses to be used. They have been used most for engineering and architectural drawings. Graphic display terminals (cathode ray tubes) have most often provided the graphic capabilities used in management information systems.

In general, document preparation devices are available with widely varying speeds and degrees of flexibility and reliability. Faster, more flexible devices cost more but usually produce copy at a lower cost per unit.

None can keep up with the internal processing speeds of an electronic computer because all these devices involve mechanical processes. Manually operated versions are subject to the greater likelihood of human error.

Film devices All devices preparing system output on film obviously must include some element that acts like a camera to imprint the data on the film. Film development may or may not be on site, but film imprinting must be.

The details of computer-outputted microfilm devices are presented in Chapter 9. Only an evaluation of microfilm as a storage device will be considered here.

Film is a fast output medium but has the disadvantage of requiring developing and reading by specialized equipment. Film is much less bulky than paper as a storage medium. With the newest techniques the entire contents of this book could be stored on a film approximately the size of this page. However, that film record could be read only with the aid of a special reader or projector (see Figure 6.16). Film is good for systems for which masses of data must be stored for consultation in the operation of the physical process but hard copies of the retrieved data are not required (catalogues or inventories, for example). Retrieval on hard copy is possible but requires special equipment. Retrieval times are slower than for all-electronic random storage systems, but costs are also much less.

Cathode ray tubes (*displays*) Cathode ray tube devices (CRTs) contain a televisionlike screen on which data can be *displayed*.

When supported by an appropriately programmed computer, CRTs can present graphs as well as tables and text (see Figure 6.17, on page 142). Some have the capability of producing an image of the displayed picture on paper. This hard-copy capability is quite expensive. The CRT display terminal is widely used with computerized storage and retrieval systems. Display devices vary widely in price and capability. Some have been joined to a microcomputer or minicomputer to create *intelligent terminals* for computer systems.

The display is best for *temporary* retrieval of magnetically stored data and for monitoring critical records while the records are being changed by input from a transaction. The size of the tube face and the character style determine how much data can be displayed on a CRT. The more data that can be displayed and the faster they can be transferred to and from the tube face, the more expensive the device. Addition of the capability either to present graphic displays or to produce hard copy can easily double the cost of the device.

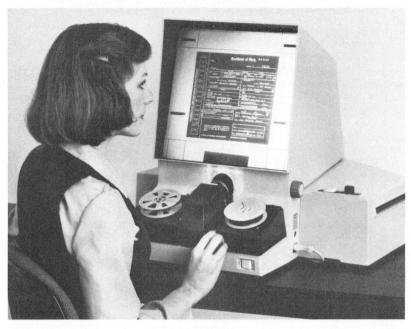

FIGURE 6.16   *Microfiche reader.* The Kodak Trimlite R reader and Trimlite printer offer variable-speed scanning and easy printmaking. (PHOTO COURTESY OF EASTMAN KODAK COMPANY)

Selecting Media and Devices

The development of an *effective* managerial information system should be the primary purpose in choosing media and devices as functional components of the system. Processing *efficiency* cannot be ignored, however. Systems can almost always be developed to provide excellent management information if cost is ignored. Similarly, excessive concern with use of the latest technology can lead to problems. Finally, we must remember that systems are operated *by* and *for* people. The system must be accepted by the people who operate it and by the people on whom it will have a direct or an indirect effect.

CRITICAL FACTORS: MEDIUM AND DEVICE CHARACTERISTICS

The brief descriptions of media and devices above make it obvious that the media and devices available for performing each of the data processing functions are many and varied. Criteria for selection among available devices are needed. The factors below have been identified as useful in choosing among these alternatives at each stage.

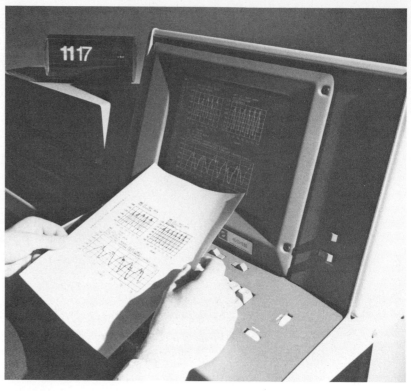

FIGURE 6.17   *Graphic display terminal.* Tektronix Model 4012 coupled with a hard-copy unit provides a hard copy of the CRT plot. (PHOTO COURTESY OF TEKTRONIX, INC.)

Speed The speed with which each device or medium-device combination can perform its function. Speed can be measured in *elapsed time* to perform a function [for example, *access time*, the time required to locate and retrieve a data element (word or record)] or in *rates* (for example, *transfer rate* measured in characters per second).

Capacity The amount of data a medium can hold. Usually measured in characters or words, both total amount and amount per unit of length or volume.

Comparison among media on capacity alone can be misleading. For example, a punched card may hold only 80 characters, whereas a single disk pack can hold 50 million characters and a magnetic tape may hold over 100 million characters. To be meaningful, the capacity of the medium must be considered together with the bulk of the medium and the speed of the device servicing the medium.

Expandability The ease with which the capacity of the device can be expanded by adding additional units or increasing the size of units.

One of the advantages of manual systems is the ease of adding another desk, typewriter, and so on, and another worker. This modular expansion capability is also built into modern electronic computers (see Chapter 8).

Bulk The physical space required to house the medium and device. This is usually expressed in general terms, although measurement of characters per cubic foot is possible.

Storage requirements for each medium vary. These requirements affect the total space needed for each medium and device. In general, the commonly used input and storage media are ordered as follows when arrayed from most bulky to least bulky:

1. Paper documents
2. Punched cards
3. Punched paper tape
4. Magnetic drums
5. Magnetic disks
6. Magnetic core
7. Microcircuit memory
8. Magnetic tape
9. Microfilm

Access mode The order in which data can be retrieved from or placed in a storage medium (including input-output media). The three major modes are *sequential* access, *random* (*direct*) access, and *modified random* (*direct*) access. (These modes are defined in Chapter 2, page 27.)

Reliability The ability of the medium and device to operate at the rated speed without error. This is considered more fully below in the section on technical feasibility.

Ease of use The need for specialized knowledge or skills in order to use the medium and device at full capacity.

CRITICAL FACTORS: SYSTEM CHARACTERISTICS
The characteristics of media and devices must be matched with the jobs to be done. The characteristics below are the features of information and data processing systems that critically influence the selection of media and devices.

Volumes Volumes are measured in numbers of transactions, file accesses or file updates, and reports expected per work period.

Transactions volume The rate at which transactions enter or pass through the system. This must be measured in number per unit of time to be useful.

The larger the number of transactions to be handled in a given work period, the more likely it will be that machine procedures are justified. Machines, including computers, cannot be avoided if transactions volumes are large enough.

File access volume The frequency (rate) at which the records in the permanent or master file(s) must be referred to. Access can be for information retrieval or record update.

File update volume The frequency (rate) at which the records in the permanent or master file(s) must be modified to bring them up to date.

If master files must be accessed continuously as part of the physical operation, they will normally be stored on some random-access (direct-access) medium. If the records must be current when accessed on a continuous basis, they must be updated as each transaction occurs. The file must be randomly accessible and available for update as transactions occur. In a department store, accounts receivable are usually updated at the end of each day's business. Sequential batch processing is normally used for this update. However, the master file records are usually directly accessible ledger cards so that inquiries (from customers, salesclerks, or management) can be answered quickly. Access to transactions occurring during each day requires (usually) time-consuming, manual access to sales tickets. For the airlines, seat inventory and reservation data by flight must be instantaneously updated as reservations are made or canceled. The airline wants to sell all available seats but does not want to sell any seat twice. Thus files are stored on online, random-access, electronic media and devices. Transactions are input via remote terminals at each ticket counter.

Report volume The rate of reporting to management.

The frequency of reports to management controls activities throughout the system. If such reports are to be timely and complete, the effects of recent transactions must be included. The timing of reports to management should be based on the control and planning needs of the physical operation being reported on. The more frequently access to master file contents is required, the more justification for random-access, machine-aided storage and retrieval systems. Automated systems are now being designed that include reporting to management "on demand," that is, whenever the manager requests it. Such systems give management direct access to the electronic files via terminals but usually involve at least three *other* types of reports: (1) *monitoring reports* are produced periodically and concentrate on comparing actual performance with planned performance; (2) *triggered exception reports* are "triggered" by the occurrence of a (critical) deviation from planned activities; (3) *planning reports* concentrate on trends and compare future courses of action.

Complexity of processing The number and complexity of processing steps to take care of a transaction and the number and complexity of analytic operations required to create management information are significant.

The more complex the processing job to be accomplished, other things being equal, the more a computer can be justified. However, complex processing jobs with no time constraints may allow the use of processing devices other than computers. Alternatively, such jobs may be accomplished by use of outside service bureau facilities. There are techniques of analysis in current use that are uneconomical or impossible to apply without computers (see Chapter 2, pages 32–34). When processing consists almost entirely of updating and summarization, accounting machines can be adequate unless volumes are too great.

TECHNICAL FEASIBILITY

The selection of media and devices for performing data processing functions must be made in the light of the true technical capabilities of the media and devices. Care must be exercised in interpreting technical claims. For example, the *rated* (advertised) capability of a card reader may be 2,000 cards per minute. However, if the reader is unreliable and malfunctions frequently, a slower rated but more reliable reader may actually read more cards per day.

A more substantive problem is being sure that the desired total processing cycle can be carried out in the allotted time. Computers are very fast machines and will do whatever they are told to do. If, however, the data to be processed must first be punched into cards and entered into the processing system via a single card reader with a maximum speed of 200 cards per minute, it may not be possible to enter the data fast enough to handle all transactions in the time available. Similarly, performing a complex analysis on a large quantity of detailed data and printing the detailed data along with the analysis on a printer operating at 300 lines per minute may require more hours of printing time than are available, thus leaving the processing element idle a large part of the time. Failure to recognize the imbalance in system components is a common technical failure. It also is wise to avoid new equipment not yet proved in use.

Guarding against complete technical infeasibility is not difficult. Visits should be made to other organizations using a similar or the same system. Technical experts other than equipment vendors should be used to evaluate the proposed design. Such experts can also be helpful in scheduling system implementation and providing training. Training is also available from equipment vendors. Probably the best safeguard is to visit other installations (not just those recommended by the vendor) and ask about their problems and their failures as well as their successes.

MANAGEMENT REQUIREMENTS

The design of a new system obviously should start with management's objectives for the system. Often these objectives provide valuable guidelines for choosing processing media and devices. However, more directly applicable are any firm ideas management may have about the media and devices to be used in the system. Managers should, however, listen to rational arguments about why their selections may be inappropriate.

General management policy can also influence media and device selection. Personnel policy may prevent firing employees no longer needed in a revised system. Such a policy can result in a slow evolution to the most desirable system rather than an immediate shift. Natural attrition can then be used to keep from having too many excess employees on the payroll after the system is put into operation.

In any case, the managers' ideas about data processing must be considered in the system's design. Unless they can be convinced that they are wrong, their wishes will prevail. Much of any existing data processing system was probably created by the current managers. They will be hard to convince that a completely new system is necessary. Systems designers must sell their ideas and should be prepared to present strong factual arguments to support their recommendations.

ECONOMIC FEASIBILITY

The cost economies of new systems are often hard to demonstrate. New systems usually are sold by the additional benefits they provide. Ideally, the new system should provide the same or more information for less money or more information for the same money. If costs are to increase, the increase must be justified by added benefits. Benefits and costs are of two types, *tangible* and *intangible*. However, care must be exercised to be sure that both the costs and the benefits are completely enumerated. The lists below are helpful in this regard.

Tangible Benefits   Obvious cost benefits to be obtained from a new data processing or information system are fairly easy to define.

1. Reducing the number of employees involved in data processing.

2. Reducing the total investment in data processing equipment.

3. Reducing the cost of maintaining data processing equipment.

4. Reducing the amount of physical space devoted to data processing.

Tangible Costs   Offsetting the tangible benefits are complementary tangible costs.

1. Added employees needed with the new system.

2. Training employees to work in the new system.

3. Lease or purchase of new equipment.

4. Maintenance of new equipment.

5. Cost of physical space used by new equipment, including remodeling and/or environmental controls.

6. Cost of developing and implementing the new system.

A common mistake is to underestimate system development time. Setting up a new system can be time-consuming, particularly if machine processes are involved. Computers and accounting machines have to be programmed. Forms and/or procedures for data capture and for output reports have to be created. Personnel have to be trained in the new way of doing things. Often, basic data files have to be transferred to a new medium. Too many times, an enthusiastic salesperson leads the inexperienced and untrained to believe that when the new machine comes in the door, all problems will disappear. Unfortunately, system development has hardly begun when the new machine arrives.

Intangible Benefits   Nonbudgetary benefits are more difficult to evaluate but are frequently the most important effects that a new system can have.

1. Improving control over the physical operation (see pages 148–151).

2. Allowing expansion of profitable activities by removing limitations in processing capacity.

3. Allowing expansion or increasing operating efficiency by reducing the time required for processing.

(Note that these first three benefits overlap, particularly the second and third.)

4. Positive effects on employee morale arising from a recognition that the system is effective and efficient. (Note that employees must feel involved in the system design effort if this effect is to be fully realized.)

5. Positive effects on external public relations. Customers and business associates like to work with an organization whose data processing systems are efficient and effective.

Intangible Costs   Complementary to the intangible benefits are a set of intangible costs, all of which can be avoided if the system is properly designed and implemented.

1. Loss of control over the activity by operating management.

2. Negative effects on employee morale and a consequent drop in employee productivity, with an increase in errors and general inefficiency. (Note that this usually arises from *not* involving key employees in the system design effort and *not* keeping employees informed of progress in system design.)

3. Negative effects on external public relations. (Note that this can result from trying to abruptly cut over to an untried new system. Parallel operation until the bugs have been worked out of the new system can result in a long-run saving. Also, the system should be responsive to the ultimate user. Keep customers and business associates in mind when designing systems.)

Note how the areas of intangible costs and benefits overlap. Note also that most of the intangible costs result from poor design of the system and/or poor management of the system implementation. The following three points can pay big dividends in gaining intangible benefits and avoiding intangible losses:

1. The rule of KISS — *K*eep *I*t *S*imple *S*tupid. The simpler the system is, the less can go wrong with it and the easier people, including employees and customers, will find it to work with.

2. People operate systems. Don't build systems to operate people.

3. Informed and involved employees are productive employees. Don't shroud systems changes in mystery. If outside experts must be brought in, explain why and use them to educate your own people.

Establishing Appropriate Controls

As indicated above, the major benefits derived from new systems tend to be intangible. They revolve around doing the data processing job more *effectively* as well as more *efficiently*. Time and volume limitations can be removed by being more efficient, but improved management control and planning doesn't happen just because processing is speeded up. Management, *top* management, must recognize that building *effective* information systems is a management responsibility. Data processing technicians cannot do the job alone. Managers must get involved. They have a special responsibility in seeing that appropriate controls are made a part of the system.

Three types of controls must be built into information systems. First, information systems are designed to produce information for use by managers in the *control of physical operations*. *Managerial controls* accomplish this. Second, data must be recorded accurately and processed properly and completely. *Internal controls* are important here. Finally, specific internal controls are applied to *data processing techniques* to prevent errors in data recording, data processing, and informational and custodial outputs.

MANAGERIAL CONTROLS

The control process is used to monitor activities and see that plans are being followed and goals realized. In general, this process consists of four steps:

1. Establishing goals or standards
2. Measuring actual performance
3. Comparing actual performance with the goals or standards
4. Taking required corrective action

In order to carry out these activities, managers must (1) analyze organizational *objectives* to identify those factors that are critical to the success of the organization and that the manager can influence, (2) identify quantifiable measurements for these factors that can be used to judge success in attaining organizational objectives, (3) set specific values as goals to be reached or as warnings of trouble, and (4) participate in the design of information systems to insure that their own "success" or "problem" measurements are properly developed and appropriately reported to them. In other words, managers should work to set up a feedback and control system (see Chapter 3, pages 45–47).

In order to accomplish these things, information systems must capture data that can be used to measure performance at each level in the organization. At the lowest levels, these data will reflect performance of individual people, individual machines, and individual products. Individual performance measurements must then be aggregated to measure performance by departments, by plants, by divisions, and by the organization as a whole. Trends in performance levels must be continuously monitored. Changes in performance levels resulting from changes in the environment or in the way jobs are carried out should result in revised performance goals. Performance in excess of the standard or goal can be just as significant as failure to attain the goal. For example, sales in excess of goals may mean that production schedules and inventory levels need to be adjusted. Expenditures running well below budgeted project costs may indicate failure to maintain project schedules or mistakes in cost estimation.

Performance goals and standards should reflect quality of performance as well as quantity. The number of defectives per 1,000 good items produced is one example. The number of errors per 1,000 transactions processed is another. Quality is also reflected in the way in which reports are made. Reports that highlight problem areas and make comparisons with comparable past periods are valuable. Often these reports need not be the result of complicated analysis. Figure 6.18 is a disguised version of a control report received by the president of a small bank. All that are contained are facts

FIGURE 6.18   *Bank president's daily report, consolidated statement*

	March 24, 1972		March 26, 1973	
Loans:				
Regular	$2,829,845		$2,934,363	
Real estate	1,805,542		2,078,687	
Consumer	906,361		1,150,746	
Student	164,423		197,485	
Overdrafts	4,428	5,710,599	22,291	6,383,572
Investments:				
Federal funds	$ 100,000		$ 650,000	
U.S. bonds	2,441,494		1,912,576	
Other bonds	1,009,058		1,164,675	
Fed. Res. stock	18,000		21,000	
U.S. govt. agencies	860,000		1,820,000	
FHA secured	278,557	4,707,109	512,186	6,080,437
Cash	$ 107,859		$ 212,767	
Fed. Res. Bank deposit	525,682		510,362	
Due from other banks	1,275,907		1,673,516	
Transit	26,360	1,935,808	69,622	2,466,267
Other assets		204,189		214,670
Total assets		$12,557,705		$15,144,946
Current income:				
Regular-loan int.	$ 87,260		$110,612	
Consumer loan int.	−897		−3,094	
U.S. bond int.	64,573		23,504	
Other bond int.	14,470		18,408	
Fed. funds int.	2,283		12,782	
Other current income	30,103	197,792	83,300	245,512

	March 24, 1972		March 26, 1973	
Less current expense:				
Interest paid	107,322		119,251	
Other expense	56,086	163,408	76,796	196,047
Current accumulated profits		$ 34,384		$ 49,465
Invested capital:				
Capital	$300,000		$350,000	
Surplus	300,000		350,000	
Undivided profits	153,481		107,450	
Bad-debt reserve	101,887	855,368	103,010	910,460
Deposits:				
Individual demand	$4,777,141		$5,928,959	
Cash over	60		−2	
Dormant accounts	3,396		3,396	
Individual savings	662,606		1,131,565	
Certificates of deposit	6,133,522	11,576,725	6,991,005	14,054,923
Other liabilities		91,228		130,098
Total capital and liabilities		$12,557,705		$15,144,946

for the current date (close of business yesterday) and the same day one year earlier. Note that changes in profits, costs, and levels of activity are clearly indicated. These year-to-year changes reflect both long-run trends and cyclical business fluctuations. The president's general knowledge of business conditions helps him to make the proper interpretation of these facts. When combined with a report on new loans, new accounts, accounts closed, and overdrafts over $50, this combination balance sheet and income statement gives the bank president a complete picture of the bank's operation each day. Note that in this small bank the president is part of the processing system. He provides data inputs from the environment in which the bank operates and combines them with internal data to produce information on which to base control actions.

INTERNAL CONTROLS

Internal controls have four purposes as defined by the American Institute of Certified Public Accountants:

1. Checking on and maintaining the accuracy of business data
2. Safeguarding the company assets against fraud, embezzlement, and theft
3. Promoting operating efficiency
4. Encouraging compliance with existing company policies and procedures

Adequately controlled systems would normally include separation of physical control and accountability, written procedures, standardized documentation, preset procedures for making changes in the system, a data security program, protection against outside intervention, and a well-developed audit program.

Separation of Physical Control and Accountability   The general procedure for separating physical control of an asset from the responsibility for accounting for that asset is reflected in data processing in that no one individual performs all aspects of data capture, processing, and output.   This also applies to design, particularly if a computer is involved.   Allowing one individual to design and program an application, prepare the input data, run the program, and proof the output gives that person ample opportunity to implement a system that converts company assets to his or her own use.   No employee should have unrestricted access to all data files and programs.   A records librarian with no operating responsibilities should keep and control computer programs.   Machine operators and other personnel should be rotated in their assignments in such a way that no person consistently controls a complete processing cycle.

Written Procedures to Guide Data Processing Activities   Good documentation provides a means for the auditor (external or internal) and for management to keep control of procedures.   It promotes operating efficiency and adherence to established policy.   All data processing systems, whether manual or machine-based, automated or nonautomated, fully integrated or applications-oriented, must be designed and documented with control and audit considerations in mind.   The participation of an auditor in systems design is imperative.

Standard Format and Standard Symbols in System Documentation   Documentation is supposed to describe the system clearly and completely.   Adherence to a standard organization for the system description is a first step in assuring a complete description.   Items to be included are indicated in Chapter 5 (page 110).   Further descriptions of documentation tools are found in Chapter 7.

Procedures for Making Changes in the System   Changes in system procedures should not be possible without prior authorization of responsible authority. For example, it should not be possible to make changes in an operating computer program without written approval from the affected department and the data processing supervisor. The internal auditor should receive automatic notification of such changes if that auditor's prior approval is not required. Changes should be completely documented and made part of the system procedure file.

Data Security Program Definite procedures should be established to control access to all data files. In addition, data files should be protected against accidental or deliberate destruction by outside forces, human or natural. Master files should be protected against destruction by fire and water. Fireproof storage vaults for the most important files should be considered. Duplicate files stored offsite may be desirable for the most critical data files. Adequate insurance should be provided to compensate for any loss. Proper identification of and control over paper or magnetic-tape files, disk packs, and so on, should be established. Waste disposal control procedures should guard against accidental destruction of important files while assuring the destruction of carbon paper, abandoned punch cards, and so on, to prevent vital company information from falling into the hands of competitors. Access to processing areas, particularly computer centers, should be strictly controlled.

Protection of Processing Procedures and Equipment Against Outside Intervention Only authorized personnel should be allowed to operate processing equipment, including computers. Access to processing sites, particularly computer centers, should be carefully controlled. Only trained, authorized personnel should be allowed access to data and programs. Changes in processing procedures should require management clearance before implementation.

Developing Auditing Procedures Auditing procedures should be developed that take advantage of system characteristics while not placing an undue burden on the system. The primary purpose of an audit is to check on the effectiveness of internal control procedures. The audit technique will vary in accordance with the manner in which the processing is performed. In largely manual, nonintegrated systems, controls will be people-oriented, depending largely on crosschecks of data between people and departments. In a computerized system, processing tends to be more centralized, and controls must of necessity be more system-oriented and included in computer programs. Checking for the presence and adequacy of such controls will differ in the two situations. (A more complete discussion of the auditing of computerized data processing systems is given in Chapter 15.)

DATA PROCESSING CONTROLS

Data must be subjected to controls that insure that all elements are recorded and processed correctly and that the resulting output is complete, adequate, and correct. There are three major areas in which controls are required — input, processing, and output.

1. *Input controls* are established to insure that data from all authorized transactions are correctly recorded at the right time and that all of these data elements enter the processing system at the right place.

Many control techniques can be used here. An illustrative sample might include the following:

Prenumbered forms. Serially numbered forms are effective in preventing the loss of input documents.

Control totals. When batch processing is used, totals can be used to prevent the loss of transactions. Either totals of meaningful data fields (such as hours worked) or "hash" totals (such as sums of employee numbers) can be used.

Record or transaction counts. Counts of the records at each processing station can help to prevent loss of any record or introduction of illegal records.

Data preaudits. Data can be checked before processing.

Such checks can be carried out in either manual or automated systems. Examples include checking for numerical data in alphabetic fields or missing data elements. *Limit checks* are based on the fact that data values must fall within certain ranges. For example, an hourly employee cannot work more than eight hours each day on regular time. *Check digits* can also be used (see Figure 6.2).

2. *Processing controls* are for the purposes of (a) preventing the loss of data or a failure to process them and (b) checking on the accuracy of processing arithmetic.

Processing controls are implemented as part of the processing system. They include some of the same controls used at the input stage. These include *record counts, limit controls,* and *control totals.* However, the counts and control totals may be developed from *processed units* and limit controls applied to *computed values* (such as gross pay).

Control techniques that are unique to processing include structural checks, sequence checks, file identification, dual processing, and operation monitoring.

Structural checks. Computed values should bear certain relationships; for example, debits and credits must occur in acceptable combinations.

These controls vary from the simple cross-footing familiar to every accounting student to reliance on very complex relationships among computed values. As examples, the totals of all amounts deducted from payroll checks when added to the total amounts computed as net pay should sum to the total of gross pay; units produced should not excessively exceed hours worked multiplied by the standard number of units produced per hour; total withholding for income tax payments should not exceed a reasonable proportion (perhaps 15 percent) of total gross pay; deductions for social security withholding should not exceed the product of gross pay times the maximum withholding rate. In sophisticated statistical or mathematical analysis, computed values often have distinct relationships. The apparent violation of such relationships may be the first warning of hardware malfunctions, rounding errors, or improper programming. Careful checking of data elements or processing when such checks fail can help to insure processing accuracy.

Sequence checks. Often input records, particularly in batch systems, are in some sequence (determined by an identifying number such as employee number or invoice number). Checking this sequencing can prevent out-of-order processing that might enter transactions data into the wrong account of cause failure to process out-of-order entries.

File identification. All files passed through the processing system should be fully identified so that they can be checked as the appropriate file.

To prevent the modification of master files by the wrong transactions data, each transactions file should be properly named and dated. This is especially important for electronic processing systems because files may be on magnetic tape or magnetic disk and therefore unreadable by humans. File labels on such tapes (or disks) should indicate file content, the length of time the file is to be retained, and, in very sensitive situations, the program that is used to process the file. The identification should not only appear on an outside label but also be entered magnetically onto the tape or disk so that it can be checked during processing. A trailer record (the last record in the file) often contains a record count and/or other control data.

Dual processing. Carrying out the same arithmetic operations independently or computing the same values by a second process can be used to check on the accuracy of arithmetical calculations. Rereading or proofreading data or information, particularly when transfer between media occurs, can catch many errors.

Dual processing is expensive, but it is used in systems producing critical results. In electronic systems two processors or repetition of calculations can be used if the additional cost can be justified. It is not uncommon for tape and disk controllers to check the accuracy with which data are magnetically recorded by automatically reading the data after they are recorded and checking them against what was to be recorded.

Operation monitoring. A *log* of processing activities actually performed should be maintained and regularly audited. When machines are used, the log of machine activities should be automatically recorded by the machine.

Operating logs can help to insure that regular processing procedures are followed. They are invaluable in spotting unauthorized processing or illegal interference in processing procedures. Computer executive programs of the current generation usually include this automatic logging of all jobs performed by the machine and of all actions by the operator. Other machines usually can be fitted with a meter that registers the amount of use in hours or operating cycles performed. Unauthorized machine time should always be investigated.

3. *Output controls* are the final controls over the propriety and correctness of the processing. They also attempt to prevent the loss of any data from the system.

Output controls apply to the final reports, documents, and data files prepared by the processing system. They include several of the same controls applied as input and processing controls. These include *record counts, limit controls, control totals, prenumbered forms, sequence checks,* and *structural checks.* At this point, the totals and limits apply to outputted results (for example, calculated net pay to an employee cannot be negative). Prenumbered forms and sequence checks prevent the loss of data in custodial processing and can also help to prevent the introduction of unauthorized documents. Structural checks are applied to final results in the same way they were during processing.

Procedures unique to output controls are *review of interested parties* and *transaction sampling.*

Review of interested parties. Input-originating parties and output-using parties can often point out errors that slip through in spite of other checks.

The data processing department should welcome the review of its suppliers and users and follow up on their reports to correct file inaccuracies or other errors.

Transaction sampling. Randomly selected transactions can be traced through the system to see if they are handled properly.

This technique is useful to internal auditors if done on a regular basis. In online electronic systems this technique can be included in the processing program to produce an *audit trail* of a sample of activities within the system by printing out interim results as processing of each sample transaction proceeds. The auditor can then follow this trail of readable results through the system to check the results.

Recognizing Human Limitations

In the design of data processing and information systems we must not forget that *systems affect people*: customers, employees, even managers. Customers get bills that, even with good controls, may be wrong. Employees find errors that must be corrected. Each manager wants special individualized responses from the system. The analyst must guard against developing a system that is *unresponsive* to humans and their problems. Billing forms must be understandable. The system that handles the responses from customers must specifically allow for reporting of errors, incorporation of changes, and response to requests for clarification. Human response by and to customers should be easily accomplished. Customers must feel that they are important and can get attention. Employees must feel that they control the system and not the other way around. They must feel needed, that they have some responsibilities apart from responses to a machine or a procedural system. Managers must be able to have access to the data bases for the operating areas they manage. System responses to managers must be in terms they understand and *want*. Again, *systems should not be designed to manipulate or control people*. Rather, they should be responsive to people and as easy as possible for people to use.

Establishing Accountability for System Results

Good systems design involves measuring the result of a system's design against clearly specified goals of the design. Broad objectives such as "speeding up processing" or "reducing errors" are not clear enough to use as standards for measuring design accomplishments. It is better to state specific goals such as "completely processing all transactions for each day against the master file within four hours of the close of the day" or "reducing the processing error rate to 1 percent or less." Stating numerical, measurable goals allows for measurement of performance.

Not only should the performance of each new system be measured against specific quantitative goals, but the *process of design* should be controlled similarly. Standards of performance in design can be established from past experience. Systems analysts and their managers can learn to estimate the time, effort, and costs of proposed design projects. They should be held accountable for producing systems against time and cost schedules in the same way that other departments are controlled. Only when truly pioneering efforts are being developed can there be any excuse for cost or time overruns of more than a few percentage points.

Good systems design also includes built-in controls over the continuation of adequate production by the system after its implementation. It involves a continuous process of checking on and evaluating system performance. Characteristics to be controlled include:

Processing cycle times. Variation in this statistic is usually an indication of poor operating controls or inadequate processing procedures.

Error rates. Statistics should be maintained on observed error rates in input preparation, processing activities, and outputs (custodial documents, master files, and reports). Excessive errors at any point are a useful indication of weak or absent control procedures.

Complaints. Unhappy customers, employees, or managers (system users) can wreck an ailing system and the organization it serves. Prompt attention to such complaints can lead to the identification and correction of system weaknesses.

Implementing the New or Modified System

The process of installing a new or modified information system should start in the initial analysis and development phases of the project by involving operating managers and other employees who will be affected by the system. The participation of such operating personnel will provide the necessary familiarity with the purposes and processes of the system. Their knowledge of operating details can be most useful. Of particular value is their knowledge of possible exceptions (unusual events) that can be expected to enter the system. This knowledge is of great value in designing controls to be placed in the system and in suggesting useful ways to test the quality of the system.

Obviously, not all the people to be affected by the new or improved system can serve on the development committee. Effort should be expended, however, to keep all those people informed. It is useful to hold periodic briefings and to review system documentation with operating personnel at frequent intervals. Formal training in interacting with the new or improved system should be provided to all employees who will have direct contact with it.

The implementation will be accomplished as one of four basic processes:

1. A new system is installed in a new operation or organization.

The basic problem here is to train employees in the organization or operation to operate the new system and use its outputs.

2. The old system is stopped and replaced totally by the new system.

This sudden "cutover" to a new system can cause a variety of problems. First, a gap in operations may occur while the switch is being made. Second, the new system may not run correctly. It is extremely difficult to develop a complex system that operates without any errors when first put into use in actual operations. Therefore, the cutover method of installation is recommended only for small systems and/or turnkey installations that have already been proved in similar operations elsewhere.

3. The new system is substituted for the old in stages.

In this procedure, the new system is phased in one piece at a time. Each minor subsystem or work station is converted as independently as possible. That such phasing in is possible does indicate, however, that the new system is no more integrated than the old system it replaces. Phasing in is usually impossible when an online computerized system replaces a batch-oriented system, whether the batch system is manual or computerized.

4. The new system is operated parallel to the old system until proved.

In this process, the new system processes the same inputs as the old system for a period. As soon as the new system has shown it is capable of handling all operations without error, the old system is shut down. Any differences in output or master record content between the two systems not attributable to the new system design must be reconciled. The duplication in processing and the efforts expended in reconciling differences make this the most expensive cutover method. However, in sensitive operations that involve direct customer or vendor contact [accounts receivable or payable, accounting and customer billing (vendor paying)] the extra expense is often justified.

Regardless of the method used for cutover to the new system, there are several tasks that must be accomplished before the cutover can be made. These include generation of new data files, selection and training of system personnel, development of any new forms for data collection or for report preparation, preparation of new facilities for equipment and/or personnel, and checking the system for completeness and freedom from error.

GENERATING NEW DATA FILES

One part of the design effort is to develop the specifications (description of design and operational characteristics) for any new master files or data bases to be used in the system. The actual creation of such files on the chosen storage media is part of the implementation effort. Current records and their status must be entered onto the chosen media in accordance with design formats. This can be a tedious and error-prone process if manual or simple machine-assisted manual processes have to be used in converting from old to new files. Tight controls must be developed and applied if errors are to be minimized.

SELECTING AND TRAINING SYSTEM PERSONNEL

New data processing and information systems can require rather wide-ranging changes in the structure of the organization and in its operating procedures. If a computer is being introduced for the first time, new jobs come with it: computer operators, programmers, data control personnel, and system analysts. Personnel employed in the operating areas that provide inputs to and receive outputs from the new system will have to be trained in the new ways of doing things. New forms and procedures for data handling have to be learned, and decision processes used in the operation can be affected. Special security procedures may be required to protect files of sensitive or personal data. All of these changes indicate that new personnel may be needed and that continuing employees may require retraining.

Employees to fill new positions may be selected from present employees or from outside the firm. Recruiting from within is preferable if the new system will result in an overall reduction in the number of employees. Highly skilled technicians, such as systems programmers (those who install and maintain the executive program that controls the overall computer operation), system analysts, and maintenance engineers may have to be hired from outside unless current personnel with appropriate aptitude and background training can be sent for extensive retraining. No matter where personnel are obtained, they must be adequately prepared to assume their new duties.

DEVELOPING NEW FORMS

New forms for data collection or for use in reporting must be developed. The placement, form, and size of each data item must be considered. The general methods for data collection, storage, and retrieval will be specified in the overall system design. The implementation process in this area will be concerned with the specific forms and with developing the exact, non-computerized procedures involved in file update and information reporting.

PREPARING NEW FACILITIES

New equipment is a normal consequence of new systems. Major redistribution of working and office space may be required to make way for the new equipment and the new employees associated with its use. Failure to plan carefully for space modifications can lead to costly delays and the added expense of overtime effort to correct the oversight. Equipment and personnel must be properly related to utilities, storage areas, and exits. Special environmental control [cooling, heating, humidity control, and removal of particulates (cleaning the air)] must be taken care of. Safety and security requirements related to fire, flood, riot, and other unwanted happenings must be considered. The physical relation of individual people to the equipment should be determined early enough to be incorporated into the training program.

CHECKING THE SYSTEM

Checks on the operation of a system are normally carried out on three levels: components, subsystems, and the total system.

Component Checks   Each piece of equipment and each form and procedure for data collection can be tested independently. New reports can also be evaluated independent of the system. Data processing controls can be independently tested as each is developed. New computer programs or program modules can be tested individually. The idea here is to isolate each component of the system and independently determine whether or not it is functioning properly.

Subsystem Tests   Each independent module (subsystem) of the total system which carries out a set of interrelated activities can be tested by itself. Smaller modules and subsystems can then be joined and tested as larger subsystems. Eventually, the total system will be tested as a unit.

System Acceptance Tests   That all components and subsystems pass all tests as individual units does not insure that the total system will operate. The interactions between these units may create error conditions rather than perform as required. Thus sales and inventory accounting systems must use the same inputs, but the accounts receivable accounting system also must interact with credit control and customer billing. Subsystems feed data back and forth, share master files, and contribute to common reports; the overall system can easily fail because of minor inconsistencies in the way that common data items are identified or interim outputs created.

Monitoring the Results

That a system begins to work is not enough. The system must continue to work. Before a processing system is accepted it should meet volume and timing standards (how much the system will do), error standards (proportion of transactions with mistakes and size of maximum error), reliability standards (the length of time each component operates between breakdowns or other failure), system effectiveness standards (ability of the system to improve management planning and control efforts), and ease of use requirements. All these factors should hold at satisfactory levels as the system continues to function.

Summary

The design of new or modified data processing or information systems really starts where systems analysis ends. The next steps are to specify the form and content of system outputs and to define alternative media and devices for capturing, recording, and processing the basic data handled by the system and for preparing those outputs (custodial documents, updated master files, and management reports). Selection among alternative media and devices is based on a matching of two sets of factors. One set describes critical characteristics of the media and devices (speed, access time, capacity, expandability, bulk, access mode, reliability, and ease of use). The other set of factors applies to the requirements of the system (volumes expressed as time rates, complexity of processing, technical feasibility, managerial requirements, and economic feasibility).

The major benefits to be derived from new systems tend to be improved controls or increased volumes. However, these things do not just happen but result from careful planning that recognizes the importance of establishing adequate controls, both managerial and internal, as part of the system. The benefits of new systems can be missed if the systems are needlessly complex (the rule of KISS) or hard to work with. (People should control systems. Systems should not be built to control people.) The process of systems design itself needs to be controlled also. Finally, performance controls should be established that will continue after the system is in operation.

Questions

1. Define the following as briefly as possible and then use a short paragraph to clarify each definition.

   a. Data processing media
   b. Media handling devices
   c. Controls
   d. System volumes
   e. System timings
   f. Technical feasibility
   g. Economic feasibility
   h. Tangible benefits
   i. Intangible benefits
   j. The rule of KISS
   k. Documentation
   l. Audit trail

m. Component checks
n. Subsystem tests
o. Point-of-action recording
p. System acceptance tests
q. Fixed data element
r. Variable data element
s. Run in parallel
t. Word processing

2. What is systems design?

3. List the major steps in systems design and write a one-paragraph description of each step.

4. Identify and briefly explain the major differences between the redesign of an existing system and the design of a new system.

5. What are the characteristics of a well-prepared form?

6. Prepare a four-column table listing, in the first two columns on the left, data recording media and related devices; in the third column, the advantages of each medium-device combination; and in the last column, the disadvantages of the medium-device combination. Include manual, machine-assisted manual, and automated devices in your table.

7. Prepare a four-column table listing storage media and devices and the advantages and disadvantages of each combination. (See question 6 for suggested format.)

8. Prepare a four-column table listing output media and devices and the advantages and disadvantages of each combination. (See question 6 for suggested format.)

9. Prepare a table showing, for the input, the processing, and the output areas, the critical characteristics of media and devices and system that should be considered in choosing components for a system.

10. How is the rule of KISS related to the need to design systems that people find easy to work with? Respond specifically in terms of employees, customers or business associates, and managers.

11. What is the basic difference between tangible and intangible benefits and costs?

12. In each pair below, which element is likely to be the more important in justifying new data processing or information systems?
a. Tangible or intangible benefits
b. Tangible or intangible costs
c. Benefits or costs
Justify your choices.

13. What is managerial control?

14. What is internal control?

15. a. What are the three types of data processing controls?
b. What is the purpose of each?

16. Prepare a list of the general types of internal controls, giving a one-sentence description of each.

17. Prepare a list of the general types of data processing controls, giving

a one-sentence description of each. Differentiate among input, processing, and output controls.

18. How can a systems designer build accountability for results into a design?

19. How should an analyst measure system volumes—
    a. In the input stage?
    b. In the processing stage?
    c. In the output stage?

20. What is the major difference between establishing control over a manual or machine-assisted manual system and establishing control over an automated system?

21. Prepare a table summarizing tangible and intangible costs and benefits to be considered in evaluating a new system design.

22. What are the major weaknesses of point-of-action recording of transactions data?

23. Why might workers deliberately sabotage factory floor data collection terminals? What could be done to reduce the chances of such sabotage?

24. Locate a document such as a regular billing from a store or credit card company or a tax return supplied by the Internal Revenue Service. Is the form well designed from the user's standpoint? What changes would you suggest? Why?

25. How might optical character recognition devices be incorporated into student registration procedures at your school?

26. Under what conditions might it be reasonable for a design team *not* to perform an analysis of the existing system?

27. Refer to question 13 at the end of Chapter 5 and answer the question after substituting the word *design* for the word *analysis* in the basic question.

28. Why are most batch processing systems designed to ignore errors and process as many good data as possible in a processing run?

29. Are there applications for which it would be unwise to follow the practice of ignoring transactions with errors (other than to point them out) and processing good transactions? If so, explain, citing at least two such applications and clearly indicating in each situation why ignoring transactions with errors would not be a good idea.

30. If it is true that top managers (as a group) do not wish to use a computer directly, how does this effect the design of computerized management information systems? Does this mean that direct-access devices cannot be used in such systems?

31. Would it ever be advisable to use a sudden cutover to a new system? Justify your answer.

32. When would it be advisable to operate a new system in parallel with the old for a time before cutover?
33. What are the major disadvantages of each of the following system implementation methods:
    a. Sudden cutover
    b. Phase cutover
    c. Parallel operation before cutover
34. Refer to your answers to parts b, c, and d of question 20 at the end of Chapter 4. Would you like to change the initial lists of questions you developed there? Include in your answer the suggested improvements for each list.

Seven

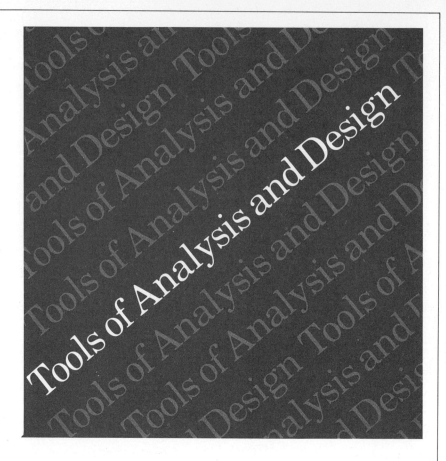

Tools of Analysis and Design

This chapter is designed to introduce the reader to a variety of tools commonly used in the analysis and design of data processing and information systems. Mastery of these tools can come only with extensive practice under the supervision of an experienced analyst. The tools to be identified and illustrated here are organization charts, interviews and questionnaires, flowcharts, decision tables, input-output matrices, simulation, and forms design.

Organization Charts

As indicated in Chapter 6, the starting place for the development of an information system must be an understanding of the organization, why it exists, and how it functions. One of our first needs is to describe the organization in general terms. A history of the specific organization and the industry of which it is a part, including an analysis of the special strengths (and weaknesses) of the organization and each of its major competitors, is

166

useful. Objectives and goals should be determined. The basic philosophies guiding the organization's management also should be identified. Major policies, general practices, and/or government regulations that affect its operation should be spelled out.

In addition to the overall organization, each major subdivision should be studied. For example, each functional area can be related to the descriptions presented in Chapter 4.

A useful device in studying the general nature of an organization is the organization chart. The organization chart in Figure 7.1 shows the major lines of authority and responsibility for a hypothetical organization. The organization chart in Figure 7.2 shows how a particular activity is organized.

Care must be exercised in developing and using organization charts. Organizations evolve, and the actual lines of authority and responsibility may differ from those shown in a chart prepared at an earlier date. However, the analyst must know who has responsibility for each particular activity and can identify the specific objectives and goals for that activity. The organization chart provides that information. It also reflects, to some extent, the managerial philosophy guiding the organization. For example, the firm whose

FIGURE 7.1   *Organization chart*

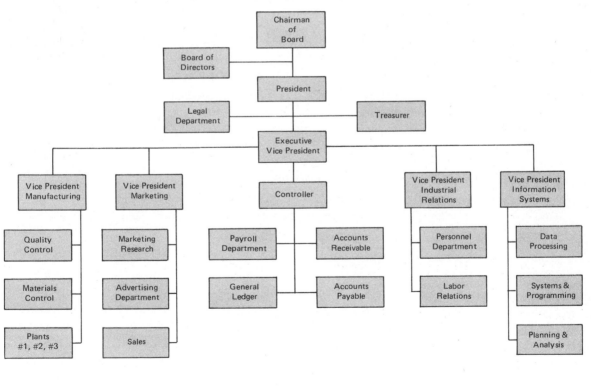

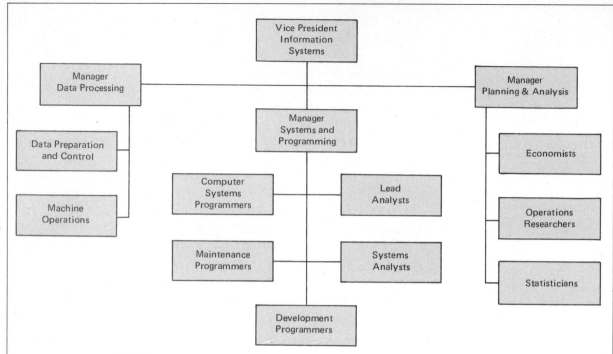

FIGURE 7.2   *Organization chart — information systems*

organization chart is shown in Figure 7.1 is organized along functional lines. It might have been organized along product lines, with each vice president in charge of the production and marketing of a particular product or product group and overseeing only the one plant producing that product or group. These basic organization structures and the more complex matrix structure have already been discussed in Chapter 4 (pp. 55–58).

Interviews and Questionnaires

Much of the initial fact finding involved in analyzing data processing or information systems takes place in interviews. When data must be gathered from large groups or from persons at a distance, questionnaires may be substituted for personal interviews. However, for determining system objectives and goals, interviews are essential. Interviews are also useful when tracing a system's procedures.

INTERVIEW PROCEDURES

Subjective interpretations or opinions are best obtained in face-to-face encounters with the person supplying the facts or opinions sought. For example, in defining system objectives, the analyst must interview the management of the physical operation served by the system under analysis as well as the supervisor of the data processing operation itself.

The most important aspect of the initial interview is to establish rapport with the person being interviewed. In fact, rapport must always be established with the person being interviewed. Rapport can be established and an interview successfully completed by observing the following:

1. Be courteous, friendly, and cooperative at all times.

Set the time for the interview at the convenience of the person being interviewed. Meet the interviewee at his or her office or desk. Be prompt and be prepared. Pay attention to what the person is saying and indicate a sincere desire to hear what he or she has to tell you. Strive for a warm working relationship that is not totally formal. Formal courtesy does not always engender confidence.

Talking down to a clerical worker and treating a top executive as a long-time buddy are both to be avoided. Allow the person being interviewed to speak freely with regard to the system under study. Solicit suggestions for design of the system. If a person's suggestion is good, say so. At least listen and thank the person for cooperating.

2. Maintain eye contact when asking questions or listening, but don't get involved in a "stare-down" contest.

3. Record factual elements of the interview.

No analyst should trust to memory for important factual data. The facts may be written down or recorded on a tape recorder, but they must be recorded.

4. Try to keep interviews short.

The best way to do this is to use an interview schedule to guide the interview. (The interview schedule is described below.) However, always accept any unsolicited facts or opinions that relate to the system being studied.

5. Avoid technical jargon.

Use language the person can understand. Ask for clarification if the interviewee uses unfamiliar terms. Technical terms often do not have obvious meanings.

6. Do not ask the person being interviewed for facts or opinions he or she would not have.

Data processing clerks probably can't state organizational objectives clearly and probably know little about the informational needs of managers. For the same reasons, top management is likely to know little about the specific problems faced at the detail processing level. Data processing managers should have a good knowledge of processing volumes and general processing procedures. They may not have operating-level technical knowledge of the latest processing procedures.

INTERVIEW SCHEDULE

The interview schedule is a printed form containing the questions to be asked during the interview. It provides a valuable guide to the logical devel-

FIGURE 7.3   *Interview schedule—regional sales managers*

BAFM Corp. sales order system

1. Identification:

   a. Region _____
   b. Name _____
   c. Years with BAFM _____ Years in present position _____
   d. Other related experience:

Type	*Period*

2. Volumes:

	This year	*Last year*
a. Number of salespeople in region		
b. Number of customers served		
c. Dollar value of sales last quarter		
d. Dollar value of sales last year		
e. Share of market held by BAFM		

3. Reports Evaluation:

Report	*Needs change*	*Explanation*
Weekly sales analysis		
Monthly sales analysis		
Quarterly sales report		
Accounting reports:		
Cost control		
Profit analysis		
Other (specify)		

4. Are there other areas for which additional information is needed?

Area	Needed	Explanation
Prospect analysis	————	————————————————
Seasonal patterns	————	————————————————
Inventory control	————	————————————————
Credit control	————	————————————————
Other (specify)	————	————————————————

5. Do you recognize any other problems associated with the data processing effect?

a. Data preparation: ————————————————————

b. Order preparation: ————————————————————

c. Customer billing: ————————————————————

d. Other (specify): ————————————————————

opment of each interview and can prevent the failure to ask all questions. It can also reduce bias by providing that all questions are stated in precisely the same words each time they are asked.

For one-of-a-kind interviews, it may seem too time-consuming to prepare an interview schedule. At the minimum, however, the analyst should have a list of facts to be obtained from the interview. Not only does this assure a productive interview, but it shortens the interview as well. Also, the person interviewed is subtly flattered that the analyst has taken time to prepare in advance for the interview.

An example of an interview schedule is shown in Figure 7.3. Note its division into major interest areas. The identification section serves as an ice breaker and gives a picture of the respondent which is helpful in evaluating the value of his or her suggestions for improvements (a person with both *depth* and *breadth* of experience will usually make better suggestions). The second section solicits background information on the region. These data can be helpful in determining future as well as present volumes. Sections 3 and 4 are extremely important. Here is where the meat of the interview is found. Note the extra space where unsolicited but important comments can be entered or extra data recorded. This kind of information can be quite helpful. It would therefore he useful to get a look at the reports received *after* they have been used by the interviewee. In connection with section 4, it may be helpful to ask if the manager has had any *special* studies done by staff, consultants, or others within the last year (or month). One should then determine if any of these studies were repetitious of previous studies. Section 5 is intended to be open-ended and to encourage the respondent to bring up any dissatisfactions with the current system.

The reader should note that the explanation of Figure 7.3 indicates a willingness to go beyond the formal questions on the interview schedule. It is always desirable to discuss the schedule thoroughly with prospective interviewers (or colleagues if you are the only interviewer) to be certain that nothing is left out and to be sure that the purpose of each question is well defined. A well-conducted interview often explores beyond the schedule when the additional information is relevant. At the same time, care must be taken *not* to get into a storytelling session that wastes time for the analyst and the respondent.

QUESTIONNAIRES

A questionnaire is very similar to an interview schedule but is intended to stand alone without interpretation by an interviewer. Good questionnaires have the following characteristics:

1. *Brevity* Do not ask for anything more than is needed. If large amounts of data must be collected, interviews should be used.

2. *Politeness and clarity* Word questions politely and clearly.

Care should be exercised not to offend the person filling out the questionnaire. Again, avoid technical jargon. Ambiguity in any form must be avoided, since there is no chance for further explanation. The questionnaire performs its task alone.

3. *Pertinence* Ask for facts that the respondent knows or has access to.

4. *Logical order* Order questions carefully to assist the respondent in recalling facts and developing answers.

It is easier for a person to recall facts if they are requested in a natural order. Later questions should build upon and extend the knowledge provided earlier. Questions should be grouped by subject matter whenever possible.

5. *Ease* Help the respondent to answer wherever possible.

Let the respondent check off answers when that is appropriate. If alternatives are to be selected from a list, present the list and allow the respondent to check off the appropriate items. *Open-ended* questions that require an elaborate response are better asked in interviews. Questionnaires are best used to gather specific facts.

6. *Rapport* Impress on the respondent that his or her answers are important and useful.

A cover letter or introductory statement is normally used for this purpose, but the tone of the questions can also subtly influence the respondent's attitude.

Flowcharts

Flowcharts are probably the most widely used general method for describing information and data processing systems. The flowchart takes on several forms, each of which has its particular uses. All flowcharts, however, are based on a single and useful concept, the *black box concept* (BBC), which was mentioned briefly in Chapter 5.

THE BLACK BOX CONCEPT

Any information or data processing system has been defined as consisting of three phases — input, processing, and output. In other words, *data inputs* are *transformed* in the processing phase into desired *outputs*. In its simplest form, any open system can be viewed in this fashion. Thus students enter the university and, if all goes well, are transformed into educated citizens. This transformation is shown graphically in Figure 7.4. Note that the nature of the transformation process (the processing) that turns a student into an educated citizen is unspecified; thus the term *black box*.

FIGURE 7.4   *The university as a black box*

In Figure 7.5 we see the university as a *set* of black boxes, each with a different output. Again the transformation processes are not explained. Students enter the law school and are transformed into lawyers. Students enter the college of education and become teachers. We still are not told how this is accomplished. Each black box represents a group of detailed activities that are individually undefined.

The process of breaking down the black box we call the university could continue. Within the college of education we could find sets of courses (curricula) leading to specific teaching degrees. Each curriculum could be defined as a set of courses, with each course designed to accomplish certain transformations of the student. Each course could be broken down into a

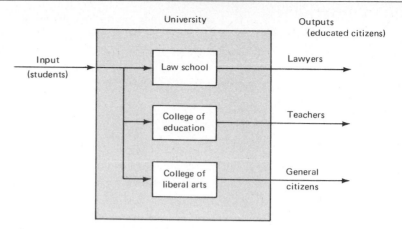

FIGURE 7.5   *The university as a set of black boxes*

set of learning modules. This process of explanation in greater detail is stopped at that set of black boxes when the details of the transformation they perform are irrelevant to the study or when we cannot penetrate the boxes and describe how those transformations are accomplished.

Thus the BBC gives us a pragmatic way to handle the complexity of the world about us. We define the major black box we are interested in and then proceed to break it into smaller and smaller black boxes until we either obtain the needed detail or are unable to penetrate the black box that remains unexplained. Of course, we must assume stability of the transformation process within the lowest-level black box.

Flowcharting is a form of black boxing, a technique for describing a process, a string of transformations. The string may or may not interact with one or more similar strings.

FLOWCHARTING SYMBOLS

The American National Standards Institute (ANSI) has adopted a standard set of symbols to be used in flowcharting. The most commonly used symbols are presented in Figure 7.6. The use of some of these common symbols is illustrated in Figure 7.7.

A complete description of a complex data processing or information system would require more symbols than those shown in Figure 7.6. Space limitations preclude a full presentation here. However, the most common of these additional symbols are shown in Figure 7.8. Their use is partially illustrated in Figure 7.9. Note that the *system chart* shown there contains major black boxes. Detailed processing features are not shown except as a total transformation process within a black box.

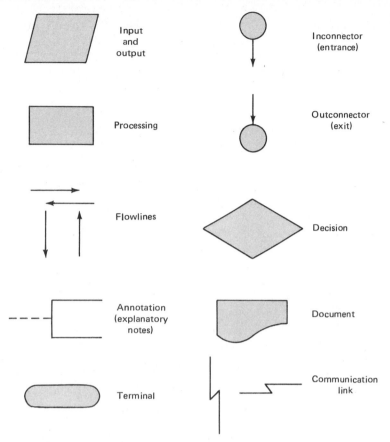

FIGURE 7.6   *Most common flowcharting symbols*

Plastic templates are available as aids in flowcharting. ANSI standard templates can be obtained from equipment vendors and office supply stores.

The distinction between a flow diagram and a system chart is important. In a *system chart*, emphasis is on the inputs and outputs produced by the sequence of actions, computer programs, and so on. *Flow diagrams*, on the other hand, focus on the sequence and detail of data transformations required to change the input data into the required output. A flow diagram is frequently only an elaborate detailing of one of the black boxes contained in a system chart.

SYSTEM CHART

A number of conventions are accepted as guidelines for developing system charts.

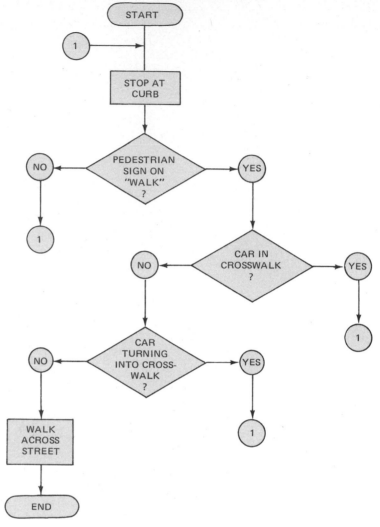

FIGURE 7.7   *How to cross the street safely*

Basic Format The system chart is a set of alternating layers of (1) data recording or development, (2) processing transformations, and (3) output. Therefore, the system chart always starts with data inputs and ends with outputs (see Figure 7.9).

Names Identifying names for data files and transformation processes in a system chart should be short but fully understandable to users of the chart. English-language names are preferred, although normally whatever names are assigned in the subject installation will be used. Consistency of use of

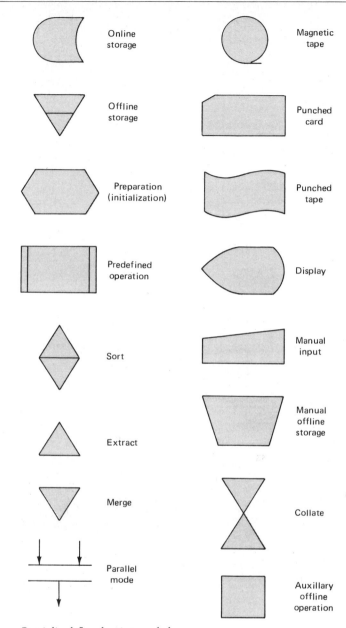

Online storage	Magnetic tape
Offline storage	Punched card
Preparation (initialization)	Punched tape
Predefined operation	Display
Sort	Manual input
Extract	Manual offline storage
Merge	Collate
Parallel mode	Auxillary offline operation

FIGURE 7.8   *Specialized flowcharting symbols*

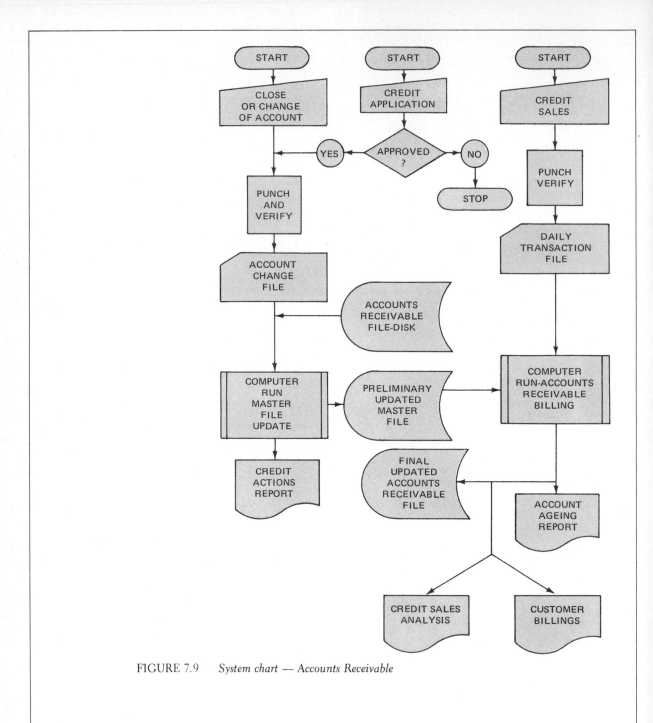

FIGURE 7.9   *System chart — Accounts Receivable*

data and process names must be practiced. The same name appearing in two or more places on a system chart must identify the same thing each time it is used.

Specialized Symbols   Uniquely identified symbols can give additional clarity to system charts and should be used to identify devices and differentiate between online and offline processes.

Connectors   System charts are normally not as long as flow diagrams. Also, they do not contain as many repeated sequences (loops) as do flow diagrams. For these reasons connectors do not appear as frequently on system charts. They can be used on long system charts to connect parts of the chart, however. The system chart format of "input-process-output and then use that output as input for a new cycle" makes it preferable to use a different method to show the connection between different pages of a system chart. This latter method is illustrated in Figure 7.10. Note the repetition of the representations for selected inputs or outputs and the associated cross-referencing between pages. Thus the account change file is repeated in pages 1, 2, and 3 with appropriate reference numbers associated with it on each page. Similarly, the daily transaction file appears on pages 4 and 5 and the preliminary updated master file on pages 3 and 5. Repetition of the output-input figures makes each page understandable when examined alone. Use of connectors with no repetition would not provide such clarity. Breaking up a chart usually makes it easier to use because it more clearly separates unconnected or parallel flows.

Annotation   Notes can clarify a system chart. They may be set in annotation figures or placed parallel to a line of figures on the chart. The use of the annotation figure provides clarity but increases the cluttered appearance of the chart. An example of the use of annotation is shown in Figure 7.11, where page 1 from Figure 7.10 is repeated with notes added. Volume and timing information are commonly shown on the system chart in this manner, as are sources and use of data files. Annotation and cross-referencing should be used where they add clarity to a system chart, but excessive use must be avoided. Chart users either get confused or tend to ignore these aids if they are used too lavishly.

FLOW DIAGRAM

A *flow diagram* ordinarily describes the procedure for accomplishing a particular processing operation within a system. Often this procedure can be

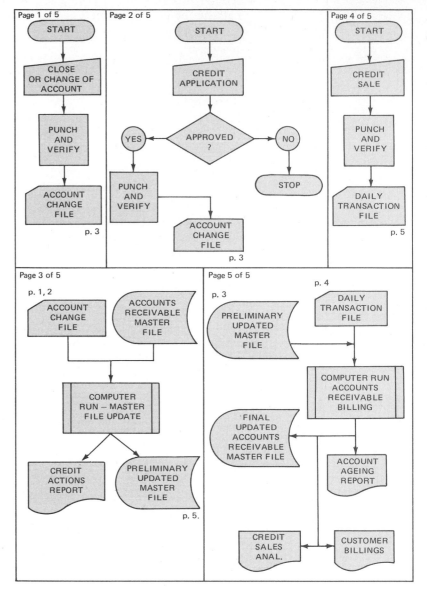

START

CLOSE
OR CHANGE OF
ACCOUNT

PUNCH
AND
VERIFY

ACCOUNT
CHANGE
FILE

p. 3

START

CREDIT
APPLICATION

APPROVED
?

YES

NO

PUNCH
AND
VERIFY

STOP

ACCOUNT
CHANGE
FILE

p. 3

START

CREDIT
SALE

PUNCH
AND
VERIFY

DAILY
TRANSACTION
FILE

p. 5

p. 1, 2

ACCOUNT
CHANGE
FILE

ACCOUNTS
RECEIVABLE
MASTER
FILE

COMPUTER
RUN — MASTER
FILE UPDATE

CREDIT
ACTIONS
REPORT

PRELIMINARY
UPDATED
MASTER
FILE

p. 5.

p. 3

p. 4

PRELIMINARY
UPDATED
MASTER
FILE

DAILY
TRANSACTION
FILE

COMPUTER RUN
ACCOUNTS
RECEIVABLE
BILLING

FINAL
UPDATED
ACCOUNTS
RECEIVABLE
MASTER FILE

ACCOUNT
AGEING
REPORT

CREDIT
SALES
ANAL.

CUSTOMER
BILLINGS

FIGURE 7.10   *Example of preferred method of breaking a system chart*

classed as an algorithm (processing procedure or formula) specifying the portions of the input data structures to be affected and the operations to be performed on them. Thus the flow diagram evolves from the system chart to
detail procedures at a work station within the system. Specification of the
media or devices involved is often ignored, since that is of secondary importance in the process description.

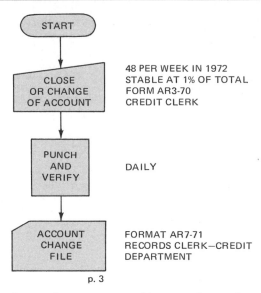

FIGURE 7.11   *Page 1 of Accounts Receivable system chart with annotation added*

Basic Format   A flow diagram is a sequence of process outlines and decision blocks connected by flowlines, or connectors. One or more input symbols will normally appear near the beginning of the diagram and one or more output symbols near the end. Usually, however, the flow diagram for a data processing operation involves looping back to repeat the same sequence of operations for each transaction processed.

Names   As in building system charts, *brevity, clarity,* and *consistency* are desirable in naming entities and processes in a flow diagram. Try to keep names short but descriptive. Use the same unique name for an entity or process each time it is mentioned. Using the same name for different entities and/or procedures is confusing and should be avoided.

Special Symbols   Since a flow diagram is a description of detailed processing activities, few special symbols are used. They should be used, however, whenever their use would lead to greater clarity and/or a medium or device is critical to the process. The annotation symbol is especially useful in flow diagrams, as illustrated in Figure 7.12.

Connectors   Connectors are important in flow diagrams for three reasons: (1) flow diagrams tend to be long, (2) flow diagrams usually involve convergent and divergent flows, and (3) flow diagrams often involve extensive use of looping. The liberal use of connectors and cross-references allows

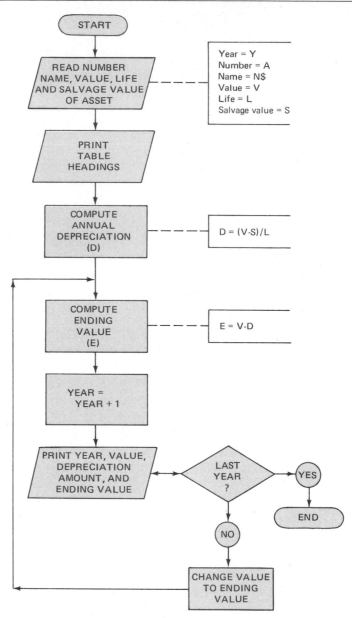

FIGURE 7.12   *Flow diagram of the computation and printing of a straight-line depreciation schedule*

flow diagrams to be shown as linear, or straight-line, flows. Each alternative path through a system may need to be presented in its entirety as a separate flow with points of convergence (entrance *from* several outside points) and divergence (exit *to* several outside points) clearly indicated.

Annotation   As seen in Figure 7.12, annotation can provide additional clarity to a flow diagram. It is particularly important at points of convergence and divergence and in identifying data entities (variables) in the process.

FLOWCHARTING GUIDELINES

The general guidelines listed below summarize and slightly expand the discussion above. They apply to both system charts and flow diagrams and should be followed at all times unless clarity requires that they be violated.

1. Choose the wording within symbols to fit the needs of the readers. Brevity is important. Charts using something close to common English are most widely understood.

2. Hold to a consistent level of detail throughout each chart. The description of a system or an algorithm is usually developed in stages at successively more detailed levels. The reader is led into greater detail by each stage. (This process is further described in Chapter 13 and illustrated there.)

3. Use identifying names consistently and keep them brief.

4. Keep the flowchart as simple and linear as possible. Cluttered charts are harder to read. Break them up if necessary (for example, compare Figures 7.9 and 7.10). Flowlines should enter or leave near the center of a flowchart figure. Collect flowlines so that only one line enters each figure wherever possible.

5. Avoid crossing flowlines as much as possible.

6. Processing handled by different means should be clearly separated. Thus manual or electro-mechanical preprocessing of data before a computer run should be clearly specified separately from the computer program. Also, initial preparation of any processing device by an operator (changing plug boards, tapes, or disk packs and setting control switches) should *not* be included in the description of the internal process (the program) to be carried out by the device, but shown in a separate preprocessing flow diagram.

7. Use cross-references liberally. Cross-references between different flows often serve to point up possibilities for greater integration of the system.

8. Flow should be from top to bottom and left to right. Initial entrances to a flow diagram should be at the top left and final exits at the bottom right.

Preferably, intermediate entrances are from the left side and intermediate exits are to the right side.

9. Use specialized symbols whenever appropriate to provide additional descriptive value to the flowchart.

10. Stick to these guidelines and the standard flowcharting symbols, avoiding all deviations.

Decision Tables

An alternate way to describe system procedures is with decision tables. A decision table is one method of specifying alternative actions to be taken and the predefined conditions under which each action alternative is to be selected. It provides a compact expression of decision rules for any multiple-action situation.

DECISION TABLE FORMAT

A decision table is composed of five elements: *condition stub, condition entry, action stub, action entry,* and *rules.* Figure 7.13 shows a decision table that describes the conditions under which a consumer loan is granted or not granted by a small bank. The first part of Figure 7.13 shows the table in its ordinary form. The quadrants of the table have been separated in the second part so that the elements of the table can be easily identified.

FIGURE 7.13   *Parts of a decision table*

Consumer loan table	Rule 1	Rule 2	Rule 3	Rule 4
Good previous credit rating	Y	Y	N	N
Loan cost ≤ 1/10 income	Y	N	Y	N
Grant loan	X			
Do not grant loan		X	X	X

CONDITION STUB	CONDITION ENTRY			
	Rule 1	Rule 2	Rule 3	Rule 4
Good previous credit rating	Y	Y	N	N
Loan cost ≤ 1/10 income	Y	N	Y	N

ACTION STUB	ACTION ENTRY			
Grant loan	X			
Do not grant loan		X	X	X

Condition Stub   The upper left quadrant of the decision table listing the predefined conditions that determine action selection is called the *condition stub*.

Condition Entry   The upper right quadrant of the decision table is called the *condition entry*. Entries in a *column* specify the mix of conditions for a specific *rule*.

Action Stub   The lower left quadrant of the decision table lists the action alternatives and is called the *action stub*.

Action Entry   The lower right quadrant of the decision table indicates in each column the action or actions to be taken for a given set of conditions (for a specific rule) and is called the *action entry*.

Rules   Each column extending through the upper and lower right quadrants specifies a *rule*. If the conditions indicated by the entries in the condition entry are met, then the actions indicated in the action entry of that same column are taken. There are four rules in Figure 7.13. (With two predefined conditions, each being true or false, there are 2^2 possible combinations, or four rules.) Note, however, that there are really only two rules. First, there is rule 1, which says that if the applicant has a good previous credit rating and the loan cost (principal payment plus interest) is no more than 10 percent of the applicant's income, then the loan will be granted. Second, there are three condition combinations that result in not granting the loan. These conditions could have been combined as a single *ELSE rule*. An example of the ELSE rule appears in Figure 7.14, which also presents a more realistic set of rules for the credit officer to follow. An additional condition covering other loan costs and an additional action allowing uncertain cases to be referred to the chief loan officer for decision have been added. If the ELSE rule were not used, there would have to be eight (2^3) rules to cover all possible combinations of conditions. Rule 4 (the ELSE) in Figure 7.14 actually combines five possible rules, all of which specify the same action. The ELSE rule can be used only in those situations in which a group of rules all specify the same action.

LIMITED-ENTRY TABLES

The tables in Figures 7.13 and 7.14 are *limited-entry tables*. That is, condition entries can only be Yes, No, or *I*mmaterial. The immaterial (I) entry as a condition entry is used when the presence or absence of a given condition will not affect the action selected.

	Rule 1	Rule 2	Rule 3	Rule 4 (ELSE)
Good previous credit rating	Y	Y	Y	
Loan cost ≤ 1/10 income	Y	Y	N	
Other loan cost ≤ 1/5 income	Y	N	Y	
Grant loan	X			
Do not grant loan				X
Refer to chief loan officer		X	X	

FIGURE 7.14   *Consumer loan decision table with expanded conditions and actions but combined rules*

EXTENDED-ENTRY TABLES

When only a part of each condition or action is stated in the stub and the remainder of each condition or action is contained in the entry portion of a row, the table is classed as an *extended-entry table*. Figure 7.15 is an example. Note how conditions and actions are completed in the rules columns.

MIXED-ENTRY TABLES

When some conditions and/or actions are questions to be answered yes or no (limited entry) and some conditions and/or actions are partially specified by the entries in the rules columns, then the table is classed as a *mixed-entry table*.

ADVANTAGES AND DISADVANTAGES OF DECISION TABLES

Decision tables possess the following advantages as a method of defining procedures:

1. They make cause-and effect relationships clear.

2. A semistandardized language is used that eliminates unnecessary verbiage.

FIGURE 7.15   *Consumer loan decision table in extended entry form*

	1	2	3	4	5	6	7	8	ELSE
Credit rating	Good	Good	Good	Good	Fair	Fair	Fair	Poor	
(Loan cost)/income	≤.1	≤.1	>.1	>.1	≤.1	>.1	≤.1	I	
(Other loan cost)/income	>.2	≤.2	≤.2	>.2	≤.1	≤.1	>.1	I	
Loan action		Grant			Grant			Don't grant	Don't grant
Refer to	Super		Super	CLO*		Super	CLO*		

CLO stands for chief loan officer

3. They are easily understood by experienced users.

4. It is possible to check that all combinations have been considered when complex tests are required to determine action selection.

5. Complex tables are easily broken into smaller tables.

6. The tables are easily used in combination by having more detailed tables called from a summary table.

7. Programs exist for converting properly structured decision tables into computer programs. The most widely known and used are FORTAB and DETAB. FORTAB converts decision tables of scientific problems into FORTRAN. DETAB converts decision table structures into COBOL. (FORTRAN and COBOL are general-purpose programming languages and are described in Chapter 14.)

The basic disadvantage of decision tables for description of information and data processing systems is that they cannot adequately describe systems. They are logically constructed to define procedures and algorithms, not general systems. When used, they supplement system charts and are used to describe the processing blocks within those charts.

Input-Output Matrices

A useful tool for checking on the completeness of data sources and for planning for management reporting is the *input-output matrix*, a table that shows sources for data used in developing custodial documents and management reports. Data sources are shown in detail on the stub of the matrix. The uses of each data element identified in the stub are shown by checking the appropriate columns on the right side. An example of an input-output matrix is shown in Figure 7.16.

Development of Figure 7.16 started with an input document, the credit sales slip. The contents of the sales slip are listed in the data elements column of the table. Each column on the right refers to a specific document or report that is affected by these data. The checks in each column identify the specific data elements that will have an effect on that document or report.

Simulation

A *simulation* is an operating representation of a real process. In other words, it is an *operating model* that represents and reproduces the characteristics of a real system. There are *three types* of simulation:

1. *Physical* A scaled replica of the real system is used to represent the real system — for example, the model airplane or the airplane wing in a wind tunnel. This approach is seldom used in simulating information systems.

DATA ELEMENTS	OUTPUT DESTINATIONS (See Key Below)									
	1	2	3	4	5	6	7	8	9	10
Sales ticket number	X	X	X	X	X	X	X			
Department number	X			X	X	X	X			
Sales clerk number	X			X			X			
Customer name	X	X								
Customer address	X	X								
Item numbers	X	X	X	X	X	X	X			
Item description	X	X	X		X	X	X			
Units sold	X	X	X	X	X	X	X			
Unit prices	X	X			X	X	X			
Total sale amount	X	X		X	X	X	X			

INPUT DOCUMENT: *Credit sales slip*   FORM NO.: *CS-1-72*
DATE: *6/30/73*   VOLUME *1860*   PER *Day*

OUTPUT DESTINATIONS KEY:

1. *Delivery order*
2. *Accounts receivable ledger*
3. *Inventory ledger*
4. *Daily sales summary*
5. *Weekly sales analysis*
6. *Monthly sales analysis*
7. *Monthly sales clerk rating*

FIGURE 7.16   *Input-output matrix*

2. *Analog* A substitute physical system that is easier and less costly to manipulate and observe is used to represent the real system. For example, electrical circuits can be used to represent fluid flow systems. Fluid velocity is represented by electrical amperage, pipe friction by electrical resistance, pump pressure by electrical voltage. Again, this approach is seldom used in simulating information systems.

3. *Symbolic or mathematical* The physical reality is represented by symbols and mathematical relationships between the symbols. Mathematical functions represent invariable relationships. Probability distributions express the uncertainties present in such systems. Mathematical simulations are widely used to analyze and design information systems. A computer is usually involved to manipulate the models, although limited simulation by less sophisticated means is possible.

Simulation of interest to systems analysts normally involves expressing the rules and relationships by which the system will operate as mathematical relationships and then trying different sets of data with the rules and relationships held constant. Then the rules for controlling system reactions are varied, and selected data sets are tried against each variation. These processes continue until satisfactory results are obtained. Care must be exercised to insure that potentially satisfactory alternatives are not missed. Operating managers of the system being studied should be deeply involved in evaluating alternatives.

Simulation as a tool of analysis and design of information and data processing systems has been applied to the following areas or problems:

1. Developing and testing control directives to be automatically applied during processing

2. Simulation of computers and other machine processing systems as part of the selection process (see Chapter 12)

3. Developing an optimum schedule for processing activities

4. Determining optimum size of work crews

5. Determining optimum equipment configurations

6. Setting optimum inventories of processing materials

7. Designing machine room or work area layouts

8. Scheduling preventive maintenance on equipment

9. Forecasting levels of activity

10. Minimizing waiting lines for data processing services

Forms Design

A *form* is a document having constant printed data or information elements and spaces to add variable data or information elements. A form is a communication medium, a link in an operational procedure. Forms vary widely in size, shape, weight, organization, and color; but most are printed on some type of paper.

Three trends are apparent in the use of business forms since the advent of the computer and its line printers, which can spew forth mile upon mile of paper covered with detailed data. First, input forms for data processing systems have expanded to include not only punched cards and punched tape, but also new document forms featuring optically read characters, magnetic-ink characters, and other specialized media. The systems person now must consider not only people's ability to use different forms of data expression but also the machine's abilities to recognize and manipulate different character forms.

The second trend is the increasing use of plain-stock (blank) paper for output. Preprinted output forms are not so important when computers can print column headings, page numbers, and vertical and horizontal lines. The computer can produce attractive reports on plain stock.

The third trend is the increasing use of direct input to and output from machine-processing systems without the use of intervening paper forms. Specialized input devices allow direct entry to the machine. Output by visual display devices and on microfilm is increasing rapidly (see Chapter 9).

CRITERIA OF GOOD FORMS DESIGN

In general, good forms must suit the purpose for which they are intended and be easy to use but avoid duplication and failure to obtain all pertinent data. Characteristics of good forms for manual data collection are presented in Chapter 6 (page 122). General technical considerations for forms design are not totally different from those listed there.

1. All fixed data and information should be preprinted on the form.

2. Abbreviations and codes used to conserve space while identifying content must be logical, nonoverlapping, and easy to comprehend.

Forms should be as self-explanatory as possible.

3. Adequate space should be provided for the insertion of data or information elements.

Most typewriters use six lines to the inch and ten character spaces to the inch. Many computer printers can be adjusted to print eight lines to the inch. Vertical line spacing when handwriting is to be entered is usually ¼ inch. Vertical lines (rulings) should be allotted at least one character space. Horizontal spaces to be filled in should be made large enough to easily contain the required data elements.

4. Horizontal rulings should be kept to a minimum. Lines above or below a single line of print are especially to be avoided.

5. Captions for boxes should be placed above and to the left so that they are visible even when the form is being filled out on a typewriter.

6. Major data elements, particularly those to be transcribed to another medium, should be highlighted and easy to find. They are best placed down the right edge and at the bottom.

7. Data elements should be logically arranged, with related data grouped and data in each group sequenced from left to right and top to bottom.

8. Multiple-part forms should use a different color for each copy to aid in the distribution and make it easy to spot copies that are in the wrong place.

9. Forms should be attractive and easy to use.

Colored inks and colored paper are usually more expensive, but they add to the attractiveness of the forms. They can also make the forms easier to use. Printing box headings, and so on, in colors other than black helps to set them off from entered data. Red ink is frequently used on forms requiring immediate attention or response. Some colors (notably blue) do not photograph well. Using a different color for each copy of a multiple-copy form makes for ease of distribution to different users.

The provision of lists and associated boxes for checking off answers is helpful to the person filling out a form. When the form goes to customers or other business associates of the firm, it is important that it be easy to use and attractive in appearance. Items to be filled in should be numbered so that instructions can be keyed to each of them by item number. If the forms are to be retained, are they easy to store? Must a specially designed storage device be used? Is it worth the cost?

10. Coordinate each form with all related forms.

One reason forms tend to proliferate in an organization is that each form tends to be developed in a vacuum and thus to overlap one or more other forms. This same concern should be applied to multiple copies. Are they all used? Is more than one filed? Should there be more than one copy filed? A form registry with a single individual responsible for reviewing all requests for new forms or revisions of existing forms can save money and reduce repetitive processing. Each form should be given a form control number to identify it on the registry. This number can be keyed to the purpose for which the form is created and where in the organization it is used. It should also indicate when the form was created and/or last revised.

11. Standardize forms design.

Form manufacturers provide specially ruled layout sheets to aid in design. Use of such standard guides helps to develop forms whose spacings fit common typewriters, printers, and other devices. Special layout sheets can be obtained for forms used with special-entry processes such as optical-character and magnetic-character readers.

System Design and Computer Program Design

The system design tools described in this chapter only incidentally include techniques for the design of computer programs. As computers have become more complex and more capable, they have tended to take over more of the processing system from original data recording to final output. In the process, computer programs have become more complex and harder to design and develop. The flowcharting and decision table techniques presented in this chapter have proven inadequate to the task when used alone. The latest design tools are *structured design*, *structured programming*, and *structured walkthroughs*. These latter techniques are described in Chapter 13 under Structured Program Design.

Summary

This chapter has reviewed some of the tools available for use in analysis and design of information and data processing systems. Tools for the collection of basic facts about the system and its objectives include interviews, questionnaires, and organization charts. Tools used to describe and document systems procedures include the two types of flowcharts (systems charts and flow diagrams), decision tables, and input-output matrices. Analysis of system efficiency and optimization of system design are aided by a knowledge of simulation and forms design techniques.

Questions

1. Define the following as briefly as possible and then use a short paragraph to clarify each definition.

   a. Organization chart
   b. Interview
   c. Interview schedule
   d. Questionnaire
   e. Black box concept
   f. System chart
   g. Flow diagram
   h. Connector
   i. Decision table
   j. Condition stub
   k. Action entry
   l. Decision table rule
   m. Limited-entry table
   n. Extended-entry table
   o. ELSE rule
   p. Input-output matrix
   q. Simulation
   r. Form
   s. Structured design

2. How is the increasing use of computers affecting the use and design of forms for business information systems? Explain.
3. What is simulation?
4. Can a decision table or a flow diagram be considered a simulation? Justify your answer carefully.
5. What might be the uses of a form? Be exhaustive, then summarize.
6. What is the objective of forms design? (This is not specifically spelled out in the text.)
7. How could a good forms design contribute to a good systems design?

8. Why should the design of a form include coordination with all related forms?
9. Refer to Figure 7.2 and extend the organization chart shown there to include the following details:
    a. Data preparation and control consists of a supervisor, two data clerks, five keypunch operators, and an electric accounting machine (EAM) operator.
    b. Machine operations consists of three lead operators and three journeyman operators.
    c. There are two systems programmers; five maintenance programmers; and three development programmers, assisted by four programmer trainees.
    d. There are two lead analysts, three systems analysts, and one analyst trainee working on systems analysis.
    e. The planning and analysis staff includes one economist; two operations researchers; and one statistician, assisted by two statistical clerks and two clerk-stenographers, one of whom acts as the department secretary.
10. As a systems analyst for SAFM Corporation you are assigned the job of improving the sales ordering system. SAFM has approximately 175 salespeople working out of fifteen regional sales offices. Several regional sales managers have indicated that the salespeople in their region are dissatisfied with the sales order form introduced six months ago. A drop in the average number of sales orders filed per salesperson per month, poorly filled-out order forms, and increasing customer complaints about service from salespeople are further indications of trouble.
    a. Would you suggest interviews or questionnaires to find what is troubling the salespeople? Why?
    b. Develop an interview schedule or a questionnaire in line with your recommendation. If you decide to use a questionnaire, include a cover letter to the salespeople soliciting their cooperation in the study.
11. Refer to Figure 7.14 and develop a flow diagram as a description of the process described there.
12. Develop a decision table for the procedure shown in the flow diagram of Figure 7.7.
13. Develop a decision table for the procedure shown in the flow diagram of Figure 7.12.
14. Develop a flow diagram for the procedure described in Figure 7.15.
15. You are designing an inventory control system for which the following rules have been specified:

a. In general, a replacement order will be sent if (1) units on hand for a product fall below the reorder point, (2) the production plant is currently producing the item, and (3) units on hand are equal to or less than the critical level (which is below the reorder point).

b. If there were no sales in the last month, then no order will be sent regardless of inventory level.

c. Highly profitable items that are expected to continue selling will be reordered when the units on hand fall below the reorder point.

Draw up a decision table and a flow diagram to describe this system.

16. You are conducting a study of the order processing department, in which the employees have been chronically late to work. You plan to interview the office supervisor and several workers about this problem. Develop one or more interview schedules to use. Write out all questions as completely as possible and indicate briefly why each is included and how the answers to each question will be used.

17. The Black Oil Company uses the following credit charge procedures:

a. Each customer is supplied with a credit card containing his or her name, address, and account number.

b. Each time the customer makes a purchase at a Black Oil service station, the credit card is presented to the attendant, who completes the sales invoice, giving one copy to the customer.

c. At the end of each week, the station manager batches the accumulated invoices with an adding-machine tape and sends them to Black Oil. The amount is verified by the company, and the station account is credited with the amount of the batch.

d. At the end of each month, the company sorts the accumulated invoices by customer number, microfilms them as a permanent record, adds the invoice amounts to each customer's account on the customer tape file, prints a billing statement for each customer, and mails each statement and the individual invoices to the customer.

e. Upon receipt of payment from the customer, the amount is verified with the payment stub, the stubs are sorted by customer number, and the payment is subtracted from the customer record on the tape file. Partial payments and overpayments are input on a special card.

Draw a system chart for this process, showing the flow of documents and data through the Black Oil credit charge system.

18. SHFM Hardware Stores, Inc., maintains eight regional warehouses in widely dispersed locations across the United States. Each regional warehouse serves twenty to thirty local SHFM hardware stores. A central warehouse in St. Louis, Missouri, keeps the regional warehouses supplied with goods. Each local store sends a weekly order to its

regional warehouse, and a copy goes to the central warehouse. In the event of unexpectedly large sales that result in an inventory shortage, the store can special order from the regional warehouse at any time. A copy of each special order also goes to the central warehouse. At the regional warehouse each weekly or special order is filled as it is received, and a confirming copy of the shipping invoice is sent to the central warehouse. Weekly, the central warehouse sorts the copies of the orders from the local stores and the confirmation copies of the shipping invoices from the regional warehouses by warehouse and matches them. For those orders with matching shipping invoices, the appropriate entries are made to adjust the regional warehouse inventory accounts. The regional warehouse inventory for each staple item is replenished whenever the inventory amount drops to the reorder level for that warehouse. A buying department at the central warehouse places orders for seasonal goods and specialty items to be sent to each store, basing order size on past sales records and on "requests" from local store managers. Monthly, each store manager is sent a "catalogue" of seasonal and specialty items to use in making store requests. Local store inventory accounts are updated weekly by resorting the filled store orders by store number and updating the store accounts on a tape file.

   a. Draw a system flowchart for this process, showing the flow of documents and data through the SHFM Hardware Stores inventory system. Follow the flowcharting guidelines on pages 182–184 in preparing your flowchart.

   b. Analyze the system description and suggest any improvements (additions or deletions) that you deem appropriate.

19. Refer to question 20 at the end of Chapter 5 and question 34 at the end of Chapter 6.

   a. Prepare an interview schedule to be used in interviewing the top managers of the chain.

   b. Prepare an interview schedule to be used in interviewing the store managers.

   c. Prepare a questionnaire to be sent to the managers of the five departments in each of the three existing stores. Include a cover letter to accompany the questionnaire designed to elicit a prompt and truthful response.

20. Prepare an input-output matrix and a flow diagram for the customer payment process of an accounts receivable subsystem. Include the following actions:

   a. Full payment (on time) of amount owed.

   b. Partial payment (on time) of amount owed.

c. Late payment of part or all of the amount owed with interest assessed at the rate of 1 percent per month for late payment (after the first of the next month following the initial billing date). Billing dates are either the first or the fifth of each month.

d. Overpayments of amount owed by customers are identified by a five-digit number and by customer name (last name, first name, and middle initial).

Part 3

The Computer: Hardware and Software

The automatic electronic digital computer is a widely used data processing device. Its use has led to a revolution in data processing procedures. With its help, the modern manager routinely applies an ever-widening array of planning and control methods of increasing power and complexity. It is also a widely misunderstood tool, underused, improperly used, improperly blamed for human failures, and just as improperly praised for human accomplishments. The computer is a tool, a powerful tool that extends the data manipulation and data analysis abilities of humans. If it is to be used properly, it must be understood and must be placed in proper perspective.

Chapter 8 provides an overview of computers as data processing devices. Functional components of the computer are identified, and their operation is explained. This is partly accomplished by tracing the changing patterns of use that have accompanied changes in computer hardware and software. Chapters 9 and 10 look closely at the specific devices available to carry out the input-output and storage functions. Chapter 11 discusses minicomputers, microcomputers, microprocessors, and teleprocessing networks. Chapter 12 uses the concepts developed in Chapters 8 through 11 as a basis for discussing the managerial problem of hardware selection. The advantages and disadvantages of lease and purchase are included in that discussion.

Software is the focus of the final two chapters in this part of the book. Chapter 13 discusses the general nature of computer programming and presents guidelines for successful program preparation with emphasis on a structured approach. Chapter 14 discusses programming languages, explaining in detail the differences between the general types of languages and discussing the general characteristics of several specific languages. Chapter 14 also deals with problems of software selection, developing guidelines for selecting from among programming languages and from among commercially available software packages for accomplishing data processing tasks.

Eight

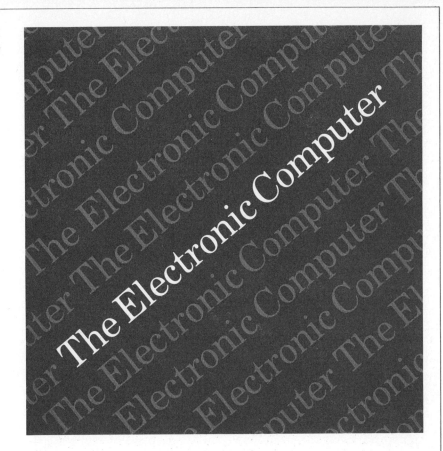

The Electronic Computer

There are two general types of electronic computers, *analog* and *digital*. Analog computers use electronic circuits and current flows as a physical representation of a process or system. Analog machines are useful in engineering planning and research and production process control. They are not used in data processing for management. Our attention will be devoted to the automatic electronic digital computer.

Definition of the Computer

The *automatic electronic digital* computer is a *machine* that utilizes *electronic circuits to manipulate data* expressed in a *symbolic form* according to *specific rules* in a *predetermined* but *self-directed* way. This complete definitional statement is somewhat hard to absorb as a whole. Let's look at its individual parts. For convenience, when we refer to *the computer*, we mean "the automatic electronic digital computer."

First of all, the computer is a *machine*. This means that it is inanimate and requires an outside power source. This also means that it can perform only those activities for which the basic capabilities have been specifically designed into the machine. In other words, it is limited to its designed capabilities and such outside direction as can be given it. If separated from its outside power source, it ceases to function.

Second, it is *automatic*. This means that once started, it continues to run without outside interference.

Third, it is *electronic*; that is, it is made up of electronic circuits and runs on electrical energy.

Fourth, the computer is a *symbol manipulator*. It manipulates data, not physical entities. These data are represented as electronic impulses within the machine. The electronic impulses are combined to form number (*digital*) representations of data. Electronic circuits are used to manipulate these symbols. Electronic devices are largely *two-state* devices. For example, a switch is either open or closed, a spot on the surface of a magnetic tape is either magnetized or not magnetized, a particular location on a punched card or punched paper tape is either a hole or not, and a particular spot on a wire at a particular instant either contains an impulse or it does not. It therefore seems natural and reasonable to use the base two (*binary*) number system as the basic data representation method in the computer. Only two digits exist in that system, 0 (zero) and 1 (one). They can easily be matched to the two states of electronic devices. Combinations of 0's and 1's can be used to represent nonnumerical data as well as numerical data. Three of the major codes for representing data (numbers and alphabetic characters) with 0's and 1's are presented in Figure 8.1. Note that it is possible to represent more characters than are shown in Figure 8.1. BCD (six bits) can represent up to 64 (2^6) characters; EBCDIC (eeb-see-dick) and ASCII-8 (asky-8) (also called UNASCII and ANSCII) can each represent up to 256 (2^8) characters.

Fifth, the computer must follow *specific rules* in manipulating data. These rules are, in the main, the rules of Boolean algebra. That is, the computer can perform *only* the processes of *addition*, *subtraction*, *multiplication*, *division*, and *comparison* (a = b, a < b, a > b), in addition to data transfer between components.

Sixth, the computer must follow a *predetermined* sequence of its allowable processes. That is, someone (the programmer) must prepare a finite sequence of the allowable individual operations (a *program*) for the computer to follow.

Finally, the computer can store the program within its own memory and then follow it through under its own direction, without further outside guidance. This *stored-program* characteristic is what differentiates the computer from other data processing machines. That is, the computer can be made,

Character	Standard binary-coded decimal (BCD)	Extended BCD interchange code (EBCDIC)	American standard code for information interchange (ASCII-8)
A	110001	11000001	10100001
B	110010	11000010	10100010
C	110011	11000011	10100011
D	110100	11000100	10100100
E	110101	11000101	10100101
F	110110	11000110	10100110
G	110111	11000111	10100111
H	111000	11001000	10101000
I	111001	11001001	10101001
J	100001	11010001	10101010
K	100010	11010010	10101011
L	100011	11010011	10101100
M	100100	11010100	10101101
N	100101	11010101	10101110
O	100110	11010110	10101111
P	100111	11010111	10110000
Q	101000	11011000	10110001
R	101001	11011001	10110010
S	010010	11100010	10110011
T	010011	11100011	10110100
U	010100	11100100	10110101
V	010101	11100101	10110110
W	010110	11100110	10110111
X	010111	11100111	10111000
Y	011000	11101000	10111001
Z	011001	11101001	10111010
0	000000	11110000	01010000
1	000001	11110001	01010001
2	000010	11110010	01010010
3	000011	11110011	01010011
4	000100	11110100	01010100
5	000101	11110101	01010101
6	000110	11110110	01010110
7	000111	11110111	01010111
8	001000	11111000	01011000
9	001001	11111001	01011001

FIGURE 8.1 *Examples of binary data codes used by the computer*

in effect, to *learn* a process, *store* the instructions in its memory, and *follow* them through *unaided* by further supervision and direction. Since the instructions are stored in the memory and the memory is accessible to a user, the instructions can be changed. The computer can thus be given the ability to handle many different jobs. It is much more flexible than the programmable accounting machines because its programs are a sequence of logic and arithmetic operations. The availability of logic (decision-making) powers allows the machine to modify its operations while working on a job, making it more versatile and giving it great power to duplicate man's cognitive mental processes.

In *summary*, then, we find that *the electronic digital computer is a symbol-manipulating machine that can be "instructed" to perform any sequence of logical or arithmetical operations on data*. Further, these instructions are easily modified, either by being replaced in total or by being modified by the machine in accordance with results it obtains during the operation.

Functional Elements of the Computer

There are five functional elements that make up the computer. The manner in which these elements are organized is indicated in Figure 8.2.

Each element in the computer has a definite function. An understanding of these functions is necessary for understanding what a computer is and what it can do for us.

INPUT ELEMENT

The *input* element of a computer performs a *translation* function. It translates data from the symbols of our language (numbers, letters, and other symbols) to the symbols (electronic impulses) used inside the machine.

STORAGE ELEMENT

The *storage* section has an obvious function, storage. But this function has *four* parts:

1. The storage of program instructions
2. The storage of input (raw) data
3. The storage of intermediate results from processing
4. The storage of final results (processed data) for output

Note particularly that data are passed directly from input to storage and must be in storage to be sent to output.

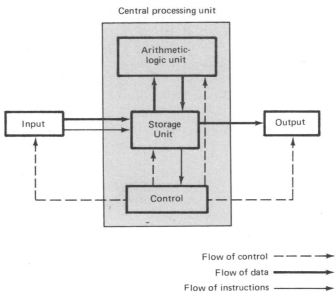

Central processing unit

Arithmetic-
logic unit

Input

Storage
Unit

Output

Control

Flow of control — — — →
Flow of data ━━━━━→
Flow of instructions ————→

FIGURE 8.2   *Functional organization of the computer*

CONTROL ELEMENT

The *control* section includes the operator's console and several registers and related control circuits. Buttons and switches on the console are used to manually start and stop the machine. Once it is operating, however, the control shifts to a program stored in memory. *Instruction registers* within the control section are used to *select* individual program instructions in the sequence specified by the programmer, *interpret* each instruction, and cause the proper operating (logic, arithmetic, and transfer) circuits of the machine to be activated to carry out that instruction and proceed to the next. It is the control section working in concert with the storage that makes possible the *stored-program concept* of machine operation.

ARITHMETIC-LOGIC ELEMENT

The *arithmetic-logic* section is the set of registers and circuits in which the actual arithmetic and comparisons (the data processing) are performed.

OUTPUT ELEMENT

The *output* section performs a translation process that is the reverse of the input function. Data and information expressed in the electronic-impulse symbols of the machine are translated to human-sensible forms or to forms that can be utilized in further machine processing.

It is particularly important to note the various paths through the computer. Refer to Figure 8.2 again. Data to be processed go from input to storage until required for processing. At that point they are sent to the arithmetic-logic section and operated upon. The results are returned to storage, from which they go to output. Instructions (the program) start along a similar path, going from input to storage, where they are held until required for interpretation and action. At that time they go to control and are interpreted and acted upon.

The computer will not take one single action without an instruction to do so. Normally, instructions are found in the computer's own memory. The switches and buttons on the console are only a very inefficient substitute for this normal mode of operation. Note also that instructions (the program) usually do *not* flow to output. The program remains in storage until erased or replaced by data or another program.

It is important to note that data and programs are both stored in the storage unit, represented by the electronic impulses contained there. Each machine represents human language symbols by a particular code. Instruction characters and data characters are both represented in the same code of electronic impulses. Either a data word or a program instruction is stored in each *word space* in the storage section. The computer can differentiate data words and program statements because, and only because, the *program* directs the computer from instruction to instruction. The instructions direct the machine where to obtain the data words to be processed. For this reason the storage is organized in an identifiable way and each (word or character) space is individually identified by an *address*. The address is like the number on a post office box; it serves to identify a specific part of the store so that it can be gone to (accessed). The sequence of the program is maintained by directing the program from location to location in the order in which the program steps are to be accomplished.

Computers as Data Processors

The electronic digital computer is easily recognized as a data processing system. Figure 8.2 illustrates the basic input-processor-output organization of the computer. The processor unit is called the *central processing unit*, or CPU. The CPU includes the control elements, the arithmetic-logic element, and the primary storage element. Data are entered through the input unit into the storage unit; taken from storage and processed in the arithmetic-logic unit in accordance with the procedures specified in the program as interpreted by the control unit; and then returned to the storage unit for transmittal to the output unit, where they are translated into usable output. Thus the computer has the standard input-processing-output form of any data processing system.

Modern computers are much more involved processors than the previous paragraph implies. Current computers have the capability to perform multiple functions at the same time. The easiest way to understand this capability is to trace the development of electronic computers and their use in data processing.

FIRST GENERATION

First-generation digital computers were much simpler than their current descendants. Based on vacuum tube technology, they were slow and bulky by today's standards. They also generated a great deal of heat and possessed limited capabilities. They had small storage capacity, with memories of 40,000 characters or less being quite common in so-called medium-sized machines. Calculations and memory accesses were timed in *milliseconds* (thousandths of a second).

The greatest limitation of these early computers as data processors was their extremely limited ability to perform more than one function at a time. When data were being entered into storage (read), no processing or outputting could take place. The machine was involved in either input, instruction interpretation (control), calculation, decision making, internal data transfer (processing), output, but not more than one of these functions at any instant in time. This lack of *simultaneity*, or *symbionts* (the ability to perform more than one function at the same time), caused underutilization of machine components, particularly the processing components (CPU). The CPU was idle because input and output units involve some mechanical devices; punched cards or magnetic tapes must be moved past the stationary (fixed) read heads, and paper must be fed through printers and characters printed on it. These mechanical operations make input-output processes much slower than the all-electronic CPU. It was not unusual to find the logic and control sections of first-generation computers idle over 90 percent of the time in data processing installations even while the machine was in use.

Another processing limitation associated with the first generation was the difficulty of programming. Programs were written primarily in *machine language*, that is, as a string of numbers. The programmer had to be aware of the idiosyncrasies of the machine being programmed in order to be at all efficient. Each program step accomplished only a single small action. For example, one instruction would load a number into an arithmetic register, a second instruction would add a second number to that same register, and a third instruction would store the sum back into memory. Another limitation of machine language programming for first-generation computers was that different machines, even from the same manufacturer, did not use the same language (instruction coding scheme).

The development of *assembly languages* eased the programming problem toward the end of the first-generation era. *Assemblers* are programs that allow the programmer to use mnemonics (usually alphabetics) to represent a machine's number codes. The assembler program reads these mnemonic codes and translates them to machine number codes. (A more complete discussion of programming languages can be found in Chapter 13, pp. 324–328.)

Early computers were developed to aid in solving scientific problems. Such problems most often involve small amounts of input data, complex manipulations of these data, and small amounts of output. Data processing problems, on the other hand, most often involve large amounts of input and output and minimal computations. Therefore the design of these early computers did not fit them for efficient data processing. Difficulties of programming, limited capacities, and lack of knowledge by users caused first-generation computers to be used primarily for accounting and clerical tasks, approaching one application (job) at a time. Thus accounts receivable billing might be programmed, then a sales analysis application that used the same input data might be developed separately. Management reports were not very sophisticated, usually duplicating the reports prepared by the replaced manual or electro-mechanical systems. Computer use was justified largely on the basis of clerical savings or the ability to expand the work load without additional expense.

SECOND GENERATION

Second-generation machines were less bulky and faster and generated less heat than their predecessors. These advantages were due to the replacement of the vacuum tube by the transistor. Speed of memory access and data transfer were measured in *microseconds* (millionths of a second). The varied storage media used in the first-generation machines were generally replaced by the magnetic core. The cores (tiny doughnut-shaped pieces of ferrite) were strung on intersecting wires in a three-dimensional grid. Core storage was faster and more reliable than earlier media.

The design of core storage units made the incorporation of additional storage units easier and permitted the development of *modular* memory design. The memory capacity of a computer could be expanded by plugging in additional *modules* of core. This modularity concept was also applied to *peripheral devices* (those devices not part of the CPU). For example, magnetic-tape drives came into common use; it became possible to add additional tape units to a machine (up to a limit, of course).

The computers also had increased capabilities. One of the more important was their ability to perform more than one function at the same time (*simultaneity*). The major design change instrumental in making both simultaneity and modularity in peripherals possible was the development of larger and more sophisticated *buffers* between the peripherals and the CPU. Figure 8.3 illustrates this concept.

FIGURE 8.3 *The buffering concept*

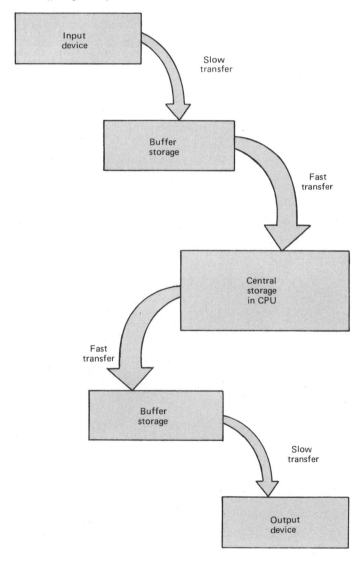

The buffer can be likened to a reservoir. Its purpose is to allow the slower electro-mechanical input or output device to keep up with the electronic CPU. This *reservoir* has a small inlet pipe from an input device or a small outlet pipe to an output device. The CPU connection, however, is a much larger pipe. The speed of transfer (*transfer rate*) between the reservoir and the CPU is much larger than the speed of transfer between the reservoir and the peripheral (input or output) device. Each reservoir is partly controlled by something other than the CPU. When used with input devices, the reservoir control is designed to attempt to run the input device continually in order to keep the reservoir completely filled. Whenever the CPU quits drawing from the reservoir and turns to computing or output, the slower input device has a chance to refill the reservoir. When the reservoir is used with an output device, an attempt is made to *empty* the reservoir. By continuing to run while the CPU is involved with input or processing, the output device has a better chance of keeping up with the central processor.

The buffering concept was important in developing modularity in peripherals. Device controllers incorporating buffer storage and control hardware were designed to control several input or output devices. Individual devices (magnetic-tape drives, card readers, line printers, and so on) could be added as required until the controller reached maximum capacity. As these control devices became more sophisticated, they took on the characteristics of small, special-purpose computers. In some cases, small general-purpose digital computers actually were adapted to this purpose, adding still greater flexibility to machine configuration possibilities. These advancements led eventually to the initial development of the multiprogrammed and time-shared computer toward the end of the second-generation era.

It was a natural development from simple buffering to more sophisticated independent device control, additional transfer circuits (*channels*) in and out of the CPU, and the ability to run peripheral input-output operations almost totally independently from the CPU. Once instituted, operations of peripherals in transferring data between peripheral devices (for example, from cards to magnetic tape or magnetic disk, from tape or disk to printer) could be continued to completion with no further attention from the CPU. Full development of this capacity did not take place until the third generation, however.

Software developments (programs and programming languages) during the second generation were as important as hardware developments. Compiler languages, first invented during the first generation, were the most important second-generation innovation in this area. *Compilers* are programs that allow the programmer to write in a *problem-oriented* language. The *source* program written in the special language is read as data by the compiler and compiled (translated) into an *object* program in the language of the machine being used. The two major compiler languages developed during this period are FORTRAN (*FOR*mula *TRAN*slator) for scientific programming and COBOL (*CO*mmon *B*usiness *O*riented *L*anguage) for business data processing. Computer manufacturers routinely began to market these compilers as part of computer systems during the second generation. These programming languages are described more fully in Chapter 13 (pages 324–328) and Chapter 14.

Special-purpose programs with wide general application were also developed during the second-generation era (for example, payroll and accounts receivable billing). *Utility programs* were developed to handle input and output tasks or to sort sets of data. A utility program could be used as a stand-alone program or incorporated as part of a larger program.

For larger computer systems, manufacturers offered *monitor* or *operating system* programs that allowed the computer to control its own work flow. Early monitors or operating systems simply accepted and queued up incoming jobs for processing, either in the order received or according to some simple priority scheme. Printing of output was similarly controlled. The most sophisticated of such systems joined two computers, with one as "master" and the other as "slave." The master controlled input and output devices and kept the operator informed of the slave machine's operations and the state of the job queue. The two machines usually shared a secondary storage device such as a large magnetic-disk file. The master loaded the shared storage with input jobs and directed the slave computer from job to job in the desired sequence. Output resulting from processing within the slave was similarly sent to the shared storage and then outputted through the appropriate device under control of the master computer. In their most sophisticated form the master-slave computers were merely different processors within a single machine, which was called a *multiple-processor machine*. As a result of the slave's being relieved of all administrative operations concerned with the operation of the ultimate input and output (I/O) devices, the workload taken care of by the slave was generally increased several times.

Data processing and information systems were affected by second-generation developments. The larger capacities, the greater flexibility of configuration, and the ability of the machine to control throughput sequence encouraged the development of integrated data processing systems and program sequences that automatically carried out *all* desired processing of a particular set of input data when it first entered the computer. Nevertheless, many second-generation business data processing installations continued to operate with the first generation's "input, then process, then output, one application at a time" philosophy. One reason was that most smaller second-generation computers did not incorporate many of the second-generation advances.

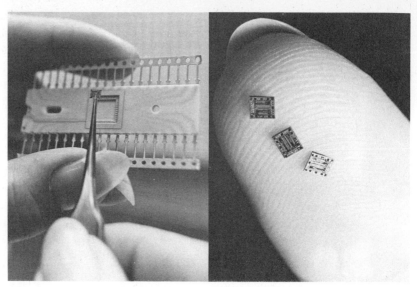

FIGURE 8.4   *Microelectronic circuits.* The small silicon chip held in the tweezers (left) and on the tip of a finger (right) typically contains 2,000 transistors that are equivalent to the number of active components found in 300 radios. (PHOTOS COURTESY OF NCR CORPORATION)

THIRD GENERATION

Third-generation machines introduced *miniaturization* and mass production of components (microcircuits); once again computers became smaller, faster, and more capable (see Figure 8.4). Third-generation machines are generally about *1 million times faster* than the first commercial computers in internal speed. Speeds in most of these machines are measured in *nanoseconds* (billionths of a second), and the very fastest operate in *picoseconds* (trillionths of a second). Such speeds are extremely difficult to comprehend. Figure 8.5 shows one attempt to make such speeds comprehensible.

Compatibility   In addition to microcircuitry, the third generation has brought "families" of computers with the ability to run the same machine language programs (*machine language compatibility*). This development is important in several ways. For the computer vendor it means greater customer loyalty. For the customer it means that a system can be expanded to a larger computer without extensive reprogramming. That is, since programs developed for a small machine (even in machine language) will run on a larger computer in the same family, capacity can be expanded merely by replacing the current computer with a larger version from the same family. Each family is a related set of computers offered by the same manufacturer.

In the computer, the basic operations can be done within the order of a

NANOSECOND

One thousandth of a millionth of a second.

Within the half second it takes this spilled coffee to reach the floor, a fairly large computer could —

(given the information in magnetic form)

Debit 2000 checks to 300 different bank accounts,

and *examine the electro-cardiograms of 100 patients and alert a physician to possible trouble,*

and *score 150,000 answers on 3000 examinations and evaluate the effectiveness of the questions,*

and *figure the payroll for a company with a thousand employees.*

and a few other chores.

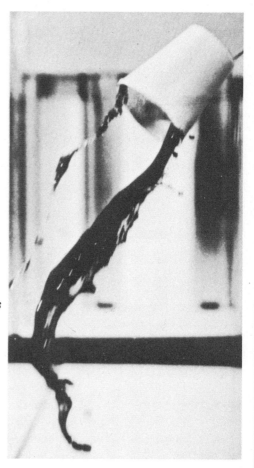

FIGURE 8.5   *An illustration of modern computer speeds.*   (PHOTO COURTESY OF IBM; DESIGN BY CHARLES EAMES)

Obviously, software compatibility downward cannot be guaranteed. A program that utilizes the full capacity of a larger computer will exceed the capacity of a smaller machine. Also, larger computers normally have a larger *instruction set* (a larger number of different machine language instructions). Compatibility also cannot be guaranteed on two computers of the same size from the same family if both machines do not have the same configuration. Thus a *disk-oriented* configuration of a computer cannot be replaced by a *tape-oriented* configuration of the same computer without reprogramming. Similarly, scientific problem-solving programs written for a configuration featuring double-precision arithmetic may not operate correctly, if at all, on a configuration without the double-precision feature. However, even with these kinds of limitations, machine language compatibility between machines in the same family has substantially reduced the need for reprogramming when going to a larger system.

Hardware *modularity* has continued to develop. In fact, it has led to *hardware compatibility*, which allows peripherals and secondary storage devices to be interchanged among machines. In many instances, the CPU and the peripherals used in a single computer configuration have been obtained from several different manufacturers.

Simultaneity, or *symbionts*, have continued to develop. Peripheral and I/O tasks (printing, data transfer among secondary storage devices, data input) for a number of jobs can be handled simultaneously. Device controllers incorporate small, special-purpose computers (microprocessors are described in Chapter 11). *Multiprocessor* machines are also more prevalent. Multiple processors are really two or more computers tied together to provide duplication of major CPU elements. Through these processes, it is now possible for many different tasks to be carried out at one time on one computer configuration.

Multiprogramming and Timesharing The further development of simultaneity and hardware modularity and compatibility in the third generation has led to the full development of multiprogramming and timesharing. Although timesharing can be considered a special form of multiprogramming, the difference between them has great significance.

In *multiprogramming*, the computer operates on job streams from several input devices simultaneously. The computer's operation is controlled by a sophisticated program called an *executive program*. The multiprogramming executive causes the machine to input from the several sources simultaneously, placing unprocessed data streams (which may be programs and associated data) in temporary secondary storage until the *first* job received has been processed. The second job is then processed. Note that the second job may use a different program than the one used by the first job. Control information, supplied by the user or the input device, will cause the new program to be brought into primary storage (to be *rolled into* the CPU) to process the associated data. The CPU is automatically moved from job to job; the appropriate processing programs are rolled into primary memory and given temporary control of the machine as required for processing the data. No program, however, is allowed to override or replace the executive, which retains ultimate control at all times. It is important to note that in multiprogramming each job is retained in the CPU in its processing phase until that processing phase is completed. Work starts on the second job only if the first job is *interrupted* for output or for more input. Whenever such an *I/O interrupt* occurs, the CPU is immediately shifted to whatever job is next in line in the processing queue.

Timesharing is a special form of multiprogramming in which the time each job is allowed to spend in the CPU (processing) on any one turn is limited. If an I/O interrupt has not been generated when that job has been in the CPU for this specified length of time, an interrupt is generated by the executive and the job is rolled out onto secondary storage to allow the next job waiting in the queue access to the CPU. The provision of the *time slice* (the limit on time in the CPU at each turn) is the difference between a timesharing executive and a standard multiprogramming executive.

The difference between multiprogramming and timesharing is illustrated in Figure 8.6. Note that both multiprogramming and timesharing attempt to keep the CPU busy at all times. In multiprogramming, however, each job completes a processing cycle before relinquishing the CPU. In timesharing, no job is allowed to hold the CPU for a longer period than the *time slice* each time that job acquires the CPU. The difference in the method of allocating CPU time results in different completion times for some units of the various jobs. For example, the first unit of job number 2 finishes later under timesharing than under standard multiprogramming. Jobs 3 and 4, however, are given more time in the CPU under timesharing than in standard multiprogramming. Job number 1 is allowed less time in the CPU under timesharing. Because of the greater decision requirements, a timesharing executive is more complex and more costly than a standard multiprogramming executive.

Figure 8.7 illustrates a hypothetical timesharing configuration. The several users, each pursuing his or her own interests, would have simultaneous access to the computer.

The differences between multiprogramming and timesharing are important to the design of data processing systems. Multiprogramming is cheaper and the obvious choice when many jobs, each requiring very little in the way of calculation and comparison, are to be run online. If the online job stream contains some jobs with lots of computation in them (these jobs are

MULTIPROGRAMMING

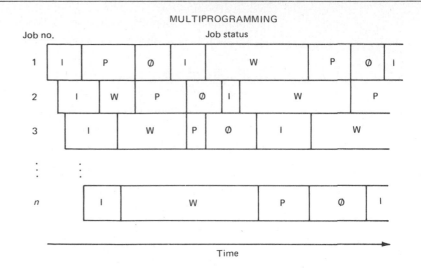

TIMESHARING

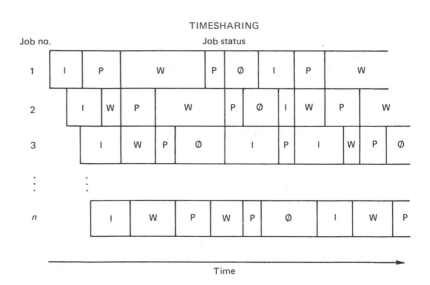

Legend: I = Input; P = Process; Ø = Øutput; W = Wait

FIGURE 8.6   *Graphic representation of multiprogramming and timesharing*

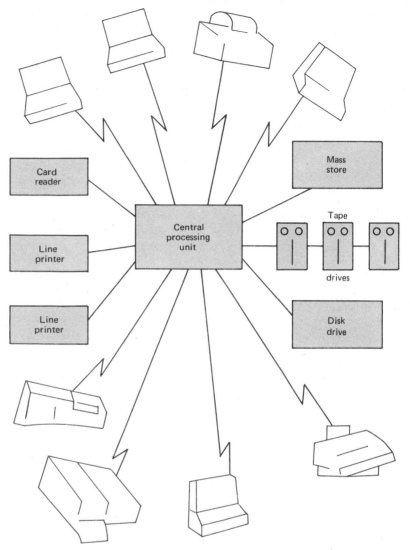

FIGURE 8.7   *A timesharing configuration*

called *compute-bound*), then timesharing is required. Timesharing has been widely used in educational institutions and in service bureaus providing online service to all who desire it. Multiprogramming is more widely used in administrative data processing in which each individual transaction (job) requires few calculations and comparisons before being outputted or before additional data are inputted.

Multiprogramming should not be confused with *multiprocessing*. In multiprogramming only one processing unit normally is involved. Two or more processing units are involved in multiprocessing systems. The processing units usually share other system elements (storage and I/O) and may be operating independently on different programs at the same moment in time. In multiprogrammed systems the software allows the single CPU to be used interchangeably by different programs.

Simultaneity and Modularity   The full development of multiprogramming and timesharing has been possible only because of the further development of simultaneity and modularity. Computers can now run numerous input and output units simultaneously with internal processing (calculations and comparisons). Also, secondary storage devices of great capacity have been developed. Removable disk packs with the capacity to hold up to 100 million characters per pack and large nonremovable disk units holding several times that amount have been developed. Large drum memories have also been widely used. Magnetic-tape drives have been increased in speed and designed to put up to 6,250 characters on 1 inch of tape. This same data density is available on disks also. Dependability and reliability of all these units have been enhanced by solid-state circuitry and other space age technology.

Hardware modularity and compatibility have also advanced to such an extent that computer systems actually can be purchased one functional unit at a time from different manufacturers to obtain whatever total configuration is suited to a specific data processing job. Peripheral devices (those outside the CPU) have been made *plug-to-plug* compatible with popular computers by other manufacturers. Costs have tended to decline because of increased competition and more suppliers.

Teleprocessing and Networks   As a complement to multiprogramming and timesharing, telephonic, microwave, and satellite transmission of data and programs (*teleprocessing*) has developed. Users dispersed over large geographic areas, even on different continents, are able to share the computational and decision-making power of a single computer. *Networks* of computers are being developed so that users can share computing power with one another. Automatic access to the computing power of large computers is provided to users possessing only a small computer by hooking the small computer into a network with a large computer. Businesses are using small computers as *preprocessors* and *data acquisition units* for larger machines that may be located anywhere on the earth.

Figure 8.8 shows a network as proposed for the educational processing function of all schools in a single state. The state contains two major universities and several smaller units in its university system. The two largest institutions and the office of education in the state capital each possess a

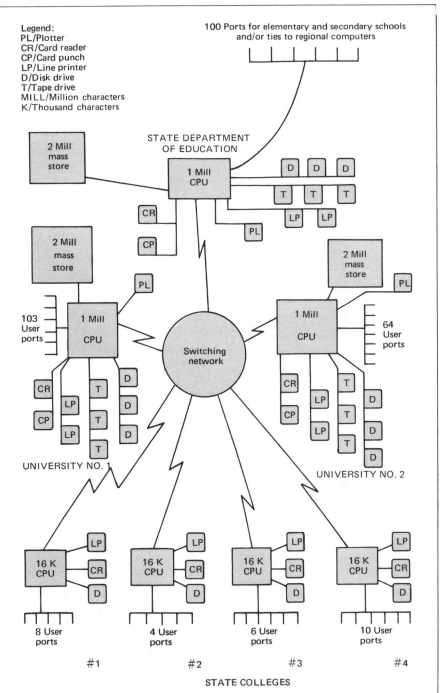

Legend:
PL/Plotter
CR/Card reader
CP/Card punch
LP/Line printer
D/Disk drive
T/Tape drive
MILL/Million characters
K/Thousand characters

100 Ports for elementary and secondary schools and/or ties to regional computers

STATE DEPARTMENT OF EDUCATION

2 Mill mass store

1 Mill CPU

D D D
T T T
LP LP
PL

CR

CP

2 Mill mass store

PL

103 User ports

1 Mill CPU

CR
CP
LP
LP
T
T
T
D
D
D

UNIVERSITY NO. 1

Switching network

2 Mill mass store

PL

1 Mill CPU

64 User ports

CR
CP
LP
LP
T
T
T
T
D
D
D
D

UNIVERSITY NO. 2

16 K CPU
LP
CR
D
8 User ports
#1

16 K CPU
LP
CR
D
4 User ports
#2

16 K CPU
LP
CR
D
6 User ports
#3

16 K CPU
LP
CR
D
10 User ports
#4

STATE COLLEGES

FIGURE 8.8   *A computer sharing network*

large computer. Each of the smaller institutions possesses a smaller computer. All the computers would be tied together by a network of telephone lines. The power of the big computers would thus be made available to all the institutions of higher learning in the state. In addition, direct transmission of large masses of data between computers in the system would be possible. Research, educational, and administrative functions within the system could be enhanced and coordinated. Excess computing power at the larger installations would be made available to users located at the small installations. This system design is a realistic goal attainable with current technology. Such networks are already operating in other areas.

Software Developments The changes in third-generation hardware have been paralleled by software (programming) developments. Control programs (executives) are at least as important as hardware in determining operating capabilities of modern machines. Multiprogramming, timesharing, and network systems could not function at their current levels of sophistication without appropriate software. Developments such as simultaneity of up to seventeen activities have been possible only because of the joint development of hardware and software features. Hardware features such as read-only memories and automatic address modification registers have been made useful by parallel software developments.

Software developments of importance in multiprogramming and timesharing are the concepts of *automatic overlay*, *paging*, and *virtual memory*. *Automatic overlay* is a process whereby a large program is automatically divided into two or more sections each of which does not exceed the capacity of primary memory. Each section is brought into primary storage as needed, *overlaying* (replacing) any section already in primary memory. *Paging* is a more sophisticated version of this process in which a program is divided into smaller sections called *pages*. Each page of the program is resident in primary memory only while it is being used. Pages can be rolled in and out of primary storage in any sequence, individually. *Virtual memory* is a development based on these concepts whereby a program can be of any size so long as it does not exceed the total online storage capacity of the entire configuration. Data being operated upon by the program are treated in a similar fashion. Thus the primary storage capacity of the machine is made to seem unlimited (virtual) to the user. Although explicit overlaying was common during the first and second generations, with users breaking large jobs into manageable pieces, the capacity of the primary memory remained an effective limit on operations. Virtual memory removes this limit. It is, however, a trade-off, since it adds to processing time because of the necessity for additional nonproductive CPU time to be used in selecting, rolling in, and rolling out appropriate program pages.

Additional higher-level languages have also been developed. BASIC (Beginners All-Purpose Symbolic Instruction Code) and APL (A Programming Language) are the most popular languages developed as timesharing or terminal-user-oriented languages. Several languages have been developed in an attempt to combine the functions of COBOL and FORTRAN in a single language. PL/1 (Programming Language 1) is the most successful and widely used. Special-purpose languages continue to be developed to make it easier to use the computer as a simulator and to manage large electronic data bases (see Chapter 14.)

I/O Developments Other developments of interest relate to faster input-output techniques. *Optical character recognition* (OCR) equipment was available in the second generation but not heavily used. It has increased in reliability and diversity and decreased in price. Microfilm is being increasingly used for both input and output. It seems particularly useful as a large-capacity, low-cost, easily retrievable storage medium for computer-organized data. *Special recorders* of many types are in use. *Terminals* have increased in versatility and speed and decreased in cost. *Incremental recorders* for magnetic tape and disk have been combined with minicomputers and microprocessors to produce programmable key-driven data input systems that speed input. They also reduce errors and increase versatility over the familiar key-driven card punch. (Additional details concerning these developments are contained in Chapter 9.)

Summary Data processing has changed in organization and scope as available hardware and software have changed during the third generation. On-line, quick-response systems have become more common. So-called management information systems featuring online storage of management information and terminal access for managers are not uncommon. Teletype, typewriter, and cathode ray tube terminals, and other special-purpose devices serve increasingly for data input. Multiprogrammed and timeshared systems are prevalent on medium to large computer systems. Telecommunications are a common feature in data processing systems of national and multinational firms. Service bureaus selling computer time often involve telecommunications, multiprogramming, and timesharing. Minicomputers and microcomputers are being used increasingly as preprocessors and data gathering devices, often in networks featuring telecommunications. These developments are more fully covered in Chapter 11.

The emphasis in the design of data processing systems is shifting to supplying management planning and control requirements while carrying out custodial processing. Greater integration of data processing with decreased human involvement is occurring.

FOURTH GENERATION

As indicated in Figure 8.9, where the discussion of computer generations is summarized, this writer finds it impossible to identify clearly the dividing line between the third and fourth generations of computers. It seems computers have been evolving to a higher-order machine with no dramatic or major change in hardware. For example, a common division has been to label as third generation those computers featuring large scale integration. Fourth generation computers feature *very* large scale integration. This division is based only on the degree of miniaturization of hardware components.

FIGURE 8.9   *Characteristics of the computer generations*

Characteristic	Computer generation			
	First 1946–1960	*Second* 1960–1964	*Third* 1964–????	*Fourth* (?) 19??–
Major circuit component	Vacuum tubes	Transistors	Microcircuits	Miniaturized microcircuits
Speed	Milliseconds	Microseconds	Nanoseconds	Picoseconds
Major storage components:				
CPU	Drums Special devices	Core	Core	Core Microcircuits
Online secondary	Very little	Tape	Disk Drums	Disk Core
Offline	Punched cards	Tape	Tape and disk	Disk and tape
Major input	Punched cards	Punched cards Magnetic tape	Incremental recorders (tape, disk) Cards	Incremental recorders Terminals Special devices
Major output	Punched cards	Line printers	Line printers	Line printers CRT Microfilm
Operating control	Manual	Queue monitor (software)	Executive (software)	Executive (software and hardware)
Major programming languages	Machine	Symbolic assemblers and compilers	Symbolic compilers	Improved compilers Data base management languages
Modularity	None	Limited	Extensive	Very extensive
Simultaneity	None	Limited	Extensive	Very extensive
Multiprogramming	None	Limited	Extensive	Routine mode
Timesharing	None	Almost none	Available	Routine mode

On this basis, most large systems are a mixture of third and fourth generation. Only a few microcomputers and minicomputers are truly fourth generation. Most of the "new" hardware labeled as "fourth generation" by some users and some vendors has been around at least since the onset of the third generation as it is defined here. The latest hardware-software developments (for example, virtual memory) have been alive and well for over a decade. For these reasons, the features of current computers and their use, which some call fourth generation, have been included in the discussion of the third generation.

Speculation about major changes in computer hardware to come in the near future are difficult. For example, laser and light memories involving film technology have been touted as the next wave for some time. Implementation dates have come and gone several times with announcement of various degrees of failure in reaching full maturity of the processes. We leave it to the future to judge what the fourth (or fifth) generation computer is or will be.

Can Computers Think?

A common fallacy of the popular press and other entertainment media is to describe the computer as a giant brain and impute human impulses to it. It is blamed for erroneous utility bills, lost reservations, and erroneous paychecks. It is billed as a super checker player that will some day rise to chess champion of the world. None of these views is correct.

A close examination of the definitions found in this chapter and a close reading of the discussion immediately above should lead to the conclusion that the computer is a wonderful machine, but it is still only a *machine*. The computer is a machine that manipulates symbols. It manipulates those symbols within a framework of the general rules of Boolean algebra and the specific framework of a set of instructions prepared by some human. A computer can process data more rapidly, more accurately, and more tirelessly than can a human being. However, the rules it uses in this processing are supplied by a human being. The logic it follows is human logic, and the computer cannot improve upon it.

The argument in the above paragraph does not mean that a computer cannot "learn" to improve on its ability to perform some task. For example, Dr. Samuels, an IBM employee, has developed and programmed into a computer a method for learning to play checkers. The computer, using this program, now plays a better game of checkers than Dr. Samuels. In reality, Dr. Samuels has figured out how to become a better checker player and has "taught" the method to a computer, and the computer is doing what it has been taught. It represents an improved version of Dr. Samuels.

The above remarks lead to one and only one conclusion. Only to the extent that we can define thinking as a step-by-step process can the computer be made to "think." However, we must recognize that the computer is a much better manipulator of symbols than humans. If a human can define tasks involving only symbol manipulation, the computer can perform them. In this way, the computer can extend the power of human intellect. Humans can often define symbol manipulation processes that they cannot carry through either in a reasonable time or with sufficient accuracy. Without the computer to carry out the necessary voluminous calculations, we could not adequately plan a trip to another planet. Without the computer to swiftly evaluate the progress of the trip, we could not carry out such a trip after it was planned.

Creative thinking is more difficult to define. Computers have been programmed to "draw" pictures by random selection of lines or colors subject to broad limits about which combinations of the lines and colors could be accepted. Similarly, computers have been programmed to "write" stories and plays by randomly selecting lines of dialogue and action within the constraints imposed by a story line. If the accidental production of acceptable results is creativity, then computers are creative. Again, however, they only manipulate symbols as instructed by some person. The only creative element is the ability to make (within limits) a random choice of symbols.

In summary, a computer can think in only a limited sense because humans understand the process of thinking to only a limited degree. However, to the extent that thinking can be defined as an explicit manipulation of symbols, computers can be made to think. Therefore, to the extent that thinking can be defined as the rational manipulation of symbols for problem solving, computers can think.

Summary

A computer is a symbol-manipulating machine that humans can control. It can only add, subtract, multiply, divide, and compare symbols in accordance with a sequence of instructions developed by some human being. It is a wondrous machine, nonetheless, performing its limited feats tirelessly at phenomenal speed. Also, it almost never makes a mistake in its performance of the manipulations described by the instructions.

As a data processing tool the computer consists of functional components that perform the functions of input, storage, logic, control, and output. The machine elements performing these functions come in a variety of forms. Computer configurations are put together from functional modules. Modern third-generation electronic data processing configurations involve special input devices, teleprocessing, multiprogramming, and timesharing.

Questions

1. Define the following as briefly as possible and then use a short paragraph to clarify each definition.

   a. Peripheral device
   b. Simultaneity
   c. Modularity (hardware)
   d. Buffering
   e. Symbionts
   f. Multiprocessor
   g. Transfer rate
   h. Nanosecond
   i. Picosecond
   j. Time slice
   k. Millisecond
   l. Microsecond
   m. Computer family
   n. I/O interrupt
   o. Virtual memory
   p. Multiprogramming
   q. Timesharing

2. List the five major functional components of a computer and define the function performed by each.

3. Why is the binary number system most often used as the basis for the internal symbol set of a computer?

4. What is the stored-program concept?

5. Both data and program instructions are placed in the storage component of a computer. How are they differentiated by the computer?

6. Can a computer think? Explain.

7. What is an automatic electronic digital computer? Try to put the answer in your own words even if it requires several sentences.

8. When inputted through the input unit, where do —
   a. the instructions go?
   b. the data go?

9. What is the CPU? What jobs does it carry out?

10. Would a nonremovable disk unit added to increase storage capacity of a computer be considered part of the CPU? Explain.

11. Turn to Figure 1.1 on page 6 and prepare a parallel diagram of a computer. What are the three corresponding sections?

12. What is computer hardware?

13. What is computer software?

14. What is hardware compatibility of computers?

15. What is software compatibility of computers?

16. Define each type of program listed below:

    a. Source
    b. Object
    c. Machine language
    d. Assembler
    e. Compiler
    f. Monitor
    g. Executive
    h. Special purpose
    i. Utility

17. What is the difference between standard multiprogramming and timesharing? Explain.

18. When would standard multiprogramming be preferable to timesharing? Why?

19. In what sense can we say that the computer is an intelligence amplifier?
20. Refer to Figure 8.1, page 201. Identify the advantages and disadvantages in using each of the three codes presented there.
21. What are the major effects of each computer generation on business data processing?
22. One major criticism of computerized processing systems is their inflexibility.
    a. What characteristics of computers would tend to cause such inflexibility? Are these characteristics being changed?
    b. What might be done to make computerized systems more flexible and thus more responsive to humans? Be specific.
23. What would be the advantages and disadvantages of an extremely fast but unchangeable memory? (Such memories do exist and are used in modern computers.)
24. Contact a local computer vendor and collect some brochures describing one or more computer systems. Identify the major components of each system. You will notice that most modern systems can be configured with several different sets of functional elements. Compare the functional capacities for different systems and the capabilities of the different configurations that result. Answer the following specific questions for each computer system for which you have brochures.
    a. How many different input devices may be used?
    b. What range of primary memory sizes is available?
    c. How many different output devices may be used?
    d. Can this computer be used in a (1) Timesharing system? (2) Network?

Nine

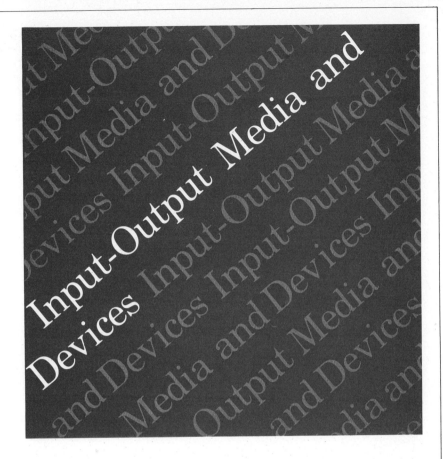

An important function in using computers is communicating with the machine. As indicated in Chapter 8, the input and output elements provide communication between the person and the machine, translating the human language into the electronic impulses of the machine, and vice versa.

This chapter will begin by identifying the types of media and devices used for inputting to and outputting from computer systems. The general criteria for comparing data processing media and devices will be developed for computer input devices, and the devices will be compared within and among types. The process will then be repeated for output media and devices. A final section will discuss the problems of balancing input-output systems.

Types of Media and Devices

INPUT

Translating human symbols and language into the symbols and language of the machine is accomplished in one of four ways:

1. *Key transcription* to a machine-sensible medium is the most widely used input process.

   The most important media involved are punched cards, magnetic tapes, magnetic disks, and punched paper tape.

2. *By-product recording* to a machine-sensible medium is gaining rapidly in popularity.

   The most widely used media are magnetic tape cassettes, floppy diskettes, punched cards, punched paper tape, and magnetic tape. These media are prepared as a secondary operation while the recording device is carrying out some primary processing operation.

3. *Character reading* of human-sensible documents allows continued use of familiar methods and represents an adaptation of machines to human procedures. The use of this method is rapidly expanding.

   These techniques vary in sophistication from reading magnetic-ink characters to optical reading of ordinary appearing paper documents prepared on typewriters or handwritten.

4. *Direct-entry devices* include simple typewriterlike terminals, display devices with a keyboard, devices incorporating various forms of optical readers, display devices capable of accepting input from light pens, and voice recognition devices.

   A large proportion of the direct-entry devices are found on multiprogrammed and timeshared computer systems, where they are often used for output as well as input. The newest direct-entry device is voice input.

   Figure 9.1 gives a general overview of computer input media and devices. The reader should spend a few minutes studying it.

OUTPUT

Output from computerized data processing systems must eventually be recognizable and usable by people. The devices that have been developed to present data and output to people can be grouped into four general types: *typewriter and typewriterlike devices, printers, visual displays,* and *voice response.*

   An overview of computer output media and devices is presented in Figure 9.2. The reader should spend a few minutes studying Figure 9.2 to get a

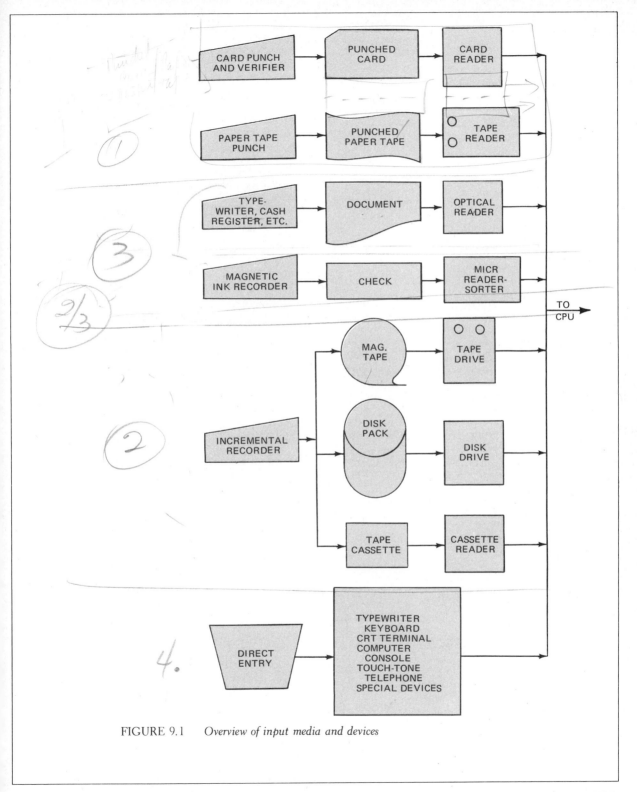

FIGURE 9.1   *Overview of input media and devices*

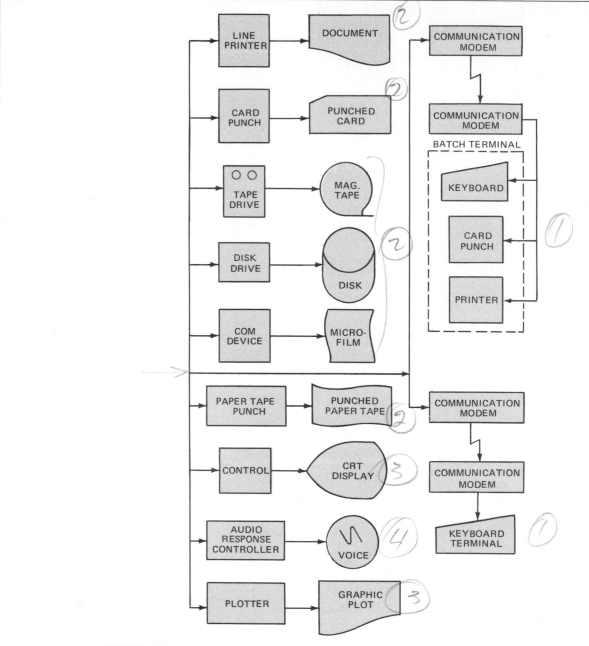

FIGURE 9.2   *Overview of output media and devices*

good idea of how these processes are carried out. The communication *modems* (*MOdulator-DEModulators*) shown are devices that translate electronic impulses from within the computer or the keying device to sound impulses to be carried over telephone lines and also translate the audio impulses back to data impulses at the other end.

INPUT-OUTPUT

Most dual-purpose input-output media and devices have already been mentioned. Dual-purpose devices include *typewriter and typewriterlike terminals, CRT keyboard terminals, intelligent terminals,* and *batch terminals.*

Characteristics of Input Media and Devices

Factors or characteristics critical to data processing medium and device selection are *speed, capacity, expandability, bulk, access mode, reliability,* and *ease of use.* (See Chapter 6 for a more detailed discussion of these factors.) When applied to computer input media and devices, these translate as follows:

1. *Speed* is —
   a. *Preparation speed* in characters per unit of time in preparing the medium for input.
   b. *Transfer rate,* the characters per second or lines per minute at which data can be moved into and out of the computer by the device. This includes *access time* on media that can be used as online storage.

2. *Capacity* is the ability of a medium to hold data measured in characters per unit of length. It still must be related to expandability and bulk.

3. *Expandability* is the ease with which the capacity of the device can be expanded by adding more units or substituting larger units.

4. *Bulk* is a loose, relative measure of physical-space requirements for the medium and the device.

5. *Access mode* is the *order* in which individual data elements can be retrieved from the medium when the medium is used as an online storage and/or input device.

6. *Reliability* is —
   a. *Accuracy,* the rate at which errors are made in preparing the media or transferring the data into the computer at reasonable levels of efficiency. Because of lack of firm data, this item does not appear in Figure 9.3 but is confined to the text discussion.
   b. *Mechanical reliability,* the ability of the device to operate at the rated capacity without a physical malfunction or breakdown.

FIGURE 9.3

Major characteristics, key transcription media and devices

Characteristic	Unit of measure	Punched card	Paper tape	Magnetic reel	Tape cassette	Magnetic-disk pack	Floppy diskettes
Speed:							
Preparation	Characters per hour	10,000 to 15,000	10,000 to 15,000	12,000 to 18,000	8,000 to 16,000	15,000 to 18,000	15,000 to 18,000
Transfer rate	Characters per second	300 to 240,000	15 to 1,000	15,000 to 320,000	20,000 to 60,000	100,000 to 1.5 million	100,000 to 1.5 million
Capacity:							
Record length	Characters	80 or 96	Unlimited	Unlimited	80 to 720	1 to 1,000	1 to 1,000
Unit capacity	Characters	80 or 96	360,000	1 million to 45 million	23,000 to 720,000	1 million to 100 million	256,000 to 1.2 million
Bulk:							
Density	Characters per inch	8	10	200 to 3,200	200 to 800	800 to 6,250	1,600 to 6,250
Access mode		Modified random	Serial	Serial	Serial	Direct	Direct
Ease of use:							
Special equipment		Keypunch Verifier Reader	Keypunch Reader	Incremental recorder Tape drive	Cassette recorder Cassette reader	Key-to-disk system Disk drive	Key-to-diskette system Diskette drive
Trained operators		Yes	Typist	Yes	Yes	Yes	Yes
Special handling		Easy to damage Humidity control	Easy to tear	Easy to damage Environmental control	Environmental control	Dust-free	Minimal
Reusable		No	No	Yes	Yes	Yes	Yes
Humanly readable		When interpreted	With difficulty	No	No	No	No

7. *Ease of use* is the need for —

    a. *Special equipment* to prepare or input the medium.

    b. *Trained operators* to enter data either onto the translation medium or into the computer.

    c. *Special handling* of the medium on which data are carried or displayed.

    d. *Reusability* (permanence) of the medium.

    e. *Human readability* of the medium.

CHARACTERISTICS OF KEY TRANSCRIPTION MEDIA AND DEVICES

The common key transcription media and the associated devices are:

Medium	Device
Punched card	Card key punch, key verifier, and card reader
Punched paper tape	Paper tape punch and tape reader
Magnetic tape	Incremental tape recorder (may be recorded on reel or cassette) and tape drive
Magnetic-disk pack	Incremental disk recorder (usually in a system involving multiple key stations) and disk drive

A summary comparison of key transcription media and devices is presented in Figure 9.3. The criteria of reliability and expandability have been omitted from Figure 9.3. Available data for the broad groupings used here do not indicate any great differences. Differences in mechanical reliability do differ for machines from different suppliers. These differences change frequently and should be taken into account whenever a system is being designed. Differences also exist by manufacturer and computer model in the number of media readers (by type and in total) that may be attached to a system. These figures also change frequently.

Punched Card The oldest of the key transcription medium and one familiar to most people is the eighty-column punch card. Other forms are a smaller ninety-six–column card and many specially designed cards of various sizes. Each card is a record, allowing easy addition, deletion, rearrangement, or replacement of individual records. Cards are easily read by humans when "interpreted" (contents printed along the edge of the card). Disadvantages are the limited record size unless records extend over more than one card, the bulkiness of cards as a storage medium, the need for a low-humidity environment to prevent the cards from absorbing moisture and swelling, and that a card cannot be corrected or reused in another operation. Cards were the most common form of data entry for computer processing, although they are declining rapidly in popularity.

Punched cards are prepared on a machine called the *card key punch*. The correctness of the initial keying is checked by having a second operator key the same data against the card on a machine called a *verifier*. The latest card punch machines perform both functions, punching and verifying.

Punched cards are read into the computer through a machine called a *card reader*. Older readers sensed holes with electrically sensitized brushes and moved the card with mechanical devices. The new high-speed readers sense the holes optically by means of photoelectric processes and move the cards in part with pneumatic (air) devices.

When all costs are considered (preparation, handling, storage, and reading time) the punch card must be considered a high-cost data entry medium on modern medium- and large-scale computer systems. Cards are economical only in low-volume operations when only a few key punches are needed or in operations using the card as a turnaround document.

Punched Paper Tape Standard punched paper tape is ¾ inch wide. Data bits (1's) are represented by holes in the tape. Holes are punched along five, seven, or nine *channels* (seven is the most common) running parallel to the tape edges. A character is represented by the combination of holes (1's) and spaces (0's) occurring across the seven channels at a particular point on the tape. Normal density is ten characters per inch. Punched paper tape has been used as a communication medium just about as long as cards. The cost of paper tape is only about one-third of the cost of a punched card on a per character basis. Nevertheless, tape is not nearly so widely used as cards, apparently because it is a slow, serial-access medium, is hard to verify after punching, and requires careful handling to prevent damage. Corrections and insertions are difficult, although record lengths are unlimited.

Paper tape *punches* and *readers* are light and relatively inexpensive. They are normally marketed as part of a unit including a typewriter producing a typed copy of all data punched or read. Several early minicomputer systems did use paper tape as their standard input-output medium. The vendors of those systems offered special high-speed readers using optical sensing. Punched paper tape has been widely used as an input medium for telecommunication systems.

Magnetic Tape Standard magnetic tape for use with computers is usually ¾-inch–wide mylar tape coated on one surface with a magnetizable substance. Widths of ½ inch and 1 inch are also used. Bits are recorded in channels running along the length of the tape. Older tapes had seven channels; newer tapes carry nine. Characters are represented by the combination of bits occurring across all channels at a particular location. Common character densities are 200, 556, 800, 1,600, 3,200, and 6,250 characters per inch. Tapes are read at speeds from 36 to over 200 inches per second. Their most common length is 2,400 feet. Pictures of a tape and a tape drive are shown in Figure 9.4.

Key-to-Tape Systems The first key-to-tape system was a buffered stand-alone unit consisting of a keyboard and a computer-compatible incremental tape drive (see Figure 6.4). The breakthrough was the ability to write on the tape *incrementally*, a few characters (in this case eighty) at a time. Tapes from several recorders were consolidated on a common tape by a "pooling" device before processing. Today systems involving minicomputer controllers with small memories supervising from one to sixty-four individual key stations are available. Other systems record on tape cassettes. The tape cassettes are usually translated to computer-compatible magnetic tape for input to the computer.

The presence of punched cards has been so ubiquitous that early key-to-tape devices recorded data on the tape in a card format of eighty characters at a time. This limited-record-size concept still exists, particularly on cassette recorders. This is partly a reflection of the fact that input data are temporarily stored in a register before being written to the tape. Record size is limited to register size by the automatic insertion of end-of-record characters by the machine.

The use of incremental tape recorders is rapidly expanding the use of magnetic tape as a transcription medium. The cassette tapes, particularly, are being increasingly seen in point-of-action offline data capture systems. Key entry of data to magnetic tapes is generally faster than entry to cards. Definitive, firm data are not available; but statements by qualified experts in industry publications indicate that average entry speeds are at least 20 percent higher. This increase in entry speed is gained from the lack of media handling and the larger number of selectable stored-record formats available. Several systems now allow key verification of input from a second keying station immediately after the data are entered. In some multiple-station installations, the supervisory station can create formats while the other stations are keying data. Thus formats for the next jobs to be keyed can be ready and waiting when the first jobs are completed. Data from individual stations can be automatically merged in preparation for computer input. Batch control counts and totals can be automatically prepared and inserted on many systems.

In general, the advantages of magnetic tape as an entry medium are that there is no natural limit to the record length, the tape has a very large capacity, and transfer rates are high. Disadvantages of magnetic tape are its

FIGURE 9.4 *Magnetic-tape drives*. The smaller "Dec-Tape" is used mostly with minicomputers. The larger drive reads and writes on longer reels of standard multichannel tape. (PHOTOS COURTESY OF DIGITAL EQUIPMENT CORPORATION)

sequential-access characteristics, which make rearrangement or insertion of records difficult, and the need for careful handling and storage. Tapes are easily erased and must not be handled roughly. Tape edges can be bent or creased and bits rearranged by careless handling. Tapes are also damaged by high humidity and by dirt, grease, or oil coming into contact with the magnetized surface. Tapes have a long life if periodically cleaned and reconditioned and handled and stored properly.

Tapes themselves are not expensive, commonly costing twelve dollars to eighty dollars a reel, but a *tape drive* is required to write and to read them. Drives are commonly connected to the computer through a *controller*, a buffering device that usually handles two to eight or sixteen individual drives. The prices of drives and controllers vary widely, and price increases with the complexity of the device. Alternatives that add to tape drive costs include echo read-and-compare for automatic error detection while writing, automatic reread if an error is detected while reading, reading in either direction on the tape, and increased transfer rate.

Magnetic-Disk Pack Magnetic disks are made of thin metal coated with a magnetizable material. Data are recorded as magnetic spots in a serial-bit structure along circular tracks (rings) around the magnetic surface. Bits are less densely packed on the outer tracks, so that each track contains the same number of bits. Characters are often represented as combinations of the single bits stored in exactly the same position on each magnetizable disk surface in the stack of disks. These sets of vertical bits are referred to as disk *cylinders* (see Figure 9.5). The outside surfaces of the disk pack are not used to record data. Access arms mounted in the drive mechanism move in and

FIGURE 9.5   *Disks and disk drives.* Each drive holds a pack with a capacity of 29.2 million bytes. Average seek time is thirty-eight milliseconds. (PHOTOS COURTESY OF HONEYWELL INFORMATION SYSTEMS)

out between the magnetized surfaces and carry the read-write heads to the various tracks. Data are addressed by cylinder number or by surface, track number, and location along the track. The disk pack is placed on a drive spindle, which spins it at a high rate of speed. The read-write heads are then inserted to pick up (read) or place (write) data at the proper locations as the heads are moved from track to track by the access arms, and the disk surfaces revolve past them.

Key-to-disk devices are mostly multiple-station systems, although stand-alone key-to-disk devices are available. One such system is shown in Figure 9.6. The disk devices are organized much like the key-to-tape systems described above. Standard key-to-disk systems are competitive with card key punches at volumes requiring six to eight card punch machines.

The newest key-to-disk system involves a so-called floppy disk and is

FIGURE 9.6   *Key-to-disk data entry system.* Pertec's PCC 1800 large-scale system accepts input to disk from up to sixty-four terminals. (PHOTO COURTESY OF PERTEC COMPUTER CORPORATION)

becoming common as a single-unit installation. The floppy disk is made of mylar, without the metal core, and is much cheaper. These disks are also being used as secondary storage in minicomputer-centered business systems.

The newest floppy is the floppy diskette. Individually packaged disks are about 6 inches in diameter and store .25 to 1.2 million characters. Diskettes cost $3 to $8 each, depending primarily on their capacity. The drive is also relatively inexpensive and diskettes are increasingly used as online/offline storage media on microcomputer and minicomputer systems. Key to diskette recorders are available to prepare input.

In general, disks are one of the most popular general-purpose random-access devices. Disk packs are widely used to provide direct-access storage in business data processing. This allows selective update of individual records in a file. Transactions data can be passed against a sequentially or randomly ordered file without being ordered in the same fashion.

Drives are available that can hold from one to eight accessible disk packs at one time, giving direct access to as many as 800 million characters online at one time. Switching one disk for another on the drive is simple, requiring less than one minute.

Disks are bulkier than magnetic tapes, although much less bulky than cards. Also, normal tape processing procedures involve the creation of a new tape file, leaving the old file intact to provide reference or system backup; in disk processing, however, the new file is created by changing the data on the existing disk file. Access speeds are faster and transfer rates larger for disks than tapes. However, disks are more expensive. A disk pack can easily cost twenty times as much as a reel of tape. The greater purchase costs of disk packs can often be offset by the greater processing efficiencies of random-order access. Disks are particularly useful in online systems and are being increasingly used for file storage.

Summary Figure 9.7 presents an overview of the three most popular key transcription processes. (Paper tape is popular only as input to communication systems and in by-product recording.) The greater use of machines in the key-to-tape and key-to-disk processes may help to explain their increasing popularity. Machine processes are more reliable and normally cost less per unit processed than operations involving more human labor. They are also faster and work well for high-volume, repetitive processes. As indicated in alternative 3 of the shared processor system in Figure 9.7, mechanistic systems also lend themselves to remote input of data via communication lines. Standard key-to-tape and key-to-disk systems become economically competitive to card punching systems at volumes requiring from five to eight card punching stations.

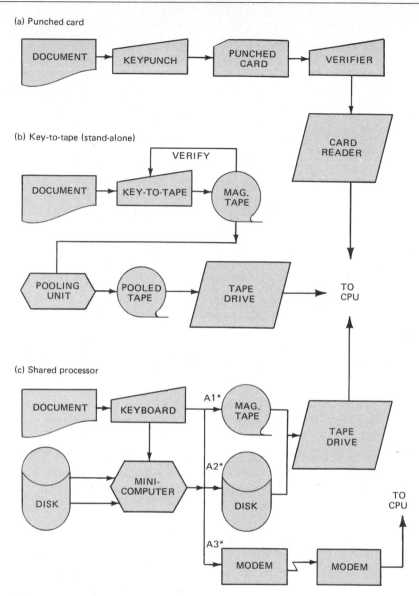

(a) Punched card

(b) Key-to-tape (stand-alone)

(c) Shared processor

*These are alternatives; normally only one would be present in a given system.

FIGURE 9.7   *Overview of popular key transcription processes*

CHARACTERISTICS OF BY-PRODUCT RECORDING MEDIA AND DEVICES

As already indicated, the media involved here tend to be punched cards, punched paper tape, magnetic tape, and magnetic disks. The preparation device (card punch, paper tape punch, or incremental recorder) is hooked to another data processing device, such as a cash register or a typewriter, and the keying involved in the basic process is used to enter the data on the medium. Bookkeeping machines have also been adapted to produce punched cards, punched paper tape, magnetic-tape cassettes, or optically readable journal tapes as a by-product. The tape cassette is being adapted in an amazing variety of ways for by-product data recording. The magnetic-tape cassettes are usually translated to computer-compatible magnetic tape in a second offline operation.

The characteristics of the media and devices mentioned here are discussed in the other sections of this chapter. The appeal of by-product recording is that the keying process that creates the initial data carrying document also produces the machine-sensible data carrying medium. It can easily be seen in Figure 9.1 how the input process would be shortened and total costs reduced. With the development of optical readers capable of reading manually written documents and those capable of translating the human voice to electronic impulses, the need for transcription keying is reduced still further.

CHARACTERISTICS OF CHARACTER READING MEDIA AND DEVICES

The major advantage of character reading devices is that a human-sensible document can be used as the input medium to the computer.

Magnetic-Ink Character Recognition (MICR) No doubt you've looked at those odd-shaped characters strung across the bottom of your checks. They are printed with a special ink containing iron particles that can be magnetized. After being magnetized, they can be read by special-character readers for computer input. Figure 9.8 shows an MICR reader-sorter. These devices read documents (checks, deposit slips, withdrawal slips, and other documents) at speeds up to 1,600 documents per minute. The MICR characters on each document are magnetized by the machine, sensed, and used to sort the document into the proper pocket. Validation processes such as the use of check digits can be incorporated into the machine. The documents read can be of different sizes and thicknesses as long as the MICR characters are placed in the proper relation to the bottom edge of the document.

MICR technology, including the shapes of the characters, was developed for the banking industry. Without this process, an army of clerks would need to be employed at each bank, use of checks would be very costly, and

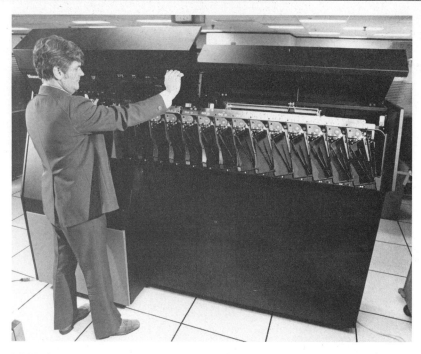

FIGURE 9.8   *MICR document reader-sorter.* (PHOTO COURTESY HONEYWELL INFORMATION SYSTEMS)

checks would clear between banks at a much slower pace. MICR has not been applied to any degree outside the banking industry. This is due partly to the development of optical reading processes, which require less cumbersome and less costly preparation equipment.

Optical Character Recognition (OCR) OCR readers use photoelectric cells to identify characters. The least costly devices recognize only the numerals 0 to 9 printed in a special type font. More expensive readers can recognize hand-printed numbers and typed numbers, letters, and special characters in several fonts. Input media read by these devices range from cash register and accounting-machine tapes in special fonts to page-size documents prepared on special typewriters. Reading speeds vary from less than 100 to 2,400 characters per second and from 180 to 1,800 documents per minute (see Figure 9.9).

The advantages of OCR, aside from use of a human-sensible medium, are cost, speed, and reduced chance of error because transcription to a different machine-sensible medium is avoided. The removal of the transcription operation can also result in greater efficiency and faster throughput for the data processing operation as a whole. However, error control depends on

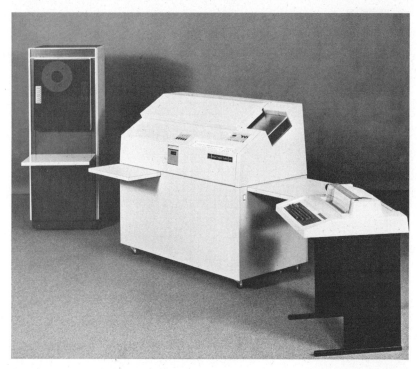

FIGURE 9.9   *Optical reader.* The Sentry 7018 system reads and interprets marks from a number two pencil on documents up to full page size at a speed of 6000 sheets per hour.
(PHOTO COURTESY OF NATIONAL COMPUTER SYSTEMS, INC.)

visual proofing and requires well-trained typists and proofreaders and close supervision over the initial recording operation.

A significant shortcoming with many OCR systems is the many restrictions placed on the user and on the paper used. Most readers require the use of paper that meets stringent specifications for reflectance, blemishes, weight, and so on. Typewriters and ribbons must be of highest quality with tight control of spacing, quality of background printing, and so on. Supplies are therefore expensive. OCR readers also may misread or reject a document because of dirt specks or wrinkles. These limitations are being reduced as the process is constantly improved.

Optical Mark Recognition (OMR)   Although not strictly a character reader, an OMR device is a simpler version of an OCR device. OMR readers optically read marks (lines) rather than characters. A single mark or a combination of marks represents particular characters or other types of data. A wide variety of marks can be read. OMR can read marks made by computer printers, hard or soft pencils, and special typewriters. These marks are humanly readable after special training.

OMR devices vary in speed and cost. Some accept only punched-card-size documents; others accept full pages. Also, some OMR readers merely translate to another machine-sensible form such as punched cards or magnetic tape.

OMR devices have been used extensively in educational testing and in automated or semi-automated warehousing operations. They are being used also in some point-of-sale recorders (see Figure 6.3, page 124). They seem particularly adaptable to any operation, such as meter reading, in which limited amounts of data are collected in the field and to operations where data are prepared by someone outside the data processing department. OMR use is expanding rapidly in point-of-sale systems in retailing operations. Packages are marked with a bar code and then read optically at the checkout stand to input price and inventory control information.

CHARACTERISTICS OF DIRECT-ENTRY DEVICES

Whenever a human being enters data directly into the computer without using an intervening input medium, *direct entry* takes place. We have already mentioned several types of direct-entry devices. Five of those will be described in more detail at this time — typewriterlike terminals, cathode ray tube terminals, voice-entry systems, intelligent terminals, and point-of-action–entry devices.

Typewriterlike Terminals The most common type of terminal for time-sharing systems is a machine with a typewriterlike keyboard. The user enters data via the keyboard, and they are transmitted to the computer over a direct cable or a telephone line. The computer responds over the same line. There is no opportunity to key-verify input. Error control is attained by having the computer edit the input and by sight-proofing the typed copy produced on the terminal. Most of these terminals operate at 10 to 30 characters per second. A few can operate at faster speeds (up to 300 characters per second) when outputting from the computer. Some have a paper tape reader and punch for use in offline data preparation, in program input, or in preserving output (such as saving a program developed online for use at another time).

The newest development in these typewriterlike terminals is portability. Models are available that weigh as little as 17 pounds. These portable units cost more than the lowest cost standard models (which are about $750), but usually not so much as the most expensive standard models (which are about $3,000). Typewriterlike terminals currently provide the lowest cost reliable means of communicating directly with a computer.

Cathode Ray Tube (CRT) Terminals A CRT terminal looks like a TV screen (a cathode ray tube) with a keyboard attached. Since the CRT is electronic, its operations are fast and silent. Thus these terminals are quieter and faster than the typewriterlike terminals. In addition, some CRTs have graphic capabilities that can be very valuable in the analysis of time flows and relationships of economic variables. Screen and print colors, sizes, and capabilities vary widely. Most CRTs do not produce hard copy or have graphic capabilities. The addition of either of these capabilities adds substantially to the cost of the terminal.

Some CRTs can accept input by the use of a light pen. Data are transmitted to the computer by pointing to a specific item or area on the screen. The interpretation of light-pen impulses is under program control by the computer. Light pens have been used by students to input answers during computer-controlled instruction; by managers to select the reports or graphs to be displayed; and by engineers to create, rotate, expand, contract, and otherwise manipulate geometric figures and engineering drawings.

Transmission speeds for CRT devices vary from 10 to almost 10,000 characters per second, with the display area varying from 200 to 2,000 character spaces. Keyboards vary from standard typewriter keyboards through keyboards arranged in alphabetic order to specialized keyboards allowing specialized inquiry or program initiation from a single key.

Voice-Input Terminals Voice-input devices are limited, recognizing only numerals and selected simple commands. They are being used in quality control, point-of-sale applications, and identification of personnel. They are currently too expensive and unreliable for general use.

Intelligent Terminals Combining a minicomputer or a microprocessor with a terminal (usually a CRT terminal) allows programming of the terminal to perform special tasks; thus the phrase *intelligent terminal*. Such a terminal can lead the user through a sequence of entry operations and/or perform many of the data editing activities normally carried out by the central computer. Some intelligent terminals also control selected peripheral devices such as magnetic-tape cassette handlers. The most sophisticated terminals are really minicomputers capable of stand-alone data processing.

Use of intelligent terminals is expanding rapidly as more and more data processing systems go online. There is a real advantage in relieving the central computer of the editing burden and providing additional data storage at the terminal. The number of accesses of the central computer decreases, and the amount of data transfer and processing associated with each access increases. Intelligent terminals tend to feature larger screen capacities and faster transfer rates, which, together with the minicomputer or microprocessor hardware, make them much more expensive than ordinary terminals.

Point-of-Action–Entry Devices Point-of-sale devices are revolutionizing retail data processing and promise to have application in other areas (materials control, transportation invoicing, and others). One device is illustrated in Figure 6.3. Included in this category are systems for factory data collection and credit card transaction recording and other forms of entry. Some systems merely involve standard keyboard terminals. Factory data entry systems are now quite sophisticated, with time and performance data necessary to job costing and control captured at online terminals involving combined plastic-card reading and key entry. Less sophisticated (usually older) systems for collecting time-card and job-status data are stand-alone devices that create punched paper tape or punched-card records or activate central tape or card punches via a simple communications network. Most of these networks are now policed by a small computer that edits input and organizes the data on a magnetic tape or disk for later processing. Current small systems handle four to sixteen remote stations and are more economical than key entry at seven or eight or more stations. Large computer (timesharing) systems generally involve at least sixteen stations and may involve as many as sixty-four stations in large factories with many work stations.

Some supermarkets are using an automated checkout counter that includes package-bottom-reading optical scanners, several of which can be controlled by one minicomputer, and a modified cash register terminal accessing the same mini. Currently used systems for point-of-sale (POS) recording online to a central computer provide automatic credit card validation as well as standard transactions processing. Most POS systems have built-in sequence control and instruction routines that guide the salesclerk through each transaction. Terminals can handle up to a dozen different transactions and include such activities as discounts, uneven trade-in, and down payment on the item purchased. Data capturing mechanisms, in addition to the optical wand shown in Figure 6.3, include electro-mechanical devices (hand-held and fixed) for reading punched tape and cards and magnetic readers for capturing magnetic-ink encoding. Some systems merely store transactions data on tape cassettes or other machine-sensible media, whereas others perform online and enter all transactions into a central computer storage device (disk or drum).

ECONOMICS OF DATA ENTRY

Data on the costs of using different entry devices vary by application and are usually considered proprietary. Available studies tend to be fragmented and are seldom scientifically designed to provide statistical measurement of their reliability. However, certain "facts" seem to be widely accepted about costs in this area.

1. Card key punching is less costly than other means at volumes of less than 10 million characters per month. This is due primarily to the low cost of card preparation and handling devices as compared to the cost of corresponding tape and disk devices.

2. Key-to-tape processes become economically feasible alternatives to card punches at volumes of about 10 million characters per month.

3. Standard key-to-disk processes require somewhat higher volumes before becoming feasible alternatives. The new floppy-disk systems are competitive at smaller volumes, however.

4. Optical character recognition systems become alternatives to card punch systems in the range of 20 million to 25 million characters per month. When special typing is not required before OCR reading, these systems become alternatives to key-to-tape systems at about 25 million characters per month.

5. Point-of-activity recorders would appear to be competitive to card punching at lower volumes than the other media transcription processes. However, the popularity of this approach seems to be based more firmly on considerations of speed, accuracy, and integrated systems design than on cost advantage.

It is interesting to note that the new minicomputer systems for business data processing tend to favor online entry even if a keying process is involved. The saving from not purchasing, punching, verifying, and storing cards and the decreasing cost of the hardware combine to make direct entry economically attractive. Direct key entry from remote-action stations to larger multiprogrammed systems is also expanding rapidly. These trends indicate that *most* systems will involve direct entry from the point of activity in the relatively near future. Key transcription will still remain to handle batch processing operations and the initial conversion of files to electronic media. Cards will remain in use as turnaround documents but are likely to be printed mechanically at the point of action and read optically when returned for processing, as is being done with gasoline credit cards. Improvements in optical readers will further simplify input processes by allowing typewriter or manual preparation of the input medium.

Characteristics of Output Media and Devices

The following are *critical factors* for selecting computer output devices. (See Chapter 6 for a more detailed discussion of these factors.)

1. *Speed* — lines per minute or characters per second.

2. *Capacity* — characters per line.

3. *Expandability* — the ease with which capacity of the device can be expanded by adding more units or substituting larger units.

4. *Bulk* — a loose relative measure of physical-space requirements for the device and any medium involved.

5. *Access mode* — the order in which individual data elements can be retrieved from the medium used for output.

6. *Reliability* — restricted to mechanical reliability.

7. *Ease of use* —
   a. Need for special equipment.
   b. Need for trained operators.
   c. Need for special handling of output media.
   d. Reusability (permanence) of the medium.
   e. Human readability of the medium.

CHARACTERISTICS OF TYPEWRITERS AND TYPEWRITERLIKE DEVICES

Widely used as timesharing terminals, these devices were discussed as input devices and will not be further discussed here except to comment that they produce paper documents and are a slow output device.

CHARACTERISTICS OF PRINTERS

Characteristics of line printers are also discussed in Chapter 6 (see pages 137–140). The major types of line printers are discussed more fully below.

Impact Line Printers The most common devices used strictly for output are line printers. They are called line printers because they print one line on each machine cycle. Most are *impact* printers, which print by forcing (impacting) the type character against the ribbon and paper. There are three major types: bar printer, drum printer, and chain printer.

The *bar printer* features a type bar at each print position, which contains all the print characters. It is the slowest of the impact printers because the bars must move to position the proper symbol for printing at each character position. At the instant that the desired character is in position, a magnetically activated hammer pushes paper and ribbon against the bar. Typical speeds are 200 to 300 lines per minute. Line length is usually 120 characters.

The *drum printer* takes its name from the horizontal drum, or print cylinder, that contains the possible print characters. Each character is repeated at each possible character position across a row on the drum. Thus each circular column around the drum contains every possible character, and there is one such column positioned at each possible character space across the printing field. Hammers at each print position strike whenever the proper character is in position, and several may strike simultaneously, so that the entire line is printed in one drum rotation. The number of different characters that can be printed varies with drum size (usually between 50 and 60). The drum printer usually features 132 characters per line and prints at speeds varying from 200 to 3,000 lines per minute, but most operate at 1,000 to 1,500 lines per minute. Very few operate at speeds above 1,500 lines per minute.

The *chain printer* uses rapidly moving chains whose links are engraved character printing slugs. The chain contains five sections of the possible characters (usually 48). As the chain moves continuously at a constant and rapid speed across the paper, hammers at each print position strike when the proper character is at that position. Printing speeds of 2,000 lines per minute are possible. Chain printers are the most common printers in use today, usually operating at about 1,200 lines per minute.

Nonimpact Line Printers The fastest printers available today are nonimpact printers. The basic theory on which most nonimpact printers are based is that a complex paper can be substituted for complex machinery to create printed copy. There are three basic types of nonimpact printers based on this idea. *Electrosensitive* printing uses a paper that is first coated with carbon, then covered with white pigment. An electronically controlled spark forms the characters by burning off the white pigment to reveal the carbon beneath. *Thermal* printing uses a similar idea. The paper is coated with a chemical that turns a dark color when heated. Images are formed when tiny heated rods in a matrix print head touch the paper. Thermal printing is widely used in portable timesharing terminals. *Electrostatic* printing uses a process common in office copiers. The paper is coated with a chemical that can hold an electric charge. The printer places the charge on the paper, which then passes through a toner with the opposite charge. The plastic toner melts and forms the image when it is exposed to high heat. The principal advantage of the thermal and electrostatic printers is the lower cost of the printer itself. This is partially offset by the higher cost of the paper. *Electrophotographic* (also called Xerographic) printing is one chemical process in which the complexity is returned to the printer. A charge-sensitive drum in the printer is charged by controlled light. Toner is then applied to the drum and the image rolled off onto the paper and fused by heating. The Electrophotographic process has been used in ultrahigh speed printers. The best known, IBM's 3800 line printer, operates at 13,000 lines per minute.

The other major nonimpact printing technique is based on *ink jet printing* in which a tiny jet shoots small drops of charged ink through a charged electrical field. The electrical field is adjusted to paint a matrix image on the paper. One version is harnessed to printing presses and uses multiple ink jets to obtain speeds between 50,000 and 60,000 lines per minute. The ink jet printers are ten to twenty times more expensive than impact line printers, the price varying primarily with speed.

The major advantages of current nonimpact printers are speed; silent operation; superior print quality; and, for those using simple printers and complex paper, lower equipment cost. The major disadvantages are their inferior ability to produce multiple copies and, for those using complex paper, high paper costs. The use of nonimpact printers is increasing rapidly, particularly in large computer installations and in the portable terminal market. Manufacturers are, however, rapidly increasing reliability and multiple-copy capability and lowering costs. The nonimpact printers that operate at 1,000 to 5,000 lines per minute are currently competitive with impact printers. This opens up the entire market from terminals to ultrahigh speeds to nonimpact printers. Most users, however, still believe that impact printers are superior for printing forms (checks, invoices, and other special documents) and for multiple-copy printing. In addition, many nonimpact printers are not compatible with a wide range of computer mainframes. These problems are bound to disappear; and the nonimpact printer is likely to become more widely used, particularly for providing single-copy, high-quality printing at high speeds. One of nonimpact printing's major competitors is Computer Output Microfilm, which is discussed in a later section of this chapter.

Summary: Line Printers   By limitation of the character set (all numerical, for example) of a line printer, faster print speeds are possible. For a given printer, actual speeds will vary depending upon whether the material being printed is all numeric, all alphabetic, or mixed numeric and alphabetic. In addition, single and double spacing will affect print speeds. Actual production rates will depend on all these factors plus the factor of idle time caused by the need to change printing forms.

Prices of printers vary widely. Price is increased for faster print speeds, for larger character sets, and for the ability to print different numbers of lines per inch. Normal line spacing is six lines per inch, but some printers can print eight lines per inch. Prices are lower if only 120 characters per line are printed rather than the more normal 132. Print quality levels (uniformity of character formation, constant line and character spacing, straightness of lines) can also affect price. Pleasing appearance, good form alignment, and high print quality are desirable in a printer preparing custodial documents.

Printer Output Media   Printer output is on paper. Standard paper for use on line printers is wider than standard letter-sized paper. To provide positive feed control, line printers and the faster character printers use *pin feed control*. The side edges of the paper (beyond the printed sections) each contain a row of holes. Pins mounted on the ends of the paper drive or the printing platen engage the holes in the paper to drive it smoothly forward with minimum chance of misalignment or wrinkling. Most computer paper comes as a continuous fanfold. Individual forms are separated by a line of perforations. After printing, the individual sheets must be separated and the pin feed edge holes removed. Multiple-part paper must be separated and the carbons removed. These tasks are usually accomplished with a machine known as a *forms burster*. The burster can also separate forms that are of less than full-page size.

Storage of computer print-out requires special storage devices. File drawers and cabinets must be larger than usual. Special binders and associated rack storage devices are also available.

CHARACTERISTICS OF VISUAL DISPLAY DEVICES

While other forms exist, such as a plotter that adds a third dimension in the form of vertical wires each clipped to an appropriate length, only cathode ray tubes and computer output microfilm are in common use.

Cathode Ray Tube (CRT) Devices   CRTs have already been discussed as input terminals and will not be further discussed here.

Computer Output Microfilm (COM)   One method of speeding output and reducing output media storage requirements is to put the output on microfilm. An overview of the COM process is given in Figure 9.10. Part (a) shows the general process, and part (b) shows how the film is recorded and used. Fiber optics are substituted for the CRT in some systems. The end of each optical fiber displays a portion of the "picture" to be filmed. A third form writes directly on the film with a beam of electrons.

Microfilm outputs are of four types as shown. The film can be used as a reel of film or cut into special film strips, normally containing twelve frames (pictures) per strip. Individual frames can be mounted on aperture cards or photographed onto a small portion of a rectangular microfiche. One 8½-by-11-inch microfiche card can store thousands of printed pages in some systems. Microfiche cards come in several sizes.

COM saves printer time, not only at output time but also in situations in which many copies are needed. With the aid of the forms overlay, custodial documents can be produced. Typical COM speeds are up to 60,000 lines per minute, which is closer to the internal transfer rate of the computer

(a) The general process

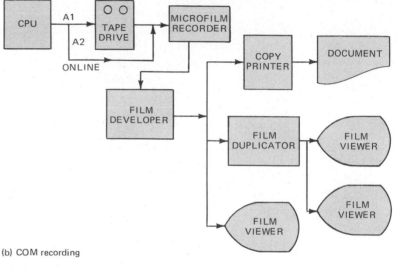

(b) COM recording

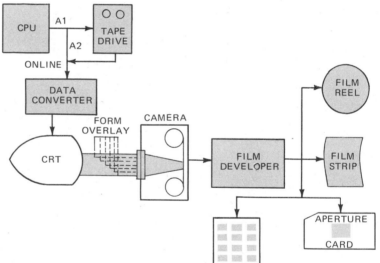

FIGURE 9.10 *Overview of COM process*

than other devices. COM-produced files are compact, and retrieval can be mechanized and made rapid and essentially direct. COM is also economical to operate, although the initial price is high. There is still some question about the reliability of COM, but the reliability of the equipment is improving rapidly and its use is expanding.

CHARACTERISTICS OF VOICE-RESPONSE DEVICES

Voice response is being used in computer-controlled inquiry systems to provide a response that does not require the operator to read the response and/or makes telephone inquiry possible. Spoken words (or syllables in more sophisticated systems) are prerecorded on a storage medium (magnetic drum, magnetic disk, and photographic-film drums are being used). Each word or syllable is given a code. The computer program composes responses to inquiries in the form of coded messages. The coded reply is sent to the audio-response device, which assembles a proper sequence of prerecorded spoken elements and transmits the message back to the station from which the inquiry came. Use of voice response is expanding rapidly. It is used in a number of credit card validation systems. At the New York Stock Exchange, the computer verbally quotes the latest price and volume information on NYSE stocks in response to telephone inquiries from subscribers to the quotation service.

The major advantage of voice response is that every touch-tone telephone becomes an inquiry station. With the addition of small portable terminals, *any* telephone can become a terminal. Complicated inquiries can be typed in and an audio response returned.

Characteristics of Dual-Purpose Input-Output Devices

Dual-purpose input-output devices that have already been discussed under input or output devices include typewriter and typewriterlike terminals, CRT keyboard terminals, and intelligent terminals. *Batch* terminals have not been discussed previously. They combine a card or magnetic-tape reader and a printer with a control terminal to provide remote access to a computer for processing of volumes of data. Sophisticated batch terminals are really small independent computer systems capable of operating in an offline mode.

Balancing Input-Output Systems

Input-output systems cannot be chosen independently. Input and output are the bottlenecks in human beings' use of the computer. Reading punched cards at 2,000 cards per minute, which is very fast, results in a maximum transfer speed of less than 3,000 characters per second. Internal transfer rates run to a million or more characters per second. Output on microfilm, the fastest output medium, approaches only one-tenth of the internal speed of the computer. Electrostatic printing at 6,000 pages per minute transfers data at about half the speed of COM, or 50,000 characters per second (if we assume 5,000 characters per page). Seldom do such input and output devices run uninterrupted for more than a few minutes. Also, seldom are all lines on an output page filled.

Input-output systems should be developed to get maximum return from the investment in the total system, including the CPU. Harnessing a fast CPU to slow punched-media devices (card or tape) wastes CPU resources. Direct input from multiple stations under multiprogrammed control from the CPU may be the answer on the input side. The output problem is best solved by doing away with unproductive output. Managers can get information more quickly from a graphic analysis, either online or printed, than from volumes of reproduced input detail. Even if all management information were provided on other devices, however, printers would continue to be necessary to create custodial documents. Computer-to-computer hookups between the firm and its suppliers and the firm and its bank are possible and are being used. Such linkups, if reproduced between consumers and banks and between banks themselves, would remove the need for many custodial documents. Although technically *possible* at the present time, assurance of data security and privacy (access control) are problems to be overcome before widespread use will develop.

Summary

This chapter has discussed the characteristics of input and output media and devices for use with the computer. Four types of input devices — *key transcription*, *by-product recording*, *character recognition*, and *direct entry* — were described and compared. Four types of output devices — *typewriter and typewriterlike devices*, *printers*, *visual display devices*, and *voice response* — were also covered. Many of these devices were defined as dual purpose, being used for both input and output. The critical factors for system I/O medium and device selection were described. (See Chapter 6 for a more detailed discussion of these critical factors.)

Current trends in use, labor cost, and prices for media and devices clearly indicate a shift to direct-entry terminals for input and to online terminals for many kinds of output. Graphics and voice response are playing an increasing role in systems outputs. These trends reflect the increasing use of multiprogrammed and timeshared systems in business data processing and information systems. Point-of-action recording systems are proliferating; and intelligent terminals, batch terminals, microcomputers, and minicomputers are extending the usefulness of computerized systems to all aspects of business data processing.

Questions

1. Define the following as briefly as possible and then use a short paragraph to clarify each definition.
   a. Key transcription
   b. By-product recording
   c. Character reading
   d. Direct-entry device
   e. Terminal
   f. CRT
   g. Character printer
   h. Line printer
   i. Graphic terminal
   j. Batch terminal
   k. Intelligent terminal
   l. Transfer rate
   m. Access mode
   n. Punched card
   o. Punched paper tape
   p. Disk pack
   q. Tape drive
   r. MICR
   s. OCR
   t. OMR
   u. Point-of-action entry
   v. COM

2. Prepare a list of the advantages and disadvantages of punched cards, punched paper tape, magnetic tape, and magnetic-disk packs as input media.

3. Under what conditions would punched cards be the *preferred* input medium? Explain. (Note that the answer "None" is possible if you can justify it.)

4. Under what conditions would *you prefer* punched paper tape as the input medium? Explain. (Do not forget to consider the answer "None,"; see question 3.)

5. Under what conditions would *you prefer* magnetic tape as the input medium? Explain. (Don't forget "None"; see question 3.)

6. Under what conditions would *you prefer* magnetic disks as the input medium? Explain. (See question 3 for hint.)

7. Under what conditions would *you prefer* direct entry of data into a computer system? Explain. (See question 3 for hint.)

8. What are the differences, if any, between key-to-tape and key-to-disk systems?

9. Under what conditions would *you prefer* by-product recording of input data? Explain.

10. What are the differences between MICR, OCR, and OMR processes?

11. Under what conditions would *you prefer* an OCR device for system input? Explain fully.

12. What are the advantages of key-to-tape and key-to-disk systems over card key punching? Be exhaustive.

13. What are the primary justifications for using line printers as the major computer output device?
14. Compare impact and nonimpact printers as output devices.
15. Compare line printers and character printers as output devices.
16. Compare plotters and graphic CRT devices as output devices.
17. Under what conditions would *you prefer* computer output microfilm (COM) as the output device? Explain.
18. What conditions favor the use of voice-response systems? Be exhaustive. Explain.
19. What is a modem?
20. What is a remote batch terminal?
21. What is a key verifier?
22. What are the advantages and disadvantages of microfilm as an output medium? Be exhaustive. (You may find it helpful to include the discussion of microfilm in Chapter 6.)
23. In what sense (or senses) is a punched card a dual-purpose medium? Can any other input media be considered dual-purpose media? Explain.
24. How might the design of a system involving the use of a turnaround document (for example, a bill that goes to the customer and is returned with payment) be affected by the continuing improvement of OCR systems?
25. Why are nonimpact line printers gaining in popularity in comparison to impact line printers?
26. Develop a college student advising and registration system involving the use of CRT displays and an OCR device.
    a. Write a narrative description of the system.
    b. Develop a system flowchart.
27. Refer to question 18 at the end of Chapter 7 and answer the following:
    a. How might remote terminals be used as input devices in the SHFM system?
    b. How might COM be used in that system?

Ten

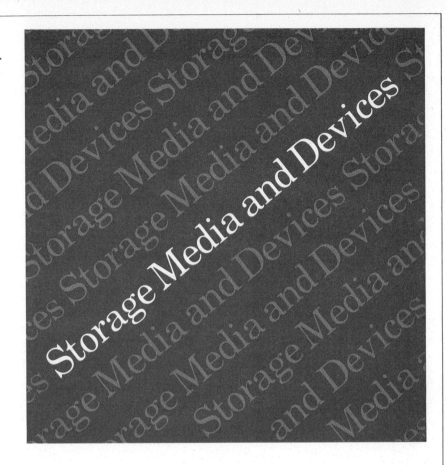

Storage Media and Devices

$\mathbf{A}$s indicated in Chapter 8, the storage element of the computer stores data (raw, partially processed, and fully processed) and program instructions. However, in the current computer generation the storage is not accomplished entirely by the primary storage units associated with the CPU. Multiprogrammed and timeshared systems tend to have more secondary storage capacity (outside the CPU) than primary storage capacity. This secondary storage performs all storage functions, being used for storing all types of data and all types of programs (executive, utility, and application).

Electronic Storage Device Concepts

A special vocabulary has been developed to describe new and modified concepts associated with storage and retrieval processes utilizing electronic devices.

STORAGE ORGANIZATION

Electronic storage devices necessarily use some form of electronic pulse to represent a binary digit. *Characters* are represented by some combination of binary digits (bits) as indicated in Figure 8.1, page 201. Characters are organized into *computer words* in one of two ways. *Fixed-word-length* machines handle a fixed number of characters as a word. *Variable-word-length* machines allow the size of words to vary, placing special *word marks* between contiguous words in the storage.

All storage devices used for primary computer memory are organized for identification of and access to each word (or character). In a fixed-word-length machine, each word stored contains the same number of characters. Each numbered storage location contains the fixed number of characters identified as a *computer word*. When an *address* is given, it refers to the entire content of that word location, either calling out or replacing all characters in the word location.

In variable-word-length machines, the location of each word is identified by the location of one of the ending characters of the word. The length of the word is specified in one of two ways. Either a word mark is added in the first character space beyond the other end of the word when the word is stored or its length is included in each instruction operating on it. When the word is retrieved from (read out of) memory, it is called for by providing the number (*address*) of the character location containing the initial end character. Reading starts at that character location and proceeds toward the other end until the word mark is found or until the number of characters specified in the instruction has been read.

PERMANENCE OF STORAGE

Each computer storage device is classed as either *volatile* or *nonvolatile*. A volatile storage device loses its contents, that is, returns to a blank state, whenever the electrical power to the device is cut off. *Nonvolatile* storage either does *not* lose its contents when the power is shut off or loses them only after a period of time (several weeks at the minimum).

While the computer is operating, it is well to have the possibility of accessing the same word or words many times. Thus most electronic storage devices are so constructed that read-out is *nondestructive*. That is, reading the content of a memory location for transfer to another computer element or to another memory location does not alter (destroy) the content of that location. When data or instructions (from the input or arithmetic-logic elements, for example) are stored, the contents of the location used are overwritten. That is, on entry the content is erased and then replaced by what is being entered.

PROTECTION AGAINST ERROR

An error in storage entry or on transfer within or from storage needs to be protected against. The most common protection is given by *parity checking*. Every character and/or word is forced to contain an *odd* (or *even*) number of bits. This is made possible by the addition of a *parity bit* to the code representing each character. If the character already contains the appropriate (odd or even) number of 1's (ones), then the parity bit is set to 0 (zero). If the character code does not contain the appropriate number of bits, then the parity bit is set to 1. This scheme protects, partially, against failure of bit representing components, misreads from electronic media, and transfer channel failures.

Types of Storage Devices

Current memory devices for primary and secondary online storage use either *fixed magnetic devices*, *moving magnetic surfaces*, or *microcircuits* as the storage medium. Experimental storage devices involving lasers, cryogenics (great cold), and light as the medium are widely discussed but unavailable at the present time. Reputedly offering greater speed, smaller size, and potential cost advantages, these devices are mentioned here as illustrations of the continuing search for better storage devices. They also indicate factors considered important in memory devices — speed, size, and cost.

FIXED MAGNETIC DEVICES

Fixed magnetic devices use magnetized elements or surfaces that do not move. Included are *magnetic cores* and *magnetic film*. Two basic types of film memory exist, thin film and plated wire. Both involve thin films of magnetizable materials.

MOVING MAGNETIC SURFACES

The surfaces of *drums*, *disks*, and *tape strips* are coated with a magnetizable material. The disks and drums spin at high speeds under read-write heads. Tape strips are retrieved from racks and wrapped on a cylinder rotating under read-write heads.

MICROCIRCUIT STORAGE

Microcircuit storage devices are produced by microminiaturization technology involving creation of memory circuits on silicon chips (semiconductors). Although they might also be classed with core and film as "fixed" devices, they are technically different, using circuit states rather than simple magnetic properties to represent bits.

READ-ONLY MEMORY

A *read-only memory* is a special-purpose memory that is used to store programs that expand or modify the capabilities of a particular computer. The content of the device is "locked in" and cannot be modified except by special procedures. These memories are used to allow one computer to accept instructions developed for some other incompatible computer and/or to provide *macroinstructions*, which are themselves a combination of instructions in the basic instruction set of the machine.

Characteristics of Storage Devices

The factors identified in Chapter 9 as critical to input and output media and device selection must be adapted to computer storage devices. (See also Chapter 6 for a discussion of these factors in relation to data processing media and devices.)

1. *Speed* — access time and transfer rate.
    a. *Access time* is the time required to locate and retrieve a data element (word or character) from storage.
    b. *Transfer rate* is the maximum number of characters that can be read out or accepted (transferred) by the device (in a sequential stream) in one second.

Access time is the more critical of these speed measurements. In fact, it is perhaps the most critical characteristic of a storage device, since the reason for storing something is to be able to retrieve it at a future time. Maximum transfer rates vary widely, but transfers seldom involve sufficient volume on each transfer for this factor to be significant in measuring device performance.

2. *Capacity* is measured in two ways:
    a. The number of characters that can be stored on one unit of the device.
    b. Total simultaneous online capacity that can be provided by the device. This seems to be continuously expanding as the number of devices that can be online to the CPU continues to increase.

3. *Expandability* is the ease with which the capacity can be expanded by adding units or by substituting larger units.

4. *Bulk* is a loose relative measure of physical-space requirements for the device.

5. *Access mode* refers to the order and comparative speed of retrieval of individual data elements from the device when it is online.

6. *Reliability* is average time to failure or average number of accesses to failure. Accuracy of recording and recall is imperative, and devices do not move into common use unless they are reliable. For this reason, this factor assumes real significance only for devices involving new techniques.

7. *Ease of use* is reduced to only two factors:
    a. *Volatility*. A volatile storage device is erased if the electrical power to the device is turned off.
    b. *Sensitivity to power fluctuations*. This is important. Some devices can experience cataclysmic failure if the voltage suddenly drops or surges. Usually this is due to a physical reaction of the drive mechanisms and moving surfaces. Such damage can be prevented by the use of properly designed intermediate power sources or special emergency power systems.

The characteristics of popular storage devices in terms of most of those critical factors are summarized in Figure 10.1. Each device is also described below, and its characteristics are further discussed. Note that the devices have been ranked on the basis of cost per character in Figure 10.1. This ranking is not reliable for all sizes of these devices. Economies of scale are not the same for all devices. For fixed magnetic devices, cost per character tends to decline as size goes up. For moving surfaces, this tendency varies in a more stepwise fashion and is harder to generalize. For all systems, total cost of the device generally varies directly with capacity and inversely with access time. Cost per character tends to decline as capacity expands but increase as access time declines. Finally, idiosyncrasies in pricing arise because of the differing reputations of suppliers and their perceived abilities to provide software and maintenance services.

CHARACTERISTICS OF FIXED MAGNETIC DEVICES
The fixed devices include magnetic core and thin film. These devices are used primarily for primary storage within the CPU, although *slow core* is used as secondary storage.

Magnetic-Core Storage Magnetic cores are tiny, doughnut-shaped rings. The rings are pressed from a ferrite and ceramic mixture and baked in an

FIGURE 10.1

Characteristics of storage devices

Characteristic	Unit of measurement	Core	Drum	Disk		Film			Magnetic strip
				Pack	Fixed	Planar	Bubble[b]	Microcircuit[b]	
Access time[a]	Microseconds	.3–8	10K–100K	30K–100K	20K–600K	.3–.8	.3–.5	.045	200K–500K
Access mode	R = random S = sequential	R	RS	RS	RS	R	R	R	RS
Capacity[a]	Thousands of characters	4–200K	100–100K	2K–400K	500–20,000K	4–1K	4–64	4–64 per chip	145K–8,000K
Expandability	Min. module (characters)	4K–16K	Add unit	Pack	Add unit	4K	4K	4K	200K
Bulk	1 = low 8 = high	5	8	7	6	1	2	3	4
Volatile		No	No	No	No	No	No[b]	Yes[b]	No
Cost	1 = low 8 = high	6	3	4	2	7	b	b	1

[a]The symbol **K** should be read as 1,000. Thus 10**K** microseconds equals 10,000 millionths of a second, or ten milliseconds (ten-thousandths of a second). Four **K** thousands of characters equals 4 million characters.

[b]The cost of bubble and microcircuit memory is currently competitive with core for smaller memory sizes and is dropping. Microcircuit memories are replacing core in many uses.

oven. Outside diameters vary from .125 inch to .018 inch. Binary digits are represented by the magnetic state of the magnetized rings. The core is magnetized by passing an electrical pulse through it and remains magnetized for at least several months. Current direction determines the magnetic state [see Figure 10.2(a)]. Differences in magnetic state distinguish 0 (zero) and 1 (one).

Cores are strung at the intersecting points on a two-dimensional wire grid to create a *core plane* [see Figure 10.2(b)]. Core planes are then stacked together to form memory modules [see Figure 10.2(c)]. A specific core is magnetized by sending one-half the required energy pulse down one of the wires intersecting at that core and one-half the pulse down the other intersecting wire [see Figure 10.2(b)]. Reading is accomplished by the use of the *sense wire* and is accomplished in two steps. Current is passed through the core. If the core changes in the direction in which it is magnetized, a pulse is picked up by the sense wire, indicating the presence of a 1 bit. The core is then pulsed again to return it to its original state. Writing is also accomplished in two steps. The core is cleared in step 1 and its magnetic state reset in step 2.

Core planes are stacked together to create a core memory module. Most commonly, they are organized for access in groups of eight- or nine-core planes so that a character may be represented by the eight- or nine-core combination at the same location on each plane [see Figure 10.2(c)]. Several such groups (for example, thirty-two- or thirty-six-planes) may be combined in a single core module.

Core storage provides fast, reliable storage in a random-access mode (all locations are accessible in about the same length of time). Access times vary from about 300 nanoseconds (billionths of a second) to around eight microseconds. The fastest core memories are found on the largest and most expensive computers. There are very few core memories with access speeds over five microseconds. Most core in use today has an access time around one microsecond. Cores also have the advantage of requiring low voltages, creating relatively little heat, and being nonvolatile.[1] This was the most common form of primary computer memory in computers produced before about 1975. It has been replaced by microcircuit memory in currently produced systems.

Fast core is the name generally given to core memories with an access time of less than two microseconds (thousandths of a second). *Slow core* has access time of two microseconds or more. Slow core is usually used as a

---

[1] Actually, cores are *current* rather than voltage devices. The current used may be substantial in order to attain very low switching times. Heat can then become a problem. Such use of cores is, however, not common.

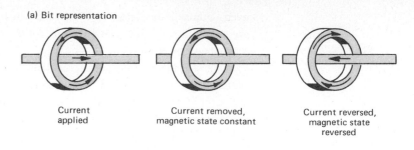

(a) Bit representation

Current
applied

Current removed,
magnetic state constant

Current reversed,
magnetic state
reversed

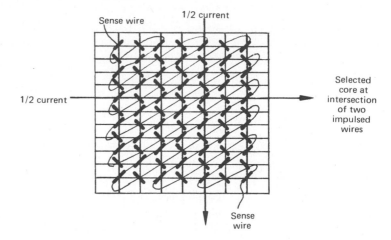

(b) Core plane, selection process

Sense wire

1/2 current

1/2 current

Selected
core at
intersection
of two
impulsed
wires

Sense
wire

(c) Core stack and character representation

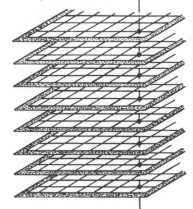

FIGURE 10.2   *Magnetic core storage*

secondary online supplement to a primary fast core memory. Fast core is manufactured from smaller magnetic cores and is less bulky as well as faster. Access speed is the single most important determinant of core cost for a memory of a given storage capacity. The faster the core, the greater the cost per character (in a given total capacity).

Film Memories *Planar,* or *thin-film,* storage is made up of flat wafers of nickel-iron alloy mounted on a very thin (ten-millionths of an inch) glass or plastic insulating base and connected by ultrathin wires. The wafers represent bits by their magnetic states, somewhat like cores, but are much smaller, having dimensions of about .05 by .025 inch. This smaller size increases the access speed. Because of the greater number of critical design factors to be controlled, planar devices are more expensive than core. They have been used for scratch pad storage in larger computers.

Plated-wire memories are formed by coating a wire with film. The wire within the coating becomes one means of accessing the store thus formed. The access across the plated wires is formed by wrapping insulated wires around those wires. In general, they have not been cost-competitive with core.

The *rod* memory is a special form of plated-wire memory in which the plated wire is a small rod. A wired grid is prepared with holes into which the short plated rods are dropped. One advantage of this method is that the manufacturing process can be automated and thus the cost is relatively low. Rod memories were able to compete directly in speed, cost, and reliability with core memories but are being replaced by microcircuit storage.

The *bubble* memory is constructed on a thin magnetic garnet film. Each "bubble" is a microscopic spot of magnetic polarization about four-millionths of an inch in diameter. These spots are controlled by means of lines of force parallel to the plane of the film in a moving magnetic field. The presence or absence of a bubble at a particular spot is used to represent a binary bit (1 or 0). A typical bubble memory module contains 100,000 to 250,000 memory bits. Bubble technology has some technical advantages over microcircuit memory modules. There are less crucial alignment tolerances, and the number of production steps is fewer. The process is still new and complex, however, and requires very precise creation and handling of the basic material. Bubble memories provide very fast access, and their use is expected to increase rapidly.

CHARACTERISTICS OF MOVING MAGNETIC SURFACES

Drums, disks, and magnetic strips share several characteristics as rotating storage devices.

Access Time   Three factors determine total access time on rotating devices:

1. *Head seek time* is the time required for a read-write head to find the appropriate track on the rotating surface. For tape strips this includes strip selection as well.

2. *Rotational delay* is the time required for the location sought to rotate under the head.

3. *Data transfer rate* is the characters transferred per second.

Head seek time is reduced essentially to zero by the provision of a head for each track on drums and disks. Multiple heads per track cut down on rotational delay. Rotational delay and transfer rate are both affected by speed of rotation. Generally, magnetic drums provide marginally faster access than magnetic disks, but both are about four orders of magnitude slower than core. They can provide an economic alternative to slow core for a limited amount of online storage. Some fixed-head disk drives are directly competitive with drums. Tape strip devices are *very* slow access, but they provide volume storage at lower cost.

Cataclysmic Failure   Rotating devices are subject to cataclysmic failure where there is a sudden power loss. The read-write heads are held above the surface of the rotating device and prevented from touching it by a cushion of air created by the movement of the device. If the device suddenly slows down, the air cushion is lost and the head drops onto the recording surface. Such a *head crash* results in the physical rearrangement of surface particles, even scoring the magnetic surface, and thus destroys the content of the device in that area. Clearances of the head from the surface are so small that the solid particulate in cigarette smoke can cause initial contact and result in a head crash. Filtering of incoming air and control of contamination (no smoking, dust control, use of lint-free paper) in the machine room are required when rotating storage devices are used.

Magnetic Drums   The magnetic drum is a cylinder spun rapidly around its longest axis. The outer surface of the drum is coated with a material that can be magnetized. Data are recorded in tracks running around the outside of the drum. Fixed heads mounted around the drum read from or write on these tracks as the drum rotates. The magnetic drum was used as the primary (CPU) storage device in several first-generation computers. It is now used for secondary storage when the user is concerned with relatively fast access to a limited amount of data. However, bulk core has now become relatively inexpensive and has begun to replace drums in this use. Drums are also disappearing because disks of similar access speed generally provide several times greater storage capacity.

Magnetic Disks Disk packs were described and discussed as input devices. They are also used for direct-access online storage.

Fixed-head disks are usually made up of several large disks permanently mounted on a revolving spindle. Read-write heads are usually fixed over each disk track. Early models had only one read-write arm and accessed only one side of one disk on any one read or write. To move to another disk required withdrawing the read-write arm, moving it vertically to the disk to be accessed next, and reinserting the arm to position the heads over the desired track. The process was very slow by current standards. The development of fixed heads has lowered access times significantly and helped to make the fixed-head disk a competitor of the drum as a direct-access storage device. The greatest advantage of disks over drums is their greater capacity.

The latest development in drives for hard disks is the Winchester drive for 8-inch disks. About the size of a bread box (the largest displayed at the 1979 National Computer Conference was about 5.5 inches by 9 inches by 19 inches), this drive has been developed to provide secondary storage capacity for microcomputer systems. By the end of 1980, users should be able to purchase a drive with almost 50 million characters of storage capacity for no more than $5000. The drives will vary widely in storage capacity and price under this maximum. Storage capacity will start at 2 million characters with 20 million characters the most common size. Cost should start at less than $1000 but the most common prices will be near $3000. Access rates and transfer rates are competitive with larger fixed-disk systems. These secondary storage systems will make the microcomputer a more viable alternative for small-business data processing systems. They may show up on some minicomputer and mainframe systems also.

Removable disk packs are described in Chapter 9 (see pages 235–237). They are widely used to provide online secondary storage, particularly in small to medium-sized systems. Because they cannot have fixed read heads (see Figure 9.5), they are generally slower than the fixed-head disks and drums. They provide the advantage of being usable for offline storage, making it possible to have a variety of files available for use online at a lower cost. The average per character cost for disk packs is only about one-fourth the average per character cost of drums.

Floppy disks are the latest development in both fixed and removable disks. As the name implies, the disk is flexible, being made of mylar (plastic) without the metal core. When spun at high speed, the disk becomes rigid and can be approached by the heads in order to read or write on the surface. The fixed-head disks have become common in small business systems. This is partly because of their much lower cost.

Floppy diskettes are the latest removable disk pack. Many record data on only one surface of the disk, but capacities of 250K to 500K[2] bytes are common. Diskettes are available that record on both surfaces of the floppy disk and provide storage for 250K to 1,200K bytes of data or programs.

Magnetic Strips Magnetic strips make use of strips of magnetizable plastic tape or film. Hundreds of these strips are hung on racks within the device. In order to read or write on the data tracks of a strip, the strip is picked off or dropped from the rack, wrapped around a rotating cylinder, and read from or written on by fixed heads mounted above the surface of the cylinder. After the reading or writing operation is completed, the strip is released from the cylinder and returned to its position on the rack. Air currents and vacuum pressure are the most common means used in moving the strips and wrapping them on the cylinder. Models are available that load the film in special cells or cartridges so that offline storage is possible. These devices have relatively high access times but store large volumes of data in a relatively small space. They are significantly lower in cost per character than either disks or drums.

CHARACTERISTICS OF MICROCIRCUIT MEMORIES

Early computer memories were mostly electrostatic. That is, bits were represented by the state of an electronic device such as a vacuum tube rather than a magnetized device. The microcircuit memory uses the electrostatic principle. A bit is represented by the state of a miniaturized circuit. However, just as magnetic cores reduced access times and memory size requirements over electrostatic devices, microcircuits are faster and smaller than cores. One silicon chip of large-pinhead size contains over 100 memory circuits.

The primary advantages of microcircuits are faster access and a 50 to 75 percent reduction in memory size. Their historical disadvantages were higher cost and volatility of storage. The current (1979) pricing process, however, does make these systems less costly than magnetic core and some are now nonvolatile. Historically, they have been used as primary memory in minicomputers and as scratch pad memory and read-only memory in larger systems. Costs of producing these memories have been declining rapidly and they are the most popular primary memory at present. It is now possible to obtain 64KB of microcircuit memory on a single silicon chip using very large-scale integration (the most advanced miniaturization) techniques.

---

[2] The symbol K represents 1,000. Thus 250K bytes equals 250,000 bytes.

Primary and Secondary Storage Devices

Primary storage has been identified as the storage element contained in the CPU. A more formal definition is needed for this term and others related to the place of use of these devices.

Primary storage is the main computer memory associated directly with the CPU. Its capacity usually can be changed by the addition or deletion of storage modules or by replacing the current modules with modules of different speed. Without such storage the computer could not operate.

Secondary storage is the storage attached to the computer by input-output channels. Changing the size of this storage can involve adding or deleting storage units on existing controllers (channels) or adding or deleting channels and the devices they control. Devices added to a system may be entirely different from existing devices. For example, a drum controller (channel) and a drum memory could be added to a system where none had been present before. Large secondary memory devices are often referred to as *mass* memory devices (see Figure 8.7, page 215). Transfer rates from secondary storage are controlled by not only the speed of the storage device but also the transfer capability (bandwidth) of the channel by which the device is accessed. Thus the number of devices accessed by a given channel affects the actual access time. A slow channel can access fewer devices in a given time interval.

Several other memories have also been mentioned. *Scratch pad memories* are used as temporary interim storage to speed processes in the central processing unit. *Read-only memories* (ROM) are special-purpose memories used to enhance or modify the capabilities of a given machine. Some now provide hardware versions of software compilers or allow use of the instruction set for a different machine. *Programmable read-only memories* (PROM) that can be more easily modified are being extensively used to provide variable capabilities for special applications and for a few general systems. Finally, many machines contain *registers*, which are limited in size

FIGURE 10.3   *Summary of place of use of storage devices*

| Place of use | Device | | | | | | | |
	Core	Drum	Disk Pack	Disk Fixed	Film Planar	Film Bubble	Micro-circuit	Magnetic strip
Primary	X				X	X	X	
Secondary	X	X	X	X				X
ROM & PROM					X		X	
Scratch pad	X				X	X	X	
Registers	X						X	

and store data elements (for arithmetic operations) and control variables, addresses, and so on, during processing. Multiple registers are used in computers designed for timesharing to handle the interrupts, paging, and so on, with maximum efficiency. Registers are often merely portions of the primary storage set aside for this use.

A summary of the uses of the various memory devices for various purposes is given in Figure 10.3.

Online and Offline Storage

The discussion of computer storage up to this point has been concerned almost entirely with *online* storage, that is, when the device is attached to and under the control of the CPU. However, it has been mentioned that several online media can be used for storing data and information offline as well (see Figure 10.3). The characteristics of those devices and media that can provide offline storage and also serve as online storage or an input medium (or both) are discussed below. Media to be discussed include punched cards, punched paper tape, magnetic tape, magnetic strips, disk packs, and other special devices.

INPUT MEDIA USED AS OFFLINE STORAGE

Input media serving as offline storage are punched cards, punched paper tape, and optically and magnetically read documents. All are discussed as input media in Chapter 9 and will be treated only briefly here.

Punched Cards Punched cards are bulky, must be stored in a semicontrolled environment, must be handled with some care to prevent damage, and can be put through processing machines only a few times before causing problems. Their contents cannot be changed, only added to on cards that are not full. Because single cards can be easily removed and replaced or new cards inserted, they have been widely used to store master copies of programs and data files. However, due to the greater I/O speeds of other media, the faster processing speeds of computers, the greater desire for integrating data processing systems, the increasing use of point-of-action recording and direct entry, and the development of key-to-tape and key-to-disk processes, punched cards are now losing favor as an input and offline storage medium.

Punched Paper Tape Because of the ease with which it can be torn, crimped, or otherwise damaged, paper tape is not widely used as a storage medium except as backup to electronically stored files and programs on timesharing and teleprocessing systems and as a cheap recording medium for capturing noncritical data, such as the results of scientific experiments.

Optically and Magnetically Read Documents Documents are probably the most widely used offline data storage medium regardless of the input medium. They have the very great advantages of familiarity and human readability. Their biggest disadvantages are bulk and ease of misfiling. When retained in large quantity or for long periods, they are often reduced to microfilm. The development of microfilm readers that can serve as input to computers, the availability of COM devices, and the continuing improvement of OCR input devices should lead to increasing use of document input, conversion to microfilm, and offline storage on microfilm. Improved devices for direct retrieval and display of microfilm from large stores should support this trend.

Magnetic-ink-encoded documents have not been widely adopted outside commercial banking, and their use is expected to decline in the future as OCR input devices and computer networking continue to improve.

INPUT MEDIA USED AS ONLINE AND
OFFLINE STORAGE

Media falling into this category include magnetic tape and magnetic-disk packs.

Magnetic Tape This was the most widely used medium for offline storage, but it has lost ground to magnetic disks. Its advantages are fast transfer rate, little bulk, unlimited record length, low cost per unit, and reusability. Disadvantages are that magnetic tape must be interpreted by a machine; it is a sequential-access medium; and it requires careful handling and a dust-free, controlled environment.

A magnetic tape cannot be fully loaded with useful data or information. Because of the speed at which it is moved when being read from or written onto, gaps are placed between records and between blocks of records. These gaps take up at least six-tenths of an inch, or about 2,000 to 2,400 characters on a 3,200-bit-per-inch tape. These gaps allow for stopping and starting the tape slowly so that it will not be damaged or characters lost.

Tapes are faster to key data to than cards but slightly slower than disk packs. However, they can be written on the computer at the maximum transfer rate of the tape drive being used. Data entered onto a magnetic tape are readable almost indefinitely (nonvolatile storage) unless the tape is damaged. A tape can be used hundreds of times in processing before it needs replacing. One ordinary 2,400-foot tape will store a maximum of 75 million characters at 3,200 bits per inch. At 6,250 bits per inch, approximately 140 million characters can be stored on a single tape reel.

Magnetic-Disk Packs   Declining costs, random-access capability, and increased capacity combine with the ability to be stored offline to make disk packs an increasingly popular data medium. Random-access files allow inline processing of transactions with immediate update of all files involved. Further, access to the files themselves is at electronic speeds. The ability to request data or information directly from the computer and receive an immediate response is an important advantage of using disk files. The disk pack makes a version of this process available on small systems. Packs stored on the shelf must be mounted on a drive before they can be accessed. Maximum capacity of packs is currently about 100 million characters. The newer *double-density* disks have increased disk pack capacities and made disk packs more economical by storing 6,250 bits per inch.

Random-access master files are much more efficient than tape when the file *hit rate* (the proportion of records accessed) is low during processing, that is, when a limited number of transactions are processed against a very large master file. Random-access files require that only the records actually affected need be handled. Such files are also efficient in high-activity applications when the file must be frequently updated. Finally, random-access devices can be used efficiently in sequential (record sequence) processing. Thus they provide flexibility and allow the analyst to choose the most efficient and effective processing mode.

OTHER ONLINE AND OFFLINE STORAGE

Only one device not used for data input has been widely used to provide offline as well as online storage. This is the tape or film strip. On some devices the strips are mounted in containers (cells or cartridges). Several containers are mounted on each read-write device and can be removed and stored offline if necessary. This offline capability has not been exploited to any great degree.

Because of their data holding capacity and slow access, magnetic-strip devices have been used on systems when online access to a large file is useful and there is not a need for very fast response. Magnetic-strip devices have proved economical in such operations.

Summary

A new vocabulary has been developed to describe the properties of electronic storage devices. We find that the devices are *volatile* (lose their content when the power is shut off) and *nonvolatile*, contain *fixed or variable word lengths*, and are organized into *locations* each of which stores a basic data unit (word or character) and has an *address*. They are protected against error by the presence of a *parity bit*, which is used to make sure that each character representation has the proper number of bits (odd or even, depending on the design).

Computer storage devices can be classified in several ways. They can be classified by type of electronic medium involved (*fixed magnetic surface, moving magnetic surface,* or *microcircuits*); by whether they are directly associated with the CPU (*primary*) or available by way of a channel to the CPU (*secondary*); or by whether they are attached to the CPU and under its control (*online*) or not (*offline*). Characteristics critical to their inclusion in a computer system include access time, access mode, capacity, expandability, bulk, volatility, and cost.

Questions

1. Define the following as briefly as possible and then use a short paragraph to clarify each definition.

   a. Primary storage
   b. Secondary storage
   c. Online storage
   d. Offline storage
   e. Storage address
   f. Magnetic core
   g. Magnetic drum
   h. Disk pack
   i. Fixed-head disk
   j. Read-only memory (ROM)
   k. Fixed word length
   l. Variable word length
   m. Volatile
   n. Nonvolatile
   o. Parity bit
   p. Planar film
   q. Rod memory
   r. Slow core
   s. Fast core
   t. Head crash
   u. Bubble memory

2. Under what conditions would magnetic tape be preferable to magnetic-disk packs for use on a computer system?

3. Under what conditions would microcircuits be preferable to fast core as the primary memory medium for a computer system? Explain.

4. What factors determine total access time for a rotating storage device? Explain.

5. When disk packs are available to provide offline as well as online storage with random access, why would fixed-head disks ever be used? Explain.

6. Since core memories are so fast, why do manufacturers continue to seek a faster device?

7. What is a PROM? What is it used for?

8. What is the purpose of scratch pad memory?

9. Under what conditions would it be reasonable to use optical or magnetic reading devices for data entry? Explain.
10. What is the most common storage medium used for each of the following? Why?
    a. Primary storage
    b. Offline storage in machine-sensible form
    c. Random-access online secondary storage
11. What would be the effects on business information processing of the development and marketing of a cheap memory device with almost unlimited capacity (say, 100 billion characters) and a very fast access (say, a basic cycle time of 100 nanoseconds)?
12. How would the effects change if the large memory device of question 11 could not be altered, that is, if the content of a location could not be changed after it was first entered?
13. What is the significance of the fact that microcircuit memories can be mass produced but fast core memories cannot?
14. Refer to question 17 at the end of Chapter 7. On what medium would you suggest that Black Oil store its customer master file? Explain. (*Note:* For control purposes, the company must have up-to-date account status to respond to telephone inquiries from stations.)

Eleven

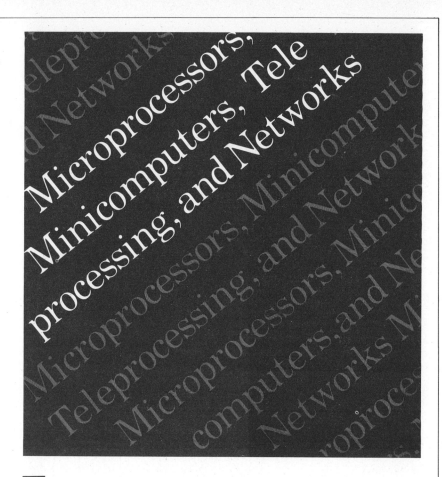

Microprocessors, Tele
Minicomputers, Tele
processing, and Networks

The *microprocessor*, a processor on a single silicon chip, may be the most significant technological development of the computer age. It is now possible to put on a single chip the size of the head of a paper match the central processor of a computer, or 64K bits of memory. Soon there will be over a million components on one chip. Such a chip can be manufactured in volume at small cost. The implications for new uses are staggering. New devices are appearing every day that incorporate this rapidly improving technology. Led by hand-held calculators and TV games, there are now electronically controlled appliances, gasoline pump meters, weapons systems, automobile ignitions, microwave ovens, and general-purpose *microcomputers*. *Minicomputers* and large computers, *mainframes*, are becoming easier to use and are given more capability through the use of *microcode* or *firmware* (software translated into hardware in microprocessor form) and improved device controllers and interfaces.

The improvements in microprocessor technology are bringing rapid expansion in the use of microprocessor-based computer systems and minicomputers in small businesses. In larger firms, minicomputers and microprocessors are being incorporated in distributed processing systems and teleprocessing networks. It is the purpose of this chapter to trace these developments and indicate their implications for the future of business information systems and their management. First, the microprocessor and the microcomputer will be discussed. Second, minicomputers will be described, followed by a short section on turnkey systems. The third part of the chapter discusses how these devices are being used in teleprocessing systems. The fourth part covers distributed processing systems.

Microprocessors and Microcomputers

The first microprocessor was developed in 1970 for use in a hand-held calculator. It provided a general computational device that could be made to serve special purposes through programming. It was not long before microprocessors were being joined with a memory and input/output circuits to create the microcomputer.

A microprocessor differs from a microcomputer.

A *microprocessor*, as its name implies, *is a general processor created using microcircuit technology* [large-scale integration (LSI) and very large-scale integration (VLSI)], *without any of the supporting circuitry and devices to provide memory, input/output, and control capabilities present in a computer system.*

A *microcomputer is a true computer built around a microprocessor by adding circuitry and devices to provide memory, input/output, and control functions.*

Microprocessors are commonly classified according to the size of the word operated on at one time in the registers that perform arithmetic operations. The most common numbers of bits in each word are 4 and multiples of 4 up to 16 (4, 8, 12, and 16). These processors are produced by the Metal-Oxide Semiconductor (MOS) production process. The 4-bit processors are usually equipped to handle arithmetic in binary coded decimal form. The 8-bit processors are the most popular microprocessors. They are common in communications applications because 8 bits can represent most of the basic communication codes. They are easier to program than the 4-bit processors and also provide greater arithmetic precision (resolution to 1 part in 256 in single-precision and 1 part in 65,356 in double-precision). The 12-bit types are popular as emulators of other computer systems. The 12-bit word provides greater arithmetic precision. However, since each instruction word of 12 bits normally contains one address along with the instruction, both the instruction set and the addressing capability tend to be reduced. The 16-bit processor is similar in character to an 8-bit processor operating on two words at a time.

A subset of 2-bit and 4-bit high-speed *bit-slice* processors using a bipolar process are available. Their primary advantages are speed and flexibility. They perform primitive operations (*microinstructions*) very rapidly. Combinations of microinstructions in the form of *microprograms* carry out *macroinstructions*. The microprograms are stored in read-only memory (ROM) associated with the microprocessor. Sets of bit-slice processors can be organized to emulate a processor of any desired word size that is a multiple of the basic word size. By changing the microprograms in the ROM, the processor can be made to emulate (act like) any other 8- or 16-bit processor. They have been used to create 24-bit processors as well.

The microprocessor is changing the nature of the computer industry. Easy to produce, they are being incorporated as controllers in peripheral devices, communication links, and processors. A *microcomputer* can be produced cheaply and sold to a mass market, making the power of the computer available to virtually every small business. Hobbyists have been quick to seize the business opportunity involved in the development of small business systems software. These computers and the related software are being marketed through retail stores, software houses, and local computer consultants. Combinations of retail stores selling the hardware and hobbyists or moonlighting mainframe computer programmers are common. Over 700 firms are now involved in producing and marketing small microcomputer-based personal and business systems. Most will not survive.

Microcomputers are full computers, with CPU, memory, and I/O. Microcomputers are physically packaged on one or more printed circuit boards. These boards are commonly about 12 inches by 7 inches. Some systems are built by combining smaller boards (cards) each of which contains one or two subcomponents. The cards are inserted into a card frame which provides the necessary electrical interconnections. When packaged in a chassis with a power supply and connectors for I/O devices, the system is complete. Many microcomputers for the hobby trade look like TV sets with a keyboard attached by a cable. The chassis containing the CRT display also contains the card frames and power supply. The keyboard provides input; the CRT provides output. When these systems are provided with devices for reading tape cassettes or portable floppy diskettes and some sort of printer, business data processing systems are created. The availability of the 8-inch Winchester disk-drive (see Chapter 9, page 265) will make these systems increasingly competitive in the small-business–systems market.

Microcomputer hardware, priced from $600 to $5,000 per system, is now available through retail outlets. Software is being provided by software houses, moonlighting programmers, and computer hobbyists. Complete accounting systems for small firms are available at minimal cost from a variety of firms. In this area, microcomputers are starting to invade the former domain of the minicomputer as the basis for small business systems. The latest move is to connect several microcomputers to produce a powerful and flexible multiprocessor computer system.

Higher level compiler languages, particularly BASIC, are now available on microcomputers. Much of this software is being incorporated as part of the hardware in a microprocessor board. That is, the program providing the language is actually a special microprocessor board. Such microprocessor compilers (firmware) are also being made available for minicomputers and mainframes.

Minicomputers

Minicomputers are not as densely integrated as microcomputers. Most minicomputers use architectural concepts developed in the 1960s. This is changing, however, as minicomputer and mainframe (large computer) architecture is being moved in the direction pioneered by microcomputer manufacturers. Minicomputer word sizes vary from 12 bits to 32 bits, with 16 bits being most common. Minicomputer primary memories are both magnetic core and microcircuit random-access memories. Some feature programmable-read-only memory (PROM), but this is a relatively expensive alternative. Very fast read-only scratch pad (cache) memories and virtual memory capability are available on sophisticated minicomputers intended to support timeshared processing systems. Minicomputers can be equipped with a wide range of peripherals and be part of multiprogrammed, time-shared, and network systems. They currently have larger instruction sets than microcomputers and better software for higher level languages. These latter advantages are disappearing, however, as new entrepreneurs apply imagination and ingenuity to the configuration of microcomputers. As hardware compilers proliferate, microprocessor capabilities in the software area are expanding rapidly. It is increasingly difficult to separate large microcomputers and small minicomputers. Both can provide computer power in excess of that provided by early middle-sized mainframes.

The differences between minicomputers and microcomputers become more obvious as the size of the system expands. The larger word size of the minicomputer allows for a larger primary memory (more locations can be addressed) and more complex configurations of peripherals. Specialized interfaces and controllers, often built using microprocessor technology, make it possible for minicomputers to invade the domain formerly reserved for large mainframes. They are no longer restricted to use as intelligent terminals and small data processing systems. Minicomputers are now common as the core of timesharing systems supporting sixty-four or more simultaneous users. They are connected in networks to provide on-site data processing for users located away from the central data processing installation. (These distributed data processing systems are described more fully below.) Minicomputers are often no longer "mini"; they possess most of the characteristics of large mainframes, except the ability to directly address large primary random-access memories. This, too, is changing as minicomputers with larger word sizes and virtual memory capability become more common.

Minimal minicomputer systems can be purchased for as little as $5,000. The largest minicomputer systems include banks of peripherals controlled by sophisticated executive programs and can cost over a quarter of a million dollars. Timesharing executives for minicomputer systems often include such features as virtual memory, dynamic memory allocation, and sophisticated compilers for higher level languages.

Minicomputer software now rivals that of the mainframes. Executives, assemblers, compilers, utilities, and data base management languages are all available. New languages are available, particularly on minicomputers and mainframes, that provide a file-handling capability that allows data processing applications programs to be built up from a series of questions posed by the user. These languages are very easy to learn and free small businesses and divisions of larger firms of the need for programmers in order to develop data processing applications programs. (These languages are discussed further in Chapter 14.)

Turnkey Systems

Turnkey systems capable of performing the specialized data processing functions of a particular small business or of a particular business function in a larger firm are available from a wide variety of firms. These systems are a combination of hardware and software needing only to be plugged into a power supply to take over the data processing application for which they have been designed. Thus the designation as *turnkey*, turn them on and they perform.

Turnkey systems are available for handling almost every one of the basic accounting systems. Specialized accounting and/or control systems are available in the areas of total accounts receivable, customer billing, inventory or general materials control, order processing and sales analysis, payroll, labor cost control, and general ledger accounting. These ready-made packages of hardware and software serve both large and small firms.

Turnkey systems are also available that provide a fairly complete data processing system for a particular type of firm. Systems are available for automobile dealerships; medical and dental clinics; wholesale distributors (automobile parts, electrical supplies, and so on); retail stores; and many more. These systems eliminate the need for small firms or divisions of large firms to design and program their own data processing and information systems. Maintenance for both the hardware and software are provided (for a fee) by the system vendor.

The quality of turnkey systems varies widely. Some are packaged and sold by large, stable firms with a history of success in software development. Some are being developed and sold out of someone's garage. Great care should be exercised when purchasing such systems to be sure that the firm is solvent and stable enough to continue to supply support over the life of the system.

Turnkey systems developed on mainframes are also available. For example, total packages for Medicare and Medicaid processing at the state level are now available. Complete data processing and information systems for large wholesalers, automobile dealers, and other industries can also be purchased.

Teleprocessing

When data are entered from remote locations via telephone and telegraph lines and, perhaps, operated upon and results returned over the same lines, *teleprocessing* takes place. The use of special-purpose minicomputers has speeded the development of business teleprocessing systems, which often have featured multiprogramming or timesharing as well. Minicomputers have been used as "front end" *communications controllers* for such systems. They poll the individual data or inquiry stations and supervise development of a full message from one station before passing it along to the central computer over one of several high-speed channels. They temporarily store output messages until the proper terminals can receive them.

MULTIPLEXORS AND CONCENTRATORS

Minis have also been used in *multiplexors* and *concentrators* to concentrate line use and reduce the need for transmission lines. If we think of a transmission line as a complex pipe that is divisible into smaller pipes, one type of *multiplexor* divides the pipe into the system of subpipes and sends simultaneous messages along each subpipe. This provides more message *carrying capacity* per unit of time. Unfortunately, the *data carrying capacity* (speed) of a line is proportional to its *bandwidth*. Dividing the line into several parallel sublines divides the bandwidth of the total line in the same way. Each subline has a significantly reduced transmission capability.

A second type of multiplexor uses the full bandwidth for each message, but several messages are pulsed intermittently (spaced in time) along the line. This type is referred to as a *time division multiplexor*.

Line concentrators differ from multiplexors in that they accept messages from a group of terminals and then pass them along (over the telephone or telegraph line) to the computer. The concentrator involves buffering and may output less data in a single unit of time than is input to it during that time unit. In contrast, multiplexors are devices that allow several stations to share a single line simultaneously, and they accept input and deliver output at the same rate.

TELEPHONE LINES

Two basic types of telephone lines are available. *Dial-up* ("switched" or "direct distance dialing") lines provide flexibility, permitting contact with any party having access to the telephone network. *Leased* lines provide a continuous connection for two or more locations. These leased (private) lines can sometimes be shared with other users, which reduces the cost. In the same way, dial-up users can often save money by purchasing Wide Area Telephone Service (WATS). WATS allows unlimited calls to be placed (or received) within the prescribed service area without individual call tolls being paid.

Choice among standard dial-ups, WATS, and leased lines depends on the volume and nature of the messages. If there are many short message exchanges with numerous points, dial-up is more economical. Leased lines are used when lengthy messages must be exchanged with a few points. WATS becomes economical when messages are lengthy and frequent and are exchanged with numerous locations.

As indicated above, speed of transmission (characters per second) is controlled by *bandwidth* of the line. Most lines in use today are so-called voice-grade lines designed to carry voice communications. The normal bandwidth is 3,000 cycles. Some lines — teletypewriter circuits, for example — are less than 3,000 cycles and are referred to as *narrowband* lines. High-speed transmission requires *wideband* or *broadband* channels of more than 3,000 cycles. Leased lines can also be *conditioned* to remove undesirable *noise*, or distortion, from the data transmission. Dial-up facilities cannot be conditioned. The maximum transmission rate for voice-grade lines is 2,400 bits per second as a dial-up line. Speeds of over 1 million bits per second are possible on conditioned leased lines. The greater the bandwidth and the more the conditioning, the greater the cost of a leased line.

A third factor to consider is *transmission mode*. A *full-duplex* line (available only on leased lines) permits simultaneous transmission in both directions on the line. *Half-duplex* mode allows movement in only one direction at one time, although nonoverlapping transmission in both directions is possible. *Simplex*, the cheapest mode, allows transmission in only one direction.

The three factors — bandwidth, conditioning, and transmission mode — must be carefully considered in selecting a communication channel. Average data volume per period, maximum rate per period, calling distance, average call time, and need for fast response will determine what combination will be most cost-effective.

A final consideration in developing a cost-effective communication channel is the *modem*. *Modems* are required on each end of the line to make it possible to send data over lines designed for voice transmission. The *modulator-dem*odulator process converts the data signals to audio at the sending end and from audio back to data impulses at the receiving end. The modems on each end of the line must operate in phase with one another. Transmission involves sending a sequence of bits constituting a data message and containing not only the codes for the actual message but parity bits and control bits as well. Bits must be received in order and properly interpreted at the receiving end. This is accomplished by using a *synchronous* or an *asynchronous* timing process. The synchronous technique is more desirable. As the data come out of the terminal, they consist of a sequence of pulses and no-pulses representing the binary 1's and 0's. Synchronous modems send pulses at regular, periodic intervals whether a message is being sent or not and no start and stop bits need be added to the message. Start and stop bits are required for asynchronous modems. Synchronous modems are faster but also more expensive. The transmission speed of a modem is also affected by whether it operates in serial or parallel mode. Parallel mode is faster and more expensive.

SATELLITE TRANSMISSION SYSTEMS

The newest method of telecommunications involves transmission via satellite. Figure 11.1 provides an overview of the possible communication systems. Note that in the land-line system in part (a), each user contacts remote sites over a physically connected wire. In the microwave system of part (b), microwave transmission is substituted for land lines between system exchanges; costs are significantly reduced. The use of satellites [part (c)] provides a more flexible system, however. Each user and remote site must be connected to ground stations only to transmit messages. Messages may be received directly over a wide area. The reason for the ground station in

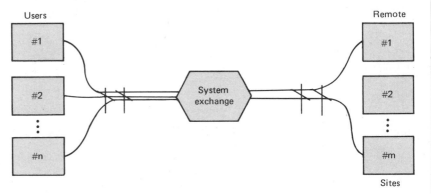

(a) Land line system

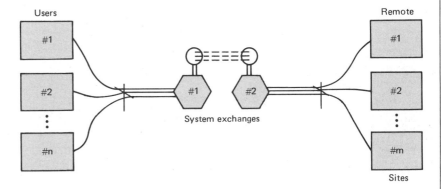

(b) Land-base microwave system

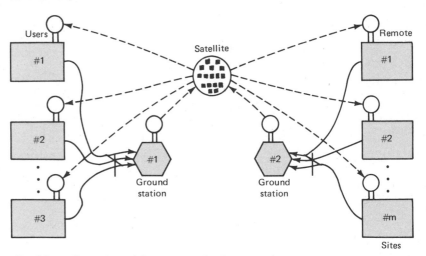

(c) Satellite system

FIGURE 11.1   *Possible configurations of data communication networks*

the sending loop is the size of the antenna required to direct the message to the satellite. The satellite and its solar-paneled power unit may weigh several tons, but it is quite a small target. Conversely, the satellite may send out a dispersed signal that can be picked up on much smaller antenna over a wide area. Through the use of microcomputers or minicomputers, each receiving site is capable of sorting out its own particular signal and retains only those messages intended for it.

Satellites are attractive as communications links between sites inaccessible by land lines or land-based microwave. Satellites can now be placed in synchronous orbit to circle the earth once in each twenty-four hours and thus appear to be stationary over a specific geographic location. The satellite is in a very high vacuum, out of the range of most human-produced interference, and is at a nearly constant temperature. The wear and tear of temperature-related expansion and contraction and atmospheric-born corrosion are absent. Thus the expensive satellite should out-perform and outlast its earthbound electronic cousins. In this way, a satellite system can be less expensive than any land-based system when communicating over long distances. Satellite systems have an economic advantage on long-distance routes. Land lines and land-based microwave are more economic over shorter distances.

When systems are expanded to provide satellite-to-satellite links, any spot on earth becomes accessible. The minimum number of satellites to give total coverage of the earth (other than the poles) is three. The only problem is that it takes a signal about one quarter of a second to travel to an orbiting satellite and back. This slight delay is increased by satellite-to-satellite links. Telephone users seem to notice only slightly the delays of up to one-half second. Persons using data networks would not be inconvenienced by delays of more than one second. (Timeshare systems are considered adequate if response times can be held to no more than three seconds.)

Two factors determine satellite performance. First, their power and sophistication is primarily dependent on their size. Second, the frequencies they use determine their signal-carrying capacity and the narrowness of their radiated beams. In order to have many satellites in orbit, the beam from each satellite must be narrow in order that the signals do not become mixed. In general, as satellites get larger, the sending and receiving antenna on earth can get smaller. Eventually, each home will be able to receive television communications directly from a satellite. Similarly, each business location can now receive messages directly from a satellite.

TYPES OF DATA SYSTEMS

Data communication systems may be simple two-terminal links (switched or leased lines), data acquisition systems, data distribution systems, or interrogation systems. Each of these systems can be online or offline. In the offline mode, the data transmission system is not connected to the computer processing system. Data would be transferred physically between the transmission system and the computer system, usually by use of punched paper tape or magnetic tape. In online systems, the communication link is attached directly to computer-controlled storage. Data may or may not be processed immediately, depending on the time constraints of the application.

Data Acquisition Systems   Data acquisition systems are of two types, the *star system* and the *branched network*. In the star system, each remote site from which data are sent is connected by a direct link to the central computer site. In the *branched network*, the message streams from individual remote sites are sent over tributary feeder lines to a major communication link connected directly to the central site. A number of slow links carrying low volumes of data are merged by zone concentrators onto a single but faster high-capacity line to the central computer site.

Data Distribution Systems   Data distribution systems are the reverse of the data acquisition systems and are used to disseminate messages from a central site to many remote locations. Multiplexing is not usually used. Rather, each remote station is normally called onto the system whenever a message is to be sent to it. The entire message is then sent in a single transmission. Several remote sites can receive the same message simultaneously.

Data Interrogation Systems   Data interrogation systems usually have been designed to enable remote users to access a central data base, usually one in which the stored data is being constantly updated. Examples would be a stock exchange price quotation system, a statewide welfare data base, and a statewide registry of automobiles and licensed drivers. Systems are now being developed that essentially reverse this process, allowing central sites and remote users to access several widely dispersed data bases.

Distributed Processing

DISTRIBUTED PROCESSING NETWORKS WITH COMMUNICATION

Data communication networks are quite common and are increasing in use. Teleprocessing networks are not quite as common but have been in wide use for a decade. There are two major types of networks. *Star networks* are so designed that all communications among network components (user terminal and the central computer, for example) must pass through the central control computer. In a *distributed network*, data can go from any one point to any other point without passing through the central location.

In *distributed processing networks*, minicomputers are found as decentralized satellite processors located at high-activity points. The central computer leaves much of the routine processing to the satellite processors. Configuration possibilities for such systems are practically unlimited. They are increasing in popularity as they increase in reliability, and their cost continues to decline. Each system tends to be uniquely designed for the use to which it is being put, but some common features are emerging.

First of all, most of these distributed processing networks involve data communication networks. The major difference from simple communication networks is the availability of computer processing capability at each node of the network. The processing at the remote sites varies from sophisticated data editing and error control and correction to full processing. The processing often involves carrying out detail record update and the creation of custodial documents. Summarized data are sent at regular intervals to the central computer site and entered into its summary data base. Summary reports (for example, balance sheets, profit and loss statements) are prepared at the central site. The detailed data base for each business account (such as a customer account receivable or item inventory) is maintained at the operating site, and its detail is forwarded to the central site only if a problem is being investigated. Customer or item records are updated, billings prepared, accounts aged, and/or inventory status analyzed at the local remote site. Only the summary statistics are forwarded to the central computer site.

In some systems, only minimal detailed processing is carried out at the operating site with data being forwarded periodically (daily) to the central site for full processing. For example, some department store chains have a computer in each store with the cash registers in the store acting as terminals for it. The transactions at each cash register are sorted and accumulated during the day. Each night, the data are presorted by item, customer, and so on, and sent to a central computer center, which updates customer and inventory accounts and prepares orders for replenishing inventory, customer billings, financial reports, and so forth.

There are commercially available distributed processing networks that anyone willing to pay the cost can attach to. Only that amount of communication and distributed computing used is paid for.

DISTRIBUTED PROCESSING SYSTEMS
WITHOUT COMMUNICATION

Another form of distributed processing system may involve no communication network or a minimal one. Minicomputer systems are being designed to handle specific applications to provide local control and relieve the central computer of part of the processing load. For example, a production scheduling and control system for a single plant may be controlled by a minicomputer at the local plant. Special terminals on the factory floor, in the warehouse, at the receiving dock, and in the receiving department provide inputs to record materials received, goods in process, amount and cost of production, and so on. The minicomputer system provides all the processing necessary to plan and control plant operations to meet output and quality requirements at minimal cost. Evaluation and control reports are prepared and forwarded to the central offices of the company at another location. Telecommunications may or may not be involved in this latter communication.

Summary

The *microprocessor*, a general processor using microcircuit technology, is the basis of many of the changes occurring in the design and application of computers. Microprocessors are being incorporated as controllers in peripheral devices, as communication links, as specialized processors, as higher level language compilers (firmware), and in microcomputers. When provided with devices for reading tape cassettes and floppy diskettes, and a printing device, microprocessors become small business data processing systems. Such systems are available through retail outlets and from consultants and software houses. Costing from a few hundred to a few thousand dollars, they put computer processing power within reach of almost every small business.

Minicomputers, also relatively inexpensive (about $10,000) at the lower end, are no longer necessarily mini. Systems with multiprogramming, timesharing, and data base management capabilities rival the power of much larger computers (mainframes) and can cost upwards of a quarter of a million dollars.

Software for minicomputers is as good and as extensive as mainframe software. Software available for microprocessors is also rapidly expanding. Both minis and micros are being designed as special-purpose systems of hardware and software to carry out a particular application (payroll, accounts receivable, inventory accounting and control, and so on). These *turnkey systems* are winning increasing acceptance as both hardware and software (and firmware) continue to improve at a rapid rate. Turnkey systems are also being developed to provide a ready-made hardware and software package to perform most of the data processing jobs for firms in a particular industry, particularly small firms.

Teleprocessing involving the acquisition, processing, or interrogation of data from a remote site over a communication system is widely practiced.

Minicomputers and microprocessors are being applied as communications controllers, multiplexors, and line concentrators in these systems. Networks of computers that create and share common data bases are bringing the power of the computer to users remote from the central data processing center featuring a large mainframe processor.

Owing to the availability of minicomputers, *distributed processing networks* are becoming common. A small computer at each remote operating site performs local processing and sends partially processed data or fully processed results to the central site. The computer at each node of a distributed system may be partially or fully online to a central computer or operate completely in a stand-alone offline mode. Thus telecommunications may or may not be involved in distributed data processing systems.

Questions

1. Define the following as briefly as possible and then use a short paragraph to clarify each definition.

   a. Microprocessor
   b. Mainframe
   c. Microcircuit
   d. Microcode
   e. PROM
   f. Macroinstructions
   g. Line concentrator
   h. Data acquisition system
   i. Data interrogation system
   j. Full-duplex line
   k. Minicomputer
   l. Microcomputer
   m. Circuit board
   n. Cache memory
   o. Microinstructions
   p. Multiplexor
   q. Modem
   r. Data distribution system
   s. Distributed processing
   t. Teleprocessing
   u. Turnkey system
   v. Firmware

2. How is the minicomputer affecting business data processing?

3. As microcomputer-based processing systems become more common, what effect will they have on firms providing computing services to small businesses?

4. Why are simplex modems and transmission lines seldom used?

5. What are the advantages and disadvantages of distributed processing networks involving telecommunications?

6. What are the advantages and disadvantages of distributed processing systems without teleprocessing?

7. Under what conditions should teleprocessing systems be considered?

8. What are the types of teleprocessing systems?

9. Under what conditions should distributed processing systems be considered?

10. What are the three factors to be considered when choosing a communication channel?

11. How are satellites changing teleprocessing economics?
12. What is (are) the relationship(s) between a modem and a communication line?
13. In a teleprocessing system, what advantages are there in handling message processing in a front-end minicomputer dedicated to this task rather than having the entire job handled by the mainframe CPU?
14. What are the common characteristics of microcomputers?
15. What are the common characteristics of minicomputers?
16. What advantages and disadvantages might be encountered if complex processing and information systems were divided into specialized functional tasks (see Chapter 4) and each of the resulting modules were handled by a separate minicomputer or microcomputer?
17. Refer to question 16 and assume that the small processors would be joined in a network, then answer the question.
18. What if the network referred to in question 17 featured a limited number of commonly used input and output devices?
19. What is the difference between software and firmware?
20. What are the advantages of firmware over software and of software over firmware?
21. What are the advantages and disadvantages of turnkey systems?
22. Identify and contrast the advantages and disadvantages of dial-up, WATS, and leased telecommunication lines.
23. How might the charge sales system of Black Oil Company described in question 17 at the end of Chapter 7 use:
    a. Teleprocessing?
    b. Distributed processing?
24. How might the hardware store chain described in question 20 at the end of Chapter 3 use:
    a. Teleprocessing?
    b. Distributed processing?
25. Develop the system chart for a turnkey system for payroll. Include labor cost distribution as part of the system. Do not forget quarterly payments to the federal government for income tax withholding, for F.I.C.A., and for unemployment insurance taxes. You need not include the actual computation of these tax amounts but show where the appropriate calculations would occur. Also include the development of the wage and tax (W-2) report for each employee at the end of the year.

Twelve

Obtaining the Proper Computer Configuration

Computer selection is a complex process. The number of alternative configurations that can be considered for a particular installation is almost unlimited. Computers are produced by nearly a hundred firms. Large computers are available from nine major manufacturers and a score of other suppliers. Minicomputers, many with capabilities that match or exceed those of medium-sized second-generation computers, are available from over sixty manufacturers. Input-output and secondary storage peripherals are available from most of these firms and many more. Each computer system comes in a variety of specific configurations from its manufacturer, and components can be substituted from many other sources. Software enhancements of hardware capabilities add another dimension of complexity to computer selection.

Wise selection requires a rational procedure. The basic procedure discussed in this chapter consists of the following steps:

Determining performance requirements

Defining alternative systems

Measuring hardware performance

Measuring software performance

Balancing hardware and software

Choosing between buying and leasing

Negotiating the contract

These steps will serve as an outline for the discussion.

Determining Performance Requirements

The purpose of determining performance requirements is to identify the general capabilities that the computer system must possess in order to accomplish the tasks it is intended to carry out. These general capabilities must then be refined and translated into the specific capabilities and characteristics the hardware must possess.

GENERAL CAPABILITIES REQUIRED

The question to be answered here is: What overall capabilities must the system possess?

1. *Nature of the processing* Does the required processing consist of complex data manipulation and scientific processing with small amounts of input and output (number crunching), of voluminous data throughput with minimal computation, or of a mix of the two?

2. *Storage and retrieval requirements* Is quick response to inquiry a characteristic the final system must possess? How many data must be stored in a machine-accessible form, online and offline?

3. *Amount of computing power* How many different users or applications can be identified? Do they have needs for the services of the computer at the exact same time? What volume of use does each have (data input, storage of data online and offline, and output reports or responses)?

4. *Locations of users* Is there a need for computing power at sites outside the computing center? What kind(s) of computing is (are) necessary at each location?

These questions are not intended to be exhaustive, only suggestive. They relate to the objectives of the organization, particularly its reasons for considering the acquisition of a computer system.

The primary objective is to specify task performance in general terms so that the definition of specific capabilities can begin. Care must be exercised at this stage *not* to preclude viable alternatives. As a first step, it is wise to specify major tasks and the types and volumes of processing each requires. This is also the place to recognize and critically examine assumptions or policy that put nontechnical restrictions on alternatives. For example, it used to be quite common for educational institutions to require separate computer systems for administrative data processing and for teaching and research. Partially because of the wider availability of timeshared and multiprogrammed systems but largely because of economic considerations, this arbitrary restriction is disappearing.

SPECIFIC CAPACITIES REQUIRED

Once the *general* nature of the computing requirements has been identified, these requirements must be refined into specific capacities. The answers to the general questions all suggest further questions.

Nature of the Processing The *nature of the processing* can be a valuable guide to determining the size of the primary memory and the access time it should have. For some applications, such as large-scale simulation, the primary memory may need to be larger to accommodate large-scale mathematical manipulation and comparison of many variables. Cycle time of the computer, the time required to carry out an instruction, should be low if the number and sizes of number-crunching processing jobs are high but can be higher for custodial processing. Primary memory access time should be balanced with the CPU cycle time so one element does not wait on the other.

Large-scale custodial processing and accounting applications involve large volumes of input and output with little computation. Primary storage requirements are dictated primarily by the configuration of system software rather than by processing volumes. Such applications also create a wide variety of reports and documents, which means a flexible printing capability must be provided. Depending on systems design, magnetic tapes or disk packs will be required for offline storage and for efficient sorting of large files. The secondary storage requirements may be met by other devices (drums or fixed disks). If batch processing is involved, with files inactive for days at a time, magnetic tapes or strips and disk packs are more efficient because they can be stored offline when not in use.

A mix of number-crunching and administrative data processing applications may indicate a need for a fast CPU, a fast and large primary store, large online and offline secondary storage capacity, and high input-output speeds. Such a configuration allows both types of processing to be efficiently carried out.

A requirement of multiprogramming or timesharing capability usually will mean a large primary memory capacity to provide simultaneous storage for the executive and the several compilers and/or applications programs. A fast CPU is needed to handle the management of the system. Otherwise, response times for individual users may not be sufficiently low to make the system feasible.

The volume of each type of processing should be established for a different reason. If one type of use is very limited, it may be less costly to obtain a leased or purchased system for the major use and then "farm out" the other use. Computer time can be purchased in a variety of ways on almost the full spectrum of machine configurations. Raw time can be bought at some service bureaus, and the purchaser's own employees can operate the system to perform the processing. At the other extreme, the entire job from data preparation to final output can be contracted out to a full-service computing organization. Timesharing services make a full range of computing power available through terminals. Common prudence should be exercised regarding the reputability, capability, and continuity of any service used.

Storage and Retrieval The *storage and retrieval requirements* indicate the volume of online storage capacity required and the type of I/O needed to obtain responses to inquiries. For immediate response, some form of terminal I/O is indicated, probably from sites away from the data processing center where the computer is located. Four levels of response speeds can be identified:

1. *Instantaneous response*, within less than two seconds, requires fast online storage (drum, disk, or slow core) and a fast CPU and primary storage (cycle time and access time of one microsecond or less).

2. *Fast response*, within ten seconds, can be accomplished by a slower CPU and almost any type of online random-access store (disk, drum, slow core, or magnetic strip).

3. *Intermediate-speed response*, within five minutes or so, can be accomplished by several microfilm retrieval systems as well as all computer systems.

4. *Slow response*, within several hours or longer, can be accomplished with manual or machine-aided manual systems and need not involve the computer.

Response time requirements must be related also to volume of requests. The lower the frequency with which response requests are received in *any* system, the lower the average response time, down to the minimum of which the system is physically capable. Type of data stored and retrieved also influences storage device selection and input-output capability. For example, are data records short or long? Is each data input lengthy? Is it coded? How much of each input or output message is really redundant, that is, not required to make the meaning of the message clear?

Inquiry stations also change with desired speed of response, volume of inquiries, and average length of each response. If each response is short (for example, Yes or No, an account balance, or O.K. or Reject) almost any terminal device can be used, including voice response. When response is more voluminous, either a CRT or a typewriterlike printing terminal is more apt to be required. CRT terminals are generally faster, but message length should be limited to what can be displayed on the screen at one time.

Amount of Computing Power *Amount of computing power* desired at one time is useful in determining CPU and primary memory speeds, primary memory capacities, numbers and kinds of I/O peripherals and their speeds, and the possible usefulness of multiprogramming or timesharing. However, it should be recognized that satisfaction of peak load demand means excess capacity at other times.

Remote Use *Remote use* is important in determining the need for terminals or other remote I/O devices or provision for several computers in the system. The nature of the processing at the remote sites and the demand for use of central computer resources (primary and secondary storage and I/O peripherals) at each site will determine if one central computer should be shared or if several smaller computer systems might be installed at different locations. The provision of remote job entry facilities and batch output terminals may be sufficient for satisfying many remote-use requirements. The ever-increasing capabilities of the so-called minicomputers cannot be ignored: timesharing and multiprogramming uses are common; virtual memory capabilities are not unknown; cycle times, access speeds, and length of instruction sets rival the large number crunchers. As a stand-alone system or as part of a *distributed processing network*, the minicomputer can provide large amounts of custodial processing and problem-solving computation at remote sites. These systems are fast, reliable, and inexpensive. If remote input and output (*teleprocessing*) is considered, a *distributed network* should be investigated. It may be less expensive to perform the bulk of the routine jobs at the activity sites, sending only the large jobs to a central computer.

System Tasks At the completion of this step, a specification of tasks to be accomplished by the system will be available. Certain minimums for the configuration will also be established. These include minimum numbers of input and output devices by type, capacity of online secondary storage, response times expected, and capacities of output devices. If multiprogramming is planned, what applications are to run concurrently? If timesharing is involved, how many simultaneous users are to be supported, and what will be the total number of terminals? If direct entry of data is planned, has the nature of the direct-entry device been established? In this regard, will the system interface in any way with other systems?

Software   What about software? What programming languages or language capabilities must be available? Would utility or special-purpose languages be desirable? Must the system run existing programs?

Future Growth   What about future growth in volume of activities or expectations for more sophisticated use of the computer system? Being able to expand volumes of transactions or file data without extensive modification of current software (programs) can be important to a dynamic, growing organization. Similarly, a change to more sophisticated forms of use (remote data entry, online response, timesharing, and so on) may be desired at a later date. No computer system can grow indefinitely, although most systems can grow over a wide range of capability. However, not all can economically provide services such as multiprogramming and timesharing.

Reliability   Finally, what about reliability? Minimum performance standards for the system must be decided on. Average length of time between failures and proportion of allowable downtime (time the system is broken down and not functioning) should be specified. This also involves questions of technical maintenance. For example, must maintenance be available on site or within one hour? Such questions must be related to the costs of downtime at different periods and the cost of preventing the downtime.

Defining Alternative Systems

If the general system specifications in terms of tasks and minimum capabilities are complete, the available systems that can meet these general specifications can be defined. Of course, the flexible nature of computer configurations means that many systems can be made to perform the tasks specified. The problem is to find the configuration that performs the prescribed tasks at the lowest cost while at the same time providing the potential for any expected future growth. The first step is usually a request for bids on the system by computer manufacturers.

REQUEST FOR BIDS

The *request for bids* ordinarily takes the form of a letter to vendors indicating an intent to acquire (buy or lease) a system meeting the established specifications. These specifications should be carefully and completely stated in as succinct a manner as possible. A due date for the acceptance of preliminary bids should be established. One person in the organization should be designated to answer prebid questions and to assemble additional information for bidders when it appears desirable. Choose this person well — someone with knowledge of your needs and of computer and data processing concepts and terms and with the strength of character to resist the blandishments and special pleas that are apt to come from the computer vendors.

In situations in which completely new or quite different computer systems are sought, the initial bid specifications may need to be modified. Also, changes in hardware or software capabilities unknown to the persons preparing the specifications may give less costly configurations the ability to do the job. For this reason, the bid specifications should put more emphasis on the tasks to be performed than on the hardware minimums.

Bid requests should be extended to as many potential vendors as possible. It may even be advisable to encourage bids on only a part of the system. In any case, vendors should be encouraged to bid separately on each part of the system, including software. Definitely, bidding should not be restricted to only a few vendors.

RECOGNIZING FUNCTIONAL TRADE-OFFS

Particularly in business data processing applications, fast input can be traded for online random-access storage of files. Transactions can then be input as they occur instead of in batches. This can reduce the need for data transcription to a machine-sensible medium in a batch operation and decrease the need for a fast input device to handle the batched transactions on the medium to which they were transcribed. When costing out system alternatives, the analyst or study team must recognize trade-offs in reduced data preparation and offline data storage available from larger online systems and from systems involving direct data entry from each operating area. The analyst must also recognize that such online input can increase the cost of detecting and correcting errors in data entry.

Larger primary memories may be replaced by larger and slower secondary memories. Sophisticated address modification hardware and virtual memory software can reduce the need for a large primary memory.

THE NECESSITY FOR FUNCTIONAL BALANCE

One of the most uneconomical computer configurations is one in which inadequate, slow I/O devices are hung on a fast processor and used for only custodial data processing. Better system balance would involve greater online storage and a larger number of direct-entry devices. Such a system could make a small but fast CPU productive. In any case, care must be taken to match functional components so that they balance — that is, so that all components are about equally productive. This should not be taken to mean that no component (or even the whole system) should ever be idle. However, an imbalance between size and type of storage, CPU size and speed, and I/O capability means some components will be worked very hard while others are idle. Many times the whole system is only as fast as its slowest component.

SAMPLING THE EXPERIENCES OF OTHER USERS

Valuable information can be obtained from past users of similar systems. Not only hardware and software performance but also the integrity and reliability of particular suppliers can be evaluated. Suppliers will normally provide a list of satisfied customers to contact. Ask competitive suppliers for names of users who have switched suppliers. Their reasons may provide valuable warnings that prevent future problems.

Measuring Hardware Performance

Selection will be based partially on the competitive bidding by vendors of system configurations capable of performing the required tasks. However, it is often advisable to measure the actual performance of the proposed configuration. The three general methods available are *benchmarking, timing,* and *simulation.*

BENCHMARKING

Those responsible for computer selection often attempt to make their analysis explicit and quantitative by comparing the cost (and speed) of performing a specific set of tasks on each alternative configuration. The same set of programs and associated data is prepared and run on each computer system. The resulting *benchmarks* are then used as a quantitative comparison of the ability of the specific computer systems to perform the programmed tasks. The least costly system of those adequately performing the benchmark tasks is normally chosen as the best configuration to acquire. If the selected mix of programs (tasks) is a true example of an *optimum* use of the new configuration, then the result is that the truly *best* system is acquired. Normally, however, the selected tasks are a sample of those performed on a configuration that is being replaced. The fact that the sample is a representative sample for the old configuration is no guarantee that it represents an optimal mix on the new configuration. If, as is often the case, the new configuration is to perform tasks not accomplished on the old configuration, a selection of the tasks performed by the old computer can seldom represent the tasks to be performed by the new configuration. The greater the difference between the tasks to be accomplished by the two configurations, the less useful a comparison based on current use. Even if the tasks do not vary greatly, the selection of a representative sample of programs is difficult.

Difficulties other than selection of an adequate sample of benchmark tasks attach to benchmarking. The most important has to do with finding a configuration of each computer that exactly matches that of the system being considered. Apparently small differences in configuration can cause significant differences in result. For example, a smaller primary memory can significantly alter performance on a large number-crunching problem or in a multiprogrammed or timeshared operation. Using disks as a substitute for tapes can lead to unrealistically fast times, and adjustments (which are difficult to do correctly) must be made. Vendors have been reputed to run benchmarks on "doctored" systems that are quite different in capacity or to "load" the proposed system. An example is the vendor who allowed a potential customer to try out a timesharing configuration from a remote terminal. It was later learned by the selection committee that the terminal used in the test was the *only* active operation on the entire million-dollar-plus configuration at the time of the test. Naturally, the test results were very good!

TIMING

All computer vendors publish timing data for their machines. The times required for each instruction and for data transfers are given. Theoretically, these data can be used to determine the time required by a particular configuration to perform a selected set of tasks. Unfortunately, rated speeds are seldom realized in an operating environment. Most authorities do use selected timings as *guides* to computer speeds, however. Selected timings for the CPU include time needed to add two numbers and store their sum back into the primary memory, primary memory access time, and instruction cycle time. Certain types of CPU architecture allow partial overlaying of simple operations and can make these simple measures misleading. For example, primary memory (and even secondary bulk memory) may be divided into blocks, with each block accessed independently and almost simultaneously. A string of two or more memory accesses may be accomplished in much less time than the sum of the individual access times. In the same manner, certain types of instructions may be partially overlayed and the set carried out in less than the sum of the independent CPU cycle times.

Timings for peripheral devices are also used in judging capability and capacity. Maximum data transfer rates in thousands of characters per second for tape and disk drives and various mass memories, access times for secondary mass storage, lines per minute for printers, and cards per minute for card readers and card punches are commonly used.

If CPU instruction times are used, some weighting scheme is required to make them representative of intended instruction mixes. This is really a form of benchmarking and is subject to the same problems of obtaining a representative sample (in this case, representative weights) as any other benchmarking procedure.

Performance of modern computer systems is determined as much by software capability and design as by hardware speeds and design. Programs are commonly prepared in some higher level language and must be compiled into machine language before being executed. Executive programs control the allocation of components in the configuration to various users. These software elements can be more significant in determining productive throughput than the hardware. The procedures used are a complex mix of hardware and software interactions that are almost impossible to separate for analysis. For this reason, hardware timing alone cannot be used to evaluate alternative systems. This is particularly true in business data processing when a data base management language is to be used to create and maintain online data bases for the system.

SIMULATION

One technique used to evaluate performance of a complex system under a given work load is *computer simulation*. Program packages are available (at a cost) that provide relatively detailed estimates of performance characteristics of a described system when carrying a specific workload. Measures provided include elapsed time for each task; percentage idle time for each component; and probability of meeting particular performance criteria, such as response time on a multiprogrammed or timeshared system.

If simulation is used to evaluate a given system, the specific philosophy and method employed by the simulation program should be checked out. Approaches vary. Some look up specific timings for the given system and use a set of equations based on observed past behavior to estimate performance of the configuration under a specific job load. Others create tasks and then process them in the appropriate sequence through the simulated components while gathering statistics on performance. Some use special languages developed for the purpose and others use a general-purpose language. Whatever their philosophy and design, however, few provide an overall measure of system performance.

Measuring Software Performance

As indicated above, evaluation of hardware alone is inadequate for most current systems. Most installations use one or more high-level languages. Multiprogramming and timesharing are common. Even in simpler systems, the user ordinarily acquires a set of standardized programs (payroll, accounts receivable, billing, and so on) and/or utility programs (input, output, file maintenance, sorting routines, and so on) with the hardware. This software must be evaluated just as thoroughly as the hardware. The methods are not totally different.

PROBLEMS

Benchmarking is probably the most widely used formal method for evaluating software. Estimates of the time required to compile and execute a representative group of programs written in one or more higher level languages are almost impossible without actual runs on equipment that is essentially the same as that being evaluated. Care must be exercised to be *certain* that the equipment is sufficiently similar. For example, increasing the times obtained on a larger computer in the same family of computers by the ratio between the CPU cycle times on the two computers and other such crude adjustments do not normally prove reliable.

Although higher level languages are supposedly machine-independent and the compilers for a given language on competing computers may have the same rating, the same program may not compile on the two systems. Random number generation and other processes on a computer usually reflect hardware characteristics (length of instruction words, for example) and may be called in different ways or produce different results on the two computers. Input and output command structures may differ as well. Finally, even if all programs compile and run, their individual times cannot be considered additive. The total time will usually be less than that sum. Compile and execution times on multiprogrammed or timeshared systems will depend upon the total job mix and will usually vary between trials of the same mix.

DOCUMENTATION

Hardware is usually *maintained* (kept in working order) by the vendor or a service organization. Software is usually maintained by the user. Suppliers of software usually get it going initially and then depart. The user obtains future changes, *enhancements*, from the supplier but not much in the way of maintenance services. It is therefore important to evaluate the documentation of *all* software received. Complete and authenticated program listings, flow diagrams, and user's manuals are needed. User's manuals should come in sets. Programmers assigned the responsibility of maintaining the systems software (executives, compilers, and utilities) need much more detailed descriptions than programmers creating and maintaining applications programs.

Balancing Hardware and Software

Obviously, hardware and software should be compatible. For example, utility input-output routines designed for a card-oriented configuration are inadequate for a configuration oriented to magnetic tapes or disk packs. Other imbalances are just as important, however. Users often accept special conversion or simulation software that can make current programs operate on the new machine. Examples can be found in which third-generation (or fourth-generation?) equipment is simulating second-generation equipment simulating a first-generation computer. The modern configuration is sometimes operating at the same speed and level of efficiency as did the first-generation computer when working on these applications. Such use can usually be shown to be a false economy over the long run. Improvements in design of the total information system are held back, and excess service from operators and in data preparation occur. The resulting higher costs of operation can often make the new system turn out to be no more cost-effective than the system it replaced. These situations serve to support the contention advanced earlier that the real economic gains to be obtained from computers are their contributions to improved information systems design that gives better management control of the business operation. This gain is realized only if the information *system* makes *effective use* of the *power* of the *computer*.

Attempting sophisticated use of inadequate hardware by the use of complex software can also be costly. Technically efficient multiprogramming and timesharing systems require specific hardware capabilities (automatic program relocation registers, for example). Hardware deficiencies can be overcome by software, but only at a cost. The multiprogramming or time-sharing executive becomes more complex and therefore harder to keep operating. Software takes longer to accomplish a task if the hardware is not architectured appropriately. Nonproductive overhead time (the time required to oversee the operation and control the sharing of system components) increases and performance decreases. Response times are slower, users must spend more time waiting for service, and errors are more frequent. The money saved by not buying (or leasing) the basic frills for a complex system can often be a false economy wiped out by higher operating costs and wasted time of users.

Choosing Between Buying and Leasing

Computers and computer components can be purchased outright, leased, leased with an option to buy, or acquired through a sale and lease-back arrangement involving a third firm. The firm or agency contemplating the acquisition of computer equipment must decide which method is best for it. This, of course, is all part of the larger decision about whether it is best to acquire a configuration or to rent computer services from a service bureau or timesharing service. The objectives are to obtain the needed computing services at the least possible cost while at the same time giving appropriate attention to considerations of privacy and control and of reliability and continuity of service.

OUTRIGHT PURCHASE

Purchasing the hardware and software has the advantage of giving the purchaser title to the equipment. Equipment may then be modified, reconfigured, or assembled from a variety of vendors. However, it is harder to negotiate maintenance contracts for modified systems and mixed vendor systems. Only depreciation and maintenance can be charged as current business expenses with purchased systems. Property taxes must be paid on the equipment. Finally, the system may become technologically obsolete and be hard to sell if replacement is contemplated.

In those cases for which the computer is expected to be retained in the contemplated use for a period beyond the rental payout period (the time required for the rental payments to accumulate to the purchase price) and obsolescence appears unlikely, purchase may be more economical.

STRAIGHT LEASE

A straight lease arrangement involves the payment of a fixed sum per period (usually monthly) for use of the equipment. Extra charges are usually levied for use beyond 176 hours per month (one 8-hour shift per day). Lease payments are a deductible business expense, but nothing of value remains on termination of the lease. Leases usually can be canceled by either party with appropriate notice (sixty or ninety days). Leasing should be favored by the user if technical obsolescence appears imminent.

LEASE-PURCHASE PLAN

Some portion of the lease payments usually can be applied on the purchase price of a computer if it is later purchased. The proportion of the lease payment to be so applied is variable, usually in the neighborhood of 80 percent in the first two years of rental but declining to less than 50 percent after five years of renting. Such plans conserve the user's capital in early years and allow a period of evaluation before commitment of capital. If the system performs well, the user may build up a significant investment in software specific to that system and want to retain it to obtain a payout on the software investment.

SALE, LEASE-BACK

It is now common for a third party, someone other than the user or manufacturer, to be involved in contracts for computers. *Leasing companies* buy equipment from the manufacturer and offer it for lease. Normally, software support and machine maintenance are still obtained from the computer manufacturer. There are two major categories of such leases, the full-payout lease and the nonpayment lease. A *full-payout lease* is one in which the user contracts to make a series of payments with a present value not less than the current value of the computer. In the *nonpayout lease*, the user contracts to make payments whose present value is less than the current value of the equipment. Full-payout leases are like secured loans, with the user of the equipment responsible for insurance, property taxes, and maintenance. Sometimes ownership is vested in the user at the end of the lease, making it a purchase contract. Alternatively, leasing companies issuing nonpayout leases often pay property taxes, take out insurance, and contract for required maintenance services.

Third-party leases may offer tax advantages and shift part of the risk of ownership. They also provide the user with credit that need not be shown as a liability on financial statements, although many accountants advise that it should be.

Negotiating the Contract

Contracts for rent or purchase of a computer or computer components are variable documents. Lease contracts are more complicated documents than purchase contracts. The discussion below is organized around the items that should be specifically provided for in purchase and lease contracts. Contracts for maintenance services are also discussed. Before getting to these specifics, however, one general warning to the buyer or lessee is appropriate. Regardless of the contract, whether for lease or purchase, all performance statements should be specified in user terms rather than in technical (manufacturer) language. Particularly in data entry, data storage (file creation and file maintenance), and data retrieval, it is important to specify performance in terms of the user's system (types and quantities of records entered, stored, and retrieved).

PURCHASE CONTRACTS

Contracts for purchase of computer systems or components should provide specifically for performance on the part of both the buyer and the manufacturer. The *exact configuration* is included, with components designated by name, manufacturer's part number, and capacity, speed, and other performance measures. *Overall performance levels* for the total configuration should also be specified. Penalties against the manufacturer for performance below specifications should be provided. The *date* of delivery or turnover by the manufacturer of an operating configuration should be stated, again with penalty for nonperformance and with the provision of alternative means of processing provided for. The manufacturer should insist on availability of the computer site with an appropriate lead time. Again, penalties should be paid for late availability. *Payment* terms should be clearly spelled out and not left to any verbal agreement.

LEASES

Rental terms are more complex than purchase agreements. They should, however, contain the same description of the total system, component by component, and provide for delivery of a working system on the agreed date the same as purchase contracts. Additional provisions should specify the contractual period, the exact nature of the rental charges and how they are computed, standard periods of use, extra use charges, and any purchase options.

The Contractual Period The length of the lease and the length of notice required to cancel the total configuration or any part of it are referred to as the *contractual period*. Nongovernment users are normally required to retain equipment for at least one year but can cancel at any time from then on with ninety days notice.

Rental Charges Lease prices are usually stated in terms of monthly payments for a one-shift operation (176 hours). Additional use may or may not require the payment of additional fees. Users should be aware of the exact provisions. A few manufacturers compute rental charges entirely from use. Meters installed on the equipment measure the amount of time each component is in operation.

Purchase Options Most manufacturers offer the alternative of applying portions of the rental payments to purchase of the equipment at any point in time. The percentage of the payment that can be applied varies with the length of the lease and the length of time the equipment has been installed. The user should check this provision carefully.

Other Services   Any *services* or *software* to be supplied by the equipment manufacturer should be completely and clearly described. Many services in this area used to be supplied as part of the lease or purchase agreement. Generally, this is no longer true. Each service, program, and so on, is separately priced and must be contracted for. If the vendor promises to train employees or assist in developing information or data processing systems (including programming), the exact nature and amount of these services should be spelled out in the contract. Otherwise the user is apt to receive a bill for the services provided or not get the services as expected. The time to clear up potential misunderstandings is when the contract is being negotiated. Unsophisticated users acquiring a major, modern computer system would do well to hire a consultant with knowledge of available services and software and experience in contract negotiation.

MAINTENANCE CONTRACTS

Normally, basic monthly maintenance charges cover parts, preventive maintenance, and remedial maintenance performed during normal working hours. For large computer systems the maintenance services are normally provided by workers stationed *on site*. For small systems remedial maintenance is usually provided *on call*. Payment for maintenance outside normal working hours is usually at a higher rate. However, users can choose as the *principal period of maintenance* an eight-hour period outside normal working hours but usually falling between 7 A.M. and 6 P.M. For large systems, maintenance is at the regular rate twenty-four hours per day but service at times outside the principal period of maintenance is on an on-call basis. Maintenance services can be obtained from firms other than the manufacturer or provided by the user. Maintenance of mixed vendor systems is usually contracted from the group of vendors, with each vendor providing maintenance for the equipment it furnished. Questions concerning the validity of manufacturer guarantees of equipment performance can then be encountered, however. In a mixed vendor system it is often difficult to attain unequivocal assignment of equipment failure to a specific component in order to receive corrective service from the equipment supplier involved.

Summary   Computer selection is a complex process. The objective is to obtain the minimum cost configuration that will provide an optimum mix of computing services for a given period. The process requires the determination of performance requirements, definition of alternative systems, measuring hardware and software performance, obtaining hardware and software balance, choosing between buying and leasing, and negotiating a contract.

The configuration acquired should depend upon the nature of the processing to be accomplished, the requirements for storage and retrieval of data and information, the amount of computing power needed, and the locations of the users.

Hardware performance can be measured by use of benchmark programs, by comparing equipment timings, and by simulation. None of these methods is foolproof, and the wise analyst uses a mix of the three in evaluating alternative configurations. Software can also be evaluated by use of benchmark program sets. An important element of the software is documentation. Inadequate documentation can make software hard to use. Whether to buy or lease is an economic question whose answer depends on evaluating risks of obsolescence and costs of the alternative plans.

Contracts negotiated with manufacturers and other firms offering computers for sale or lease now include penalty provisions for failure to perform as specified. Care should be exercised in negotiating contracts to be certain that the computer investment is adequately protected. Contracts for equipment maintenance are also necessary unless the user plans to supply the maintenance.

Questions

1. Define each of the following as briefly as possible and then use a short paragraph to clarify each definition.
   a. Functional trade-off
   b. Functional balance
   c. Benchmarking
   d. Cycle time
   e. Straight lease
   f. Lease-purchase plan
   g. Sale, lease-back plan
   h. Hardware maintenance
   i. Software maintenance
   j. Number crunching

2. List and briefly describe each of the seven steps in the computer selection process.

3. How does the nature of the processing required influence —
   a. Performance specifications?
   b. Computer configuration?

4. a. What are the four levels of response speed?
   b. What does each speed level imply about the computer system configuration?

5. How is the required amount of computing power determined?

6. How does the amount of computing power required affect —
   a. Performance specifications?
   b. Computer configuration?

7. Why is it important to determine the locations of the potential computer users?

8. Under what conditions would it be desirable to measure hardware and software performance separately? Explain fully.
9. Why is software documentation important?
10. How can hardware and software incompatibility lead to increased cost?
11. What are the advantages and disadvantages of outright purchase of a computer system?
12. What are the advantages and disadvantages of leasing computer equipment?
13. What are the differences between a full-payout lease and a nonpayout lease?
14. What should be specifically included in a purchase contract?
15. What should be specifically included in a lease contract?
16. What is a maintenance contract? What does it provide?
17. Develop a list of criteria to be used in selecting a computer system for the information system of the hardware chain described in question 20 at the end of Chapter 3. (Refer also to questions 20 of Chapter 5, 34 of Chapter 6, and 19 of Chapter 7.)
18. Develop a list of the tasks to be performed and some capacities to be handled for the credit charge system of the Black Oil Company (see question 17 at the end of Chapter 7).

Thirteen

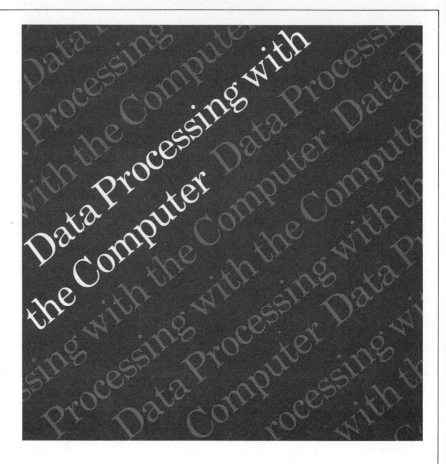

Data Processing with the Computer

$\mathbf{T}$his chapter describes in more detail just how a computer operates on data. Details of the electronics and of the EBCDIC, ASCII, and binary coding are ignored. The conceptual framework introduced in Chapter 8 is expanded, and a fuller explanation of programming languages is given.

Computer Instruction Execution

A program consists of a set of instructions for accomplishing a particular task. The exact form of each instruction and what it causes the machine to do depend upon many factors. The earliest programs were written in the language of the specific machine being used. Most programs are now written in machine-independent, problem-oriented languages and are converted to machine language by a special program (compiler). In all cases, however, programs cause the execution of a sequence of machine instructions. This section explains how each instruction is executed.

COMPUTER INSTRUCTION

A *computer instruction* is made up of two parts, an *operation code* and one or more *addresses*. All are numbers. The *operation code* usually contains two or three digits. Address size varies, but four or more digits in each address are common. Instruction words are examined and identified by a special register (or set of registers) called the *instruction register*.

INSTRUCTION REGISTER

Within the control element of the computer is a special register called the *instruction register*. It is one or more special-purpose storage locations found within the CPU. Its purpose is to analyze each program instruction in the proper sequence and determine which operation is to be executed during each CPU cycle. When analyzed in this register, the instructions are in machine language; that is, they are a series of 1's and 0's. The instruction register usually involves two or more subsidiary registers.

Address Register   The storage address of the data to be operated on by the command (*operand*) is stored in an *address register*. In simple terms, an *operand* is a location in storage the content of which is to be changed or the address of the location where results are to be placed. Depending on architecture and word size, computers may use one-address, two-address, or three-address instructions. In one-address-instruction CPUs, the address generally refers to a data location in storage. Instructions are stored in sequential primary storage locations, and the next instruction to be executed is usually in the sequentially next word location. The address register is really a counter that is incremented by 1 each time an instruction is brought into the CPU. The address thus created is the location of the sequentially next instruction that will be executed next unless a *branch* is specified. A *branch* instruction is a decision-making instruction that may cause the computer to execute an instruction other than the sequentially next instruction. The address given in a branch instruction is the address of the instruction to be executed next in the event the branch is actually made. For example, one number (say 10) may be subtracted from another (say 8). Then an instruction is used that tests the content of the register containing the difference to see if it is a negative value. In this case the content is -2 and the condition specified is met. Therefore the branch is executed, and the computer goes to the address named in the branch instruction for its next command. Any location in the store can be named in the branch instruction. If the condition tested for by the branch instruction is *not* met (if 8 is subtracted from 10 and the result is $+2$), the normal sequential pattern is maintained and the next program step to be executed is located in the immediately following word location specified in the counter.

Two-address instructions normally contain an operand and the address where the next instruction can be found. Instructions need not be stored in sequential locations. Branch instructions cause the computer to execute the instruction specified by the operand address rather than that specified by the next-instruction address. The three-address instruction normally contains *two* operands and a next-instruction address.

Operations Register This register decodes the actual coded instruction portion (the *operation code*) of an instruction word. Its identification of the operation code causes the activation of the circuits designed to carry out the defined operation.

LOGIC AND ARITHMETIC REGISTERS

The circuits and registers in the arithmetic and logic element vary widely from one machine to another. There may be one major register or several, but the activities discussed below must be provided for.

Addition and Subtraction Subtraction is merely the complement of addition, so both are carried out by the same register (often called an *accumulator*). This register is most often as long as a storage word plus sign and an overflow bit. Addition (as well as subtraction) is accomplished in *series*, one digit at a time, or in *parallel*, all digits at the same time. Parallel adders involve more hardware, are faster, and usually are more expensive. However, the development of microcircuit logic components has made them the most common type. With chip technology, the hardware costs are little different.

Multiplication and Division Multiplication and division are carried out as repeated addition and subtraction, respectively. Each of the operations requires two registers, however, unless a storage location in primary memory is used as a register.

Comparison Data items and instructions can consist of letters, numerals, special characters, or some combination of two or more of these character types. Characters are represented by combinations of binary digits and can be compared to find which comes earlier in alphanumeric sequence. Many machines allow for comparing entire words in one operation.

OTHER INSTRUCTIONS

Arithmetic and compare instructions comprise a minority of all the machine instructions available. Branch instructions have already been discussed. Other major categories are *shift*, *load*, and *store* instructions.

Shift instructions move a word right or left one or more characters within a logic register. They are used to align words before comparison or addition and in accomplishing rounding. Shifting far enough in one direction causes characters on that end of the word to "drop" out of the register and be lost while 0's are entered at the other end of the word.

Load instructions cause words to be entered into logic registers from storage. The content of the storage location normally is unchanged after the load.

Store instructions are used to enter the content of the CPU register into a general storage location, replacing the previous content of the location. The content of the register normally is not changed by a store.

I/O instructions control input and output processes. *Special* instructions recognize interrupts signaling the end of some I/O process or generate interrupts when signaled to do so by a CPU clock.

The instructions above and often others make up the *instruction set* for a particular computer. Obviously, the more the instructions, the more expensive the machine.

Knowledge of the manner in which a computer accomplishes basic operations can be important to programmers, especially those developing executive programs and compilers. For example, it is faster in most machines to ask the machine to add a value to itself $(A + A)$ than to multiply the value by 2 $(2 \times A)$, because multiplication is repeated addition. We will have more to say on this topic when discussing software selection in Chapter 14.

OPERATING CYCLE

An *instruction execution cycle,* or *operating cycle,* for a computer is the complete sequence of activities involved in carrying out an instruction, including fetching the next instruction from primary storage. To illustrate, suppose the computer is to execute an instruction located in storage location 0101. The next instruction is stored in location 0102. Say that the instruction 0101 is supposed to cause the content of location 1056 to be added to the arithmetic register (the accumulator). Note that we are assuming a single-address machine, which is the most common type. Assume that the content of 0101 has been entered into the instruction register. The activities making up an operating cycle would be:

1. Increase the instruction address register by 1 to 0102, to indicate the address of the next instruction.

2. Decode the operation code (add).

3. Identify the location of the operand (1056).

4. Actuate the circuits to cause the content of location 1056 to be brought into the arithmetic-logic unit.

5. Actuate the adder circuit to cause the word brought from 1056 to be added to the content of the accumulator.

6. Load the content of storage location 0102 into the instruction register.

Note that some of the above activities may be accomplished simultaneously. Also, the cycle might be started at a different point to provide a fetch, execute sequence. In any case, to initiate any activity, the machine must receive an initial instruction that at least indicates the location of the next (first) instruction to be executed. This can be accomplished through switches on the control console or through action of the controlling executive program.

CONTROL CONSOLE

The operator communicates with the computer through the *control console*. This can be a set of switches and display lights but can include a typewriter and/or keyboard CRT and other items. By appropriate switch settings or through instructions entered on the control keyboard, the operator can enter an initial instruction to start the machine operating. The console is also used for *clearing* the machine in case of malfunction, bad data, or bad instructions. It is also used, along with test equipment, to identify machine malfunctions and to initiate maintenance checks. Some machines, however, have special maintenance consoles.

The console can also be used to enter data and to test and correct (*debug*) programs. These latter uses are declining. Modern systems are too fast and complicated to be harnessed to the slow keying processes of the control console. The CRTs or typewriters at the console are used to keep track of what the machine is doing (what jobs are on the machine and the status of each), to record machine activity and operator interruptions, and to communicate with the operator. Modern large-system software control programs (executives) allocate system resources partly by informing operators of the need to change tapes or disk packs and that the printer needs more or different paper.

Structured Program Design

Tools for use in designing computer programs are discussed in Chapter 7. However, the emphasis there is on systems design, and computer runs are described as *work stations* in a processing system. This section looks at the specific task of translating a processing procedure into a working computer program. We recommend a *structured* approach.

Computer programming is as much art as science, but some methods have been developed to guide in program development. The processes listed below have proved helpful to programmers:

1. Define the problem.
2. Establish the general approach.
3. Specify the procedural detail.
4. Code the sequential procedures.
5. Make the program work.
6. Use a "structured" approach.

Professional programmers do not agree on the specific, detailed, techniques to be used at each stage. Again, the techniques suggested below have proved helpful.

DEFINING THE PROBLEM

The obvious first step is to understand the task that the computer is going to be given. One advantage gained from learning to program any computer in any language is an improved ability to recognize the precise nature of problems and to more easily suggest a logical solution procedure. Tools useful here include *verbal description* and *input-output schematics*. The first step normally is to obtain agreement between the person with the problem and the programmer on a verbal description of the program, preferably in writing. The description need not specify solution algorithms or detail processing steps.

Verbal Description   Consider a program to compute gross pay, tax withholdings, and net pay for hourly employees and produce a weekly check register. The verbal description follows:

The problem is to use hourly work records to compute gross pay, tax withholdings, and net pay for each hourly employee. Output is to consist of a weekly check register and a year-to-date statement. The hourly work record for each employee contains employee number, regular and overtime hours worked, hourly wage rate, number of dependents, and year-to-date withholdings. The check register is to show, by employee number, gross pay, income tax withholding, social security withholding, and net pay for the current week. Weekly grand totals for all employees for each category are also to be outputted. The year-to-date statement is to show, accumulated in the year to date for each employee by employee number, gross pay, income tax withholding, social security withholding, and net pay. Accumulated year-to-date totals for all employees should also be shown for each category.

It is obvious that a complete verbal description is lengthy and can easily become hard to follow. Even though the description can be simplified when a standard solution method (linear programming simplex algorithm, for example) is to be applied (by calling for its use at that point), the description of all inputs and outputs can become tedious and confusing. The input-output schematic is suggested as a more easily understood problem descriptor. This does not mean that the verbal description should not be used, however. It is a starting point, even if it is never developed in full detail.

Input-Output Schematic This tool is particularly useful when developing custodial processing programs. It consists of listing *required outputs* and *specified inputs* in two columns and providing information connecting the columns to show that the required outputs can be obtained from the specified inputs (see Figure 13.1).

Inputs are divided into two categories, data inputs and program inputs. *Data inputs* are facts about each transaction or problem that the program is to process. These data inputs, as defined here, include both transactions data and the file records that are being modified by the transactions. *Program inputs* are numerical constants or algorithmic formulas used in processing data inputs.

Figure 13.1 presents an input-output schematic for our simplified hourly payroll program. Note that the data inputs vary with each employee pay record processed, but the program inputs (income tax computation scheme, FICA withholding rules, and so on) apply equally to all records. Note also that the year-to-date input data, hourly pay rate, and number of dependents would come from an employee payroll master file.

Outputs are also divided into two classes. *Direct outputs* are those obtained by direct manipulation of the inputs. *Indirect outputs* require manipulation of direct outputs. Inputs may or may not enter directly into the development of indirect outputs. The distinguishing characteristic of indirect outputs is that they require the previous computation of direct outputs. Thus in Figure 13.1 the weekly totals for gross pay, tax withholdings, and net pay require the previous calculation of these values for each hourly employee. All input and output items are numbered, and the numbers following each output item show what input and/or direct-output items are used in obtaining that output item.

ESTABLISHING THE GENERAL APPROACH

The *block diagram* is a special type of system chart intended to show in general terms the *major* tasks to be accomplished. Figure 13.2 presents the

Inputs	Outputs
Data inputs (work record)	*Direct outputs (check register)*
1. Employee number	13. Employee number (1)
2. Regular hours	14. Gross pay (2, 3, 4, 10)
3. Overtime hours	15. Income tax withholding (14, 5, 11)
4. Hourly pay rate	16. Social security withholding (6, 14, 12)
5. Number of dependents	17. Net pay (14, 15, 16)
Year-to-date (Y-T-D):	*Indirect outputs (check register)*
	Totals (weekly)
6. Gross pay	
7. Income tax withholding	18. Gross pay (14)
8. Social security withholding	19. Income tax withholding (15)
9. Net pay	20. Social security withholding (16)
	21. Net pay (17)
Program inputs	
	Direct outputs (Y-T-D table)
10. Overtime pay formula	
11. Income tax table	22. Employee number (1)
12. Social security formula	
	Accumulated Y-T-D:
	23. Gross pay (6, 14)
	24. Income tax withholding (7, 15)
	25. Social security withholding (8, 16)
	26. Net pay (9, 17)
	Indirect outputs (check register)
	Totals (Y-T-D)
	27. Gross pay (23)
	28. Income tax withholding (24)
	29. Social security withholding (25)
	30. Net pay (26)

FIGURE 13.1   *Input-output schematic, hourly payroll*

block diagram for our hourly payroll program. Each block defines a major subtask in the overall program but does not specify the detail of how it is to be accomplished. Use of block diagramming encourages and facilitates a *modular* approach to programming a process. The total program is divided into *modules* which can be programmed independently. The modules are then combined to obtain a total program.

SPECIFYING THE PROCEDURAL DETAIL

The third step in program development is to take each major block and specify *exactly* how that subtask is to be accomplished. The tool to be used

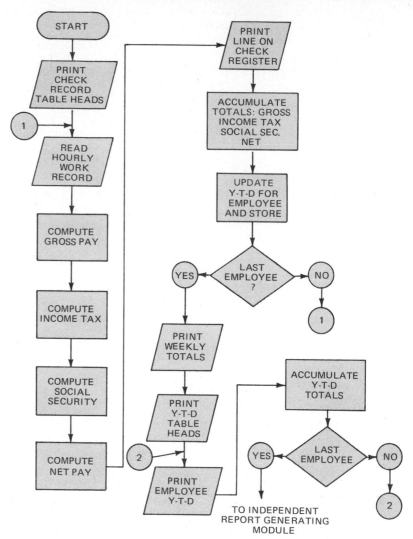

FIGURE 13.2   *Block diagram, hourly payroll program*

here is a flow diagram or a decision table.   Note that the flow diagram indicates the order in which each procedure is to be accomplished.   The flow
diagram covering the first two blocks shown in Figure 13.2 is given in Figure 13.3.   The remainder of the flow diagram is left as an exercise for the
reader.   (See questions 14, 15, and 16 at the end of the chapter.)

The reader should look at Chapter 6 and note that the approach to
programming parallels the process of system design described in that chapter.   The block-diagram–to–flow-diagram approach is a form of black box
analysis.   Up to this point, program development is merely a general form
of system analysis.

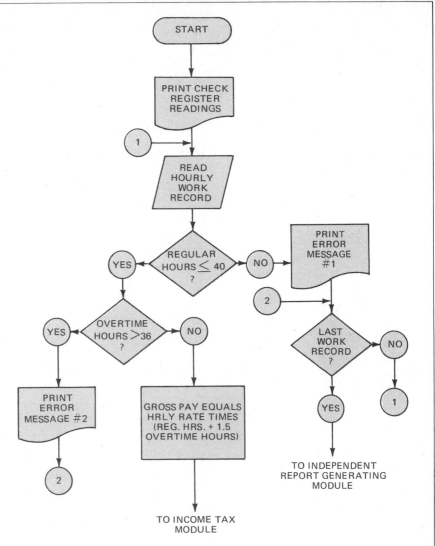

FIGURE 13.3   *Partial flow diagram, hourly payroll program*

CODING THE SEQUENTIAL PROCEDURES

After the problem has been fully defined and the solution specified in detail, it is time to cast the process into a form that the computer can use. At this point, the flow diagram or decision table is translated into a language that the computer can understand. The actual program may be written in a machine language or a higher order language.

The process of translating a detail flowchart or decision table into a program is not as simple as it sounds. The resulting program can be designed to be an efficient user of the computer, to be easy to understand and use, or to be easy to compile. It is extremely difficult for it to possess all these characteristics simultaneously. The programmer performing the translation needs a detailed knowledge of the language into which the process is being translated and a clear understanding of the process to be coded.

MAKING THE PROGRAM WORK

Programs seldom operate correctly, if at all, as initially written. Computers are very fast and powerful, but they are also limited. They cannot understand that a command RED D at a particular point in the program is *obviously* an input command telling the machine to input (READ) a variable (data word) called D. The computer would need to be specially programmed or designed to interpret RED as "READ" whenever it could be considered a program instruction. This too might cause problems. The simplistic consistency of the computer means that misplacing or forgetting a comma, transposing two characters, or other such simple errors can cause the program to malfunction partially or totally. The process of removing the errors, some of which may be logic errors, is called *debugging the program*.

Desk Debug The process of rereading the program in search of errors is called *desk debugging*. The most useful part of this technique is *playing computer*, that is, each instruction is manually executed with sample data to see what results. An example of playing computer is illustrated in Figure 13.4.

Part (a) of Figure 13.4 presents a detailed flow diagram for a program to add five numbers and print the sum obtained. Part (b) gives a computer program for accomplishing these tasks. The program is written in the BASIC language. Note that the numbers that identify each program line in part (b) have been placed alongside the corresponding part of the flowchart in part (a). A step-by-step explanation of the program is given in part (c) on page 318. Part (d) presents the normal form of a playing-computer table for such a program. Note that all one does is to follow the program through and perform the operations called for, keeping track of what happens as each instruction is executed.

Test Data Data sets can be prepared and run through the computer to test the program. These test data should be carefully designed to exercise every part of the program. That is, ideally these data will contain every major combination that can occur in the real data the program must process. For example, test data for the hourly payroll program should contain data for employees who reportedly worked less than forty regular hours and for those

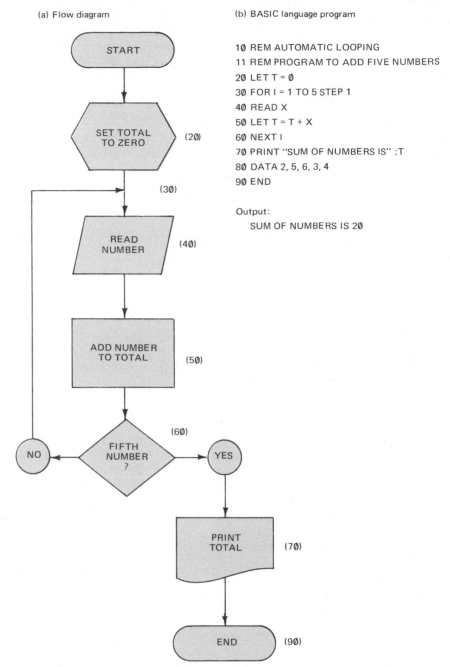

(a) Flow diagram

START

SET TOTAL TO ZERO (20)

(30)

READ NUMBER (40)

ADD NUMBER TO TOTAL (50)

FIFTH NUMBER ? (60)

NO

YES

PRINT TOTAL (70)

END (90)

(b) BASIC language program

```
10 REM AUTOMATIC LOOPING
11 REM PROGRAM TO ADD FIVE NUMBERS
20 LET T = 0
30 FOR I = 1 TO 5 STEP 1
40 READ X
50 LET T = T + X
60 NEXT I
70 PRINT "SUM OF NUMBERS IS" ;T
80 DATA 2, 5, 6, 3, 4
90 END
```

Output:
    SUM OF NUMBERS IS 20

FIGURE 13.4   *Flow diagram and BASIC language program for adding five numbers with illustration of playing computer* (continued on page 318)

(c) Step-by-step explanation of the program

Statement number	Explanation of statement	Values of variables (in order of appearance)		
		T	I	X
1∅-11	A "remark" to anyone reading the program.			
2∅	Clearing the adder.	∅		
3∅	Open a loop to be repeated five (5) times.		1	
4∅	Set X equal to value of next data word in the data list (line 8∅).			2
5∅	Add X to Total (T).	2		
6∅	Close loop (change I by STEP value and repeat loop [go back to 3∅]			
3∅	if I < 5.)		2	
4∅	Define next X.			5
5∅	Add X to T.	7		
6∅-3∅	Return if I < 5.		3	
4∅				6
5∅		13		
6∅-3∅			4	
4∅				3
5∅		16		
6∅-3∅			5	
4∅				4
5∅		20		
6∅	I = 5, so leave loop.			
7∅	Print output.			
8∅	Inoperable statement defining data.			
9∅	End of program—stop.			

(d) The normal playing-computer table

Value of each variable in loop as I changes:		
I	X	T
		∅
1	2	2
2	5	7
3	6	13
4	3	16
5	4	2∅

FIGURE 13.4 (cont.)

who reportedly worked exactly forty regular hours during the week. Some employees may have overtime, and others may not. All limits in the program should be tested. More than forty regular hours cannot be worked in one week; does the program satisfactorily handle such an occurrence? Can the program recognize and report excess overtime hours, too large hourly rates, impossible gross pay amounts, negative net pay, and so on?

Program Tracing To find logic errors in the program, it is necessary to know exactly how it is proceeding from step to step. This can be accomplished by temporarily inserting output commands to print interim results that show (*trace*) the sequence of activities in the program. Such a trace is particularly useful when no final output or pure garbage (pure nonsense) is being outputted as the regular output from the program. Some compilers for some higher level languages contain special *snapshot* routines that print out all interim results by the insertion of a single command. These provisions are not standard, however. In fact, they are quite rare.

Diagnostics Compilers do contain *diagnostic routines*, which check each program statement for syntax errors and incompleteness. *Syntax errors* include misspellings; improper sequence within or among commands; failure to complete an operation (for instance, not closing a sequence that loops back repeatedly to process the next transaction); and missing punctuation or other characters. The diagnostic routines cannot check logic, however. If all commands are a legal form for the language being used and do not violate syntactical sequence rules, the program will be accepted even though it accomplishes nothing at all.

Modular Programming A long program usually divides naturally into subunits (*modules*), each carrying out a part of the total task. During program preparation each program module should be treated as a separate, independent program accepting inputs and producing outputs. Errors in program logic are thus easier to identify and correct. An additional advantage is that different modules can be assigned to different programmers. This can reduce the difficulty of completing large, complex programs; but it also increases the coordination problem. Team programming is impossible without a clear, complete, and well-documented program design. In addition, names of data elements and procedures common to more than one module must be identified in precisely the same way in all modules. Large, complex programs are almost impossible to debug if a modular programming approach is not used.

The greatest problem for the programmer in using a modular approach is to find a logical way to divide the program into modules. The major block diagram is the most useful tool for identifying essentially autonomous modules. Care must be exercised to avoid dividing the task into separate parallel flows. The use of several parallel modules, each operating in a different way on the same inputs and passing common outputs to a subsequent module or set of modules, compounds the coordination problem and also encourages the development of inefficient processing procedures in the program. It is usually wise to divide a job into serially related modules with each module accepting inputs from the preceding module and passing outputs to a subsequent module.

Programming Guidelines   If every programmer would learn and follow the same general guidelines, programming would improve, partially because each programmer could more easily understand another's program.

1. Document fully and carefully.
   a. Verbal description and/or input-output schematic
   b. Block diagram
   c. Detailed flow diagram or decision table
   d. Complete program listing keyed to the flowcharts and/or decision tables
   e. Sample inputs and outputs that illustrate exactly how the program is used
   f. Complete running instructions for the computer operator and others interacting with the system on how to operate the program

This last step is absolutely necessary if any tapes or disks must be mounted or outputs are provided in nonnormal ways. For example, if the output is via the line printer in the computer center for a program designed to be entered from a terminal, the user should know this. Similarly, if the program is operated from a terminal but can accept data from a file on an electronic storage device, the user should be given detailed instructions on how to use this alternative.

2. *Comments to the reader* as part of the program are provided for by most higher level languages. They should be used in the program to indicate sections where major and minor subtasks are performed. During program development, these comments can guide the programmer in placing temporary output statements for tracing program operation.

3. Make programs modular and avoid interlocking modules as much as possible. Avoiding unnecessary complexity in program flow pays dividends in readability and in debugging ease.

4. Make each program loop unique. Do not close two or more loops with the same command.

5. Use all possible aids to increase readability of the program.

a. Break up complex formulas into several commands.
b. Use parentheses liberally to provide clarity in arithmetic expressions.
c. Name program variables in as logical and natural a way as possible.
d. Avoid the use of two variable names for the same entity and avoid giving two different variables the same name.
e. Number statements in logical order.
6. Prepare as much documentation as possible *before* writing the program.

USE A STRUCTURED APPROACH

The structured approach to program development consists of the use of three basic techniques, *top-down design, structured programming,* and *structured walk-throughs.* These techniques have been widely acclaimed for improving programmer productivity, for increasing the chances of obtaining a working program, and for providing better control over the programming function. Each of these techniques is described briefly below.

Top-Down Design In top-down design, the functional specifications of a program and the code to carry them out are developed literally from the top down. Modules are developed starting at the top or broadest level of the program. Lower-level modules which have not been coded are represented by *program stubs.* This is illustrated in Figure 13.5. The major control routine of the program is designed to call up one of three major subroutines. Subroutine A is complete except for Module A-2. This latter module is represented by a stub. The stub may be only a program statement that returns the message, "Module A-2 called at this point." Similarly, Subroutine C is totally undeveloped and the stub would consist of the minimum

FIGURE 13.5   *Use of program stubs in top-down development*

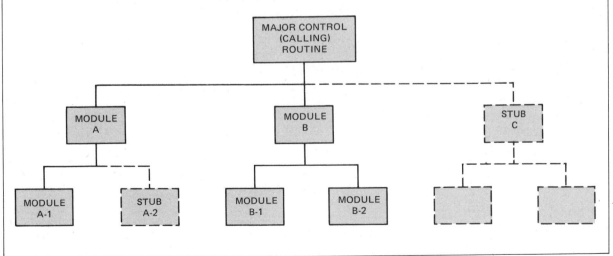

code that would allow the major control routine to function. Detailed coding at lower levels is deferred until the higher modules are working. Sometimes, the stub must generate data to be used by higher modules, but this should be avoided wherever possible. Note that this is a logical extension of the modular approach to programming.

Structured Programming   Only three basic logic "structures" are required to develop any computer program. The most basic logic structure is the *sequence structure*. It provides for each of the processes in the program to be completed in the order in which they appear. A process, once started, must be completed before a new process or sequence can be begun. Practically, this means that each module must have only *one entry* point and *one exit* point. The sequence structure is illustrated graphically in Figure 13.6(a).

The second logic structure is the *choice* or IFTHENELSE structure. It consists of a logical choice between processing sequences and is illustrated in Figure 13.6(b). Note that one of the processes shown in the diagram may be a "null" process which merely passes control to the next module. Again, note that there is only one entry point and one exit point.

The third allowable logic structure is the *looping* or DOWHILE structure. It really consists of a combination of the first two structures which provides for repetition of a process, as is required in so many processing operations. The looping structure is represented in Figure 13.6(c).

The three allowable structures may be combined in any order to perform any necessary processing. Restricting programmers to these three structures makes program modules easier to design. It also makes programs easier to read and understand. This results in easier debugging, easier maintenance, and easier control over program development and programmer activity.

Structured Walk-Throughs   This is a process for formal review of program development efforts at each major stage of that development. Walk-throughs are used to review program (system) specifications with the user, to review the design to ensure that the specifications are being met, to review coding to be sure that the agreed-upon design is being followed, and to review planned tests and test data to ensure their adequacy.

To illustrate the process, let us suppose that Susan P. Coder is assigned to code a module of a larger program. She knows the specifications the module must meet. When she is ready, she arranges a walk-through session to review the way she is handling the data interfaces between her module and the other modules in the system. The walk-through consists of the following:

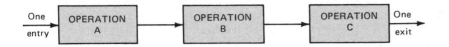

(a) Sequence structure

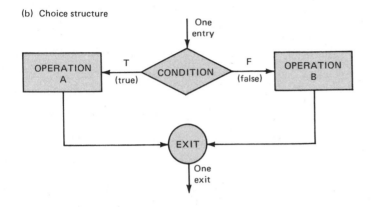

(b) Choice structure

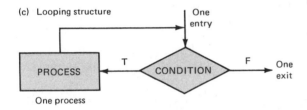

(c) Looping structure

One process

FIGURE 13.6   *Basic logic structures for computer programs*

1. A scheduled meeting, with all participants formally advised of the purpose of the meeting.

2. Each participant is provided with copies of all pertinent materials (specifications, assumptions, logic flows, and so on) to review *before* the meeting. Further, each participant is expected to be familiar with these materials by the time of the meeting.

3. The review session is conducted by a moderator. This may be Susan herself or one of the other participants. It is *not* Susan's supervisor, who does *not* attend the meeting.

4. Errors discovered during the session are recorded but not corrected. One participant acts as official recorder and develops a list of the errors found. A copy of the list is given to each participant.

5. The above process is repeated as necessary until everyone is satisfied that Susan has properly designed and executed the data-handling interfaces in her module. Only then may Susan proceed to the next phase of development of the module she has been assigned.

There are several key characteristics that make the structured walk-through effective. First, all participants understand the purpose and each is properly prepared to carry it out. Second, the walk-through is a help session, not a performance review. Third, all technical members of the project team have their work reviewed at each stage of development before subsequent stages are begun. This structure provides protection against error. The walk-throughs contribute positively to progress and provide positive reinforcement of that progress. Perhaps because of the positive support it provides, the use of structured walk-throughs is reported to motivate personnel to higher levels of more error-free performance.

Regardless of the specific techniques used for describing programs and program modules and of the debugging aids available, the use of the structured approach has been demonstrated to increase programmer productivity. Its use is strongly recommended.

Programming Languages

There are four levels of programming languages. The lowest level is that of *machine* language. The second level is that of *assembly* language. The third level is that of *problem-oriented compiler* languages. The fourth level involves *special-purpose compiler* languages such as those used for writing computer simulations. These specialized compiler languages are discussed briefly in Chapter 14.

MACHINE LANGUAGE

To illustrate machine language, consider a mythical two-address computer with a double-word-length accumulator for arithmetic and logic. Words are ten digits. Instructions break down like this:

Operation code	Operand address	Next instruction address
Ø1	1ØØ1	ØØØ5

Suppose we wish to code a program to add a series of number pairs. The steps to be accomplished are shown in Figure 13.7 on the left. The code to accomplish each step is shown on the right. Note the difference between

Step	Description	Instruction location*	Coded instruction
1	Read first and second words.	ØØØ1 ØØØ2	Ø1 Ø2ØØ ØØØ2 Ø1 Ø2Ø1 ØØØ3
2	Clear accumulator and enter first word.	ØØØ3	1Ø Ø2ØØ ØØØ4
3	Add second word to accumulator.	ØØØ4	11 Ø2Ø1 ØØØ5
4	Store result.	ØØØ5	2Ø Ø2Ø2 ØØØ6
5	Print result and return to read next number pair.	ØØØ6	Ø6 Ø2Ø2 ØØØ1

* The instruction locations are not part of the instruction. They are shown to facilitate following the program.

FIGURE 13.7   *Machine language program to add pairs of numbers*

the clear and load accumulator instruction (1Ø) and the add instruction (11). If the add code (11) had been used for step 2, any value present in the accumulator would have been added into the sum. Even if the accumulator were clear (set to zero) when the program started, all sums after the first would include the sum of all numbers read previously. Also, the accumulator holds two words and each is addressed individually. The instructions in steps 2, 3, and 4 refer to the lower half of the accumulator only. If we had wished to do this work in the upper half of the accumulator, the codes for steps 2, 3, and 4 would have been 15, 16, and 25, respectively. Machine language programming requires an intimate knowledge of the particular machine. The programmer must know the best way to accomplish each activity to take advantage of special machine features. This can be an advantage as well as a disadvantage, however. Programs can be made to use the machine in the most efficient way.

Another disadvantage of machine language programming is the need to learn the arbitrary operation codes. Why should a read command be 01? Why not 02? Also, each operation performed by the machine is a very small step in the overall process.

ASSEMBLY LANGUAGE

The first step in making program languages easier to use was the development of assemblers. An *assembler* is a program written in machine language that allows the programmer to write in a pseudoindependent language. Early assemblers required a one-for-one correspondence between the program written in assembler language and the program written in machine language. Assemblers in use today include pseudoinstructions or macroinstructions (macros) which translate as more than one machine lan-

Step	Machine language	Assembly language
1	Ø1Ø2ØØØØØ2	START RDD RØ1
	Ø1Ø2Ø1ØØØ3	RDD RØ2
2	1ØØ2ØØØØØ4	RAL RØ1
3	11Ø2Ø1ØØØ5	ALO RØ2
4	2ØØ2Ø2ØØØ6	STL PØ1
5	Ø6Ø2Ø2ØØØ1	PRI PØ1 START

FIGURE 13.8 *Machine and assembly language programs to add pairs of numbers*

guage instruction. In any case, operation codes and addresses are stated in alphabetic *mnemonics*, which are easier to remember. For example, the program of Figure 13.7 has been restated in Figure 13.8 in machine language on the left and in a mnemonic assembly language on the right. Note how much more easily the assembly language program can be read. RDD means *ReaD* a *D*ata word, RAL means "reset the lower accumulator and add a data word into it (*R*eset and *A*dd *L*ower)," ALO stands for "*A*dd to the *LO*wer," and so on. Only those instructions that do not follow in sequence need be given names. The first instruction is named so that the last instruction can send the control back to begin the whole process over again.

COMPILER LANGUAGES

The next refinement in languages made them problem-oriented. Programmers were allowed to write in a language very near to the way they would state a problem. The *compiler* program accepted the program in the problem-oriented language (called a *source program*) and converted it (compiled it) into machine language (an *object program*). Figure 13.9 charts the general assembly and compiler process.

The compiler language differs from an assembly language in that each program statement in the problem-oriented language is related to a problem task and may compile as several machine language instructions. Figure 13.10 restates the sample program of Figures 13.7 and 13.8. Note that the program requires only five statements. The statements have been placed opposite the steps in the original program that they replace. Note also that the fifth statement is a special statement whose purpose is to tell the compiler that the program is complete. Without such an ending statement, the compiler cannot complete all of its checks on program syntax.

A special kind of compiler has been developed for use in timesharing. This is the interpretive compiler, more commonly referred to as an *interpreter*. Unlike standard compilers, an interpreter compiles programs one statement at a time without reference to other statements except when clos-

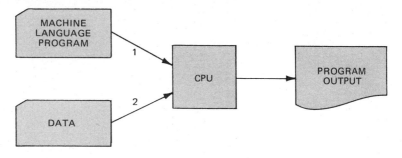

(a) Machine language process

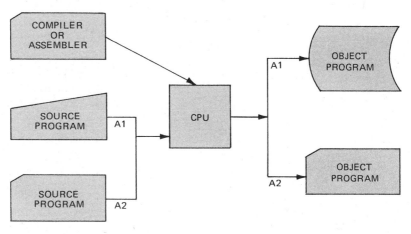

(b) Assembler and compiler process

Phase 1—compile source program to object program

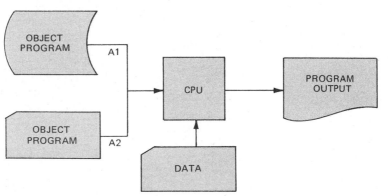

Phase 2—execute the object program

FIGURE 13.9   *Machine language and assembler and compiler processes*

Step	Machine language	Compiler language (BASIC)
1	Ø1 Ø2ØØ ØØØ2	1ØØ READ A,B
	Ø1 Ø2Ø1 ØØØ3	
2	1Ø Ø2ØØ ØØØ4	11Ø LET C = A + B
3	11 Ø2Ø1 ØØØ5	
4	2Ø Ø2Ø2 ØØØ6	
5	Ø6 Ø2Ø2 ØØØ1	12Ø PRINT C
		13Ø GO TO 1ØØ
		14Ø END

FIGURE 13.10   *Machine and compiler language (BASIC) program to add pairs of numbers*

ing a loop or creating a data table or data list for which space has been reserved. This step-by-step process means that an interpreter does not provide as powerful a language as a regular compiler. It is only in sophisticated uses and in advanced file handling processes that this weakness becomes a real handicap, however. The advantages of the interpreter is shorter compile times and easier identification of some programming errors. Interpreters are usually used in a load-and-go mode. That is, the object program is never printed out but the program is executed on the same computer run as it is being compiled.

Higher level languages ease the task of writing a computer program. They speed program development and encourage programmers to pay more attention to getting a good problem solution than to writing a machine-efficient program. However, some compilers on some machines do compile slowly and do use the machine very inefficiently.

Summary

A computer program consists of a set of instructions for accomplishing a particular task. Programs may be written in a *machine language,* an *assembly language,* or a *compiler language.* The computer directly executes only machine language. A program written in an assembler or a compiler language (*source program*) must be translated into a machine language program (*object program*) by the assembler or compiler. Assemblers and compilers are programs that accept source programs as data and convert them to machine language for machine execution. Developing a computer program requires that the problem be fully defined, the general solution procedures be identified, the procedural details be specified, the sequential procedures be translated into a programming language (coded), and the program be debugged (made to work). Verbal descriptions and input-output schematics are useful in problem identification. Block diagrams serve to specify general solution procedures. Their use also encourages a *modular* approach to programming, with major sections (modules) of the program developed independently. Flow diagrams or decision tables are used to specify the procedure in detail before coding. Debug tools include desk debugging and using test data, program-tracing outputs, and diagnostic statements from compilers and assemblers.

The process of programming is made more scientific and the efforts of programmers more productive through the use of a structured approach. Top-down design, structured programming, and structured walk-throughs provide programs which are easier to read and maintain and provide them more quickly as well.

Questions

1. Define the following as briefly as possible and then use a short paragraph to clarify each definition.

   a. Computer instruction
   b. Operation code
   c. Operand
   d. Operating cycle
   e. Program debug
   f. Block diagram
   g. Desk debug
   h. Instruction register
   i. Control console
   j. Assembler
   k. Compiler
   l. Input-output schematic
   m. Machine language
   n. Modular programming
   o. Structured programming
   p. Top-down design
   q. Structured walk-through
   r. Interpreter

2. What are the differences between assemblers and compilers?
3. How does programming in a machine language differ from programming in
   a. an assembler language?
   b. a compiler language?
4. What are the major advantages of programming in
   a. machine language?
   b. assembler language?
   c. compiler language?
5. What are the advantages and disadvantages of modular programming? When should it be used?
6. What are the three major elements in the structured approach to developing computer programs?
7. What are the three basic elements of structured programming?
8. What are the advantages of structured programming?
9. What are the advantages of structured walk-throughs?

10. Prepare a table listing the advantages and disadvantages of programming in
    a. machine language
    b. assembly language
    c. compiler language
11. Is it more important to save programmer time or machine time? Why?
12. Turn to Figure 7.12 (page 183) and prepare a verbal description and input-output schematic for the problem described there.
13. Develop a verbal description, input-output schematic, block diagram, and detailed flow diagram for a program to compute the arithmetical average age (to the last birthday) of all students in your class.
14. Social security withholding is levied at 6.13 percent on the first $22,900 of income each year. Develop a detailed flow diagram for computing the social security withholding for the hourly employees. (Hint: some workers will pay tax on only part of their current pay during some week each year.)
15. Assuming that the following tables describe the weekly tax withholding schedule, develop a detailed flow diagram for computing weekly income tax withholding for the hourly employees.

Weekly income tax withholding table

Taxable income = gross pay − $17.00 for each dependent

a. Single persons

Taxable income (TI)		Tax liability		
Over	but not over	Base amount	plus Percentage	of TI over
$ 5	$ 15	$ 0	14	$ 5
15	25	1.50	15	15
25	100	3.00	17	25
100	185	16.00	20	100
185	250	33.00	25	185
250		50.00	30	250

b. Married persons

Taxable income (TI)		Tax liability		
Over	but not over	Base amount	plus Percentage	of TI over
$ 5	$ 25	$ 0	14	$ 5
25	100	3.00	15	25
100	185	15.00	17	100
185	250	28.00	20	185
250	370	41.00	25	250
370		71.00	30	370

16. Assume that the payroll system of questions 14 and 15 is structured as follows: The *master hourly employee payroll file* contains all permanent and year-to-date data and is stored on a magnetic tape in employee number order. A *payroll change file* contains all data on new hires and changes in pay rate, job assignment, number of dependents, and nontax deductions and is also on magnetic tape in employee number order. The *time card file* is a set of optically readable cards, one for each hourly employee in each department, and the cards come to the electronic data processing (EDP) department arranged by employee number within each of five departments with hourly employees.
    a. Develop a system flowchart for this payroll system.
    b. Develop a block diagram for a program to compute and print out the weekly payroll checks and create a final updated master hourly employee payroll file.
    c. Develop a detail flow diagram for the weekly payroll program.
17. Refer to question 16 and develop a block diagram and a flow diagram for a report-generating block for the hourly payroll system described there. Include a labor cost distribution by department and an employee withholding report (withholding by the following categories: federal income tax, state income tax, FICA, union dues, Christmas Club, United Way Contribution, medical insurance, group life and disability insurance, employee credit union share purchases, and employee credit union loan payments).
18. Refer to question 17 at the end of Chapter 7 and prepare an input-output schematic for the credit charge system of Black Oil Company.

Fourteen

Comparing Programming Languages

See various items top 354

General-purpose higher level programming languages are each different, but they do have many points of similarity. Part of the purpose of this chapter is to show their similarities. First, the general organization of computer programs and the effects of these generalities on higher level languages (from the user's viewpoint) are discussed. A program written in FORTRAN is then compared to a COBOL version of the same program to show the similarities and differences in general language structure. FORTRAN and COBOL were chosen for the comparison because they were developed for two different using groups and because they are widely used. The reader should be able to follow the discussion even without any prior knowledge of FORTRAN or COBOL.

Other higher level languages are briefly described and their uses indicated. A final section discusses the problem of language selection.

The Organization of Data Processing Programs

In general, data processing programs input transactions data and file records, update the file record, summarize and analyze the transactions and/or the current state of the file, and output the results. To accomplish these tasks, most data processing programs proceed in four general steps:

1. Initialization
2. Input
3. Process
4. Output

The last three steps tend to be repeated once for each transaction and once for each report. Output is often delayed until the end of the program when no individual custodial documents, such as payroll checks or customer billing statements, are being prepared.

As a first example of the four-phase process, refer to Figure 13.4(b), page 317. Note how the total is set to zero and the loop opened to run five times at the beginning (the FOR statement, number 30). This is *Initialization*. Then a value of X is read (*Input*) and added to the total (*Process*). Finally, after repeating the input and processing once for each of the five numbers, the result is printed (*Output*).

Figure 13.2, page 314, presents a more complex example. In this case the block diagram does not indicate any initialization except the printing of output table headings before input begins. However, at the end of the processing loop for each employee paycheck (each transaction), how can it be determined whether all employees have been processed? Control information usually would be inputted at the beginning of the program for this purpose, an initialization process.

Note how the program would loop back for each employee in developing and printing individual check records. Then the year-to-date table would be printed out in a *second* loop, line by line. If reports (for example, labor cost distribution) were developed as part of the total program, the same general four-step process could be considered to have been followed for each of those reports even though each unit of transactions data would have been inputted only once to obtain the several outputs.

The Nature of General-Purpose Higher Level Languages

All general-purpose higher level languages must perform each of the activities required for data processing. All of them therefore contain the same set of general statements designed to accomplish the same set of general tasks. The major tasks to be accomplished are used below to organize the discussion and identify the specific capabilities available in such languages.

INPUT AND OUTPUT

Master files and transactions data must be input to storage elements of the computer to be available for processing. Input commands perform this activity. Output commands must be available to make the results of processing available to managers and other users. Input command words vary, but the most common are READ and INPUT. The most common output command words are PRINT and WRITE. Some languages essentially allow an entire file to be entered or outputted with one complex command (see line 101 of Figure 14.4(a), page 345).

ARITHMETIC COMPUTATION

Languages must include commands making it possible to perform the arithmetic operations (addition, subtraction, multiplication, division, and exponentiation). All higher level languages have such capabilities.

DECISION MAKING

The branch, or *transfer*, commands make it possible to have the exact character of further processing depend upon specified or calculated conditions. For example, the computer can decide if all items are processed or if the value of some variable is less than, equal to, or greater than some other variable or control constant. (See the IF statement in line 45 of Figure 14.3(a), page 340.) The looping instructions (lines 30 and 60) of Figure 13.4(b) (page 317) are another example of a specialized decision-making instruction. All higher level general-purpose languages provide for looping in one or more ways. They also provide for such decisions as the tests for excess regular and overtime hours called for in Figure 13.3, page 315. (See also Figure 14.4, lines 108 and 109.) Comparisons of alphabetic words can also be made to perform tasks such as identifying legal users of a timesharing system by name and/or password, identifying accounts by customer name, or making it possible to sort on an alphabetic or mixed alphabetic and numerical key to arrange records in a desired order.

OTHER COMMON LANGUAGE FEATURES

In addition to providing for input, output, arithmetic computation, and decision making (including looping), higher level general-purpose languages usually contain several other common features. For example, *variables* usually may be *called by mnemonic names*, with the compiler converting these names to actual storage locations. The same generic (common) name may be assigned to a list or table of values, and provision is usually made for reserving storage space for such lists or tables when the source program is being compiled.

Provision is made for having *subroutines* or *subprograms* so that a process used several places in a program may be written once by the programmer and "called" whenever it is needed elsewhere in the program. At least during development of a complex program, each module of the program can be designed as a subroutine, with the so-called main line program consisting primarily of a series of "call" statements.

Subroutines or subprograms should not be confused with *mathematical functions* that can be called for use at any point in a program to perform standard mathematical functions (such as extracting square root, obtaining an absolute value, or producing a random number). For example, see the AINT (*A INT*eger) function in line 60 of Figure 14.3(a).

Most general-purpose languages provide for the *exact* description of input and output records. They also require that language statements follow an exact format with spaces, commas, and symbols in a precise order in each statement line. The trend, however, is to remove such restrictions to make the programmer's job easier. Restrictions on the form of language statements and exact descriptions of data files are being eased in the new languages and in newer versions of the older languages. In BASIC, for example, statements are generally free format. The spaces between the words and symbols in the statements found in Figure 13.3 (page 315) are there only to make them more easily read by people. The compiler does not require them. Data to be read by BASIC programs are essentially free form, the general requirement being that data words be separated by a comma or a space. Current versions of FORTRAN also allow for inputting data files that have not been described in detail but include commas to separate data words. The standard mode requires FORMAT descriptions of all input data (see Figures 14.3 and 14.4).

Major Differences Among General-Purpose Languages

The major differences among general-purpose languages tend to reflect the purposes for which the languages were developed. All general-purpose languages are intended to make the program (and the programmer) *machine-independent*, that is, to allow the programmer to ignore (or not even know) the characteristics of the specific machine(s) on which the program will be executed. However, each language has been developed for a specific group of computer users. For example, FORTRAN (*FOR*mula *TRAN*slator) has been developed to assist in coding scientific problems involving, primarily, numerical computation. COBOL (*CO*mmon *B*usiness *O*riented *L*anguage) has been developed as a file-oriented language directed at the needs of the

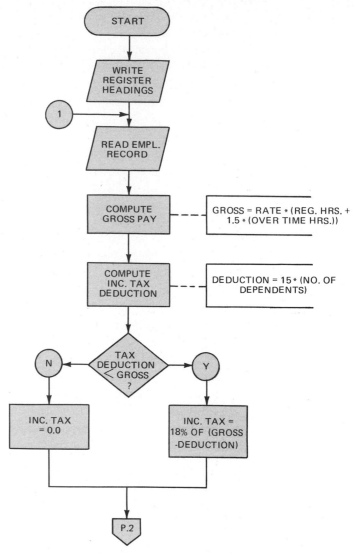

FIGURE 14.1   *Flow diagram of simplified hourly payroll program*

business data processor. The major differences between these two languages are in the way they organize a program and the form of program statements themselves. Also, COBOL is intended to be more easily understood (to be *self-documenting*).

To contrast the two languages, a very simplified hourly payroll program has been programmed in both languages. Figure 14.1 presents a flow diagram of the program. Figure 14.2 presents the data to be processed by the programs.

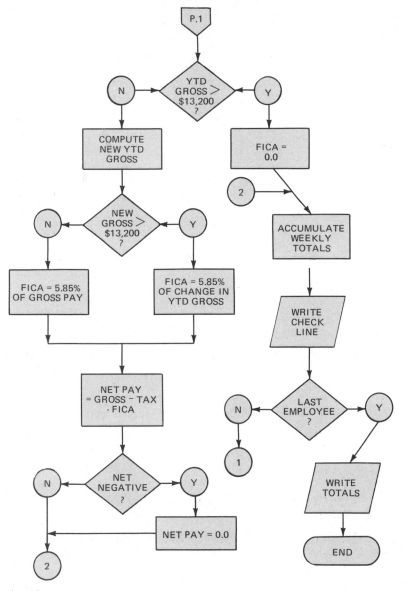

FIGURE 14.1   (cont.)

Field name						
Name	Soc. sec. number	Hrly. rate	Dep.	Reg. hrs.	O-time hours	Y-T-D gross
Beginning column number						
01	21	31	34	36	41	46
Karen Baron	333222111	300	04	04000	00000	0800000
Peter Singer	111333222	500	02	04000	00000	1200000
Tom Mueller	112210102	400	01	04000	04000	1310000
Juanita Perez	584132987	700	01	04000	04000	1310000
Maria Ricci	593761617	600	06	04000	03000	1350000
Joe Friedman	789912834	400	01	04000	02000	0700000
Mike Tomcheff	111222333	550	10	04000	04000	1100000
Jan Dobinsky	444555666	999	01	04000	04000	1320000

FIGURE 14.2   *Payroll records for processing by the payroll programs*

FORTRAN PROGRAM

A FORTRAN language version of the program diagrammed in Figure 14.1 is presented in Figure 14.3. Note the general organization of the FORTRAN program. FORTRAN is oriented to individual statements. Reference among the statements is accomplished by numbering each statement that is referred to by one or more other statements. Thus the READ statement in the third line of part (a) refers to the FORMAT statement in the fourth line (which is numbered as 4). Similarly, the WRITE statement in the sixth line refers to the FORMAT statement in the seventh line (numbered as 2). Note that statements need not be numbered in any specific order.

Several *types* of statements are found in FORTRAN. Let's examine them in their order of first appearance in Figure 14.3(a). The first two statements are *comments*, which serve to guide the reader. A "comment" statement has been used to define each major section of the program. The READ statement is used to enter data (input) described in an associated FORMAT statement. The FORMAT statement describes each data record to be read. For example, statement 1 (fifteenth line) defines the form of the time card records found in Figure 14.2. Specifically, the description within the parentheses says each record will consist of the following:

Four five-character alphabetic words (4A5). The name field of twenty characters is read as four different fields because the FORTRAN compiler used allows each alphabetic field to contain up to six characters.

A nine-digit whole number (integer) (I9). The employee number.

A blank space (1X).

A floating-point, three-digit number with two places after the decimal (F3.2). The hourly rate, which has a maximum value of $9.99.

Another blank space (IX).

A floating-point, two-digit number (F2.0). The number of dependents.

Another blank space (1X).

Two floating-point, five-digit numbers with two places after the decimal and a blank space following each number — 2(F5.2,1X). The regular and over-time hours worked.

A floating-point, seven-digit number with two places after the decimal point (F7.2). The year-to-date gross pay.

Compare statement 1 to statement 90, which describes a check register line. See the similarity in form of the two FORMAT statements? Note, however, that the nine-digit employee number is now described as a ten-digit integer. This is to allow for the sign attached to the number within the computer. The sign will be printed only if it is negative. Note also, the 1H0 at the beginning of the description. This is read "One Hollerith (alphanumeric) character to follow." The first Hollerith character, the 0 (zero), is a carriage control for the printer. A zero causes the printer to double-space before printing the line described in the FORMAT statement.

Statement 3 (ninth line) is a FORMAT statement containing a table heading. Note how this line is reproduced in the output in part (b) of Figure 14.3. Here the Hollerith statement contains a *literal* to be printed out. Note that the carriage control character is *not* printed.

The FORMAT statement in statement 4 of Figure 14.3(a) describes a four-digit integer that is inputted by the preceding READ statement. That number, N, is used to identify the number of records in the input file. (Special note: The number 0008 was added as the first word in the data file before it was read by the FORTRAN program. This control word is not used in the COBOL version of the program and was removed from the file before running the COBOL program.)

Note, again, how the comments (the lines starting with a C in the first character position) divide the FORTRAN program into logical sections and identify what each section does.

Find the section in which the loop to process the time records is opened (eleventh line). The DO statement says to repeat the lines from there through line 85 N times. N was defined as the number of time records (eight) in the third line. Read the comments in order down to line 85 and see how the program progresses through the loop:

1. Repeat steps 2 to 8 N times.

2. Read a record.

```
C  SIMPLIFIED HOURLY PAYROLL PROGRAM
C    READ NUMBER OF EMPLOYEES TO BE PAID
          READ (1,4) N
      4 FORMAT (I4)
C    WRITE CHECK REGISTER HEADINGS
          WRITE (3,2)
      2 FORMAT (40H1                              **CHECK REGISTER**  )
          WRITE (3,3)
      3 FORMAT (1H0,'EMPLOYEE',16X,'NUMBER',6X,'GROSS',6X,'TAX',7X,'FICA',
        15X,'NET')
C    OPEN LOOP TO PROCESS TIME RECORDS
          DO 85 I = 1,N
C    READ RECORD
          READ  (1,1)  NAME1,NAME2,NAME3,NAME4,NUMB,RATE,DEPND,RHRS,OHRS, YTDGR
      1 FORMAT  (4A5,I9,1X,F3.2,1X,F2.0,1X,2(F5.2,1X),F7.2)
C    COMPUTE GROSS PAY
          GROSS = RATE*(RHRS + 1.5*OHRS)
          GROSS = (AINT((GROSS + .005)*100))/100
C    COMPUTE TAX DEDUCTION
          DED = DEPND*15.0
          IF (GROSS - DED) 20,25,25
     20 TAX = 0.0
          GO TO 30
     25 TAX = (GROSS - DED)*.18
     30 TAX = (AINT((TAX + .005)*100))/100
C    COMPUTE FICA DEDUCTION
          IF (13200.0 - YTDGR)    40,40,45
     40 FICA = 0.0
          GO TO 60
     45 IF ( (13200.0 - YTDGR) - GROSS) 50,55,55
     50 FICA = 0.0585*(13200.0 - YTDGR)
          GO TO 60
     55 FICA = 0.0585*GROSS
     60 FICA = (AINT((FICA + 0.005)*100))/100
C    COMPUTE NET PAY
          PAY = GROSS - TAX - FICA
          IF (PAY) 70,80,80
     70 PAY = 0.00
C ACCUMULATE WEEKLY TOTALS
     80 TGRCSS  = TGROSS + GROSS
          TTAX = TTAX + TAX
          TFICA = TFICA + FICA
          TPAY = TPAY + PAY
C    WRITE CHECK LINE
     85 WRITE (3,90) NAME1,NAME2,NAME3,NAME4,NUMB,GROSS,TAX,FICA,PAY
     90 FORMAT (1H0,4A5,1X,I10,4(2X,F8.2))
```

FIGURE 14.3   FORTRAN *language version of simplified hourly payroll program and associated output*

```
C   ALL EMPLOYEES PROCESSED, WRITE WEEKLY TOTALS
        WRITE (3,105) TGROSS,TTAX,TFICA,TPAY
    105 FORMAT (31H0                      TOTALS        ,2X,F9.2,3(1X,F9.2) )
        END
```

(b)   Program output

CHECK REGISTER

EMPLOYEE	NUMBER	GROSS	TAX	FICA	NET
A. SANDY BEACHCOMB	333222111	120.00	10.80	7.02	102.18
SMODEY T. BEAR	111333222	200.00	30.60	11.70	157.70
JULIUS A. CEASER	112210102	400.00	69.30	5.85	324.85
JAMES H. DOUGH	584132987	700.00	123.30	5.85	570.85
MUNNEY EARNER	593761617	510.00	75.60	0.00	434.40
WILL I. FINDITALL	789912834	280.00	47.70	16.38	215.92
SHURELY A. LOSER	111222333	550.00	72.00	32.17	445.83
PENNEY SAVER	444555666	999.00	177.12	0.00	821.88
TOTALS		3759.00	606.42	78.97	3073.61

FIGURE 14.3   (cont.)

3. Compute gross pay.

4. Compute (income) tax deduction.

5. Compute FICA deduction.

6. Compute net pay.

7. Accumulate weekly totals.

8. Write check line.

Note the algebraic form of the FORTRAN processing statements. For example, statement 25:

$$TAX = (GROSS - DED)*.18$$

This is not really an algebraic statement. Rather, the expression on the right of the equals sign is to be evaluated (worked out) and its value stored away into the location labeled "TAX."

Refer to statement 45. This is an IF statement, a decision-making statement. Statement 45 says, "If the value of the expression within the outside parentheses, '(13200.0 − YTDGR) − GROSS,' is negative, go next to statement 50; but if the value is equal to zero or is greater than zero (positive), go next to statement 55." Can you understand the entire section in which the FICA deduction is computed? Try flowcharting it. (See question 15 at the end of the chapter.)

COBOL PROGRAM

A COBOL program is divided into four divisions. The first three divisions do not perform any data processing but serve only to describe the equipment and files to be used by the program. We might say that these divisions perform "initialization." The *identification division* [the first seven lines of the program in Figure 14.4(a)] serves to identify what is being programmed, by whom, and when. The *environment division* [lines 8 through 16 in Figure 14.4(a)] specifies the computer or computers involved and the elements of the computer configuration being used by the program. The *data division* provides an exact description of the data files used by the program. Lines 23 through 35 describe the *input* data records. Lines 36 through 41 and 55 through 91 describe *output* lines. Lines 42 through 54 describe *working-storage* files internal to the program where results are developed for transfer to the output files.

The *procedure division* is the working portion of a COBOL program. This division describes the processing that is to be carried out. Note how the operating program proceeds. First the output table headings are printed (lines 93 through 99). Then a loop is opened at line 101 that reads the data card for an employee, computes the paycheck (lines 101 through 114), accumulates the weekly totals (lines 114 through 119), prints a line on the check register for that employee (lines 120 through 132) before returning to read the next record. This loop is repeated as instructed in line 101 until all data records have been processed. Line 133 closes the loop.

Try to read the program division by division. Can you understand it? Can you flowchart the procedure division? (See question 16 at the end of this chapter.) Note the way computation is carried out in the procedure division. COBOL is supposed to be a self-documenting language understandable by managers. Does it seem so to you?

Let's look more carefully at Figure 14.4(a), division by division. The first two divisions (identification and environment) are simple enough if one knew what computer is referred to as a PDP-10 and that DSK stands for "disk unit" and LPT for "line printer." But did you notice the periods at the end of each line? COBOL statements are organized into "sentences"

```
0001        IDENTIFICATION DIVISION.
0002        PROGRAM-ID. HOURLY-PAYROLL.
0003        AUTHOR. GEORGE BRABB.
0004        DATE-WRITTEN. MAY 1 1974.
0005        REMARKS.
0006              THIS PROGRAM COMPUTES A SIMPLIFIED HOURLY
0007              PAYROLL AND PRINTS A CHECK REGISTER.
0008        ENVIRONMENT DIVISION.
0009        CONFIGURATION SECTION.
0010        SOURCE-COMPUTER. DECSYSTEM-10.
0011        OBJECT-COMPUTER. PDP-10.
0012        INPUT-OUTPUT SECTION.
0013        FILE-CONTROL.
0014              SELECT FILDAT ASSIGN TO DSK
0015              RECORDING MODE IS ASCII.
0016              SELECT FILE-OUT ASSIGN TO LPT.
0017        DATA DIVISION.
0018        FILE SECTION.
0019        FD  FILDAT
0020              VALUE OF IDENTIFICATION IS "FILDATCOL"
0021              LABEL RECORDS ARE STANDARD
0022              DATA RECORD IS CARD-IN.
0023        01    CARD-IN.
0024              02 NAME-IN        PIC A(20).
0025              02 EMP-NO         PIC 9(9).
0026              02 FILLER         PIC X.
0027              02 RATE           PIC 9V99.
0028              02 FILLER         PIC X.
0029              02 DEPEN          PIC 99.
0030              02 FILLER         PIC X.
0031              02 REG-HRS        PIC 999V99.
0032              02 FILLER         PIC X.
0033              02 OT-HRS         PIC 999V99.
0034              02 FILLER         PIC X.
0035              02 YTD-GR         PIC 9(5)V99.
0036        FD    FILE-OUT
0037              VALUE OF IDENTIFICATION IS "REGISTER "
0038              RECORD CONTAINS 72 CHARACTERS
0039              LABEL RECORDS ARE STANDARD
0040              DATA RECORD IS PRINTOUT.
```

FIGURE 14.4   *COBOL language version of simplified hourly payroll program and associated output*
(continued on pages 344–346)

```
0041      01    PRINTOUT            PIC  X(72).
0042            WORKING-STORAGE SECTION.
0043      77    FICA-LIMIT          PIC  9(5)V99 VALUE 13200.00.
0044      77    GROSS-PAY           PIC  9(4)V99 VALUE IS ZEROES.
0045      77    DEDUCTION           PIC  9(5)V99 VALUE IS ZEROES.
0046      77    FED-TAX             PIC  999V99 VALUE IS ZEROES.
0047      77    FICA-1              PIC  999V99 VALUE IS ZEROES.
0048      77    DIFFERENCE          PIC  9(5)V99 VALUE IS ZEROES.
0049      77    NET-PAY             PIC  9(5)V99 VALUE IS ZEROES.
0050      77    TAX-AMT             PIC  9(4)V99 VALUE IS ZEROES.
0051      77    TGROSS              PIC  9(6)V99 VALUE IS ZEROES.
0052      77    TTAX                PIC  9(4)V99.
0053      77    TFICA               PIC  9(4)V99 VALUE IS ZEROES.
0054      77    TNET                PIC  9(4)V99 VALUE IS ZEROES.
0055      01    PRT-HDG.
0056            02  HEAD-1          PIC  A(17) VALUE "       EMPLOYEE NAME".
0057            02  FILLER          PIC  X(4).
0058            02  HEAD-2          PIC  X(10) VALUE "ID-NUMBER".
0059            02  FILLER          PIC  X(2).
0060            02  HEAD-3          PIC  X(7) VALUE "GR-PAY ".
0061            02  FILLER          PIC  X(2).
0062            02  HEAD-4          PIC  X(5) VALUE "W-TAX".
0063            02  FILLER          PIC  X(4).
0064            02  HEAD-5          PIC  A(5) VALUE " FICA".
0065            02  FILLER          PIC  X(2).
0066            02  HEAD-6          PIC  X(7) VALUE "NET-PAY".
0067      01    PRT-HDG-1.
0068            02  FILLER          PIC  X(22).
0069            02  HD-1            PIC  X(41) VALUE "****CHECK REGISTER****".
0070      01    DET-LINE.
0071            02  NAME-0          PIC  A(20).
0072            02  FILLER          PIC  X.
0073            02  EMP-NUMB-0      PIC  9(9).
0074            02  FILLER          PIC  X.
0075            02  GROSS-0         PIC  $(6).99.
0076            02  FILLER          PIC  X.
0077            02  W-TAX-0         PIC  $(4).99.
0078            02  FILLER          PIC  X.
0079            02  FICA-0          PIC  $(4).99.
0080            02  FILLER          PIC  X(2).
```

FIGURE 14.4   (*cont.*)

```
0081          02  NET-PAY-0        PIC    $(4).99.
0082    01    TOT-LINE.
0083          02  TOTAL-0          PIC    X(17) VALUE "                TOTALS".
0084          02  FILLER           PIC    X(14).
0085          02  TGROSS-0         PIC    $(6).99.
0086          02  FILLER           PIC    X.
0087          02  TTAX-0           PIC    $(5).99.
0088          02  FILLER           PIC    X.
0089          02  TFICA-0          PIC    $(4).99.
0090          02  FILLER           PIC    X.
0091          02  TNET-0           PIC    $(5).99.
0092    PROCEDURE DIVISION.
0093    BEGIN.
0094    OPEN INPUT FILDAT, OUTPUT FILE-OUT.
0095    PRINT-HEAD.
0096          WRITE PRINTOUT FROM PRT-HDG-1 AFTER ADVANCING 6 LINES.
0097          MOVE SPACES TO PRINTOUT.
0098          WRITE PRINTOUT FROM PRT-HDG AFTER ADVANCING 3 LINES.
0099          MOVE SPACES TO PRINTOUT.
0100    COMPUTE-1.
0101          READ FILDAT AT END GO TO FINISH.
0102          COMPUTE GROSS-PAY ROUNDED = RATE * (REG-HRS + 1.5 * OT-HRS).
0103          MULTIPLY DEPEN BY 15.00 GIVING DEDUCTION.
0104          IF GROSS-PAY > DEDUCTION SUBTRACT DEDUCTION FROM GROSS-PAY
0105          GIVING TAX-AMT, ELSE GO TO FICA-ROUTINE.
0106          MULTIPLY TAX-AMT BY .18 GIVING FED-TAX ROUNDED.
0107    FICA-ROUTINE.
0108          IF YTD-GR < FICA-LIMIT SUBTRACT YTD-GR FROM FICA-LIMIT
0109          GIVING DIFFERENCE, ELSE GO TO NET.
0110          IF DIFFERENCE > GROSS-PAY MULTIPLY GROSS-PAY
0111          BY .0585 GIVING FICA-1 ROUNDED, ELSE MULTIPLY DIFFERENCE BY .0585
0112          GIVING FICA-1 ROUNDED.
0113    NET.
0114          COMPUTE NET-PAY = GROSS-PAY - FED-TAX - FICA-1.
0115    TOTALS.
0116          ADD GROSS-PAY TO TGROSS.
0117          ADD FED-TAX TO TTAX.
0118          ADD FICA-1 TO TFICA.
0119          ADD NET-PAY TO TNET.
0120    PRINT-OUT.
```

FIGURE 14.4   (cont.)

```
0121          MOVE SPACES TO PRINTOUT.
0122          MOVE NAME-IN TO NAME-0.
0123          MOVE EMP-NO TO EMP-NUMB-0.
0124          MOVE GROSS-PAY TO GROSS-0.
0125          MOVE FED-TAX TO W-TAX-0.
0126          MOVE FICA-1 TO FICA-0.
0127          MOVE NET-PAY TO NET-PAY-0.
0128          WRITE PRINTOUT FROM DET-LINE AFTER ADVANCING 3 LINES.
0129          MOVE SPACES TO PRINTOUT.
0130          MOVE ZEROES TO FED-TAX.
0131          MOVE ZEROES TO TAX-AMT.
0132          MOVE ZEROES TO FICA-1.
0133          GO TO COMPUTE-1.
0134     FINISH.
0135          MOVE SPACES TO PRINTOUT.
0136          MOVE TGROSS TO TGROSS-0.
0137          MOVE TTAX TO TTAX-0.
0138          MOVE TFICA TO TFICA-0.
0139          MOVE TNET TO TNET-0.
0140          WRITE PRINTOUT FROM TOT-LINE AFTER ADVANCING 3 LINES.
0141          CLOSE FILDAT, FILE-OUT.
0142          STOP RUN.
```

(b)   Program output

****CHECK REGISTER****

EMPLOYEE NAME	ID-NUMBER	GR-PAY	W-TAX	FICA	NET-PAY
A. SANDY BEACHCOMB	333222111	$120.00	$10.80	$7.02	$102.18
SMODEY T. BEAR	111333222	$200.00	$30.60	$11.70	$157.70
JULIUS A. CEASER	112210102	$400.00	$69.30	$5.85	$324.85
JAMES H. DOUGH	584132987	$700.00	$123.30	$5.85	$570.85
MUNNEY EARNER	593761617	$510.00	$75.60	$.00	$434.40
WILL I. FINDITALL	789912834	$280.00	$47.70	$16.38	$215.92
SHURELY A. LOSER	111222333	$550.00	$72.00	$32.18	$445.82
PENNEY SAVER	444555666	$999.00	$177.12	$.00	$821.88
TOTALS		$3759.00	$606.42	$78.98	$3073.60

FIGURE 14.4   (cont.)

and "paragraphs." This sentence and paragraph structure is easiest to see in the procedure division.

Let's move to the data division. Input is to be by time records, each containing one employee record consisting of seven data fields and five blank fields as follows:

1. Employee name — twenty alphabetic characters (line 24)

2. Employee identification number — nine numerical characters, no decimal (line 25)

3. One blank space (line 26)

4. An hourly wage rate — three numerical characters with two places after the decimal (line 27)

5. One blank space (line 28)

6. The number of dependents — a two-digit whole number (line 29)

7. One blank space (line 30)

8. Regular hours worked — five digits with two places after the decimal (line 31)

9. One blank space (line 32)

10. Overtime hours worked — five digits with two places after the decimal (line 33)

11. One blank space (line 34)

12. Year-to-date gross earnings — seven digits with two places after the decimal (line 35)

Refer to Figure 14.2 and check the structure of the data file. Is it described above? Now, can you read lines 42 to 54, which describe the working-storage variable values and initially set several of them to zero? How about the lines describing the output records?

Finally, note the arrangement of the statements across each line. See how each division and its major subdivisions (paragraphs) all begin at the same point on the line. Note how subsidiary lines are either indented or numbered. COBOL requires strict adherence to rules of placement on the line.

Other Languages

Higher level languages are of two general types, general purpose and special purpose. *General-purpose* languages are designed to carry out *any* data processing job, but they may still have characteristics favoring their use for specific problems or by specific users. COBOL and FORTRAN are general-purpose languages. Each can be used for programming *any* problem.

But COBOL is a business data processing, file-oriented language, while FORTRAN is better suited for scientific problem solving (solution by formula).

OTHER GENERAL-PURPOSE LANGUAGES

The additional general-purpose languages to be discussed here include ALGOL (ALGorithmic Oriented Language), APL (A Programming Language), BASIC (Beginners All-Purpose Symbolic Instruction Code), PL/1 (Programming Language 1) and RPG (Report Program Generator).

ALGOL   The arithmetic capabilities of ALGOL are similar in type and in operations to those of FORTRAN. ALGOL, however, is a more sophisticated mathematical language than FORTRAN. It is the most popular scientific programming language in Europe and has been used as machine language for one series of computers (Burroughs B-5000, B-5500, B-6000, B-7100, B-8100).

APL   Designed as a timesharing language, APL's greatest weakness for unsophisticated users is its use of mathematical notation including Greek letters. Its use requires a special terminal keyboard. It is a powerful language for scientific problem solving and has been used primarily in education and research applications. A business data processing version is now available.

BASIC   BASIC is the most popular of the timesharing languages. It was designed to be used by students working at online terminals. Initially it was a subset of FORTRAN with major omissions freeing the programmer from having to describe input and output records in detail. This is not an unmixed blessing, however, since well-organized output reports have been more difficult to produce using BASIC. Newer versions are overcoming this weakness. Its biggest advantage is the ease with which it can be learned. Partly because of the interaction between the programmer and the compiler, beginners produce complete, meaningful programs after as few as two hours of formal instruction. BASIC is available from most timesharing service bureaus and is being used in industry for both scientific problem solving and administrative data processing, particularly on microcomputers and minicomputers. Its most common use is as a student programming language. Its use in business data processing is expanding rapidly with the increasing use of microcomputers and minicomputers in business. Business versions of BASIC make it easier to process files containing decimal data.

PL/1   As a response to what was considered an undesirable proliferation of languages in the 1960s, PL/1 was developed at the International Business Machines Corporation and initially was available only on IBM computers.

It is a very complex and sophisticated language designed to include the best features of ALGOL, COBOL, and FORTRAN. This strength is also a weakness, making PL/1 more difficult to master (or use) in its entirety than other general-purpose languages. One advantage of PL/1 from the user's viewpoint is the lack of rigid rules of form, so that no special coding forms are required. In response to user demand, PL/1 has been implemented on (programmed for) several computer families other than those manufactured by International Business Machines Corporation.

RPG As its name implies, Report Program Generator started out as a way to quickly and easily manipulate data files in order to prepare standard reports. Later extensions have expanded its capabilities, so that it is a general problem-solving language. However, it retains its report-generator origins, with three major sections in each program. The data file is described first, the necessary processing is detailed second, and the format of the output (report) is detailed in the last section. Note the similarity of this structure to the structure of COBOL. Both are business data processing languages. RPG is being made available for most business minicomputer systems.

SPECIAL-PURPOSE LANGUAGES

The exact number of programming languages that have been developed for different purposes is not known, but it is *large*. At least a score of special-purpose languages are in general use. We will not attempt to identify all these languages, but we will give examples of the major types. The discussion below is organized by major language types.

Simulation Languages The computer is a powerful simulation tool, but the complexity and extensive detail involved in large simulations makes special-purpose languages designed to take care of routine details and major (general) functions very desirable. In general, the languages provide the programmer with a set of modeling concepts (entities, events, levels, flows, and so on) by which to describe the system being simulated. These descriptions are then converted into a computer program by the language. The systems being simulated are usually described as either *continuous* or *discrete,* and each simulation language is designed to handle one or the other.

Popular examples of *discrete* system simulation languages are GPSS (General Purpose System Simulator) and SIMSCRIPT. Other discrete languages are in use. Examples are GASP and SIMULA. Discrete simulation languages are available for every major computer system.

The most widely used *continuous* system simulation language is DYNAMO, the language developed to handle the Industrial Dynamics models of Jay Forrester. Another example is CSMP (Continuous System Modeling Program), which has been implemented on various IBM computer systems.

List Processing A variety of languages have been developed that emphasize features making it possible to link up, or *chain*, groups of interconnected items (lists). A *pointer* is attached to each data word or record identifying the next and/or previous item in the chain. Various ways of modifying lists (*push-down* and *pop-up* structures, for example) are also added. These features make it possible to make chain searches of related files for information. One access of a set of files can retrieve all related facts from each file in the total set. Thus an inquiry directed initially to an inventory file to ascertain the availability of an item can obtain, in addition to the number of finished units in inventory, units in production and unfilled orders on file. The most popular languages of this type are LISP and SNOBOL.

Data Management Languages Partly a pragmatic development of list processing languages are the languages developed to handle large, integrated data base files. List processing languages ease the job of modifying all records in separate but integrated files. Pointers on each record in each file (for example, customer file) link each record to related records in other files (for example, order file and inventory files). In addition, the data management languages provide automatic organization of data structures within files. Programmers are freed from the necessity of describing data files in detail at each use after the files have been initially developed. The file manager follows preset procedures and preset descriptions to store or retrieve data words, fields, or records within each file on the system whenever the field or record is called for by putting its logical name in a program instruction.

Over a score of file management systems are available for purchase or rent. Languages can be found that are based on COBOL, FORTRAN, PL/1, or some unique special language. The value of such systems is great. They reduce programming cost, reduce the time required to respond to special data requests, and ease the job of keeping an electronic data base up to date. Additional data management systems are introduced frequently.

The latest data base management systems are making use by nonprogrammers relatively easy. These languages are *nonprocedural*. They do not require the user to specify each procedure to be used (table look-up, sort, print using a specified format, and so on). Rather, the user can specify, in simple Englishlike statements, what is wanted. Data retrieval paths are developed from data names in the request. Sorting and formatting to develop responses are automatically performed in standard ways unless the user chooses to override this feature and supply other sorting and/or formatting specifications. Using these request-based languages, a nonprogramming user can develop simple but complete applications programs to process data contained in a data base and create usable reports.

Programming Assistance   Computer scientists continue to work toward the goal of a computer that programs itself. At least, it is hoped that we can merely describe any problem in some simple fashion to the computer and the computer will develop a program to solve it. The special-purpose languages, in particular, are the result of efforts along this line. The ultimate goal is to allow the programmer to use natural language (English) to express problem solutions. Progress has been slowed by the ambiguities of the English language. The new request-based DBMS languages are about as close as we've come, but they are far from the English language. A second approach has been to describe the solution procedure in a general way with flowcharts or decision tables and let the computer write the program code from this description. Work with flowcharts has not been too successful, primarily because of the difficulties of developing unambiguous input descriptions in flowchart form. Languages do exist that translate decision tables into machine code. The most widely used of these languages is called DETAB. DETAB translates decision tables into the COBOL language.

Programs do exist that develop flowcharts from source programs written in a higher level language such as FORTRAN or COBOL. These programs can be helpful in providing documentation. However, flowcharts should be prepared *before* the program is coded, not after.

Choosing a Programming Language

Four classes of programming languages have been identified: *machine* language, *assembly* language, *general-purpose higher level* language and *special-purpose higher level* language. Each computer system has its own machine language. Except for limited computer families, machine languages differ for each computer. Assembly language instructions usually bear a one-to-one relationship to machine language instructions, so they also differ from machine to machine, but they still have a great deal of similarity. This is partly because machine language has tended to become more standardized. The higher order languages (procedural or problem-oriented) are *supposedly* machine-independent; but they do vary slightly from computer to computer, particularly in handling input and output. In addition, there are many candidates available as general-purpose higher order languages. The purpose of this section is to guide the user in finding a way through this maze to a *suitable* problem-language match. (Note that we said *suitable*, not *optimal*.)

MACHINE LANGUAGE

About the only programming done in actual machine language is an occasional correction to an operational machine language program. The lowest level of programming language in common use for problem solving is the one-for-one assembly language. Any machine language that is used is obviously machine-dependent, requiring the user to learn the idiosyncrasies of the particular computer on which the program will be run.

ASSEMBLY LANGUAGE

Assembly language has two levels. Assembly languages require, in general, that each assembly language instruction be compiled as a single machine language instruction. However, most assembly languages have been extended to include macroinstructions. Each macro produces more than one machine language instruction. Even so, all assembly languages are machine-dependent, generally indicating machine operations mnemonically and using symbolic machine addresses in each instruction. Like machine languages, assembly languages tend to be detailed and arbitrary and therefore hard to learn. Program coding in assembly language tends to be a slow, tedious, and error-prone process. The programs are hard to read, making program maintenance difficult. However, assembly language programs can be more easily made *machine-efficient*. That is, they can be made to perform the required machine operations in a minimum of elapsed time and with a minimum of total machine language (object) code.

Problems of any type or complexity can be coded in assembly language. The flexibility of the language is limited only by the architecture of the machine being used. Complex programs, however, are time-consuming to write and debug in assembly language. Assembly languages tend to be used to produce input-output and other data handling utility programs. Compilers, timesharing executives, and most instantaneous-response systems also are written in assembly language. Production programs that require frequent and lengthy machine runs are sometimes written in assembly language, although most application programs are written in a higher level language. The relative costs of programming effort and computer use favor efficiency of programming over efficiency of computer use.

GENERAL-PURPOSE HIGHER LEVEL LANGUAGES

Higher level languages allow the user to prepare the program in a language procedurally oriented to the problem being solved. They are generally easier to learn and easier to use than assembly language. Programs can usually be developed and debugged with less effort. Maintenance is easier because the programs are easier to read and understand; that is, the higher level languages are more self-documenting. Although any problem can be programmed in any general-purpose higher level language, each language tends to favor particular problem types. COBOL is a business data processing language; FORTRAN and ALGOL are designed for scientific problem solving; and PL/1 contains elements of all three, including elementary list processing. PL/1, however, seems biased toward scientific rather than business problems. It looks more like FORTRAN or ALGOL than like COBOL.

Special problems arise with higher level general languages. The compilers that convert the source programs to object code cannot be expected to produce optimal object code for all source programs. Object programs tend to be longer and to use more computer time than programs developed in assembly language to do the same job. In addition, some compilers can be quite slow at compiling the object code, particularly those compilers that attempt to optimize the object code. The additional machine time required to compile and execute the programs and the additional storage required to hold the additional object code are costs to offset against the lower costs of program development and maintenance.

Higher level languages obviously are preferable to assembly language for programs that are to be run only once or at infrequent intervals. They, obviously, are favored by problem solvers who are *not* professional programmers but have a need to program. Most applications programming, even by professional programmers, is performed in higher level languages. However, only when higher level languages produce machine code approaching assembly language code in efficiency of machine use will the use of assembly languages for production programs completely disappear.

SPECIAL-PURPOSE HIGHER LEVEL LANGUAGES

Special-purpose languages have the characteristics of general-purpose higher level languages except for the limited scope of the problems they can be used on. They are relatively easier to learn and easier to use. They also tend to be easier to read and more self-documenting. This makes them easier to maintain.

CRITERIA FOR LANGUAGE SELECTION

The above discussions indicate the following criteria as appropriate for guiding language selection for a computer installation and for a particular programming problem. In each case the object is to choose the language that will do the job at the least cost *in the long run*.

Language Selection for a Computer Installation To make a higher level language available to programmers at a particular installation requires the acquisition (rent, purchase, or on-site development) of supporting software (assembler or compiler, manuals, and so on) and maintenance of that software. Factors to consider in justifying costs of these requirements include:

1. The type of problems being handled (number and frequency of programs of each type)

2. The cost of the software alternatives

3. The maintenance provided by the supplier, including the handling of any future changes in the language

4. Cost and availability of programmer training in the language

5. The efficiency of the compiler or assembler:
   a. Satisfaction expressed by previous users
   b. Compilation speed
   c. Object code efficiency (run time and number of instructions in the object program)
   d. Support for structured programming

6. Special hardware required to use the language efficiently, including costs of acquisition and of maintenance

7. The likelihood of a future change in hardware that could require machine-dependent programs to be rewritten

In general, the languages chosen for use in a computer installation will be determined by the major jobs to be accomplished. For example, assume a general-purpose data processing language, a simulation language, and a data management language are to be chosen. The languages in each of these three categories available for the computer system being used and capable of handling the work in each area must then be compared. Cost of acquisition and maintenance of each language, amount of programmer training required, cost of training programmers, the efficiency of each compiler available for the hardware in use, and costs for any additional hardware must be determined for each alternative. After all costs for each language alternative have been summed, the prime candidate is determined. If the prime candidate does not commit the installation to a language likely to become obsolete soon enough that the cost of the programming cannot be recaptured, that language should be chosen. Higher order languages are less likely to be outdated by new hardware developments.

Language Selection for a Particular Problem In addition to the above factors influencing language selection for an installation, language selection for a specific problem should consider:

1. Programming skills available

2. Frequency of use of the finished program

3. Time available for program development

Choice of a language for a particular problem is simpler than choice of a language for an installation. Higher order languages that reduce program development effort are preferred for complex one-shot programs. Assembly languages can become competitive when jobs are run frequently and require a great deal of computer time and are usually preferred for developing utilities and other basic system software. However, a change in hardware can force reprogramming of jobs written in assembly language. A higher order language procedurally oriented to the specific problem is usually the best choice.

Summary

Although programming languages differ, they all must provide for input and output, processing (arithmetic and data transfer), transfer of control for decision making, looping, and subroutines or subprograms. A comparison of FORTRAN and COBOL illustrated this fact. Parallel similarities could have been shown for assembly and machine languages. Machine and assembly languages reflect the characteristics of the specific computer on which they are used. They are therefore more detailed and harder to learn and use than higher order languages but tend to produce a more machine-efficient object code. Higher order languages have been developed to allow the user to concentrate on the problem without regard to the idiosyncrasies of the specific computer being used. They are usually not completely machine-independent, however, particularly with regard to input and output processes. Higher order languages are preferred for complex one-shot programs and to prevent future reprogramming because of a change in hardware. Most applications programs are written in a higher level language. Assembly language is still used for frequently used or lengthy production programs and in preparing basic system software. Costs of program development, compilation, and operating runs must be considered in determining language selection. Programming skills available and time available for program development can influence choice of language for programming particular problems.

Questions

1. Define each of the following as briefly as possible and then use a short paragraph to clarify each definition.
   a. Programming language
   b. Compiler
   c. COBOL
   d. General-purpose language
   e. DETAB
   f. Software
   g. Assembly language
   h. Higher level language

i. FORTRAN   l. Data management language
j. Format   m. RPG
k. Simulation language   n. Machine-dependent

2. What are the four classes of programming languages?
3. When should an assembly language be used for programming?
4. When should a general-purpose programming language be used?
5. When should a special-purpose programming language be used?
6. What were called decision-making statements in this chapter have also been classed as *conditional-transfer* statements. Justify the use of the latter classification.
7. List and briefly discuss each of the factors listed as criteria for selection of programming languages.
8. What three factors are involved in determining compiler efficiency?
9. Prepare a table ranking assembly language, general-purpose higher level language, and special-purpose higher level language on each of the following factors (use 1 for best, 3 for worst on each factor):
   a. Ease of learning
   b. Ease of program development
   c. Ease of debugging
   d. Ease of maintenance
10. Refer to the table prepared for question 9. What general conclusions can you draw from it?
11. What are the advantages of an easy-to-read programming language?
12. Compilers furnished with several computer systems are imbedded in the hardware. That is, the compiler is executed by use of microprogrammed hardware instructions instead of being composed of the usual software assembly language instructions. What are the advantages and disadvantages of such a compiler?
13. a. Should a top manager of even a small firm be expected to write programs? Explain.
    b. If a top manager were to write programs, what kind of language should be used? Explain.
14. What criteria should be used in evaluating the job performance of applications programmers?
15. Prepare a detailed flowchart for the section in which the FICA deduction is computed in the FORTRAN program of Figure 14.3.
16. Flowchart the procedure division of Figure 14.4. Compare your diagram to Figure 14.1. Are they the same? They should be.
17. Compare your results for questions 15 and 16. Which language was easier to flowchart? Why?
18. Is computer time more valuable than programmer time? If so, why are

higher order languages so popular? If not, why are any programs written in machine or assembly language?

19. Refer to question 17 at the end of Chapter 7 and specify whether the system described there would be better programmed in FORTRAN or in COBOL. Fully explain your choice of language.

20. Refer to question 18 at the end of Chapter 7 and specify what programming language would best serve for implementing that system on a computer. Justify your choice in detail.

Part 4

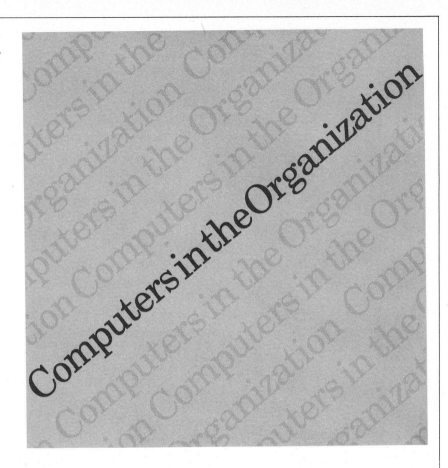

Computers in the Organization

Computers have had significant impact on organizations. In many cases, the introduction of computerized processing into the organization has led to improved performance. In other cases, the move has been labeled unsuccessful or even disastrous. Firms have even abandoned attempts to computerize after large expenditures. Such costly mistakes can be avoided. This section is intended to provide guidance to managers to prevent such costly errors.

The accounting function is an important element in any business organization. Accounting records provide a basic source of managerial information. Computers are frequently introduced into business data processing systems to perform the clerical aspects involved in the accounting function. There have been several recent stories of fraud and embezzlement made possible by computerized accounting systems. Chapter 15 discusses the important area of computers and accounting. The changes in accounting procedures induced by the computer are indicated, and control (auditing) procedures for electronic systems are discussed.

Chapter 16 discusses the computer and the management function. The effects on the organization (structure) of management and the practice of management are explained. A final section discusses the special problems involved in managing the information system function itself.

Fifteen

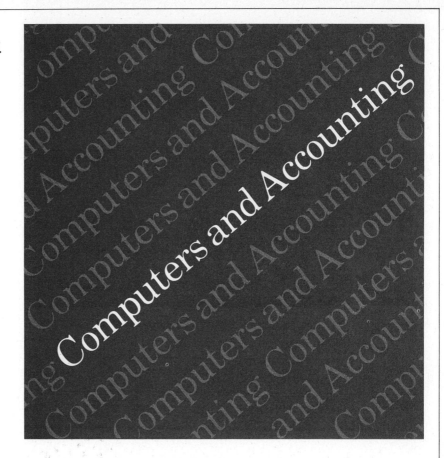

Computers and Accounting

It is the purpose of this chapter to identify the purposes of the accounting function and consider the ways in which this discipline is affected by the computer. The changes that occur in accounting systems when the computer is used to perform accounting procedures are identified. A special section discusses the auditing of electronic accounting systems. A final section briefly discusses the special problems encountered in accounting for computer use.

The Accounting Function

The accounting subsystem is a record-keeping, information-providing system. It provides a model of the organization and provides information in terms of that model that is useful to stockholders and other investors, to managers of the organization, and to governmental control and taxation agencies. Books of record developed originally to preserve facts for use in evaluating the results of an economic activity and to fairly distribute the economic gains or losses from that activity. Now the language of accounting is largely financial, and accounting reports are developed partly for users outside the firm. The measurements of results are in financial terms. Historical records of resource inputs are in financial terms. Reports on operating activities are normally in financial terms (profit, loss, cost per unit, return per unit). Physical measurements of activities are converted to reflect their impact on the financial situation for the firm.

The above comments seem to imply that the accounting system is at least a large *part* of the information system of a firm. Accounting systems are the most complete models of the firm available to us, and accounting reports do provide the majority of management's operating (control) information. It is therefore important to assess the impact of computerization upon this function. However, it must be recognized that the accounting system is a subsystem of the management information system.

Procedural Changes

The use of computers to perform business data processing means that all input data must, at some point, be available on a machine-sensible medium. In small systems, transactions data may still be captured on manually prepared documents and then transferred to punched cards, punched paper tape, magnetic tape, magnetic disks, and so on. In larger volume systems or systems with severe time constraints on response, transactions are being captured online. In either case, the bookkeeping is done by the machine. Since the machine does only what it is told, this need not change the nature of the books at all. However, the two processes usually differ in several ways.

SYSTEM DESIGN

A manual bookkeeping system can be implemented by getting a set of ledger books; designing a straightforward set of double-entry accounts (each transaction results in a *debit* entry offset by a *credit* entry); and then waiting for transactions documents. As unusual or nonroutine items occur, procedures are developed to handle them. However, because an electronic accounting system is implemented on one or more machines, it must be planned down to the last detail before implementation. Provision must be made to take care of unusual and nonroutine transactions as well as routine transactions. Plans must be fully developed before the system can be programmed and implemented.

DATA INPUT

In a manual accounting system, inputs are usually entered directly from individual transactions documents or from documents summarizing a group of transactions. In a computerized system, data must be converted to machine symbols for entry. This can be accomplished by direct online entry or by offline data conversion (to cards, tape, or disk). With some small business computers, it is common to perform online key entry from transactions documents to magnetic memory (disks) and perform edit processing and some bookkeeping at the same time. Customer, supplier, or product accounts are updated as invoices are entered. Summary reports are then produced by the machine.

Data are often *coded* for entry. Customers, inventory items, employees, transaction types, and so on, are given identifying number codes. Alphabetic names and descriptions are already stored in the permanent electronic file and only identification codes (item or account number) and data varying with each transaction (quantity, price) need be entered.

In manual systems each input document tends to pass through several hands. For example, a sales invoice is written by a salesperson; it then may be seen by a warehouse worker, a ledger clerk, and a file clerk. This division of labor with its multiplicity of observations of input documents decreases the chance of posting errors. With the computer, all these functions can be performed by the computer. All data tend to flow to one spot, the computer, and are processed there. The natural checks and balances of the manual system must be replaced by system controls designed into computer programs.

INTEGRATION OF THE SYSTEM

In addition to a tendency to centralize processing, the computerized system encourages integration in processing. Each transaction tends to result in changes in several permanent records. For example, a credit sale causes changes in accounts receivable, inventory, and sales records. Files tend to be centralized in the data processing center to ease this integration process.

Manual systems are different. They tend to be organized by business function (purchasing, billing, sales, production), often with a complete duplication of much of the information in separate systems and files. Data do not flow across operational department lines but tend to be processed fully within an operational department. Only summaries and analyses (reports) cross departmental lines in most manual systems.

RANDOM-INQUIRY RESPONSE

It is generally easy for a manual system to respond to an unexpected request for information stored within the system. Electronic systems must be carefully designed to provide easy response to random inquiries. Unless files are stored in online random-access electronic storage, the electronic system cannot respond quickly and easily. However, when planned to answer such responses, the computerized system is superior.

In batch-oriented systems, random inquiries must often wait for the next scheduled run of the file being interrogated. Many online systems do not retain very much detail in the online file. Inquiries about transactions details often must be answered by special processing runs or by manual search of the initial transactions records. Some electronic systems (particularly direct-entry systems) keep no record of transactions detail (it's too costly) and cannot answer such inquiries.

DATA ANALYSIS

As symbol manipulators, computers are outstanding. Electronic accounting systems can easily be designed to create involved statistical reports. For example, past trends, operating standards, and exception analyses can be obtained on a routine basis. This feature of the computer is important in reducing the volume of management reports. Detailed data can be sifted and manipulated to reveal information content. Management reports need contain only the information that results. Detailed data required for making decisions or implementing decisions at the operating level can be obtained from later specific inquiry. Thus only a portion of the detailed data available will ever be seen by management. Given the speed possible with electronic systems, reports can also be much more timely than in a manual system.

TYPES OF ELECTRONIC ACCOUNTING SYSTEMS

Two general types of computerized accounting systems exist. In *batch-oriented unit record systems* each transaction becomes a record that is processed in several different ways. The number of times the record enters the system depends on the degree of integration in the system. Fully integrated batch systems enter the record once and update all files in a single pass. Usually the files in a fully integrated batch system would be on random-access electronic storage media such as magnetic disks. Input records would be on cards, tapes, or disks. Capture of transactions data on machine-sensible media might sometimes be involved, but data conversion from transaction documents is much more common in batch systems. The computer performs the bookkeeping and routine clerical functions. Usually batches of input data are proofed offline before entry, and output reports are analyzed offline also. Routine reports are prepared on the computer; but random inquiries or special analyses are often performed by humans, perhaps with computational help from the computer. Reports tend to be made at regular calendar intervals and summarize activity for a prior accounting period.

Online integrated systems feature random-access storage and direct-data entry. Transactions data are captured by online devices and used to keep all online files updated. Very few systems are totally integrated online systems, but many large subsystems (inventory and customer orders, for example) are. In the online system, the computer performs all the functions of the bookkeeper and the accounting clerk, keeping the accounts updated and preparing reports. Normally, the computer also handles all random inquiries to the system and is responsible for proofing input data and recognition and reporting of unusual or unwanted developments. Of course, the computer must be programmed to do these things, which can be a difficult and costly task.

Accounting files for a batch-oriented unit record system often differ little from manual ledgers, except that they are stored on a machine-sensible medium. Transactions data are often available on input documents. Online integrated systems tend *not* to retain transactions detail in any form, and a ledger account is apt to contain only a summarized account balance.

Systems controls must be built into online systems to a greater degree than in unit record systems because transactions data are lost. It cannot be assumed, however, that unit record systems can be controlled by *exactly* the same procedures used for manual systems. They too must have controls built into the computer programs.

Two basic problems must be faced in using the online system. The first is the problem of adequately and correctly identifying each transaction at its point of capture. If more than one type of transaction is carried out at an activity station, transaction types must be kept clearly separate. The second problem is of control. If data are entered directly into the computerized system, how do we prevent errors? How do we audit the system? These questions are discussed more fully below.

Auditing Electronic Accounting Systems

Traditional control and audit techniques do not suffice for electronic accounting systems. However, the same principles still apply.

Auditing is a process of examining information with the intent of establishing its reliability. The process is normally performed by someone other than the preparer or user of the information. The auditor reports his or her findings so that the information can be understood and used properly. Auditing of accounting information systems is concerned with the correctness of accounting records and financial reports. System procedures, system controls, data sources, and the manner in which financial statements have been developed are examined in detail. To properly carry out this examination, the auditor must know the firm and its operations, be intimately familiar with its financial information system, and be thoroughly aware of generally accepted accounting principles and conventions. There are two types of auditors, internal auditors and external auditors.

THE INTERNAL AUDITOR

The internal auditor is an employee of the firm who is given the responsibility for seeing that accepted accounting practices are followed and that adequate internal and data controls are included in the accounting systems of the firm. An internal auditor does not make third-party audit reports to anyone other than management within the firm.

THE EXTERNAL AUDITOR

External auditors are ordinarily certified public accountants (CPAs). Their primary responsibility is in determining that the financial statements of a firm give a fair and honest picture of the financial position of the firm. They are not primarily involved in the initial design of systems but, rather, in examining the accounting systems used to develop the financial statements. External auditors (CPA firms) often perform the internal auditor function for firms that do not have an internal auditor.

THE AUDIT PROCESS

Regardless of who is performing an audit, an internal or an external auditor, the audit has the same purposes. Internal controls are examined to see that they do in fact —

1. Check on and maintain the accuracy of business data.
2. Safeguard the company assets against fraud, embezzlement, and theft.
3. Promote operating efficiency.
4. Encourage compliance with existing company policies and procedures.

Accounting systems are then reviewed carefully to see that accepted principles and procedures are being used in preparing financial statements.

THE PROBLEMS

The control problems of electronic systems can be defined as follows:

1. Data and records are captured and stored as invisible magnetized spots on magnetic tapes, disks, or strips.

2. Interdepartmental and interpersonal crosschecks on data accuracy are not present.

3. The processing procedures are stated in computer programs that also carry them out. These programs are written in special languages and stored on a machine-sensible medium.

4. Online integrated systems retain only the current status on each account. Transactions documents and daily journals usually do not exist to provide an audit trail.

5. Electronic accounting systems are frequently developed by nonaccountants (systems analysts and programmers) as part of a total information and custodial processing system.

The methods for overcoming these difficulties are complex, but they can be summarized in three general approaches.

AUDITING "AROUND" THE COMPUTER

When auditing "around" the computer, the auditor proves the accuracy of transactions data inputs, demonstrates that those inputs actually should result in the outputs obtained, and concludes that the processing system is correct. Input controls are examined and tested, and a sample of actual inputs is selected. The results of processing the sample inputs are calculated and checked against the actual values existing as computer output in the system. If the calculated results and the outputs in the system agree, the system is declared valid.

Auditing around the computer has the obvious advantage of not requiring any knowledge of how to unravel a flowchart or a program listing. Its major weakness lies in its failure to assess the processing system. Vital system controls against fraud may be missing. Data input controls may be absent or inadequate. Also, processing may be done in inefficient and costly ways. The auditor should spot such deficiencies in the system. Because of its weaknesses, auditing around the computer is an inadequate technique for auditing modern computerized systems.

AUDITING "THROUGH" THE COMPUTER

The inadequacies of auditing around the computer were obvious. It performed only adequately for even the simple nonintegrated systems on first-generation computers. With the advent of online random-access storage and online input in the second and third generations, the around-the-computer approach became impossible to apply. The dissatisfactions and inadequacies led, starting in the first generation but concentrated in the second generation, to the development of techniques designed to audit "through" the computer. In this process, the auditor verifies the input and processing parts of the system and then assumes that the output must be correct.

The techniques developed for auditing through the computer are many and varied. The major techniques include reading programs, using test data, and using auditor-maintained master programs.

Reading Programs　　It has been suggested that auditors learn programming and actually check the programs. However, two programmers working from the same flowchart or decision table can prepare quite different programs. Small differences in program logic make it difficult to understand programs written by others. The size and complexity of programs currently used are also a factor. The interaction of processing programs with executive programs in modern multiprogrammed and timeshared systems is complex, and the exact result is sometimes difficult to predict. Auditors *should* review program documentation to check for obvious omissions of adequate control procedures, but auditors *cannot* expect to actually read the programs themselves as a general audit technique.

Test Data　　A common technique used by programmers when debugging new programs is to devise a set of test data involving the alternatives the program is designed to handle. The results of processing these test data are computed prior to their use and used to check the computer results. When controls in the program are being tested, invalid as well as valid data must be included. The process is a difficult one in a large, complex system. The number of data combinations that should be included gets quite large; and the audit test run can become a major, time-consuming operation.

A major problem in relying on test data is the possibility of substitute programs or *program patches* — temporary changes in the program — being inserted by the machine operator during standard operating runs. To guard against this possibility, the auditor must check the adequacy of separation of duties and responsibilities in the processing center. Are there controls guarding against unauthorized program changes? Do programmers or employees responsible for data preparation operate the computer? Are all interruptions from the computer console automatically logged? Does *any* employee have access to both programs and data?

Using test data in auditing online systems can be particularly difficult.

Records affected (such as customer or supplier accounts) must be legal elements in the system. Fictitious test entries cannot be allowed to interfere with normal operations. Reversal of such fictitious entries requires special procedures that are not normally a part of the system. Yet it must be possible to make test runs unannounced. Ideally, test data would go through the system as part of the normal input stream. The use of special false accounts for testing the system is inadequate. Real accounts are then open for manipulation.

Auditor-maintained Programs A special technique for guarding against program modification is for the auditor to maintain a special copy of the operating program under personal control. At irregular intervals this program is used to reprocess actual input data. The results obtained are compared to the records and reports obtained in regular processing runs. A major weakness in this process is that programs change frequently and maintaining two separate master programs is expensive. Another weakness is that it may be difficult or even impossible to interrupt processing to reprocess input data with the special program. In online systems the programs are large, complex, and in constant use. Input data captured online are often not retained and are unavailable for reprocessing.

AUDITING "WITH" THE COMPUTER

It is now recognized that the computer can be a powerful ally in the auditing process. Many of the jobs done by auditors and their staffs can be performed by computers. Often the computer can do the job better than humans can. It is relatively easy to program the computer to scientifically sample online files or incoming data streams. In sensitive areas every record in a file can be examined for undesirable characteristics.

Auditing Programs There are two types of auditing programs, *special programs* prepared by the audit staff for use on the system of a particular client and *prepackaged audit programs*. Prepackaged audit programs are really special-purpose languages that make it easy to tailor standardized programs for testing any electronic system. Using these special-purpose languages, programs can be quickly prepared to screen files for exceptionally large or small account balances or other unusual activity. Verification letters for customer or supplier accounts can be automatically prepared for a properly selected sample (or even *all*) of the accounts in the file. Activity levels on customer or supplier accounts can also be checked with ease. The standardized programs are economically feasible for use in situations in which the time and expense involved in preparing a special audit program would not be justified.

Continuous Audit   The auditing of online integrated systems cannot be adequately performed at infrequent intervals unless an audit trial is maintained. Storing the data for each and every transaction along with the resulting changes in all files is prohibitively costly. If input data do disappear, making it impossible for the auditor to reconstruct the sequence of activities, how can the auditor attest to the accuracy of the final record? Several alternatives exist.

Sampling can be used to preserve the audit trail. A random sample of transactions, statistically calculated to be of adequate size, can be preserved. The path of each of these transactions through the system can be traced and recorded. A second alternative is to select a sample of accounts in each file and record in detail all activities affecting the sample accounts. When combined with system snapshots obtained by routine storage dumps, such samples provide an adequate trail. For a snapshot, contents of all files are read onto magnetic tape, preserving a complete picture of all files at that instant.

Unusual transactions (unusually large or small, frequent or infrequent, reversing entries for previous transactions, adjustments, and so on) can be identified and recorded. In this fashion the computer is used to alert the auditor to possible fraudulent activities or to an unusual frequency of errors requiring correction.

Automatic recording of interruption of processing or of accesses to executive programs can be useful. Most large systems include a clock, and interventions can be traced easily if recorded by time. However, the system should be so designed that anyone interrupting processing or accessing the control executive must be clearly identified by location of access, name, password, and so on, and also be authorized to perform that activity before being allowed to proceed.

Finally, an effective electronic system, particularly an online system, must provide *procedures for recovery* in the event of hardware or software failure. For example, snapshots are taken periodically in most online systems to protect against file loss in case of system failure. Also, key transactions may be recorded on tape and stored offline to assist in updating the last snapshot. The logic underlying those procedures should provide an auditor with opportunities for building audit trails and for determining the correctness of the current status of system files.

PARTICIPATION IN DESIGN

In general, each of the three methods of auditing a computerized accounting system should be in the auditor's tool kit. However, the auditor's most important tool is not one of those. That tool is *participation in systems design*. The auditor should be involved in the design of the system to insure the presence of adequate system controls. Computer specialists have been slow to accept the auditor as a member of the team because auditors have not been knowledgeable about computer processing. This condition is being rapidly corrected. Many accountants are trained in computer use, and the number is increasing rapidly. Auditors have alienated computer specialists and management in some cases by insisting on the preservation of a complete and detailed audit trail. This is an excessively costly process and defeats the purpose of many online systems. The use of sampling on such systems is relieving this problem.

The auditor should insist upon standard internal and data controls being included in the system design. Important internal controls include:

1. Separation of activities within the information systems department

2. Standardized and complete systems documentation

3. Control over system changes

4. Protection of data and programs against fire, flood, or other damage

5. Control over console intervention

6. Prevention of unauthorized access to data and to processing equipment

7. Adequate data and processing controls (see Chapter 6)

8. Auditor participation in systems design

Accounting for Computer Use

If any resource is to be efficiently utilized, the cost of each alternative use of that resource must be known. Most computer suppliers provide some sort of job accounting information as part of their executive control programs. A number of independent software suppliers have developed various accounting programs or extensions to suppliers' software to assist in accounting for computer use on large systems. These normally supply data in the three areas of job accounting and control, resource utilization monitoring, and individual user billing.

JOB ACCOUNTING AND CONTROL

The flow of jobs through the computer system is traced by job accounting and control systems. Jobs can be suspended or modified on the basis of variations from predetermined system use standards or computed run times. Resource utilization data and job billing based on resources used can be obtained from most of these programs. Billings are computed on the basis of rates established by the computer operations department. A control useful here is the checking of authority for requesting particular priority levels for each job (based on budget account number).

RESOURCE UTILIZATION MONITORING

Data on resource use can be summarized and analyzed for each major device in the system. Such data are a valuable aid to planning and control of resource acquisition and future hardware systems design. Cross-classifying resource use by job and programmer can help programmers to plan for more efficient use of the total system. Knowledge of device downtime, frequency of operational errors, and so forth, are valuable aids in acquisition and control of hardware devices.

INDIVIDUAL USER BILLING

Computers are seductive. The unwary can easily be trapped into using the computer to perform jobs that could be done more economically in other ways or that might better not be done at all. Charging users can help to curb these misuses. The allocation of costs, by job and by department, is routine on most large computer systems. Costs of each resource and how to charge for each are not standardized, however. The vendor-supplied programs merely keep track of usage and allow the user to supply the per unit charge rates to obtain dollar cost data if they are desired.

Chargeable Items Available programs vary in regard to chargeable items. Most programs provide for costing the following:

1. *CPU time.* The user pays for processor time plus interrupt processing charges.

In timeshared systems, the number of interrupts (and the associated charges) will vary with the number of users on the system. The user thus pays a higher fee for running the same program when the system is particularly busy. Unfortunately, a timeshare system user can pay for more time when the other users on the system are of higher priority even though there are few users on the system.

2. *Input-output* (also called *spooling*). The user is charged for cards or records read and lines printed.

Input-output charges often include charges for job control statements, the number of which is determined by the system executive.

3. *Media mounting.* A charge is made for each tape or disk mounted by the operator.

4. *Other resource use.* Elapsed time of use of *peripherals* (tape and disk drives) and volume of storage required can also be priced. Special surcharges may be included for resource use over an established limit when

such use affects performance capabilities of multiprogrammed or timeshared systems.

5. *Priority*. Basic usage charges for each element can vary depending on the speed of response or throughput requested.

6. Currently, most timesharing and multiprogramming systems provide for billing for *connect time* (time the remote user is online) and for memory use. Memory use charges are variable and include any or *all* of the following: total space used, number of references, and time spent in the primary memory.

Most of the available programs are inadequate in providing billing information. Not all systems provide itemized billings by programmer, job, and date within multiple levels of account numbers. Some do not even provide totals by this level of detail for an accounting period. Many systems are inflexible in the length of the accounting period used.

Setting Charges Few billing systems allow flexible modification of billing algorithms. Charge coefficients can be varied easily, but not the basic formula. Such modifications may be useful in establishing a billing system that truly reflects an efficient *and effective* allocation scheme for a particular computer system.

In general, charges should be set to obtain maximum benefits from the available resource. If idle time is being paid for, any job whose returns cover out-of-pocket running expenses will provide net positive benefits. The computer operations department should, ideally, set internal use charges at the level that causes total user demand to equal total resource availability.

Summary

Accounting provides the *financial* information system of a firm. Its function does not change if computers are introduced, but procedures and the forms of records do. Transactions data are entered into the system to modify accounts stored on electronic storage devices. Detailed transactions data exist only on input documents or media. In online systems, when transactions data are entered directly, details tend to disappear entirely with account records showing only net balances. Electronic systems tend to be more integrated than manual systems, which each input data element being recorded once and used in updating many accounts.

These changes tend to centralize processing and reduce automatic cross-checking of records. Systems must be carefully designed to include adequate controls in computer programs. Auditors must participate in this design. Systems are best designed to include the computer as an auditing tool (*audit with* the computer). Audit trails can be preserved in online systems by preserving details of samples of individual transactions or account activities. Auditors can also employ aspects of the *audit-around* and *audit-through* techniques in testing simpler batch-oriented EDP systems.

Accounting for computer costs is a developing field. Accounting programs currently available as part of system executives provided by computer vendors are not complete. They do, however, provide valuable information on resource utilization and the capability to turn this into very useful cost data.

Questions

1. Define the following as briefly as possible and then use a short paragraph to clarify each definition.
   - a. Accounting
   - b. Test data
   - c. External auditor
   - d. Spooling
   - e. Auditing
   - f. Internal auditor
   - g. Job accounting

2. What is the difference between—
   - a. Accounting and data processing?
   - b. Accounting systems and management information systems?

3. *Outline* the ways in which electronic accounting systems differ from manual accounting systems.

4. How do batch-oriented and online integrated electronic accounting systems differ?

5. What is (are) the purpose(s) of auditing?

6. What is the difference between an internal auditor and an external auditor?

7. Define the general assumptions and procedures for —
   - a. Auditing around the computer.
   - b. Auditing through the computer.
   - c. Auditing with the computer.

8. What are the advantages and disadvantages of using test data in auditing EDP systems?

9. What are prepackaged auditing programs?

10. What are the weaknesses of each of the following EDP auditing techniques?
   - a. Auditing around the computer
   - b. Reading programs
   - c. Auditor-maintained programs
   - d. Special audit programs

11. List some of the techniques useful in a continuous audit of online systems.
12. List the important internal controls that should be included in any EDP system.
13. Read the discussion of systems controls in Chapter 6 (pages 151–157). Would you add any controls to the list given in your answer to question 12 above? Explain fully.
14. What are the three types of data normally supplied by accounting programs designed to account for computer costs?
15. How should computer use charges be determined?
16. Refer to the flow diagram for an hourly payroll program in Figure 13.3 (page 315). Develop a set of employee records to be used in testing the program. Be sure to test for regular and overtime hour limits, partial or zero FICA deductions, negative taxable pay, and negative net pay. How many pay records had to be created?
17. Refer to question 17 at the end of Chapter 7.
    a. Specify control features that should be included in any computerized processing developed for the system described there.
    b. Develop a test file to use in testing a computerized version of the system including the controls you have identified.
18. Refer to question 18 at the end of Chapter 7.
    a. Specify control features that should be included in any computerized processing developed for the system described there.
    b. Develop a test file to use in testing a computerized version of the system including the controls you have identified.

Sixteen

Computers affect management in three areas. Probably the most important effects are on the ways in which managers perform their duties, the *operational effects*. Second, there have been effects on the *organization* of the management function, particularly the organizational placement of the information system function. Last, but far from least, the computer has brought general management in most firms the special problems associated with the management of a highly creative and technically oriented work force, the *information specialists* and the *information system* they create and operate.

Operational Effects of Computers

The effects of computers on the content of managerial jobs, the *way* management performs, are due primarily to the (relatively) new capabilities of computers as suppliers of management information. These new capabilities have, in turn, led to the development and application of new management tools.

THE NEW CAPABILITIES OF COMPUTERS

Three specific capabilities of computers have had an impact on management practice. The capabilities are the *speed* with which computers perform, the *accuracy* with which they perform, and the *complexity of analysis* they make possible.

Speed The ability to perform millions of calculations in one second has obvious implications for management practice. Transactions data can be summarized, compared to historical trends, checked for other relationships, and reported quickly. This means that the managerial control cycle can be shortened. At least two things must be present for this effect to be realized.

First, operational data must be entered into the computer system and processed in time to make real-time control possible. Computers can be and are being used in batch-oriented systems in which transactions documents are accumulated and then translated to machine-sensible media in a processing cycle unrelated to the physical cycle time of the operation. Even though the computer collapses the processing time, the change is not significant because the processing system has not been designed to provide informational outputs in time to reflect the current status of the physical operation.

Second, the system outputs must be designed as *information* in the sense used here: *as communicated knowledge in a form that is immediately useful for decision making*. To meet this definition, the output must be in a form that the recipient is willing and able to use for guiding decisions. Emphasis on *exception reporting* is one of the best ways to provide the brevity and clarity required to make management information reports effective.

Accuracy Modern computer hardware is extremely reliable. If properly programmed, computers can be safely assumed *not* to make mistakes in processing. Note, however, that we said *if properly programmed*. Computers do as they are told and will produce bad results with great speed if incorrectly programmed. Also, hardware failure is *possible*, even though infrequent; procedures for recognizing and recovering from such failures should be provided. Software failure is much more likely, however. Failure to provide recovery procedures can mean lost records, inaccurate billings, lawsuits by irate customers, and so on.

It is also true that the input must be correct for output to be correct. The computer can be programmed to edit incoming data, checking format, structural relationships, and so on (see Chapter 6), in order to recognize and reject (or even correct) as many erroneous entries as possible. Some data errors cannot be recognized. Even so, experience has shown that computerized processing systems generally commit fewer errors than manual processing systems. Machines are more reliable than humans. They are designed that way. If the information system is designed to enter correct data and use adequate programs, the outputs usually can be relied upon. However, as has been so correctly stated, "a computer can make more errors in one second than one human can make in a lifetime." These infrequent errors must be guarded against.

Complexity of Analysis Because of their speed and accuracy and their decision-making capabilities, computers can carry out very complex analyses in brief periods of time. Management is finding it possible to apply the complex mathematical tools of management science (statistics, operations research, mathematics, decision analysis, and so on) as a routine part of operational data processing. Factories capable of producing multiple products are having their production schedules developed by use of mathematical programming. Work schedules for production jobs and product development programs are being developed by the use of critical-path analyses. Investment decisions concerning new capital facilities or investment in existing corporate entities are being guided by complex analytic models. Sales performance is being checked against projections based on historical patterns (long-term trends, cyclical fluctuations, and intrayear seasonal patterns). Developing problems can be recognized; and modifications in sales efforts, inventory levels, and production rates can be made in time to prevent excessive loss. Inventory levels for standard stock items are being based on the results of analysis with a variety of models (demand estimates based on exponential smoothing, economic order quantity, economic reorder point, economic lot size, and so on). Advertising expenditure and ventures into new markets are routinely evaluated by complex mathematical and statistical models. Few of these tools could be used on a routine basis if the computer were unavailable. Without the computer, large simulations of firms, industries, and the total economy would not be useful analytic tools. The calculations are too voluminous and the chances for error too great.

CHANGES IN MANAGEMENT PRACTICE

The implications of new capabilities for managers are obvious. To compete effectively with their counterparts in other firms and other industries, today's managers must be able to utilize the results of the analyses referred to above. They must insure that their information systems take advantage of the new techniques made available by the computer. They do not need to become mathematicians, statisticians, or operations researchers. They do need to become aware of the new tools that are available and how to use them. They must assure themselves that they are receiving competent technical advice and assistance in applying and interpreting these new analytic techniques. The manager must not fall into the trap of abrogating responsibilities in this regard by depending *totally* on the knowledge and skills of trained specialists. To the professional specialist, all problems *tend* to be seen from the perspective of his or her specialty. Problems tend to be narrowly and incompletely analyzed. Hard-to-quantify factors, often of overriding importance, can be assumed away and erroneous results obtained. Unless the manager knows enough about the tools of the specialist to ask proper questions and to participate in the development of analytic models, the results will most likely be inadequate.

The application of computers in guiding management decisions should do three things:

1. Assist managers to make decisions where the decision processes are only partly structured, that is, where complete decision algorithms are unavailable.

2. Support managerial judgment in decision making rather than replace it.

3. Improve the *effectiveness* of decision making as well as its efficiency.

Formal management information systems, as presently constituted, tend to perform these functions only where tasks have been structured and the major payoff is in improving the efficiency with which those structured tasks are performed. Seldom do the reports and data furnished to management focus specifically on the decision each manager must make. Further, the system frequently is not under the manager's direct control and not responsive to his specific unstructured and, largely, not previously determined, needs. Computerized systems designed for these specific purposes are being developed. They are being called *decision support systems*. The development process is being supported and intensified by the growing use of time-sharing, distributed processing, and other forms of more personal computing.

Organizational Effects of Computers

The organizational effects of computers are twofold. First, the potential effects of the computer on the placement of decision-making power in an organization must be understood. Second, the importance of the location of the information system function must be recognized.

OVERALL ORGANIZATION

Two general philosophies of management organization exist. Debate has developed over whether the use of computerized information systems favors a *centralized* or a *decentralized* management structure.

Centralized Management The philosophy of *centralized management* is *to push all decisions as high in the organizational structure as possible.* Authority and responsibility are centralized in the managers or executives at the top of the organizational hierarchy. Supervisors and foremen do not participate in planning or goal-setting activities. Middle managers tend to be involved almost entirely in operations and participate little in planning and goal setting. Middle managers carry out plans and strive after goals developed almost entirely by top management.

Decentralized Management The philosophy of *decentralized management* is *to push all decisions as low as possible in the organizational structure.* All levels of management participate in planning and goal setting to the maximum extent possible. Each manager then attempts to attain the plans and goals that have been developed. Middle managers tend to run autonomous departments.

Computers and Centralization of Management A debate has developed on whether or not computers favor (promote) centralized management. It is asserted that computers centralize and speed up data processing. Data for the entire organization tend to be collected and analyzed at one location. Therefore, centralized (top) management can stay abreast of operational details for all parts of the organization. Proponents of this view believe that authority is given up by any manager only reluctantly. Without the computer, top management of large enterprises had no choice but to give some authority to lower level (operating) managers. Lower level managers were the only ones close enough to the situation to know what was going on. With computerized, quick-response, real-time systems, however, the top-level manager can be made aware of lower level problems and be given the information necessary to make the required operating decisions. Many students of management believe that top managers will be unable to resist the opportunity to recentralize decision making.

The arguments in favor of decentralization also recognize the ability of the new information systems to provide better and more complete information to top management. It is argued that the computer can be used to improve the performance of the lower level manager. Use of automatic control by exception designs in the electronic information system will improve control of routine operations and give operating managers more time to concentrate on planning, goal setting, and personnel relations. Top management can therefore have greater confidence in the ability of lower level managers to use wisely any authority delegated to them. Top managers also can be more confident of their own ability to control the performance of lower level managers because better information can be obtained more quickly about the effects of the decisions made by lower management. The conclusion, then, is that decentralization will be supported and promoted by the use of computerized information systems.

Careful analysis of the above arguments leads to the conclusion that the computer itself favors neither centralization nor decentralization. The level at which decisions are to be made is determined by where authority and responsibility are assigned. Information from a computerized system can be reported to whoever is to use it. In fact, if the definition we've established for information is to be realized, the pertinent, useful, timely facts *must* be reported to the person or persons responsible for using them in decision making. Otherwise information is not created!

When the current increasing uses of teleprocessing, particularly distributed networks, and timesharing and multiprogramming are considered, no *distinct* trend toward decentralization or centralization can be clearly identified. Centralization and decentralization of processing are both occurring. All forms of processing are being used to support both centralized and decentralized management structures.

EFFECTS BY MANAGEMENT LEVEL

All managers perform the functions of planning, organizing, staffing, and controlling. The computer is expected to take over more of the controlling function, primarily through application of the concept of control by exception. Responses to many exceptions (reaching the inventory reorder point, for example) can be predetermined and left to the computer. Routine planning (such as work scheduling) can also be programmed for accomplishment by the computer. Managers will have more time to recognize opportunities and plan to capitalize on them. More time can be devoted to personnel relations and communication. Employee morale and productivity should therefore improve.

The effects of these developments on the different levels of management are being debated by students of management. One group sees a greater challenge for managers at the middle level. Lower level managers are not expected to be affected as much because their jobs are primarily supervisory. Middle managers, however, will be expected to exercise closer control over operations and react more quickly to both problems and opportunities. It may well be that middle managers, generally, will be given greater responsibility and authority for planning and for making strategic policy decisions.

The conclusion of the group of management experts who feel that this may happen is that middle-management jobs will be made more challenging and candidates for those positions will have to be better educated, more creative, and ready to assume responsibility for strategic decisions.

Another group of management experts sees the middle-manager job as composed in large measure of the application of standardized responses to repetitious problems. Computers will tend to perform these routine functions while increasing the planning and decision-making capabilities of top management. The number of people employed in routine clerical activities supervised by middle managers will also decline as the computer takes over these activities. Those positions that remain will be highly specialized. At the lowest level will be the production-level employees who prepare data and material inputs and supervise machine functions in data processing and production. A higher level group will be the specialists performing systems analysis and design, engineering design, programming, and nonroutine data and material processing. At the top will be the top managers who receive informational outputs and make planning and strategy decisions. There will be limited transfer among these three levels. Middle managers will virtually disappear.

An intermediate view is held by the majority of management experts, who agree that management jobs will become more challenging (including those of middle management) and the number of middle managers will decline, perhaps significantly. (However, those authorities who believe that computers will result in greater decentralization of authority actually see an *increase* in the number of middle managers.)

PLACEMENT OF THE INFORMATION FUNCTION

Historically, the information function has tended to be fragmented, with each functional component of the organization (production, marketing, finance) responsible for its own information system. The pressure for integration of these systems brought by the computer has tended to concentrate the information function in a data processing department. Recent developments in networking, the increasing capabilities of minicomputers, and timeshared and multiprogrammed systems may be modifying these trends. The evidence is not completely clear. However, one thing is clear: the location of the *responsibility* for the information function is changing.

The most common organizational placement of the electronic data processing (EDP) department has been to locate it in another department, usually finance. The second placement has been to make it a service department serving all the functional departments. The location of the computer in the finance area usually results when the computer is initially acquired to perform large-volume clerical applications such as hourly payroll or customer billing. In firms involved with large scientific research or engineering projects, the computer has been located in the engineering or research department because that department provided the initial impetus for acquisition.

There are several disadvantages to having the computer located in the sponsoring department even if that department is and will continue to be the major user. First of all, the operation tends to be staffed by personnel drawn from or with the same viewpoint as the host department. This leads to a *less than companywide viewpoint* and a *lack of objectivity* in selecting applications and setting job priorities. Location in a user department also *reduces the status* of the data processing operation. Because their authority derives only from the host department, the manager of data processing and the systems analysts find it difficult to design technically efficient systems and to enforce high standards for data preparation.

The second most common location of the EDP department is as an independent service center department. Often the center reports to a committee representing the using departments. This can give objectivity (depending on how the manager is selected and on the charge given to the department). However, the department usually has no authority for rational planning or long-term development of the information system. Jobs are brought to the department by the operating departments. Integration of systems is not fostered. Systems work is directed toward individual applications for "customer" departments. Chaotic and costly development of overlapping applications that do not utilize the full capabilities of the computer are the almost inevitable result.

A third alternative is being utilized to an increasing degree. This involves the establishment of the *information system function* (ISF) as an independent department reporting at the top level in the firm. Although not clearly best for all firms of all sizes in all industries, this location tends to overcome the weaknesses of the other two locations. First, the establishment of a separate, major department headed by a member of top management reflects the importance of the information system function. Second, it also promotes a *companywide viewpoint* that promises an unbiased evaluation of project proposals. Job priorities set by such a department can be expected to reflect company goals. Integration and continual improvement in the information system are encouraged. Personnel within the department are encouraged to think in innovative terms and to seek continually for improvement of the current system.

The independent major department is not without some drawbacks. Hardware and software technicians can easily get carried away with innovation and the desire to have control of a big hardware system. "Empire building" can occur in the area of computer hardware or online information systems just as in other areas. That is why great care must be exercised in the selection of subdepartment managers within the function and the top-level executive to whom they report. The department should be subjected to the same controls as any other function, clearly justifying whatever system it may seek to develop. On balance, however, advantages appear to outweigh disadvantages for this location of the information system function.

Information System Personnel

The information system function (ISF) involves application of specialized technical knowledge and skills. Personnel involved in this function speak a technical jargon that is a foreign language to most general managers. Special problems arise in recruiting, training, and supervising these technicians as they design, develop, and operate data processing and information systems.

Technical personnel are not the only problem faced by ISF management. The complexity of modern hardware and software systems leads to special problems in monitoring and controlling their performance. Also, the concentration of sensitive, proprietary data and information and the vulnerability of the operations to various forms of industrial sabotage create a need for special security measures. Understanding the specialists and their work is absolutely necessary for good management of the ISF. Personnel characteristics differ by job level and job assignment.

THE INFORMATION SYSTEM FUNCTION MANAGER

The recognized importance of the ISF, the cost of most information systems, and the complexity of the systems to be managed have created the need for a manager with special skills. Historically, data processing managers have come primarily from two sources. Some worked their way up through operations or programming and systems analysis. Others were chosen from the major using department and, most frequently, were accountants. The increasing emphasis on *information systems* and the recognized importance of the ISF to the organization have led to a change. Professional managers from all operating areas are being placed in charge of the extended information system departments. They are being charged with objectively developing plans and an organization that promises a profit-oriented information system and close managerial control over the costs of developing and operating that system. This means that the ISF manager must possess the following knowledge and skills:

1. A complete knowledge of the organization, its objectives and goals; the physical or economic activities it is engaged in; how it is organized to carry on those activities; and the rationale for its organizational structure

2. The knowledge and skills to motivate and control a group of highly skilled technicians; in other words, the manager must understand the personal motivations and aspirations of all types of information systems personnel and know how to lead and control them in the application of their specialized skills

3. A working knowledge of management practices, including the tools of management science and accounting

4. A general knowledge of data processing techniques, including types of available hardware and software

TYPES OF INFORMATION SYSTEM PERSONNEL

The activities involved in carrying out the information system function can be grouped as:

Systems analysis and design

Computer programming

Data processing operations

Data management

Each activity is normally performed by a group of employees possessing certain unique characteristics. Successful selection, training, and supervision of each group requires the recognition of the unique characteristics of the members of each group.

SYSTEMS ANALYSIS AND DESIGN

The nature of systems analysis and design activities are covered in some detail in Chapters 5, 6, and 7. The persons performing these activities are called systems analysts. *Systems analysts* should possess the following characteristics:

1. A general knowledge of the organization, including its objectives and goals; the physical or economic activities it is engaged in; how it is organized to carry on those activities; and the rationale for that organizational structure

2. A knowledge of management practices, including the tools of management science and accounting

3. A working knowledge of data processing techniques, including computer programming

4. An up-to-date, broad knowledge of data processing hardware, including both electronic and nonelectronic devices

5. A high level of disciplined creativity, including the ability to express ideas clearly and persuasively in person and in writing

6. An orientation to detail work that does not inhibit creativity

7. An ability to work cooperatively and effectively with technical (programmers) and nontechnical (operations) personnel and managers

Systems analysts must be able to develop innovative improvements to current systems and sell those improvements to data processing management and the managements of operating departments. They should have a broad knowledge of currently available equipment of *all* types. Given such knowledge, they are less likely to uneconomically restrict the systems to electronic equipment.

Experienced analysts are often assigned the responsibility of project leadership. *Project leaders* are responsible for the analysis, design, development, and implementation of an application system. They lead a team of analysts and programmers doing the technical work. They also work closely with the operating personnel in the departments affected by the system. Leadership abilities are just as important as technical skills for such persons. If analysts are to be expected to assume such responsibilities, they should be given opportunities to develop leadership skills.

Systems analysts are the most highly trained information systems personnel, usually being college educated. As a group, they tend to aspire to management positions. Encouraging them to train for functional or systems management positions is helpful in keeping them on the job. Closing such career paths to them encourages systems analysts to seek these positions in other organizations. Management training also tends to improve their ability to understand the problems of operating managers and to be able to establish effective communication with them.

COMPUTER PROGRAMMING

There are three levels of programmers at work in most installations: *systems programmers*, *applications programmers*, and *maintenance programmers* (see Chapter 13). All of these programmers should possess certain characteristics:

1. A thorough knowledge of the language or languages in which programs will be written at the installation

2. A knowledge of general programming techniques and general relationships between program and hardware features

All programmers should understand and be able to use general techniques such as structured programming. They should also be aware of significant interactions that can exist between programs and hardware and between programs and the system executive. For example, for the use of virtual memory systems to be most efficient, programs run under the executive must be properly designed. To prevent excessive executive overhead, swapping of program "pages" between primary and secondary memory should be minimized. In other words programs must be designed to reduce interactions between widely separated portions of the program. In some instances (for some executive operating systems) it may pay to reproduce frequently used subroutines at several points in a program. Hiring programmers only on the basis of their knowledge of a specific language or set of languages can lead to ineffective use of hardware.

Failure to use good programming techniques will lead to problems. All programmers in an installation must understand and follow a consistent and rational set of programming guidelines (see Chapter 13).

3. A strong orientation to detail

Programmers must possess the patience to spend the time to assure that every symbol in a program is correct. A misplaced comma, reference to the wrong variable in a little-used subroutine, or failure to include an infrequently exercised control routine can cause expensive system failure or a managerially ineffective system. This detail orientation is especially important during program debugging and maintenance.

4. A disciplined, logical creativity

Programmers must translate flow diagrams and decision tables to computer code without unauthorized embellishment. An excessive desire to develop innovative coding will lead to programs that are extremely difficult to maintain at best and can cause system failure at worst. At the same time, a lack of creative development in new programs makes the development of innovative new systems impossible.

Programmers tend to fall into two general categories regarding career aspirations. One group desires to become system analysts and, eventually, managers. The other group enjoys the technical challenge of programming. These latter persons tend to avoid social interaction, including receiving close direction, and have no interest in a management position. Systems programmers tend to fall into the second category.

In addition to the common characteristics outlined above, each type of programmer should possess certain special characteristics.

Systems Programmers Systems programmers should have the following characteristics:

1. A detailed knowledge of the hardware system and the system software that controls it

In addition to maintaining the system software, systems programmers should be involved in decisions concerning hardware additions and deletions. They also help to train applications and maintenance programmers in the use of system software and provide them with assistance in debugging complex applications programs.

2. A firm base in the theory of computer language structure and syntax

Systems programmers are expected to maintain compilers and assemblers, develop enhancements to them, and develop needed utilities. A knowledge of the principles of language development and structure is essential to the efficient performance of such duties.

In short, a systems programmer should be a full-fledged programming professional trained in computer science. Care must be exercised to be sure the systems programmer has a sufficiently pragmatic orientation to be interested in furthering the objectives of the organization, not just an interest in pushing back the frontiers of computer science. Experimentation with esoteric and untried software techniques can be very costly. It is true that a computer can be made to do almost anything in the way of symbol manipulation, but that does not mean that it should be put to every task that might be suggested. Dedication to achieving optimal fine tuning and enhancement of the system executive for a multiprogrammed or timeshared system containing features such as dynamic storage allocation and virtual memory can lead to excessive experimentation. The resulting downtime and loss of production are often of greater cost than the benefits realized from the successful software changes.

Applications Programmers Applications programmers should possess the following characteristics:

1. A general knowledge of the objectives of the organization and the activities involved in pursuing those objectives

2. At least an introductory knowledge of accounting and management science if involved with administrative data processing or management information systems

With only a knowledge of coding techniques, programmers can experience difficulty in properly interpreting flow diagrams and decision tables.

Lack of communication among management, systems analysts, and programmers often can be traced to lack of knowledge of the organizational activities by the programmer. In one installation, the hourly payroll program required excessive maintenance. It had been designed and programmed by two systems analysts–programmers with backgrounds in teaching high school mathematics and English literature. Pay scales were written into program instructions rather than being entered as variable parameters subject to change. Obvious control checks were omitted from the program, resulting in one employee receiving a check for a negative amount for a pay period in which he worked only a few hours. Unfortunately, neither the employee nor the bank where the check was presented for payment was bothered by the minus sign on the amount. The later adjustments that were required had to be carried out entirely by hand. Reprogramming would have been required to perform all the adjustments on the computer. The payroll program had to be completely redeveloped to correct those and other deficiencies.

Maintenance Programmers Program maintenance activities are extremely important. An enormous number of elements are involved in most computer systems. Most large programs are *never* completely debugged. There is a continuing need for enhancement or repair of major programs. Skills of value in maintenance programming include:

1. Experience in program development

2. A high level of analytic ability

Almost nothing of substance has been written on debugging techniques. Substantial skill and experience are required to develop an excellent maintenance programmer.

Program maintenance is made feasible by complete and consistent documentation supplemented by a *program maintenance history*. The history describes each corrective or enhancement change, with emphasis on the techniques used to isolate any bugs discovered. Since some bugs are a result of corrections of other bugs during maintenance, the corrections made should be described in detail. Major computer programs interact in complex ways with themselves, with system software (executives, compilers, and utilities), with the hardware, and at times with other application programs. Small changes in a major program can result in failure of some other software element. Careful collection of bug types, their frequency of occurrence, and the isolation and correction techniques proved to be successful can pay dividends in improved maintenance.

DATA PROCESSING OPERATIONS

Clerical Workers and Machine Operators Machine operators who key data onto cards, tapes, or disks for batch applications will probably continue to make up the bulk of clerical workers and machine operators. Also involved in card-using systems are the operators of the other card processing machines (sorters, reproducers, tabulators, etc.). In online systems, data are entered directly from operating stations. Regardless of the entry point, all workers involved in data entry should be carefully trained to reduce the incidence of errors in data entry. In online systems, the systems designers must give special attention to simplifying data entry and developing intensive editing procedures that forestall the entry of erroneous data to the maximum extent technically and economically feasible.

Media Librarian Someone must maintain control over tape, disk, and card files of data and programs. This person should be separated from programming and machine operation to provide adequate control. Access to stored master files and programs by programmers and operators should be closely controlled.

Scheduler A scheduler who plans daily work flows in data preparation and batched computer processing may be required for large installations.

Computer Operator Operators set up the machine and mount and remove tapes, disks, and printer forms as required by jobs being processed. On multiprogrammed and timeshared systems, control over a large part of this activity is channeled from users through the system executive program. The operator appears to perform as directed at the console (by messages on a typewriter or CRT). However, operators of modern, complex computer systems are trained technicians interacting with a sophisticated operating system to attain maximum efficiency from the hardware. Even so, they usually receive their training as apprentice operators and seldom have a college education.

Maintenance Engineers Electronic equipment requires preventive maintenance on a regular schedule as well as repair in the event of breakdown. The technicians responsible for this activity require background training in electrical engineering and mechanical maintenance and specific training in routine maintenance procedures for the equipment contained in the system being maintained. Generally maintenance is obtained on contract from the equipment supplier, but it can be provided by user personnel. If maintenance is to be supplied by employees of the user, they should be intensively trained by the equipment supplier or suppliers. In mixed vendor systems in which components from a number of suppliers are intermixed, fewer problems are encountered when maintenance is carried out by user employees.

DATA MANAGEMENT

As indicated in Chapter 2, data are managed in the modern business firm. Managers now recognize data as a valuable business resource.

Historically, each data element belonged to the application or department where it was first captured or created. The new philosophy underlying the integrated data base turns this up-side-down, assigning the application, as an attribute, to the data element. In order to accomplish this shift (reversing) of philosophy, the following tasks must be accomplished:

1. Identification of the *data elements* available in the organization and the source, form, and reliability of each of them.

2. Identification of *data and information requirements*; where, in what form, and with what frequency and speed are they needed.

3. Organization of the availability and the need for information into a *descriptive model of the organization's data system*.

4. A plan for sharing the available data: data base designs, data entry procedures, inquiry response mechanisms.

5. *Keep the whole system up-to-date*.

Data inventory	Data elements (Form, Reliability, Source)
Analysis	Data and information needs (Frequency, Form, Speed)
Design	Data base, data entry procedures, retrieval processes, processing devices and general processing techniques
Maintenance	Volume changes Requirement changes (kinds, form, frequency) Availability changes Technological advances

These new tasks are carried out by the *data administrator* and the *data base administrator*.

Data Administrator The person occupying this position is responsible for this overall process of data management. This position interfaces with all parts of the firm in developing and maintaining an adequate, up-to-date inventory of data in whatever forms and degrees of access that may be required by users. The data administrator is not responsible for the technical aspects of file and data base design and maintenance, however. That task is reserved for the data base administrator. Any competent administrator familiar with the firm and possessing some knowledge of data processing and information systems can serve as data administrator.

Data Base Administrator The person occupying this position needs a high level of technical expertise in file structure and file handling. This person is responsible for the technical aspects of design and maintenance of individual files and data bases in the firm. Only if this individual performs at a highly expert level will a firm be able to approach the ideal of a single integrated management information system.

SELECTION OF PERSONNEL

The first step in successful recruiting of appropriate personnel is the preparation of complete, detailed job descriptions and job specifications for all positions. A *job description* describes the work itself, defining in detail the duties to be performed, any machines to be operated, the amount of supervision to be given and received, and the general conditions under which the work is performed. A *job specification* identifies characteristics job applicants must possess. It describes the physical, educational, training, and experience qualifications required for successful completion of the job. Job descriptions and job specifications are also useful in carrying out wage and job evaluations and in defining career paths (promotional opportunities for employees) when planning for staffing needs.

Positions in the ISF may be filled from within the organization or with outside applicants. In a new installation and in implementing new systems that will result in work force reductions, recruiting from within is preferable, particularly for machine operation, data preparation, and applications programming. The danger in filling systems analyst positions initially from within is that most of the employees to be removed will have had experience only in a single department of the company and will possess very limited knowledge of data processing equipment and processes. The training courses provided by computer vendors and most private short-term schools concentrate on EDP systems. Often all that is obtained is an ability to develop flowcharts for use in programming an application and a rudimentary knowledge of some programming language. The result is an employee with limited knowledge of alternatives.

If personnel are recruited from within the company, the positions available should be announced and all interested employees allowed to apply. Review of personnel records to develop a list of qualified persons will undoubtedly miss interested persons with qualifications as good as those on the selected list. Knowledge of the best background for each job in data processing is not definitive. Who would believe that a person trained to teach American history in secondary schools would develop into a top-flight systems programmer (largely through self-study) within three years after being accepted as a programmer trainee? As another example, one of the best systems programmers the author has ever met had only a high school education.

In a new installation, highly skilled technicians (systems programmers, maintenance engineers) may have to be hired from outside. Other personnel can often be selected from present employees who can then be specifically trained for the positions they will fill. Machine operators and clerical personnel are easy to train and usually require no more than a high school education. Systems analysts and programmers are in a different category. If the installation is to involve a large, complex system, some of these people must have a background in the work. In a small system restricted largely to routine processing, the advantage in having analysts and programmers who know the business may well outweigh the disadvantage of lack of technical skill. Experience seems to indicate that the technical skills can be learned quickly but knowledge of the business takes time to acquire.

Identification of potential programmers and systems analysts is difficult. Inexperienced candidates for programming or systems analyst positions are often given an aptitude test, and those scoring sufficiently high are interviewed and their educational and work records checked carefully. Aptitude tests have not proved to be an infallible indication of programming ability. Proficiency tests are sometimes administered to experienced programmers; but personal interviews, examination of work and training records, and direct contact with former employers are more common.

Tests measuring manual dexterity, mechanical aptitude, and/or clerical aptitude have generally yielded satisfactory results in choosing computer operators and data preparation personnel.

EMPLOYEE TRAINING

All employees at the supervisory level and above, whether or not they are involved in computer processing, should receive some information systems training. In fact, it would be well to include key personnel in all operating departments in this group. This training should include an introduction to basic concepts of information systems, computer hardware and programming, and the implications of computer usage for management practice and operating procedures. Such training can be important in reducing resistance to change to new systems. Training programs of this type are available from consulting organizations, computer vendors, professional associations, and colleges and universities. They also can be provided within the organization when employees with proper skills are available to teach the courses.

Programmers and programmer trainees also can receive training in courses offered by computer vendors, technical schools, consulting firms, professional societies, and colleges and universities. However, much more training is given within user organizations. Experienced programmers and analysts train their less experienced colleagues while they are involved in projects or in formal classes.

Systems analysts have more limited opportunities for training. A review of the skills and knowledge required by analysts indicates that such skills cannot be easily obtained in part-time or short-term study. A college degree in business administration supplemented by intensive training in data processing techniques and equipment seems a reasonable prerequisite. Working under an experienced analyst on several projects after formal training is completed is recommended before an analyst is considered fully trained. Training programs are being developed in a few colleges and universities that involve actual project experience along with classroom training. However, familiarity in a particular industry and firm gained from two or more years of experience is advisable before considering the analyst to be fully trained.

SUPERVISION OF PERSONNEL

Turnover rates among data processing employees have tended to be higher than for other office workers. This has reflected a rapidly growing market for their skills. This turnover can be cut and productivity increased if these employees are managed as creative people with a strong desire to expand their potential. The supervisory practices discussed below have been found useful:

1. Make the work challenging but not overwhelming.

The manager who expects his employees to produce and clearly communicates that expectation in a nonthreatening manner will have more productive employees. Clerical employees are happier and more productive when they know exactly what management wants from each assignment. Even experienced programmers can be affected by the way assignments are stated. Programs can be produced to meet a variety of goals, such as (a) minimum programming time, (b) minimum length, (c) maximum efficiency of machine use, (d) clarity of output, and (e) clarity of program. Some of these objectives are in conflict (minimizing programming time conflicts with writing an easily read program and one of minimal length). Programmers are happier and more productive when programming management clearly indicates which objectives are most important when a programming project is assigned.

2. Involve employees in decision making.

Creative people like to feel important. Letting them participate in decision making accomplishes this. One way programmers can participate is by being involved in laying out the schedule for a programming project. After all, they should be a good source for estimates of development time and computer debug runs. Also, programmers, analysts, and operations personnel should work together to design processing systems.

3. Give employees a chance to expand their abilities.

Well-developed career paths for employees together with a training program available to all gives employees incentive and opportunity to improve.

4. Keep employees informed at all times.

In the absence of full knowledge about what is happening in an organization, the employee rumor mill works overtime. The most negative interpretations of events seem to spread most rapidly and are given the greatest credence. In any time of change, employees throughout the organization must know what is going on.

5. Good working conditions should be maintained.

Adequate space, good lighting, sufficient equipment, good pay, and a friendly environment all pay dividends in employee productivity. Employees are human beings and should be recognized as such and treated humanely. Recognizing positive achievements with a word of praise and offering criticism, even if it is constructive, only in private are only two examples. Even clerical workers like to know that their efforts are observed and evaluated in a friendly atmosphere.

Internal Organization of the Information System Function

The information system function (ISF) is usually organized functionally but often operates by project. In some instances, systems personnel are housed in the operational departments rather than in an ISF department.

COMPOSITION OF THE INFORMATION SYSTEM FUNCTION

The organization chart in Figure 7.2 (page 168) indicates the functions to be performed in an ISF operation. Large departments will normally be organized around these functions as indicated in Figure 7.2.

Planning and Analysis This activity includes the collection of data and the development of data relating to economic fluctuations. Long-term trends and short-term deviations from trends for the national economy, the local economy, the industry, and the individual firm need to be currently available. Studies on such things as investment opportunities, facilities locations, new product potential, and other specialized problems need to be performed. The special knowledge and skills of economists, operations researchers, and statisticians are useful here.

Systems and Programming The specific activities included here are systems analysis and design, development programming, maintenance programming, and systems programming. In larger departments, systems analysis and design has its own manager and so does programming.

Data Processing This section comprises machine operations and data control activities. They are often under separate management in larger departments. Operators of computers and other data processing equipment, data control personnel, and media librarians work in this section.

EFFECTS OF SIZE OF OPERATION

Small firms using only electronic accounting machines or minicomputers may not have a separate information systems department. The functions indicated above must still be carried on, however; and this should be recognized in the assignment of responsibility and delegation of authority to personnel within the firm. Planning and analysis may be carried out by the manager of a small firm with only occasional help from an outside expert (certified public accountant, economist, management scientist, or other information system specialist). Even so, the function must be performed and the internal information structure developed to serve it.

Very large firms may subdivide the information systems activities to an even greater degree than the organization shown in Figure 7.2. For example, separate groups may be responsible for data base file maintenance, specialized data collection and preparation, near-term systems development, and long-range systems development. A separate specialist or group may have responsibility for planning and controlling the development of the hardware system while another handles software development.

In any case, the functions described above must be performed regardless of the size of the operation. The exact structure used to organize the activity is unimportant so long as the need for performance of the total information systems function is met.

PHYSICAL LOCATION OF SYSTEMS ANALYSTS

The emergence of data processing personnel as an elitist group has given them almost monopoly control over information systems development in many organizations. Data processors have frequently ignored the basic tenets of management and organization in designing the processing systems that serve as the basis for the management information system. More loyal to their elitist discipline than to the organization that employs them, these people have often striven for the latest (and biggest) hardware utilizing the fanciest software. Some, unfortunately, appear to have striven to delay balanced development of the ISF, preferring the comfort of outmoded and managerially ineffective but easy-to-operate data processing systems. Information systems have been oversold, overdesigned, and underdeveloped. Projects have been started and abandoned with little regard to their worth to the organization. Operational departments lacking in data processing knowledge have been at the mercy of the data processing elite.

An attempted solution to the unresponsiveness of the data processing elite has been to place one or more systems analysts in each operating department. These analysts, hired by and responsible to the manager of an operating department, are, it is argued, loyal to the interests of that department. Also, the analyst(s) in each operating area can fully understand the processing and informational needs of that home department. The systems designed by a resident analyst reflect the procedural and informational requirements of that operation. Training and experience within the departments develop analysts attuned to and responsive to user needs. This alleviates the past tendency to design systems for technical efficiency but with little regard for the intended function of supporting the decision-making activities of management.

Among supporting arguments for locating analysts in operating departments is the alleged inability of computer personnel to work effectively with each of the many functional (operating) departments of an organization. Because of their training and their position as part of the data processing elite, systems personnel tend to think of their work as dealing with data processing problems, not business problems. Many systems analysts and programmers were originally trained in nonbusiness fields such as engineering and mathematics. Their subsequent training in systems analysis often omitted practical business orientation, emphasizing data processing procedures instead. Even the analyst who has received business training has seldom had any practical experience in most of the operating areas where he or she is expected to work.

Disadvantages of user departments acquiring their own systems analysts do exist. Integration within the information system is hindered. Improvements in methods for processing data are slow to be adopted. Standards for documentation, design, and programming are hard to enforce. Decentralized personnel tend not to keep up with technical developments in their field. Activities within a centralized processing department (economies of scale still favor a single department) are difficult to schedule when user departments determine development schedules and systems timing features. Of course, a data processing department that does not adjust its schedules to the needs of users is labeled as "unresponsive" and finds expansion of processing systems is inhibited. Nevertheless, the need for some central coordination of information systems is undeniable. Standards of quality must be enforced on the work of every analyst. Analysts also must be kept informed of what is being done elsewhere. Knowledge of the current systems in related areas is vital to efficient and effective design of processing or information systems in a given area.

PROJECT MANAGEMENT FOR SYSTEM DEVELOPMENT

Most information systems incorporate custodial processing as well as data retrieval and analysis and are quite complex. Design and development of such systems is naturally difficult and time-consuming. Project management has proved successful as a technique for planning and controlling information system development.

Project management involves the planning and carrying out of an integrated effort leading to the attainment of a specific limited objective. A special organization (project team) is established to plan and carry out the activities required to meet the specific objective and is dissolved after the objective is attained.

Project management initially involves planning of the work to be done and development of the team required to carry it out. Objectives, schedules, and budgets must be set out in considerable detail. First, the total project must be broken down into measurable work units. Expected cost, completion schedule, performance quality, and resource requirements are then developed as standards for each work unit. Organizational units of the project team are assembled and assigned responsibility for particular work units. It is desirable that all work groups (especially systems analysts and programmers) participate in the development of the performance standards for the work units assigned to them. During project implementation, a project management control system monitors progress in terms of the established standards.

The entire project management process usually proceeds in five general steps:

1. Preliminary project analysis

This step consists of a quick look at a possible new system to evaluate, without formal study, the technical and economic feasibility of the project. If the systems representative and the user decide the idea has merit, step 2 is undertaken.

2. Formal feasibility assessment

In this stage the real need for the change, its managerial effectiveness, the time required to complete the project, and the probable cost of development and operation of the system are determined. Assuming the project appears to assure benefits commensurate with the effort required in its development, the third step is taken.

3. Planning the system project

Computer-based techniques, such as linear programming and critical-path planning, including PERT, are valuable in this phase. Computer programs are available that make personnel assignments on the basis of job requirements and skill levels for systems analysis and programming personnel.

4. System analysis and design (see Chapter 6)

5. System implementation

This phase includes programming the system and training the personnel working in the system and the users of the system.

Except on small projects, the use of a computer program to keep track of schedules, costs, and personnel assignments is required. The entire project, starting with step 3, can be planned and monitored by some programs. These programs incorporate planning techniques such as critical-path analysis (PERT) to schedule projects, develop detailed budgets, and then assess progress against these schedules. These so-called project management systems differ widely in effectiveness. Some are highly inflexible, making the modification of project schedules difficult. In the performance monitoring area, some systems report performance in detail and provide little real information about deviations from projected schedules. A good project management system, whether computer-based or not, should provide for participation of project personnel in setting goals, time schedules, and individual personnel assignments and provide continuous project status information (work units completed and costs incurred) while assuring orderly completion of the project.

Alternatives to the Internal Computer Processing Department

Many general managers feel that management of computerized data processing requires a level of technical capability that is difficult to acquire. These managers have searched for ways to "farm out" their processing activities. Two basic modes have developed. Most widely used has been the outside *service bureau*. A more recent development has been *facilities management* firms.

SERVICE BUREAUS

There are three general types of service bureaus. One type provides general data processing services including data preparation, computer processing, computer programming, and raw computer time. A growing number of service bureaus designed to provide specialized computing services to firms in a particular industry constitute a second type. The third type of service provides general processing services via timesharing hookups. A few large national service bureau firms provide all three types of service.

General-Purpose Service Bureaus The general-purpose service bureau developed initially to provide computerized processing for firms that did not feel justified in acquiring an in-house computer. In order to broaden their customer base, the service bureaus also provide systems analysis and design services and programming. Raw computer time is often sold to individuals or firms that have developed their own systems and programs. Many firms prefer this arrangement, being reluctant to allow proprietary company data to be processed by other than their own employees. Purchased computer time can also provide backup for firms with the same hardware.

General service bureaus also provide one-of-a-kind services. For example, they may contract to translate an organization's files to electronic media at the time the firm converts to a computerized system. They may also provide supplemental input data preparation capacity for users.

Some service bureaus now provide for remote data input. Most of these service bureaus are providing specialty services within timesharing as their major service. Most general-purpose service bureaus receive input from users via some form of surface transportation. Much of the input requires translation to a machine-sensible medium before computer processing.

Specialty Service Bureaus In about the mid-1960s, entrepreneurs began to recognize that groups of users with similar processing needs existed in various industries and professions. Specialized systems were developed to service these groups. Many service bureaus specialize in providing billing and other accounting services to doctors, dentists, and other professionals. One such specialty bureau obtains daily transaction inputs via the touch-tone telephone and handles the entire billing and accounting process from there. Through a connection with a bank, the service bureau even collects on the bills and provides an investment trust service for its clients. Most such services are not so complete, being content to provide standard accounting and/or billing services for customers in a given grouping (parts wholesalers, clothing retailers, professionals, fuel dealers, or savings and loan associations, for example.)

Timesharing Services Several national firms provide generalized timesharing services to anyone with telephone service and a terminal. Local dial-up service is provided in major cities. Users located in less populated areas often find the cost of the telephone connection to a local dial-up service area to be prohibitive.

Most national timesharing networks also provide certain specialized systems. For example, wholesalers and retailers may be able to access and utilize a package of programs that provide standard accounting services tailored to their needs. General ledger accounting and payroll systems are generally available to all users. In addition, the user can access the general problem-solving capabilities of a large computer, usually with the assistance of preprogrammed algorithms for many applications such as multiple regression, mathematical programming, and present value. Such services can provide a powerful supplement to a modest in-house processing capability.

FACILITIES MANAGEMENT

Facilities management firms (FMFs) contract to operate a data processing facility for a firm. Contractual arrangements vary; but usually they provide that the client will buy or lease the equipment and that the FMF will hire, train, and supervise the employees required to utilize the system. General managers are free, supposedly, to concentrate on running the business operation. They need not get involved in supervising the group of technicians, including systems analysts and programmers, involved in providing the technical service. Other advantages are that the FMF can hire better people because it provides greater opportunities for advancement within the specialty area. It also should be able to acquire a pool of specialized talent to draw upon for the solution of technical processing problems.

The greatest weakness in using an FMF is that management tends to view the information system function as primarily custodial data processing. The full power of the computer for creating profit by improving management decisions may not be realized. Emphasis tends to be placed on operating efficiency rather than managerial effectiveness.

Reports on the experiences of users of FMFs have been mixed. Some firms have abandoned the system after a short trial; others are well satisfied. Any manager contemplating such a move should examine the advantages and disadvantages carefully. Particular attention should be paid to the contract with the FMF. The exact volume, quality, and timing of services promised should be determined to insure managerial effectiveness as well as processing efficiency.

Summary

Computers are a powerful management tool. They provide the possibility for shortening control and reporting cycles, speeding up business operations, and handling large volumes of transactions processing with speed and accuracy. Their ability to be programmed to provide complex analyses of operating and environmental data means that managers can do a better job of planning and have closer control over day-to-day operations. The resultant changes in the practices of managers can have significant impacts on organizational structures. Computers make possible greater centralization or decentralization of management, depending on how they are used. In either case, they can take over certain routine, well-defined decision processes and allow all levels of management more time for planning, personnel relations, and communication.

The *information system function* (ISF) should be placed at a high level in the managerial hierarchy of an organization. Such placement recognizes the importance of the function and encourages ISF personnel to adopt an organizationwide viewpoint in planning and developing information and data processing systems. Care must be exercised that the department does not develop into an empire for a power-hungry data processing elite.

The ISF is difficult to manage. Specialists speaking technical jargon and engaged in highly technical work create special problems in recruitment, training, and supervision. The manager of the ISF must recognize the differing skill levels required by systems analysts, programmers, and operating personnel and must also be aware of the differing career aspirations of individuals within these job classifications in order to obtain maximum effort and cooperation from them.

Internal organization of the ISF has usually been along functional lines. The exact organizational groupings are not critical so long as the need for planning and analysis, systems analysis, programming, machine operation, and data control are provided. Some organizations have found that locating systems analysts in user departments makes for a more responsive ISF, one more clearly oriented to the solution of management problems than to achieving technical efficiency.

Project management has proved to be an effective means of organizing systems development efforts within the ISF. This process involves the creation of a special organization (team) for planning and carrying out an integrated effort leading to attaining a specific limited objective, such as a particular ISF subsystem.

Alternatives to an internal, computerized data processing department include service bureaus (general purpose, specialty, and timesharing) and use of the services of a facilities management firm. Such alternatives free general managers from the need to supervise ISF technicians performing highly technical tasks. However, they do not relieve general managers of the responsibility for assuring that the ISF is oriented toward promoting managerial effectiveness as well as data processing efficiency.

Questions

1. Define the following as briefly as possible and then use a short paragraph to clarify each definition.
   a. Centralized management
   b. Decentralized management
   c. Systems programmer
   d. Applications programmer
   e. Maintenance programmer
   f. Job description
   g. Job specification
   h. Information system function
   i. Project management
   j. General-purpose service bureau
   k. Specialty service bureau
   l. Timesharing service bureau
   m. Facilities management
   n. Data administrator
   o. Data base administrator

2. What are the operational and organizational effects of computers on management?

3. What characteristics of computers have been significant in determining their operational effects on management? Explain.

4. What are the advantages and the disadvantages of locating the ISF high in the organizational hierarchy?

5. Argue that computers favor centralization of management.

6. Argue that computers favor decentralization of management.

7. Will middle managers be replaced by computers? Explain fully.

8. What specific skills should be possessed by each of the following?
   a. ISF manager
   b. Systems analyst
   c. Systems programmer
   d. Applications programmer
   e. Maintenance programmer
   f. Data administrator
   g. Data base administrator

9. Why should systems analysts be encouraged to develop managerial skills?

10. List the major practices that have been found useful in supervising ISF personnel.
11. Refer to the list developed for question 10. Do these practices appear warranted for use for other groups of employees? Why or why not?
12. What are the subfunctions that comprise the ISF? Explain each briefly.
13. What are the advantages and disadvantages of locating systems analysts in user departments?
14. List and briefly explain the five steps in the project management approach to systems development and implementation.
15. What are the advantages and disadvantages of using data processing service bureaus?
16. What are the advantages and disadvantages of using the services of a facilities management firm?
17. What is the major problem to be solved in managing the ISF? Explain.
18. Several studies of computer use in business firms have indicated that the top managers of medium to large firms are almost unaffected by the introduction of a computer into the firm.
    a. Is this an expected outcome? Explain.
    b. Is this a desirable outcome? Explain.
    c. Will this change in the future? If so, will the change be due to new technological (hardware and software) developments? Explain.
19. Develop advancement criteria for each of the following career steps:
    a. Computer operator to programmer trainee
    b. Applications programmer to lead applications programmer
    c. Lead applications programmer to system analyst
    d. Systems analyst to lead systems analyst
    e. Media librarian to data administrator

Selected Bibliography

SELECTED PERIODICALS

The periodicals presented are chosen from those the author has found helpful in keeping abreast of developments in the information systems area in general and in electronic systems in particular. The periodicals listed here should be comprehensible to persons reading this text.

Byte. Subtitled *The Small Systems Journal.* Monthly. 70 Main Street, Peterborough, N.H. 03458. Publishes articles on applications, design, and components of personal or small business computer systems.

Computer Characteristics Quarterly. Quarterly. Charles Adams Associates, Cambridge, Mass. Descriptions of currently marketed computers.

Computer Decisions. Monthly. Hayden Publishing Company, Inc., 50 Essex Street, Rochelle Park, N.J. 07662. (Free)

Computerworld. Weekly newspaper. 797 Washington Street, Newton, Mass. 02160. Like any newspaper, it must be read regularly over time to be fully comprehensible. Very comprehensive.

Creative Computing. Bimonthly. P.O. Box 789-M, Morristown, N.J. 07960. Reviews, applications, and software for personal computing.

Data Management (formerly *Journal of Data Management*). Monthly. Data Processing Management Association, 505 Busse Highway, Park Ridge, Ill. 60068. Business-oriented articles on data processing topics. (Free to members of DPMA)

Data Processing Digest. Monthly. Data Processing Digest, Inc., 1140 South Robertson Boulevard, Los Angeles, Calif. 90035. Summaries of current articles on data processing from a wide selection of journals and magazines. Sometimes carries feature articles on timely topics written specifically for this magazine.

Datamation. Monthly. Technical Publishing Company, 1301 Grove Avenue, Barrington, Ill. 60010.

EDP Analyzer. Monthly. Canning Publications, Inc., 925 Anza Avenue, Vista, Calif. 92083. In-depth articles on developments in data processing.

Harvard Business Review. Bimonthly. Graduate School of Business Administration, Harvard University, published at 108 Tenth Street, Des Moines, Iowa. Articles on topics of interest to managers.

ICP Quarterly. Quarterly. International Computer Programs, Inc., 2506 Willowbrook Parkway, Indianapolis, Ind. 46205. Each issue in two volumes: vol. 1 covers software products for the management of hardware, software, data, and systems creation; vol. 2 covers data-based and algorithmic-based applications software. The *Quarterly* keeps tabs on about 3,000 software products available from over 1,000 different suppliers.

Infosystems. Monthly. Hitchcock Publishing Co., Hitchcock Building, Wheaton, Ill. 60187. (Free)

Interface Age. Monthly. Box 2654, Clinton, Iowa 52735. Microcomputer topics for home and business applications.

Journal of Systems Management. Monthly. Association of Systems Management, 24587 Bagley Road, Cleveland, Ohio 44138. (Formerly *Systems and Procedures Journal* and Systems and Procedures Association.) Contains articles of interest to managers of systems department.

Modern Data. Monthly. Modern Data Services, Inc., 5 Kane Industrial Drive, P.O. Box 369, Hudson, Mass. 01749. (Free)

INFORMATION ON HARDWARE AND OTHER ITEMS

The journals listed here regularly feature articles that explain an equipment item and/or list current models available from manufacturers, discuss new developments in information systems, or summarize current knowledge on some topic.

Item	Journal
Computer hardware	
Complete systems	*Infosystems*
	Computer characteristics quarterly
Minicomputers	*Modern data*
	Datamation
	Byte
	Creative computing
Peripherals	
Disks	*Computer decisions*
Mass storage devices	*Computer decisions*
Printers	*Modern data*
Keyboard teleprinters	*Modern data*
Terminals	*Infosystems*
Point-of-sale terminals	*Computer decisions*
Computer-outputted microfilm	*Computer decisions*
Modems and multiplexors	*Modern data*
	Computer decisions

Item	Journal
Computer software	*ICP quarterly*
Other topics	
Annual EDP salary surveys	*Infosystems*
Computer fraud	*Datamation*
Networking	*Datamation*
Timesharing services	*Computer decisions*

SELECTED REFERENCES

Presented here is a brief list of recent works of value in studying the areas specified, which are keyed to major sections of the text.

Part I. Concepts of Information Systems

Ackoff, R. L. "Management Misinformation Systems," *Management Science*, December 1967, pp. B147–B156.

Ackoff, R. L., and Patrick Rivett. *Manager's Guide to Operations Research.* John Wiley & Sons, Inc., 1963.

Anthony, R. N., *Planning and Control Systems: A Framework for Analysis.* Graduate School of Business Administration, Harvard University, 1965.

Davis, Gordon B. *Management Information Systems: Conceptual Foundations, Structure, and Development.* McGraw-Hill Book Company, 1974.

Forrester, J. W. *Industrial Dynamics.* M.I.T. Press, 1961.

Head, R. V. *Real-Time Business Systems.* Holt, Rinehart and Winston, Inc., 1964.

Martin, F. F. *Computer Modeling and Simulation.* John Wiley & Sons, Inc., 1968.

Martin, James. *Principles of Data Base Management.* Prentice-Hall, Inc., 1976.

Sanders, D. H. *Computers in Business: An Introduction.* 4th ed. McGraw-Hill Book Company, 1979.

Society for Management Information Systems. *What Is a Management Information System?* Report No. 1, 1971.

Part II. Analysis and Design of Information Systems

Alexander, M. J. *Information Systems Analysis.* Science Research Associates Inc., 1974.

American National Standards Institute (ANSI). *Flowchart Symbols and Their Usage in Information Processing, ANSI.* American National Standard X3.5–1970.

Blumenthal, S. G. *Management Information Systems*. Prentice-Hall, Inc., 1969.

Chapin, Ned. *Flowcharts*, Auerbach Publishers Inc., 1971.

Cougar, J. Daniel, and Robert W. Knapp, eds. *Systems Analysis Techniques*. John Wiley & Sons, Inc., 1974.

Daniels, Alan, and Donald Yeats, eds. *Systems Analysis*. Science Research Associates Inc., 1971.

Murdick, R. G., and J. E. Ross. *Information Systems for Modern Management*. 2nd ed. Prentice-Hall, Inc., 1975.

Optner, S. L. *Systems Analysis for Business Management*. 2nd ed. Prentice-Hall, Inc., 1968.

Pollock, S. L., H. T. Hicks, Jr., and W. J. Harrison. *Decision Tables: Theory and Practice*. John Wiley & Sons, Inc., 1971.

Part III. The Computer: Hardware and Software

Doll, Dixon R. *Data Communications: Facilities, Networks, and Systems Design*. John Wiley & Sons, Inc., 1978.

Kanter, Jerome. *Management Guide to Computer Systems Selection and Use*. Prentice-Hall, Inc., 1970.

Sammett, Jean. *Programming Languages: History and Fundamentals*, Prentice-Hall, Inc., 1969.

Sanders, D. H. *Computers in Business: An Introduction*, 4th ed. McGraw-Hill Book Company, 1979.

Sharpe, W. F. *The Economics of Computers*. Columbia University Press, 1969.

Part IV. Computers in the Organization

Allen, Brandt R. "Computer Security: Part I," *Journal of Data Management*, 10, No. 1 (January 1972), 18–24.

Allen, Brandt R. "Computer Security, Part II," *Journal of Data Management*, 10 No. 2 (February 1972), 24–29.

Davis, Gordon. *Auditing and EDP*. American Institute of Certified Public Accountants, 1968.

Gibson, Cyrus F., and Richard L. Nolan. "Managing the Four Stages of EDP Growth." *Harvard Business Review*, 52, No. 1 (January–February 1974), 76–88.

McFarlen, F. W., R. L. Nolan, and D. P. Norton. *Information System Administration*. Holt, Rinehart and Winston, Inc., 1973. (Text and cases.)

McRae, T. W. *The Impact of the Computer on Accounting.* John Wiley & Sons, Inc., 1964.

Orlicky, Joseph. *The Successful Computer System.* McGraw-Hill Book Company, 1969.

Weinberg, G. M. *The Psychology of Computer Programming.* Van Nostrand Reinhold Company, 1971.

Weinwurm, G. F. *On the Management of Computer Programming.* Auerbach Publishers Inc., 1970.

Glossary

This glossary of selected terms reflects current and approved usage. Definitions marked with a dagger are reproduced with permission from "American National Dictionary for Information Processing, X3/TR-1-77." Copyright © 1977 by Computer and Business Equipment Manufacturers Association. All rights reserved. Items marked with an asterisk (*) are taken from the above source but are modified or abbreviated to better serve the users of this particular book. Items with no preceding symbol have been supplied by the author.

ABACUS A device for performing arithmetic calculations by sliding beads or counters along rods.

* ABSOLUTE ADDRESS 1. An address that is permanently assigned to a storage location. 2. A pattern of characters that identifies a unique storage location. Also called machine address, specific address, physical address.

ACCESS *See* Direct (Random) Access, Remote Access, Serial Access.

* ACCESS ARM A mechanical devive on a storage unit that holds and/or positions one or more reading and/or writing heads (mechanisms).

* ACCESS TIME 1. The time interval between the instant at which data are called for from a storage device and the instant at which delivery is completed. 2. The time interval between the instant at which data are requested to be stored and the instant at which storage is started.

* ACCOUNTING MACHINE A machine that prepares accounting records and usually is key-activated. Automatic accounting machines read data from offline storage media such as cards or tapes, and automatically produce accounting records or tabulations, usually on continuous forms.

* ACCUMULATOR A register in which the result of an arithmetic or logic operation is formed.

ACCURACY The degree of freedom from consistent error in a given direction (bias). Contrast with Precision.

ACRONYM A word formed from the first letter or letters of all or most of the successive words of a multiple word term.

ACTION ENTRY The lower-right quadrant of a decision table, which indicates for each rule the actions to be taken if the set of conditions specified by the rule are present.

ACTION STUB The lower-left quadrant of a decision table, which lists the possible actions that may be taken.

* ADDER A device whose output is a representation of the sum of the quantities represented by its inputs.

* ADDRESS An identification, as represented by a name, label, or number, for a register, a location in storage, or any other data source or destination such as the location of a station in a communication network. See Absolute Address, Indirect Address, Relative Address.

* ADDRESS REGISTER A register in which an address can be stored.

ADP *See* Automatic Data Processing

* ALGOL (ALGorithmic Oriented Language). A language primarily used to express computer programs by algorithms.

* ALGORITHM A prescribed set of well-defined rules or processes for the solution of a problem in a finite number of steps.

* ALPHABETIC CODE A code according to which data is represented using an alphabetic character set that consists only of letters and associated special characters.

* ALPHABETIC STRING A character string represented only by alphabetic letters and associated special characters.

* ALPHABETIC WORD A word consisting solely of letters and associated special characters from the same alphabet.

ALPHAMERIC *See* Alphanumeric.

† ALPHANUMERIC Pertaining to a character set that contains letters, digits, and usually other characters such as punctuation marks. Synonymous with alphameric.

AMERICAN STANDARD CODE FOR INFORMATION INTERCHANGE (ASCII) A standard eight-bit code used for exchanging data among data processing systems, communication systems, and associated equipment. Same as USASCII.

AMPLITUDE MODULATION   In communications, the distortion of the amplitude of a carrier signal waveform to represent the message. *See* Modulate.

* ANALOG   Refers to use of continuously variable physical quantities to express representation.

† ANALOG COMPUTER   1. A computer in which analog representation of data is mainly used. 2. A computer that operates on analog data by performing physical processes on these data. 3. Contrast with Digital Computer.

* ANALYSIS   The methodical investigation of a problem involving (usually) the separation of the problem into smaller related units for further study. *See* Systems Analysis.

* ANALYST   A person who defines problems and develops formulas and procedures for their solution. *See* Systems Analyst.

† ANNOTATION   An added descriptive comment or explanatory note.

APPLICATION PROGRAM   A data processing program unique to a specific type of processing job (for example, payroll). Contrast with Executive, Supervisor, and Utility Program.

ARGUMENT   The reference factor (variable) necessary to find a desired item or value in a table or from a function.

* ARITHMETIC UNIT   The unit of a computing system containing the circuits that perform arithmetic operations. *See* Arithmetic-Logic Unit.

ARITHMETIC-LOGIC UNIT   The unit of a computing system containing the circuits that perform arithmetic and logical operations.

* ARRAY   An arrangement of data elements in one or more dimensions. For example, a list or a table.

† ARTIFICIAL INTELLIGENCE   1. The capability of a device to perform functions that are normally associated with human intelligence, such as reasoning, learning, and self-improvement. 2. Related to machine learning.

ASCII   *See* American Standard Code For Information Interchange.

ASR   *See* Automatic Send and Receive.

* ASSEMBLE   To prepare a machine language program from a symbolic language program by substituting absolute (machine) operation codes for symbolic operation codes and absolute (machine) or relocatable addresses for symbolic addresses.

ASSEMBLER   A computer program that carries out assembly. *See* Assembly Language.

ASSEMBLY LANGUAGE   A source language that is translated to machine language by an assembler.

ASYNCHRONOUS   1. Having a variable time interval between successive bits. 2. In asynchronous transmission each character (sometimes word or block) is individually synchronized, usually by start and stop elements. The gap between each character or word is not of a fixed length. Called start-stop transmission.

AUDIT TRAIL   The visible (hard-copy) trail or path left by a transaction as it is processed.

AUDITING   The process of checking source data, processing procedures, and output documents for validity and error control (accuracy).

AUTOMATIC COMPUTER   A computer that is able to perform a sequence of individual operations without the help of a human operator.

AUTOMATIC DATA PROCESSING (ADP)   Data processing that is carried out mostly by automatic machines and, by extension, the discipline that deals with methods and techniques involved in automatic-machine data processing.

AUTOMATIC SEND AND RECEIVE (ASR)   Usually applies to a terminal device which can be used to originate, receive, or transmit data. Commonly consists of a keyboard printer with paper tape punch and reader.

* AUTOMATION   1. The implementation of any set of processes by automatic means. 2. The theory, art, or science of making a process more automatic. 3. The conversion of a procedure, a process, or equipment to automatic operation.

* AUXILIARY STORAGE   A storage that supplements a main storage. Contrast with Main Storage. Also called secondary storage.

† BACKGROUND PROCESSING   1. The execution of lower-priority computer programs when higher-priority programs are not using system resources. 2. Contrast with Foreground Processing.

* BAND   1. A group of circular recording tracks on a storage device such as a drum or disk. 2. In communications, the frequency spectrum between two defined limits.

BANDWIDTH   1. The difference in cycles per second (Hertz) between the highest and lowest frequencies in a band. 2. The range of frequencies available for signaling. 3. The carrying capacity of a circuit or channel.

* BASE ADDRESS   The given address from which an absolute address is derived by combining the base address and a relative address. Also called address constant.

BASIC (Beginners All-purpose Symbolic Instruction Code)   An interpretive compiler language initially designed for use by students working on a timeshared computer system.

BATCH PROCESSING   A technique by which data items or transactions and programs to be processed are collected into groups prior to processing each group in a single computer run.

BAUD   A unit of signaling speed. The number of basic signal elements, commonly binary digits (bits), per second. Same as Bit Rate if the basic signal element is a bit.

BCD   *See* Binary-coded Decimal.

BENCHMARK   1. A reference element. 2. In evaluating computer systems or computer programming processes, a benchmark problem is a problem chosen to represent a set of problems in evaluating the system or process.

* BINARY   1. Pertaining to a selection or condition in which there are two possibilities. 2. Pertaining to a number representation system with a radix of 2 involving the binary digits 0 and 1.

BINARY-CODED DECIMAL (BDC)   A system of number representation in which each decimal digit is represented by the four binary-digit positions representing 8, 4, 2, 1 (or 0).

* BISTABLE   Pertaining to the capability of a device to assume either one of two stable states.

BIT   Contraction of *binary digit*, it is the smallest unit of information, particularly in a binary system.

BIT RATE   A data transfer rate expressed in bits per second.

BLACK BOX   A generic term used to describe an unspecified device or work station which performs a particular function in which known inputs produce known outputs in a fixed relationship.

BLOCK   1. A set of data elements (bits, characters, words) handled as a unit. 2. In the hierarchical structure of data, a set of records handled as a unit.

* BLOCK DIAGRAM   A diagram of a system, instrument, or computer in which the principal parts are represented by suitable geometric figures to show the basic functions of the parts and the functional relationships between the parts. A type of flowchart.

* BOOLEAN   Pertaining to the operations of formal logic, particularly the processes used in an algebra formulated by George Boole.

BPI   Bits per inch.

BPS   Bits per second.

* BRANCH   1. A set of instructions executed between two decision instructions. 2. To select a branch, that is, to make a conditional jump.

BUBBLE MEMORY   An electronic data storage device which stores binary digits as microscopic spots (bubbles) in a thin garnet film controlled by lines of force parallel to the plane of the film in a moving magnetic field.

* BUFFER   A storage device used to compensate for a difference in rate of flow of data or time of occurrence of events when transmitting data from one device to another.

* BUG   A mistake or malfunction, usually in a computer program.

* BURST   1. To separate continuous-form paper into separate sheets. 2. In data transmission, a sequence of codes counted as one unit in accordance with some specific criterion or measure.

† BUSINESS DATA PROCESSING   Data processing for business purposes, for example, recording and summarizing the financial transactions of a business.

BYTE   A set of consecutive binary bits operating as a unit. Most frequently, eight bits that represent one character.

CACHE MEMORY   Temporary interim storage devices used to speed processes in the central processing unit of a computer. Also called scratch-pad memory.

CALCULATOR   A device capable of performing arithmetic. Usually, a device requiring frequent intervention by a human operator.

* CALL   In programming, to transfer control to a specified closed subroutine. Also called subroutine call.

CARD   *See* Punched Card.

CARRIAGE CONTROL   The device or process that controls vertical and lateral positioning of the output of a printing device.

CATHODE RAY TUBE (CRT)   A device that presents data in visual form by means of controlled electronic beams "writing" on the surface of a glass tube. (Think of a TV picture tube.) Also called display.

CDP (CERTIFICATE IN DATA PROCESSING)   A certificate issued by the Institute for Certification of Computer Professionals to persons successfully completing an examination covering data processing and related subjects. The CDP was initially administered by the Data Processing Management Association.

† CENTRAL PROCESSING UNIT (CPU)   A unit of the computer that includes the circuits controlling the interpretation and execution of instructions. Synonymous with central processor and mainframe.

CHAD   The piece of material removed when the hole is punched in a storage medium such as a punched card or a punched paper tape.

CHANGE FILE   A data file containing changes to be

made in the records of a master file in a particular processing cycle.

* CHANNEL   1. One or more parallel paths treated as a unit along which signals can be sent. Also called circuit, line, or cable. 2. The portion of a storage medium that is accessible to a given reading or writing station. For example, a path parallel to the edge of a tape along which data can be stored. Also called track and band. 3. A unit that controls the operation of one or more I/O units.

CHARACTER   1. A letter, digit, or other symbol used in the representation of data. 2. The coded representation of an alphabetic letter, numerical digit, special symbol, or control function. A character is composed of one or more bits in accordance with the coding scheme being used.

* CHARACTER PRINTER   A device that prints a single character on each machine cycle.

CHECK DIGIT   A redundant (extra) digit computed from the digits of a word or number and carried along to provide a check on the accuracy of those digits. The check digit is recomputed and the new and old check digits compared during data transfers.

CIRCUIT   1. The conductor or system of conductors through which an electronic current is intended to flow. 2. In communications, a path for carrying data both ways between two or more points.

* CLOCK   A device that measures and indicates time. In computing, this may be a device that generates periodic signals or a register whose content changes at regular intervals.

* CLOSED SHOP   A computer facility in which most programming is performed by professional programmers rather than the problem originators. The use of the computer itself also may be described as closed shop if trained operators rather than user programmers operate the computer. Contrast with Open Shop.

CLOSED SUBROUTINE   A subroutine that can be stored at one place and connected into (used in) a main routine by linkages at one or more points of the main routine. Contrast with Open Subroutine.

COBOL (Common Business Oriented Language)   A higher-level computer language designed for use in business data processing.

CODE   1. A set of unambiguous rules for representing data. For example, the standard code for information interchange (ASCII). 2. To write a routine in a programming language.

* COLLATE   To combine items from two or more ordered sets into one set that is not necessarily ordered the same as any of the original sets.

COLLATOR   A device for collating sets of punched cards.

COM   See Computer Output Microfilm.

COMMON CARRIER   An organization that rents or leases wires or transmission lines for communication purposes.

COMPILE   To translate, via the logic structures of the program, a computer program written in a problem-oriented or procedure-oriented language into machine language. It usually involves generating multiple machine instructions for each of the higher level language statements.

COMPILER   A program that compiles.

COMPUTER   See Automatic Computer.

COMPUTER INSTRUCTION   A machine instruction designed for a particular computer.

COMPUTER OUTPUT MICROFILM (COM)   Pertaining to a process for placing computer output on microfilm.

COMPUTER PROGRAM   A series of instructions or statements prepared in a form acceptable to a computer that will yield a planned result.

* COMPUTER WORD   A sequence of bits or characters treated as a unit and capable of being stored in one computer location. Also called machine word.

CONDITION ENTRY   An entry in the upper-right quadrant of a decision table that indicates for a particular rule a condition that must occur if the rule is to be applied.

CONDITION STUB   The upper-left quadrant of a decision table, which lists the possible conditions that may occur.

* CONDITIONAL JUMP   A jump that occurs if specified criteria are met. Also called Branch and conditional transfer.

CONDITIONING   In communications, the addition of equipment to a leased voice-grade channel to provide minimum values of line characteristics required for data transmission.

* CONNECTOR   On a flowchart, a symbol that represents a break in a flowline for continuation in another area. See Inconnector and Outconnector.

† CONSOLE   A part of a computer used for communication between the operator or maintenance engineer and the computer.

CONTROL UNIT   In a digital computer, the part that causes the retrieval of instructions in proper sequence, the interpretation of each instruction, and the application of proper signals to the arithmetic and logic unit and other system components in accordance with the interpretation.

CORE   See Magnetic Core.

* COUNTER   A device, such as a register or storage loca-

tion, that can represent the number of times an event occurs.

CPI   Characters per inch.

CPS   Characters per second.

CPU   *See* Central Processing Unit.

CRT   *See* Cathode Ray Tube.

CUSTODIAL PROCESSING   Data processing whose purpose is to carry out organizational activities usually involving the creation of custodial documents such as customer billings, employee paychecks, purchase orders, and so on.

† CYBERNETICS   The branch of learning that brings together theories and studies on communications and control in living organisms and machines.

* CYCLE   An interval of time in which one set of events is completed or a set of operations repeated regularly in the same sequence.

DATA   Raw facts and their representations for communication or processing.

DATA ADMINISTRATOR (DA)   The person(s) responsible for managing the data resources of an organization.

DATA BANK   A comprehensive library of files or data bases. The totality of files and data bases for an organization.

DATA BASE   An integrated collection of two or more files where each record in each file has at least one data item in common with a related record in each of the other files.

DATA BASE ACCESS LANGUAGE.   *See* Data Base Inquiry Language.

DATA BASE ADMINISTRATOR (DBA)   The person(s) responsible for designing, building, and maintaining the data bases in an organization.

DATA BASE INQUIRY LANGUAGE   A language that provides the ability to access data stored in a data base by reference to the logical organization and meaning of the stored data. Also called data base access language. *See* Data Base Management Language and Data Base Management System.

DATA BASE MANAGEMENT LANGUAGE (DBML)   A computer language that provides for addition, deletion, modification, and retrieval of data stored in a data base by reference to the logical organization and meaning of the stored data. May be divided into a data definition language, a data manipulation language, and a data base access (data base inquiry) language.

DATA BASE MANAGEMENT SYSTEM (DBMS)   A software system that allows addition, deletion, modification, and retrieval of data items, records, or files as an interface between users or programs and a data base. Often consists of data definition language, data manipula-

tion language, and data base inquiry language. Also called data base manager.

DATA DEFINITION LANGUAGE   A language used to describe or define the data items included in a data base. May be part of a data base management language. Contrast with Data Manipulation Language. *See* Data Base Management System.

DATA DICTIONARY   A listing of all the data elements found in an organization's data files. The listing shows each data element's name, location, meaning, and uses. Also called the data inventory.

DATA MANIPULATION LANGUAGE (DML)   A language used to transfer data between a data base and application programs. May be part of a data base management language. Contrast with Data Definition Language. *See* Data Base Management System.

* DATA MEDIUM   The material in or on which a specific physical variable represents data.

* DATA PROCESSING   The execution of a systematic sequence of operations performed upon data. Also called information processing. *See* Automatic Data Processing.

* DATA PROCESSOR   A device capable of performing data processing functions; includes desk calculators, punched-card machines, and computers.

DBML   *See* Data Base Management Language.

DBMS   *See* Data Base Management System.

* DEBUG   To detect, locate, and remove errors from a routine or malfunctions from a computer program.

DECIMAL   Pertaining to the numeration system with a radix of 10.

* DECISION TABLE   A table of all the contingencies to be considered in the description of a problem, along with the actions to be taken for each contingency set.

* DECK   A collection of punched cards. Also called card deck.

DEMODULATE   To retrieve the original signal (intelligence) from a modulated carrier wave; the reverse of *modulate*.

DENSITY   The number of characters or bits that can be stored in a given unit of length.

† DESTRUCTIVE READ   A reading that also erases the data in the source location.

DETAB   A computer programming language used to translate decision tables into the COBOL language.

DEVICE   A machine or unit that performs a function in a data processing system. *See* Input Device, Output Device, Storage Device.

DIAGNOSTIC   The message outputted by a compiler describing a programming mistake.

DIAGRAM   *See* Block Diagram.

* DIGITAL   Pertaining to data in the form of digits. Contrast with Analog.

* DIGITAL COMPUTER   A computer in which discrete numerical (digital) representation of data is mainly used. Contrast with Analog Computer.

* DIGITIZE   To use numerical characters to express or represent data, for example, to convert an analog representation of a physical quantity to a digital representation of the quantity.

DIRECT ACCESS   Refers to the locating of data in storage where the time required to obtain an element from storage or place an element into storage is independent of the location of the element most recently obtained or placed. Also called random access.

DISK   See Magnetic Disk.

DISK DRIVE   A device on which one or more removable disks may be mounted for use as secondary storage in a computer system.

DISK PACK   An assembly of magnetic disks that can be removed from the disk drive and stored offline.

* DISPLAY   A visual display of data or a device for presenting data visually. See also Cathode Ray Tube.

DISTRIBUTED PROCESSING   The provision of processing capability at two or more using locations, rather than at one central location.

DISTRIBUTED PROCESSING NETWORK   A network of computers providing on-site data processing for users located away from the central data processing center. Such networks often feature the use of a shared data base or data bases.

DML   See Data Manipulation Language.

DMS   See Data Base Management System.

DOCUMENT   A medium and the data or information recorded on it for use by man or machine.

DOCUMENTATION   1. The written and diagrammatic descriptions of a data processing operation, for example, verbal descriptions, flowcharts, program listings, run instructions. 2. The creating, collecting, organizing, storing, citing, and disseminating of descriptions of data processing operations.

* DOWNTIME   The time interval during which a device is inoperable.

DRIVE   See Tape Drive, Disk Drive.

DRUM   See Magnetic Drum.

DRUM PRINTER   A printing device that uses a drum embossed with the character set. As the drum rotates, a hammer strikes the paper from behind at the instant that the desired character on the drum passes the line being printed. One drum rotation is required to print a single line.

* DUMP   To copy the contents of all or part of a storage, usually from an internal storage into an external storage.

* DUPLEX   In communications, pertaining to a simultaneous two-way independent transmission in both directions. Contrast with Half Duplex. Also called full duplex.

† DYNAMIC PROGRAMMING   In operations research, a procedure for optimization of a multistage problem solution wherein a number of decisions are available at each stage of the process. Contrast with Integer Programming, Quadratic Programming.

* DYNAMIC STORAGE ALLOCATION   A storage allocation technique in which the location of programs and data is variable and determined by criteria applied at the moment of need.

EAM   See Electric Accounting Machine.

EBCDIC   Extended Binary-Coded Decimal Interchange Code.

EDP   See Electronic Data Processing.

EFFECTIVENESS   In systems analysis, refers to the capability of a processing or information system to meet management objectives, that is, to provide control and management information.

EFFICIENCY   In systems analysis, refers to the economic and physical (people, machines, energy) requirements for accomplishing a given task or process.

† ELECTRICAL ACCOUNTING MACHINE (EAM)   Pertaining to data processing equipment that is predominantly electro-mechanical, such as keypunches, mechanical sorters, collators, and tabulators.

ELECTRONIC DATA PROCESSING (EDP)   Data processing that is carried out mostly by electronic devices.

† ELEVEN-PUNCH   A punch in the second row from the top on a Hollerith punched card. Synonymous with x-punch.

ELSE RULE   A rule found in the right-hand column of a decision table that specifies the action(s) to be taken if none of the conditions specified in the previous rules occur.

* EMULATE   To imitate one system with another so that the imitating system accepts the same data, executes the same programs, and achieves the same results as the imitated system. Normally involves a hardware feature such as a read-only memory. Contrast with Simulate.

EMULATOR   A device or computer program that emulates.

EXECUTIVE   Referring to a routine or program that controls the execution of other routines or programs. Also called supervisor, monitor, and operating system.

FEASIBILITY STUDY   A preliminary systems analysis

whose purpose is to determine the potential for cost savings, time savings, increased capacity, and improved managerial control resulting from the computerization of processing.

† FEEDBACK LOOP   The components and processes involved in correcting or controlling a system by using part of the output as input.

* FIELD   In a record, a specified area used for a particular category of data, for example, a group of character spaces used to represent a customer's name.

* FILE   A collection of related records treated as a unit. For example, one line of an invoice forms an item, a complete invoice forms a record, and the complete set of such records forms a file; the collection of inventory control files forms a data base, and the data bases used by an organization are known as its data bank. *See* Master File, Transaction File.

FILE BUCKET   A division of a file capable of storing a fixed number of records.

FILE KEY   The field used as the identifier for each record contained in a file. Also called control field. *See* Major File Key.

* FILE MAINTENANCE   The activity of keeping a file up to data by adding, changing, or deleting data elements, fields, or records.

FILM   *See* Magnetic Thin Film.

FIRMWARE   Software translated into hardware in microprocessor form.

FIXED POINT   Refers to a system of positional representation in which each number is represented by a single set of digits, the position of the radix point being fixed, according to some convention, with respect to one end of the set.

* FLOATING-POINT   Refers to a numeration system in which each number is represented by a pair of numerals and equals one of those numerals multiplied by a power of an implicit fixed positive integer base where the power is equal to the implicit base raised to the exponent represented by the other numeral.

Common notation
$$\overline{0.0001234 \text{ or } (0.1234) \times (10^{-3})}$$

A floating-point representation
$$\overline{1234E\text{-}03}$$

* FLOWCHART   A graphic representation for the definition, analysis, or solution of a problem, in which symbols are used to represent operations, data, flow, equipment, and so forth. See Block Diagram.

* FONT   The set or assortment of characters of a given size and style.

* FOREGROUND PROCESSING   The automatic execution of a computer program that pre-empts the use of the computing facilities. Usually a real-time program. Contrast with Background Processing.

* FORMAT   The arrangement of data on a data medium.

† FORTRAN (Formula Translation)   A programming language primarily used to express computer programs by arithmetic formulas.

* FRAME   An area, one recording position long, spanning the width of a magnetic or paper tape perpendicular to its movement. Several bits or punch positions may fit into a single frame through the use of different recording positions across the width of the tape.

FREQUENCY MODULATION   In communications, to vary the frequency of a carrier signal as a way of transmitting a message.

FREQUENCY DIVISION MULTIPLEX (FDM)   In communications, a transmission method in which a separate message modulates each of a series of separate subcarriers that are simultaneously transmitted on a single channel. *See* Multiplex.

FULL DUPLEX   *See* Duplex.

† GENERAL-PURPOSE COMPUTER   A computer that is designed to operate upon a wide variety of problems.

* GENERATE   To produce a program by selection of subsets of code from a master set of skeletal coding under the control of parameters.

* GRAPHIC   Refers to the production of symbols by a process such as handwriting, drawing, or printing.

* HALF DUPLEX   In communications, pertaining to the ability to transmit in only one direction at a time.

HARD COPY   A printed copy of machine output in humanly readable form.

* HARDWARE   Physical equipment in data processing, as opposed to the computer program or how it is used, for example, mechanical or magnetic devices or electrical circuitry. Contrast with Software.

* HEAD   A device that reads, writes, or erases data on a storage medium.

HEADER RECORD   A record that contains information about the records that follow.

HERTZ   A measure of frequency or bandwidth that indicates the number of basic message units per second.

HEURISTIC   Refers to exploratory methods of solving problems wherein the progress toward the final result is evaluated to uncover solutions. Contrast with Algorithm.

* HIT   A successful comparison of two items of data.

* HOLLERITH   Pertaining to a data code or a punched card utilizing twelve rows per column and, usually, eighty columns per card.

I/O (Input-Output)   Input or output or both.

Identifier   A symbol used to identify, indicate, or name a data item.

Idle Time   A period of time during which available hardware is not being used. Opposite of operating time.

† Inconnector   1. In flowcharting, a connector that indicates a continuation of a broken flowline. 2. Contrast with Outconnector.

* Index   1. An ordered reference list of the contents of a file or document together with keys or reference notations for identification or location of those contents. 2. To prepare such a list. 3. A symbol or a number used to identify a particular quantity in an array of similar quantities. For example, the terms of a subscripted array represented by $X(1)$, $X(2)$, . . . $X(100)$ have the indexes 1, 2, . . . 100 respectively.

* Index Register   A register whose contents may be added to or subtracted from an operand address prior to or during the execution of a computer instruction.

Indexed Sequential   A file organization in which the records are organized sequentially within indexed blocks.

* Indirect Address   An address that designates a storage location that contains either a direct address or another indirect address. Also called multilevel address.

Information   In management information systems, communicated knowledge that is in a form that makes it immediately useful for decision making.

Information Processing   See Data Processing.

† Information Retrieval   Methods and procedures for recovering specific information from stored data.

Information Theory   The discipline that involves studying the probability of accuracy in the transmission or communication of messages that are subject to transmission failure, distortion, and noise.

* Initialize   To set counters, switches, addresses, and variable values to zero or other starting values usually at the beginning of a computer routine.

Inline Processing   Processing of data transactions in the order in which they occur.

* Input   Pertaining to a device, process, or channel involved in the insertion of data or states, or to the data or states involved. See Input Data.

* Input Data   Data to be processed. See Input.

Input Device   The device or collective set of devices that translates data into a form useable by another device, which is usually a computer.

* Inquiry Station   User terminal equipment used primarily for inquiry into an automatic data processing system.

* Instruction   A statement that specifies an operation and the values or locations of its operands. In this context, the term *instruction* is preferable to the terms *command* and *order*. *Command* should be reserved for electronic signals, and *order* should be reserved for sequence, interpolation, and related usage. See Computer Instruction, Machine Instruction, Macro Instruction.

* Instruction Address   The address used to fetch an instruction. The location where an instruction is found.

Instruction Code   See Operation Code.

† Instruction Counter   A counter that indicates the location of the next computer instruction to be interpreted.

* Instruction Register   A register that stores an instruction for interpretation and execution.

Instruction Set   The set of operations that can be represented in a given machine language.

* Integer Programming   In operations research, a class of procedures for locating the maximum or minimum of a function subject to constraints, where some or all variables must have integer values. Contrast with Mathematical Programming, Nonlinear Programming, Quadratic Programming.

* Integrated Data Processing (IDP)   Data processing in which coordinated procedures for data acquisition and manipulation are combined in a coherent system. For example, a data processing system in which data for orders and for purchasing are used together to accomplish scheduling, invoicing, and accounting.

* Interblock Gap   An area on a data medium used to indicate the end of a data block. Also called block gap. Contrast with Interrecord Gap.

* Interface   A shared boundary.

† Interleave   To arrange parts of one sequence of things or events so that they alternate with parts of one or more other sequences of things or events and so that each sequence retains its identity.

* Internal Storage   Addressable storage that is under direct control of the central processing unit of a computer.

* Interpreter   1. A computer program that translates and executes each source language statement before translating and executing the next one. 2. A device that prints on a punched card the data punched in the card.

Interrecord Gap   An area on a data medium used to

indicate the end of a record. Also called record gap. Contrast with Interblock Gap.

* INTERRUPT   1. To stop a process in such a way that it can be resumed. 2. The signal for accomplishing an interrupt.

INVERTED FILE   A file in which the file index is constructed from attribute values and record content identifies the record(s) in the primary file that possess the specified attribute.

† JOB   A set of data that completely defines a unit of work for a computer. A job usually includes all necessary computer programs, linkages, files, and instructions to the operating system.

* JUMP   A departure from the normal sequence of executing instructions in a computer. Synonymous with branch. *See* Conditional Jump.

* JUSTIFY   1. To adjust the printing positions of characters on a page so that the lines have the desired length and that both the left- and right-hand margins are regular. 2. By extension, to shift the contents of a register so that the most or the least significant digit is at some specified position in the register. Contrast with Normalize. *See* Left-Justify, Right-Justify.

k   An abbreviation for the prefix kilo, which means 1,000 in decimal notation.

K   In automatic data processing, loosely, 2^{10} (two to the tenth power), 1,024 in decimal notation.

* KEY   One or more characters within a record that are used to identify it or control its use. *See* Major Key.

* KEYPUNCH   A keyboard-actuated device that punches holes in a punch card to record data.

LABEL   One or more characters used to identify a record or a file.

* LANGUAGE   A set of representations, conventions, and rules used to convey information. *See* Machine Language, Problem-oriented Language, Procedure-oriented Language, Programming Language, Source Language.

LARGE-SCALE INTEGRATED CIRCUITS (LSI)   Refers to miniaturized circuits containing many circuits on a single chip (semiconductor). A single LSI circuit storage chip can store 64K bits.

* LATENCY   The time interval between the completion of the interpretation of an address and the start of the actual transfer from the addressed location. Latency includes the delay associated with access to storage devices such as magnetic drums and disks.

* LEFT-JUSTIFY   1. To control the printing positions of characters on a page so that the left margin of the page

is regular. 2. To shift the contents of a register so that the most significant character is at a specified position in the register. Contrast with Normalize.

† LETTER   A graphic character that, when used alone or combined with others, represents, in a written language, one or more sound elements of a spoken language, but excluding diacritical marks used alone and punctuation marks.

* LEVEL   The degree of subordination of an item in a hierarchy.

LIBRARY   A collection of related files. *See* Data Bank.

LIBRARY PROGRAM   A proved program that is maintained in a program library. Also called library routine.

* LINEAR PROGRAMMING (LP)   In operations research, a procedure for locating the maximum or minimum of a linear function of variables that are subject to linear constraints.

* LINE PRINTER   A device that prints a line of characters as a unit. Contrast with Character Printer.

* LINKAGE   In programming, the part of a program that connects two separately coded portions of the program.

* LINKAGE EDITOR   A utility program that combines independent program modules to create a translated, loadable program.

* LIST   An ordered set of items.

* LIST PROCESSING   Refers to methods of processing data arranged in the form of lists. Data records are connected by "pointers", that is, chained together, so that the logical order of items can be changed without changing the physical locations of the items.

* LOAD AND GO   An operating technique in which there are no stops between the loading and execution phases of a program.

* LOCATION   An identifiable unit in which data may be stored.

* LOGICAL RECORD   A meaningful collection of items, a record, independent of its physical environment. Portions of the same logical record may be located in different physical records.

* LOGIC ELEMENT   A device that performs a logic function.

* LOGIC INSTRUCTION   An instruction that executes an operation that follows the rules of symbolic logic.

LOGIC UNIT   That part of a computer that performs the logic functions of Boolean algebra.

* LOOP   A set of instructions that is executed repeatedly until a terminal condition prevails.

LSI   *See* Large-Scale Integrated Circuits.

MACHINE ADDRESS *See* Absolute Address.

MACHINE CODE An operation code that a machine is designed to recognize.

MACHINE INSTRUCTION An instruction that a machine can recognize and execute.

MACHINE LANGUAGE A language that is used by a computer without translation.

* MACHINE-READABLE MEDIUM A medium that can convey data to a given sensing device for input to a computer.

MACHINE WORD *See* Computer Word.

* MACROINSTRUCTION An instruction in a source language that is to be replaced by a defined sequence of machine instructions.

† MACROPROGRAMMING Computer programming with macroinstructions.

* MAGNETIC CARD A card with a magnetic surface on which data can be stored by selectively magnetizing portions of the surface.

* MAGNETIC CORE Most frequently, a doughnut-shaped configuration of ferrite placed in a spatial relationship to current-carrying conductors and used to concentrate an induced magnetic field as in a transformer induction coil, or armature, to retain a magnetic polarization for the purpose of storing data. It may be made of such material as iron or iron oxide as well as ferrite and in such shapes as wires, tapes, toroids, or thin film.

* MAGNETIC DISK A flat circular plate with a magnetic surface on which data can be stored by selectively magnetizing portions of the flat surface. Also spelled *disc*.

* MAGNETIC DRUM A circular cylinder with a magnetic surface on which data can be stored by selectively magnetizing portions of the curved surface.

* MAGNETIC INK Ink that contains magnetic particles that are detectable by magnetic sensors.

* MAGNETIC-INK CHARACTER RECOGNITION (MICR) The machine recognition of characters printed with magnetic ink.

† MAGNETIC STORAGE A storage device that utilizes the magnetic properties of certain materials.

* MAGNETIC TAPE A tape with a magnetic surface on which data can be stored by selectively polarizing portions of the surface.

† MAGNETIC THIN FILM A layer of magnetic material, usually less than one micron thick, often used for logic elements or storage elements.

MAIN FRAME *See* Central Processing Unit. Also refers to a large computer.

MAIN STORAGE The general-purpose storage of a computer. Usually, it is the fastest storage in the system and is directly accessed by the operating registers. Contrast with Auxiliary Storage.

* MAINTENANCE Any activity intended to eliminate faults or to keep hardware or programs in satisfactory working condition, including tests, measurements, replacements, adjustments, and repairs. *See* File Maintenance, Preventive Maintenance.

MAJOR FILE KEY The field serving as the primary identifier for each record in a file. *See* Key.

MANAGEMENT INFORMATION SYSTEM (MIS) The persons, machines, and procedures organized to provide information to management.

* MAP To establish a correspondence between the elements of one set and the elements of another set.

* MARK SENSING The electrical sensing of manually recorded conductive marks on the nonconductive surface of a data medium.

† MARKOV CHAIN A probabilistic model of events in which the probability of an event is dependent only on the event that precedes it.

* MASS STORAGE DEVICE A device having a large storage capacity, most frequently a magnetic disk.

* MASTER FILE A file that is used as an authority in a particular job and that is relatively permanent.

* MATCH To check for identity between two or more items of data. *See* Hit.

† MATHEMATICAL MODEL A mathematical representation of a process, device, or concept.

* MATHEMATICAL PROGRAMMING In operations research, a procedure for locating the maximum or minimum of a function subject to constraints, at least one of which is an inequality. *See* Dynamic Programming, Integer Programming, Linear Programming, Nonlinear Programming, Quadratic Programming.

† MATRIX 1. A rectangular array of elements, arranged in rows and columns, that may be manipulated according to the rules of matrix algebra. 2. In computers, a logic network in the form of an array of input leads and output leads with logic elements connected at some of their intersections. 3. By extension, an array of any number of dimensions.

MEAN-TIME-BETWEEN-FAILURES (MTBF) The arithmetic average length of time between two successive failures of a device or element.

MEAN-TIME-TO-REPAIR (MTTR) The arithmetic average length of time required to correct a malfunction or breakdown of a device.

MEDIUM The material, or configuration of material,

on which data are recorded and stored, for example, paper tape, cards, magnetic tape. Also called data medium.

MEGABYTE (MB) One million bytes (characters).

MEMORY Storage.

MERGE To combine items from two or more similarly ordered sets into one set that is arranged in the same order.

METAL OXIDE SILICON (MOS) Pertaining to a miniaturization process in microelectronic production whose end product is a silicon chip containing many circuits. *See also* Large-Scale Integrated Circuits.

MICR *See* Magnetic-Ink Character Recognition.

MICROCODE *See* Firmware.

MICROCOMPUTER A computer built around a microprocessor by adding circuitry and devices to provide memory, input/output, and control functions.

MICROINSTRUCTION The simplest instruction carried out in a computer.

MICROPROCESSOR A general processor created with microcircuit technology and used as the basis of many electronic devices including use as the central processing unit of a microcomputer.

MICROSECOND One millionth of a second.

MILLISECOND One thousandth of a second.

MINICOMPUTER A class of computers that use architecture developed mainly in the 1960s and that feature more limited instructions sets than large computers (main frames).

MIS *See* Management Information System.

* MISTAKE An action that produces an unintended result.

† MNEMONIC SYMBOL A symbol chosen to assist the human memory, e.g., an abbreviation such as "mpy" for "multiply".

* MODEM (MODULATOR-DEMODULATOR) A device that modulates and demodulates signals transmitted over communication facilities. Most frequently, changes electrical impulses to signals specifying sound or sound signals to electric impulses in order to transmit data codes over telephone lines.

MODULAR PROGRAMMING An approach to computer programming that separates the total program into modules and writes and debugs each module independently before combining the modules into a single program.

MODULATE In communications, to vary some characteristic (amplitude, phase, or frequency) of one signal or wave in accordance with another wave or signal.

* MODULE 1. A program unit designed to be written and debugged independently before being combined into the main program. 2. A program unit that is discrete and identifiable with respect to compiling, combining with other units, and loading. 3. An independent functional hardware unit designed for use with other components.

MONITOR See Executive.

MONTECARLO METHOD A technique that uses random numbers to approximate a solution to a numerical problem.

MOS *See* Metal Oxide Silicon.

MOVE Same as transfer, transmit.

MTBF *See* Mean-Time-Between-Failures.

MTTR *See* Mean-Time-To-Repair.

† MULTIADDRESS Pertaining to an instruction format containing more than one address part.

MULTILEVEL ADDRESS *See* Indirect Address.

MULTIPLE PUNCH The presence of more than one hole in the same column on a punched card.

* MULTIPLEX To interleave or simultaneously transmit two or more messages on a single channel. *See* Frequency Division Multiplex and Time-Division Multiplex.

* MULTIPROCESSING Pertaining to the simultaneous execution by parallel processing of two or more computer programs or sequences of instructions by a computer or computer network.

MULTIPROCESSOR A computer that can execute one or more computer programs employing two or more processing units under integrated control of programs or devices.

* MULTIPROGRAMMING Pertaining to the concurrent execution of two or more programs by a computer involving automatic and continuous alternation among the programs by a single processor under the control of a supervisor or executive program. Contrast with Timesharing and Multiprocessing.

NANOSECOND One billionth of a second.

* NATURAL LANGUAGE A language whose rules are based on current usage rather than prescribed usage.

* NEST To embed subroutines or data in other subroutines or data at a different hierarchical level.

NETWORK The interconnection of a number of points by communication facilities. The switched telephone network is the network of telephone lines normally used for dialed telephone calls. A computer network is two or more computers interconnected by communication facilities.

* NOISE 1. Random variations of one or more characteristics of any entity such as voltage, current, or data.

2. Loosely, any disturbance likely to interfere with the normal operation of a device or system.

* No Op   An instruction that causes the computer to do nothing other than to proceed to the next instruction in sequence.

* Nondestructive Read   A read process that does not erase the stored data being read.

* Nonlinear Programming   In operations research, a procedure for locating the maximum or minimum of a function of variables that are subject to constraints, when either the function or the constraints or both are nonlinear. Contrast with Dynamic Programming, Integer Programming, Linear Programming, Mathematical Programming, Quadratic Programming.

* Normalize   1. To make an adjustment to the fixed-point part and, correspondingly, to the exponent in a floating-point representation to ensure that the fixed-point part lies within some prescribed range; the real number represented remains the same. 2. Loosely, to scale.

† Numerical Analysis   The study of methods of obtaining useful quantitative solutions to problems that have been expressed mathematically, including the study of the errors and bounds on the errors in obtaining such solutions.

* Numerical Control   Automatic control of a process performed by a device that interprets numerical data that is generally introduced as the operation is in process.

* Object Code   Output from a compiler or assembler that is itself executable machine code.

* Object Program   A fully compiled or assembled program that is ready to be carried out by the computer. Also called target program.

OCR   See Optical Character Recognition.

Octal   1. Pertaining to the attribute of having eight possibilities of selection, choice, or condition. 2. Pertaining to the numeration system with a radix of eight.

* Offline   Pertaining to equipment or devices not under direct control of the central processing unit.

* Online   Pertaining to equipment or devices physically attached to and under the direct control of a central processing unit.

* Open Shop   Pertaining to the operation of a computer facility in which most problem programming is performed by the problem originator rather than by a group of professional programmers. The use of the computer itself also may be described as open shop if the user/programmer also operates the computer, rather than using a full time trained operator. Contrast with Closed Shop.

Open Subroutine   A subroutine that must be relocated and inserted into a routine at each place it is used. Contrast with Closed Subroutine.

* Operand   That which is operated upon. In computer processing, an operand is usually identified by an address part of an instruction.

* Operating System   Software that controls the execution of computer programs. Software may provide scheduling, debugging, input-output control, accounting, compilation, storage assignment, data management and related services. Also called Executive, Monitor, and Supervisor.

* Operation   1. A defined action, namely, obtaining a result using one or more operands in accordance with a rule that completely specifies the result for any permissible combination of operands. 2. The action that a single computer instruction specifies. 3. A processing step undertaken or executed by a computer, for example, addition, multiplication, extraction, comparison, shift, transfer. The operation is usually specified by the operation code part of an instruction.

* Operation Code   A code used to represent specific operations. Also called instruction code.

Operations Analysis   See Operations Research.

* Operations Research (OR)   The application of the scientific method to provide criteria for decisions concerning the optimal use of people, machines, and other resources in a system. Also called operations analysis.

Operator   A person who operates a machine.

* Optical Character Recognition (OCR)   Machine identification of printed characters through use of light-sensitive photo-electric cells.

Optical Scanner   A device that uses light to examine patterns usually for the purpose of generating their digital equivalents.

* Order   The arrangement of items according to any specified set of rules.

† Outconnector   1. In flowcharting, a connector that indicates a point at which a flowline is broken for continuation at another point. 2. Contrast with Inconnector.

Output   1. The data or states generated by a process. 2. Pertaining to the data or states received from a process or to the devices, processes or channels through which they are received.

Output Data   The data delivered from a device or

program, usually after some processing. Also called output.

OUTPUT DEVICE   The device or collective group of devices that conduct data out of another device, which is usually a computer system.

OVERFLOW   The part of an operation's result that is beyond the capacity of the unit of storage being used.

* OVERLAY   The technique of repeatedly using the same blocks of internal storage during different stages of a program such that a new routine can take the place of a routine, or part of a routine, that is no longer needed in storage.

* PACK   To store data in a compact form by taking advantage of known characteristics of the data in such a way that the original form of the data can be recovered, for example, to compress data in a storage medium by using bit or byte locations that would otherwise go unused.

PAGING   An automatic overlaying technique used in timesharing and multiprogramming in which program and data blocks (pages) are transferred from secondary storage into main storage whenever required in processing a program.

* PARALLEL   Pertaining to the simultaneous or concurrent operation of two or more devices, occurrence of two or more activities (processes), or processing of two or more parts of a whole.

* PARAMETER   A variable that is given a constant value for a specific application.

PARITY BIT   A binary digit appended to a set of bits to make the sum of all the bits always odd or always even.

* PARITY CHECK   A check that tests whether the number of 1's or 0's in a set of binary digits is odd or even. Also called odd-even check.

* PASS   One complete cycle of processing of a body of data.

* PATCH   To modify a computer routine or program in a rough or expedient way.

† PATTERN RECOGNITION   The identification of shapes, forms, or configurations by automatic means.

* PERIPHERAL EQUIPMENT   In a data processing system, any equipment, distinct from the central processing unit, that may provide the system with additional capacities or communication.

PHASE MODULATION (PM)   A way of modifying a signal to make it carry information in which amplitude of the carrier wave remains constant but its phase is varied in amplitude by the modulating signal.

PHYSICAL ADDRESS   See Absolute Address.

* PLUGBOARD   A perforated board into which manually inserted plugs may be placed to complete electrical circuits that provide control over the operation of equipment. Also called control panel.

POLISH NOTATION   See Prefix Notation.

POLLING   To interrogate (check on) devices in a computer or data processing system to determine their current status with regard to their readiness to participate in system activities.

* POSITIONAL NOTATION   A numeration system in which a number is represented by means of an ordered set of digits, such that the value contributed by each digit depends upon its position as well as upon its value. Also called positional representation.

* PRECISION   The exactness with which a numerical value is stated. For example, a two-digit numeral discriminates among 100 possibilities, but a three-digit number among 1,000.

* PREFIX NOTATION   A method of forming mathematical expressions in which each operator precedes its operands. In prefix notation, the expression "(a plus b) multiplied by c" would be represented by x + abc. Also called Lukasiewicz notation, parentheses-free notation, Polish Notation.

* PREVENTIVE MAINTENANCE   Maintenance carried out to prevent faults from occurring during subsequent operation.

* PROBLEM-ORIENTED LANGUAGE   A programming language that is especially suitable for the expression of a given class of problems.

* PROCEDURE-ORIENTED LANGUAGE   A programming language that facilitates the expression of procedures used to solve a wide class of problems.

* PROCESS   A systematic sequence of operations carried out to produce a specified result.

* PROCESSOR   1. In hardware, that part of a machine system that operates upon data. 2. In software, a computer program that performs the compiling, assembling, translating, and related functions for a specific programming language, for example, COBOL processor, or FORTRAN processor.

* PROGRAM   1. A series of actions proposed to achieve a certain result. 2. A computer routine or program. 3. To design, write, and test a program or routine. See Computer Program, Object Program, Source Program.

* PROGRAM LIBRARY   An organized collection of available computer programs and routines.

PROGRAM MODULE   See Module.

PROGRAMMABLE READ-ONLY MEMORY (PROM) A read-only memory whose content can be changed by special procedures but not by the use of standard programming processes.

* PROGRAMMED CHECK   A check procedure designed by the programmer specifically as a part of the program.

† PROGRAMMER   A person who designs, writes, and tests computer programs.

† PROGRAMMING FLOWCHART   A flowchart representing the sequence of operations in a computer program.

* PROGRAMMING LANGUAGE   An artificial language used to express computer programs.

PROM   See Programmable Read-only Memory.

† PSEUDO CODE   A code that requires translation prior to execution.

* PSEUDORANDOM NUMBER SEQUENCE   An ordered set of numbers, determined by a defined arithmetic process, but satisfactorily random for its given purpose, such as an ordered set of numbers that satisfies one or more of the standard statistical tests for randomness.

PULSE CODE MODULATION (PCM) In communications, modulation of a pulse train in accordance with a code.

* PUNCH.   A perforation, for instance in a punched card or paper tape. Also, the device for making such perforations. See Keypunch, Eleven-Punch, Twelve-Punch, Zone Punch.

† PUNCH POSITION   A defined location on a card or tape where a hole may be punched to record data.

* PUNCHED CARD   A card punched with hole patterns that represent data.

PUNCHED TAPE   A tape punched with holes or cuts in a pattern that represents data.

PUSH-DOWN LIST   A list arranged such that the most recently stored item in the list is in position to be retrieved next, last in, first out. Also called stack.

PUSH-UP LIST   A list arranged such that the oldest item still in the list is in position to be retrieved next, for example, first in, first out. Also called pop-up list.

* QUADRATIC PROGRAMMING   In operations research, a particular case of nonlinear programming in which the function to be maximized or minimized is a quadratic function of the controllable variables. Contrast with Dynamic Programming, Integer Programming, Linear Programming, Mathematical Programming.

* QUEUED-ACCESS METHOD   Any access method that automatically synchronizes the transfer of data between the program using the access method and input-output devices, thereby eliminating unnecessary delays for input-output operation.

* RADIX   In positional representation, that integer, if it exists, by which the significance of the digit place must be multiplied to give the significance of the next higher digit place. For example, in decimal notation, the radix of each place is 10; in a biquinary code, the radix of the fives place is 2. Also called base.

* RADIX NOTATION   A positional representation in which the ratio between the weight of one digit place and the weight of the next lower digit place is a positive integer; permissible values of the digit in any position range from zero to one less than the radix of that position.

* RADIX POINT   In radix notation, the location that separates the characters associated with the integral part of a numeral from those associated with the fractional part.

RANDOM ACCESS   See Direct Access.

RANDOM-ACCESS DEVICE   A device in which the access time is effectively independent of the location of the data. Also called direct-access device.

* RANDOM NUMBERS   A series of numbers obtained by chance. See Pseudorandom Number Sequence.

† RANDOM-WALK METHOD   In operations research, a variance-reducing method of problem analysis in which experimentation with probabilistic variables is traced to determine results of a significant nature.

† READ   1. To acquire or interpret data from a storage device, from a data medium, or from another source. 2. See Destructive Read, Nondestructive Read.

READ-ONLY MEMORY (ROM) A storage device that stores data (or instructions) and is not alterable by computer instructions. Also called read-only storage, fixed storage.

REAL TIME   Pertaining to the performance of a computation (during the same time period when the related physical process is taking place) fast enough that results of the computation can be used in guiding the physical process. That is, obtaining control feedback from an operating system in time to maintain operating stability in the system.

* RECORD   A collection of related items of data, treated as a unit. For example, a charge sale may form a transaction record; a complete set of such records for a given period of time may form a transaction file.

RECORD GAP   A space between records on a storage device such as magnetic tape or magnetic disk.

* RECORDING DENSITY   The number of bits in a single

linear track per unit of length of the recording medium, for example, bits per inch.

* RECORD LAYOUT   The arrangement and structure, or description thereof, of data in a record, including the sequence and size of the components.

RECORD LENGTH   The length of a record, usually measured in words or characters.

REENTRANT PROGRAM   A computer program that may be reentered repeatedly so long as neither its internal parameters nor any of its instructions are modified during its execution. In timesharing, reentrant compilers and executive programs are reentrant and may be used by more than one computer program simultaneously.

REENTRANT ROUTINE   A routine that may be used simultaneously by more than one program or entered repeatedly by the same program as long as neither its internal parameters nor any of its instructions are modified during its execution.

* REGISTER   A device capable of storing a specified amount of data, such as one word. See Address Register, Index Register, Instruction Register.

* RELATIVE ADDRESS   An address expressed as the difference between the absolute address and the base address.

* RELIABILITY   The probability that a device will perform its intended function without failing for a stated period of time or amount of usage.

* RELOCATE   To move a routine from one portion of storage to another and to adjust the necessary address references so that the routine can be executed in its new location.

REMOTE ACCESS   Access to a data processing facility via a station or stations located outside that facility.

* REMOTE STATION   Remote-access data terminal equipment.

* RERUN   A repeat of a machine run.

* RESET   To restore a storage device to a prescribed initial state.

RESPONSE TIME   The elapsed time between the transmission of the last character of a message (usually an inquiry or request for service) from a remote terminal and the receipt of the first character of the response at the terminal.

* RIGHT-JUSTIFY   1. To control the printing positions of characters on a page so that the right margin of the page is regular. 2. To shift the contents of a register so that the right-hand–most character is at some specified position of the register.

ROLL IN   To restore to main storage data or a program segment located in auxiliary storage.

ROLL OUT   To record on an auxiliary storage device the contents of main storage.

ROM   Read-only memory.

ROUNDING ERROR   An error resulting from roundoff. Contrast with Truncation Error.

* ROUNDOFF   To delete the least significant digit or digits of a numeral or positional representation and to adjust the part retained in accordance with some rule.

* ROUTINE   An ordered set of instructions that may have some general or frequent use. (A routine may be a program.) See Executive, Library Program, Subroutine, Utility Routine.

RPG (Report Program Generator)   An interpretive computer language designed for programming business data processing applications.

RUN   A single, continuous performance of a processing routine.

* SAMPLING   1. In statistics, obtaining a sample from a population. 2. Loosely, using a subset of the items that make up a whole to represent that whole.

* SCALE   To adjust the representation of a quantity by a factor so that its range will fall within prescribed limits.

† SCALE FACTOR   A number used as a multiplier in scaling.

SCAN   To examine parts in sequence.

SCRATCH-PAD MEMORY   See Cache Memory.

* SEARCH KEY   Data to be compared to specified parts of each item for the purpose of finding one or more items possessing the characteristics described by that data.

* SEMANTICS   The relationships between symbols and their meanings.

* SEQUENTIAL   1. Pertaining to the occurence of events in time sequence, with little or no simultaneity or overlap of events. 2. Pertaining to the occurrence of events in some order, for example, alphabetic or numerical.

SEQUENTIAL ACCESS   See Serial Access.

* SERIAL   Pertaining to the sequential or consecutive occurrence of two or more related activities in a single device or channel or the sequential processing of the individual parts of a whole, such as the bits of a character, the characters of a word, or the records in a file using the same facilities for successive parts. Contrast with Parallel.

* SERIAL ACCESS   Pertaining to the process of obtaining

data from or placing data into storage where the time required for such access is dependent on the location of the data and on a reference to data previously accessed. Contrast with Direct Access. *See* Sequential Access.

SERVICE ROUTINE *See* Utility Routine.

* SERVOMECHANISM 1. An automatic control system that uses feedback to govern the physical position of an element by adjusting either the values of the coordinates or the values of their time derivatives. 2. Any feedback control system in which at least one of the signals represents mechanical motion.

SHIFT REGISTER A register in which stored data can be shifted to the right or left.

SIGNAL The event or phenomenon that conveys data from one point to another.

SIGN BIT A binary digit occupying the sign position and representing the algebraic sign of the numeral to which it is attached.

* SIGN POSITION A position, normally located at one end of a numeral, that contains an indication of the algebraic sign of the number represented by the numeral.

* SIMULATE To represent certain features of the behavior of a physical or abstract system by the behavior of another system.

* SIMULATION The representation of certain features of the behavior of a physical or abstract system by the behavior of another system, for example, the representation of physical phenomena by means of a set of mathematical functions or by operations performed by a computer.

* SIMULATOR A device, system or computer program that represents certain features of the behavior of a physical or abstract system. Most frequently, a software feature that allows one computer system to imitate another.

SIMULTANEITY The ability of a computer system to perform more than one functional operation simultaneously.

* SINGLE ADDRESS Referring to an instruction that contains only one address part. Also called one address.

* SNAPSHOT DUMP A selective dynamic dump of the contents of a specified storage area performed during a machine run.

SOFTWARE The media and documents that relate to the operation of a data processing system by specifying computer programs, procedures, and rules, for example, compilers, library routines, manuals, circuit diagrams. Contrast with Hardware.

* SOLID-STATE Referring to components whose operation relies on the control of electrical or magnetic phenomena in solids, for example, transistors, crystal diodes, ferrite cores.

* SORT To segregate items into groups according to some definite rules. *See* Order.

* SORTER A person, device, or computer routine that sorts.

SOURCE LANGUAGE The original language of a statement that has been translated (assembled or compiled).

* SOURCE PROGRAM A program written in a source language.

* SPECIAL CHARACTER A graphic character that is not a letter, not a digit, and not a space character.

† SPECIAL-PURPOSE COMPUTER A computer that is designed to operate upon a restricted class of problems.

* STATEMENT In computer programming, a meaningful expression or generalized instruction.

* STATIC DUMP A dump that is performed at a particular point in a machine run, often at the end of a run.

STORAGE 1. Referring to a device into which data can be entered and retained for retrieval and use at a later time. 2. Loosely, a data-storage device. Also called memory. *See* Auxiliary Storage, Internal Storage, Read-Only Memory, Volatile Storage, Working Storage.

* STORAGE CAPACITY The amount of data that a storage device can contain.

* STORAGE DEVICE A device into which data can be inserted, in which they can be retained, and from which they can be retrieved.

* STORE 1. To enter data into or retain data in a storage device. 2. A storage device.

* STORED-PROGRAM COMPUTER A computer controlled by internally stored instructions that can synthesize, store, and subsequently execute instructions with the capacity to alter those instructions during execution.

* SUBROUTINE A routine that can be part of another routine or program. *See* Closed Subroutine, Open Subroutine.

SUBROUTINE CALL *See* Call.

* SUMMATION CHECK A check based on the sum of the digits of a numeral. Usually, the sum is compared with a previously computed value.

SUPERVISOR *See* Executive.

* SWITCH A device or programming technique for making a selection among paths for continuation of a process, for example, a toggle, a conditional jump.

SWITCHED NETWORK A nationwide complex of telephone channels and switching equipment that automatically routes messages between the caller and the persons or data equipment being called after dialing is completed. Also known as the direct distance dialing, or DDD, network.

* SYMBOL   A thing that represents another thing by reason of relationship, association, or convention. *See* Mnemonic Symbol.

* SYMBOLIC ADDRESS   An address expressed in symbols for the convenience of the programmer.

SYMBOLIC CODING   Coding that uses a symbolic language for routines and computer programs.

* SYMBOLIC LOGIC   The discipline that deals with valid arguments and operations by using a formalized artificial language or symbolic calculus designed to avoid the ambiguities and logical inadequacies of natural languages.

* SYNCHRONIZATION PULSES   In communications, pulses introduced by transmitting equipment into the receiving equipment to keep the two equipments operating in step.

* SYNTAX   The structure of expressions in a language.

SYSTEM   1. A combination of elements, their attributes, and their interrelationships that are organized in the pursuit of a common objective. 2. In electronic data processing, a computer configuration.

* TABLE   A collection of data wherein each item is uniquely labeled, positioned relative to the other items, or otherwise identified.

* TABLE LOOK-UP   The procedure of referring to a table of values to find the value corresponding to an argument.

* TABULATE   1. To put data into the form of a table. 2. To print totals.

TAPE   *See* Magnetic Tape, Punched tape.

TAPE DRIVE   A device that moves tape past a head. Also called tape transport.

TARGET PROGRAM   *See* Object Program.

* TELECOMMUNICATIONS   The transmission of signals over long distances.

TELEPROCESSING   A form of data processing involving the use of telecommunications.

* TEMPORARY STORAGE   In programming, storage locations used only for intermediate results. Also called working storage.

* TERMINAL   1. A point in a system or communication network at which data can either enter or leave. 2. A device for entering data into or outputting data from a communication network or computer.

TIME DIVISION MULTIPLEX (TDM)   In communications, a technique that allows several message

channels to share a common physical channel by separating the transmitted messages in time by interleaving either the bits or characters of the several messages on the carrier channel. *See* Multiplex.

TIMESHARING   1. The interleaved use of the time of a device for two or more purposes. 2. In electronic data processing, the interleaved use of the elements of a computer system with a limitation on the time (a time slice) that each program can use the central processor on each access of the CPU. That is, a form of multiprogramming involving the use of the time slice to control CPU use.

TIME SLICE   The maximum length of time that each using program is allowed to retain control over the central processor each time the program is allowed to use the central processor in timesharing.

* TRACING ROUTINE   A routine that records specified events in the execution of a program.

* TRACK   The portion of a moving storage medium, such as a drum, tape, or disk, that is accessible to a given reading-head position. Also called channel, band.

* TRANSACTION FILE   A file containing relatively transient data pertaining to related business transactions to be processed in combination with a master file. For example, in a payroll application, a transaction file indicating hours worked might be processed with a master file containing employee name and rate of pay. Also called detail file.

* TRUNCATION ERROR   An error resulting from deletion or omission of a leading or trailing portion of a numeral or other character string. Contrast with Rounding Error.

TURING MACHINE   A mathematical model for computer-like behavior. *See* Universal Turing Machine.

TURNKEY SYSTEM   A data processing system, including hardware and software, capable of performing the data processing functions of a small business or of a particular business function in a larger business.

† TWELVE-PUNCH   A punch in the top row of a Hollerith punch card. Synonymous with Y-Punch.

* TWO-ADDRESS   Referring to an instruction format containing two address parts.

* TYPE FONT   The collection of type of a specified size and style, for example, ten-point Electra.

* UNDERFLOW   The condition that may occur if a machine computation yields a nonzero result that is too small to be stored in the intended unit of storage.

UNIVERSAL TURING MACHINE   A mathematical model that can simulate any turing machine.

USASCII (USA STANDARD CODE FOR INFORMATION IN-

TERCHANGE) *See* American Standard Code for Information Interchange.

UTILITY ROUTINE A routine or program that provides some type of general support of the operation of a computer. For example, input-output, diagnostic evaluation of a program, tracing or monitoring. Also called service routine, utility program.

† VARIABLE A quantity that can assume any of a given set of values.

* VARIABLE-LENGTH RECORD A record whose length is not constrained.

* VARIABLE-POINT REPRESENTATION A positional representation in which a special character explicitly indicates the position of the radix point. Contrast with Floating-Point Representation.

* VERIFY To determine whether data transcription or some other operation has been performed accurately. Specifically, to confirm the results of keypunching.

* VOLATILE STORAGE A storage device whose stored data are lost when the power is removed, for example, a microcircuit store.

* WORD A character string or a bit string considered as an entity. *See* Computer Word.

WORD LENGTH The size of a word, usually measured in characters or binary digits.

* WORKING STORAGE 1. Same as temporary storage. 2. In COBOL, the location of the results of interim calculations.

* WRITE To record data in a storage device or on a data medium. The recording need not be permanent; it may be transient, such as on a cathode ray tube display device.

X-PUNCH Same as eleven-punch.

Y-PUNCH Same as twelve-punch.

* ZERO SUPPRESSION The elimination from a numeral of nonsignificant zeros.

ZONE PUNCH A punch in row eleven, row twelve, or row zero of a punched card.

Index

Bucket, *see* File bucket
Buffer, 206–208
Bulk, of media, 143, 259
By-product recording, 123, 239

Capacity (media and devices)
  input, 142, 229
  output, 143, 246
  storage, 258
Card, *see* Electro-mechanical processing machines;
    Punched card
Career path, 392
Cathode Ray Tube (CRT), *see* Terminals
Central processing unit (CPU), 204
  time, 372
Chain line printer, *see* Line printer
Channel, 208, 232
Character, 18
Character printer, 137, 246
Check-digit, *see* Data controls
Classification, in data processing, 9
COBOL (computer language), 209, 342–347, 350,
    351, 353
  divisions, 342
  example program, 343–346
Communication
  controller, 278–279
  in data processing, 11
  networks, 278–285
Compatibility
  hardware, 212, 216
  software (language), 210–211
Compiler
  defined, 208
  languages, *see* Programming languages
Complaints, 158
Component checks, 161
Compute-bound, 214–215
Computer
  accuracy, 377–378
  address, 204
  analog, 199
  automatic electronic digital, 199–202
  central processing unit, *see* Central processing unit
  complexity of analysis, 378
  as data processor, 204–205
  effects of
    on accounting, 362–365
    on centralization of management, 380–381
    by level of management, 381–382

    on management practice, 378–379
    operational, 376–379
    organizational, 379–384
  families, 210–211
  first generation, 205–206
  functional elements
    arithmetic-logic, 203
    control, 203
    input, 202
    output, 203–204
    storage, 202–203
  hardware, *see* Hardware
  instruction, *see* Instruction
  instruction set, *see* Instruction
  language, *see* Programming language
  leasing, 300–303
  and management, 376–403
  operator, 390
  performance requirements, 289–293
  peripheral devices, 206–207
  processing, *see* Processing
  purchase, 300
  second generation, 206–209
  selection, *see* Computer selection
  simulation, *see* Simulation
  simulation of, 297
  software, *see* Software
  speed, 211 (Fig.), 377
  stored-program concept, 200–201
  and thinking, 221–222
  third generation, 210–219
  vendors, 146, 293, 296, 303
  see also, Firmware; Hardware; Input; Microcompu-
    ter; Minicomputer; Modularity; Output; Pro-
    gram; Programming; Simultaneity; Storage
Computer-output microfilm, *see* Output media and de-
    vices
Computer selection, 289ff
  alternative systems, 293–294
  benchmarking in, 295–296
  functional tradeoffs in, 294
  request for bids, 293–294
  steps in, 289
Concentrator, *see* Line concentrator
Console of Computer, 310
Contract, *see* Lease contract; Maintenance contract;
    Purchase contract
Contractual period, 302
Control
  and accountability, 157–158

Control (*Cont.*)
of computer costs, 371–373
console, 310
by exception, 47
field, 20
of forms, *see* Forms
internal, *see* Internal controls; Data controls
of intervention, 153, 371
limits, *see* Internal control
managerial, *see* Managerial controls
models, 34
operational, 43, 149–151
totals, *see* Internal control
over system changes, 152–153, 371
over unauthorized access, 152–153, 371
see also Auditing; Controls; Internal control; Managerial controls
Controller
communications, 278–279
device, *see* Media and devices
see also Concentrator; Multiplexor
Controls
data, *see* Data controls
data processing, 154ff, 371
input, *see* Data controls
internal, *see* Data controls; Internal controls
managerial, *see* Managerial controls
output, *see* Data controls
processing, *see* Data controls
Core, *see* Magnetic core
Costs
of computer use, 371–373
intangible, 148
processing, 13–14, 27, 29
tangible, 147–148
and value of information, 13–14
Counts
record, 154, 156
transaction, 154
see also Data controls
CPU, *see* Central Processing Unit
Custodial processing, 4–5
Cybernetics view of MIS, *see* Management information system
Cycle time
computer, *see* Instruction
information system, 46
of physical operation, 46
processing, 158
see also Instruction execution cycle

Data
administrator, 391–392
analysis, 10–11, 391
analysis of uses, 30
bank, 48–50
base, *see* Data base
block, 18
capture, *see* Data recording
controls, *see* Data controls
defined, 11
dictionary, 29–30, 391
entry, economics of, 244–245
field, 18
file, 18, *see also* File
historical, 5
input, *see* Input-output media and devices
inventory, 29–30, 391
maintenance, 391
management, 391–392
preaudit, 154
processing, *see* Data processing
record, 18
recording, 8, 121, 127
direct entry, 121, 123, 124–127, 226, 242–244
machine-assisted manual, 122–124
manual, 122
point-of-action, 121, 123, 124–127, 226
point-of-sale, 28, 124 (Fig.)
security program, 153
structure, 18–19
systems, *see* Data systems
transactions, 3, 48
transfer rate, 195, 258, 264
word, 18
Data base, 29–31
administrator, 392
concept, 29, 391
defined, 29
design, 30–31
inquiry language, 350
integrated, 29
maintenance, 31, 391
management language, *see* Programming languages
management system, 391–392
Data controls, 123–124, 154–157, 371
check digit, 123–124
control total, 154, 156
dual processing, 155–156
file identification, 155
input, 154

Resource use monitoring, *see* Monitoring resource use
Response, *see* Management reporting
Response speed, categories of, 291
Retrieval and reporting
    defined, 9–10
    devices, 135–140
    on-demand, 145
    volume, 144–145

Samuels, Dr., 221
Satellite systems, *see* Telecommunications
Schedules, 390
Schematic, *see* Input-output schematic
Scratch-pad (cache) memory, 276
Selection of computer, *see* Computer selection
Separation of physical control and accountability, 152, 371
Sequence checks, *see* Data controls
Sequential
    access, 27
    file organization, 20
Service Bureau
    general-purpose, 400
    special-purpose, 400–401
    timesharing, 401
Simplex, 280
Simulation
    analog, 188
    applications, 189
    computer, 33–34
    of computer, 297
    defined, 187
    languages, *see* Programming languages
    physical, 187–188
    symbolic or mathematical, 188–189
Simultaneity (symbionts), 205, 207, 212
Skills inventory, *see* Personnel function
Software
    balance with hardware, 299
    benchmarking, 298
    defined, 208
    development with hardware
        first generation, 206–207
        second generation, 208–209
        third generation, 218–219
    documentation, 298–299
    maintenance, 298–299
Sorting, 9
Source program, 208
Special-action path, 105, 107

Speed
    access, 142
    input, 142, 229
    media and devices, 142, 229
    see also Transfer rate; System design
Spooling, 372
Standard
    control, 149–150
    format and symbols, 152
Stochastic models, 33
Storage
    access, *see* Access
    access time, *see* Access
    address, 256
    computer, 255ff
    devices, *see* Storage devices
    mass, 267
    offline, 268–269
    online, 269–270
    organization, 256
    permanence, 226
    primary, 267
    secondary, 267
    types of devices, 257–258
Storage and retrieval, 9–10
Storage devices, 127–130, 255–271
    automated, 129–130
    bubble, *see* Bubble memory
    cache (scratch-pad), 276
    characteristics, 258–266
    core, *see* Magnetic core
    disk, *see* Disk pack; Floppy disk; Magnetic disk
    film, 263
    fixed magnetic devices, 259–263
    machine assisted manual, 127–128
    manually operated, 127
    microcircuit, 266
    moving magnetic surfaces, 263–266
    nonvolatile, 256–257
    offline, 268–269
    online, 269–270
    primary, 267
    scratch-pad, *see* Storage, cache
    secondary, 267–268
    tape, *see* Magnetic tape
    volatile, 256–257
    see also Data processing operations; Programmable read-only memory (PROM); Read-only memory (ROM)
Stored program concept, 200–201